The
Bachs
1500 – 1850

By the same author

HANDEL (Master Musicians series)

VAUGHAN WILLIAMS

ELGAR, O.M.

MASTERS OF MUSIC SERIES

WORLD CONDUCTORS

ZOLTÁN KODÁLY: A HUNGARIAN MUSICIAN

J. S. BACH

TRAGIC MUSE: ROBERT SCHUMANN, LIFE AND WORKS

THE CHORAL TRADITION

etc.

The Bachs

1500 – 1850

Percy M. Young

THOMAS Y. CROWELL COMPANY

NEW YORK · ESTABLISHED 1834

To my friends in
Halle and Göttingen

Printed in the United States of America
Library of Congress Catalog Card No. 73–108991

Preface

WHETHER this book proves anything or not I do not know. That is for the reader to decide. It does, however, have relevance to certain matters of permanent interest and importance, not all of which fall within the limits of a particular discipline.

What weight, for instance, should we give to factors of heredity? What is the meaning and validity of nationality? Where does the artist (or anyone else) stand in relation to society? What is the place of the arts in education? To what extent is music a reflection of philosophy? To what extent are stylistic differences explicable by psychological analysis or accidents of environment? These are among the abiding questions which I have attempted to ask myself in respect of one family across three centuries.

The Bachs represent a unique phenomenon in European, indeed in world, history. Their tradition is without parallel in any field. Without exception the members of this family—or rather clan—were very ordinary people, indistinguishable from those with whom they generally associated, except that some of them have been allowed by posterity to have been touched with a kind of divine fire. The greatest of them were markedly blessed with a spirit of independence, confident that by making the best use of their talents as they saw fit they were most usefully fulfilling themselves.

They were not lofty people in isolation from their fellows. They were among those who were committed to the belief that society was a balance of reciprocal forces and interests, and that within the pattern they had their own part to play. On the whole they believed that their special duty lay in extending the spiritual frontiers of those with whom they lived, and thus positively improving their lot. What is described as musical genius was the connection of innate ability to skills acquired by constant application, idealism and opportunity.

This book is, so to speak, an account of the rise and fall of a dynasty. I have tried to show the members of this dynasty as human beings, with failings as well as virtues, in their ordinariness. They are set against the larger background of history, so that the effects on them and their work of social and political tendencies and events become apparent. I have also devoted a good deal of space to the so-called 'Bach Revival', showing the not inconsiderable part played in this by my own countrymen. Of these there were some who felt that in the art of music nationalist impulses were out of place, and that in the end the great artist belongs not to one people but to all.

This leads at least to one conclusion: that music not only can be, but is, a unifying force.

Over many years I have been privileged from time to time to work in Germany, and this book is some small token of the considerable debt owed to friends and colleagues in many parts of that country. Through them I have learned to appreciate that what may be called the spirit of the Bachs endures, and that in the general sense this is the hope of the future.

I have been generously received in all the places associated with the Bachs, and those acknowledged below have responded to my importunities with unfailing kindness and consideration.

P.M.Y.

November 1969

Contents

Preface

List of Illustrations

List of Music Examples

Acknowledgments

1 THURINGIA IN THE SIXTEENTH CENTURY
   Landscape and economy 1 Political and religious background 3 Emergent Bachs 6 Aspects of Lutheranism 10 Nationalist impulses 13 The German Passion 16 Notes to chapter 1 17

2 THE THIRTY YEARS WAR
   Divine displeasures 21 Influx of new ideas 23 Influence on music 25 War and its consequences 29 A war generation of Bachs 32 Notes to chapter 2 36

3 MIDDLE GERMAN BAROQUE
   The popular tradition 39 The aristocratic tradition 42 Confluence of traditions in Mühlhausen 43 Sons of Johann Bach 46 Sons of Christoph Bach 47 Sons of Heinrich Bach 49 Notes to chapter 3 61

4 JOHANN AMBROSIUS BACH OF EISENACH
   Court life in Eisenach 63 Johann Ambrosius Bach, citizen of Eisenach 65 Johann Christoph Bach, guardian of Johann Sebastian 69 More Bachs in Eisenach 70 In Ohrdruf 71 Lüneburg and the Court of Celle 73 Return to Thuringia 77 Emigrants 80 Notes to chapter 4 83

5 COURT MUSICIAN
   The Berlin–Dresden axis 87 The Courts of Weimar 89 Citizens of Weimar 90 J. S. Bach achieves prominence 92 Progressive government in Köthen 96 The composer's vocation 100 Notes to chapter 5 107

6 ENLIGHTENMENT AT JENA AND MEININGEN
   Liberal studies in a Thuringian university 110 Johann Nikolaus Bach as a teacher 113 Johann Nikolaus Bach as a composer 116 Musicians at Meiningen 123 Johann Ludwig Bach, a stylist 125 Notes to chapter 6 128

7 LEIPZIG

The city and its Kantors 130   Household affairs 135   The trials of a schoolmaster 138   Music and the Church 143   Civic and University affairs 150   The stature of Bach of Leipzig 155   Notes to chapter 7 158

8 FREDERIC THE GREAT

Prussia and Saxony 162   The Enlightened Despot 165   Emanuel Bach at the Prussian Court 167   The intellectuals of Berlin 170   Musical life in Berlin 171   Matters of style 176   Notes to chapter 8 181

9 THE HALLE BACH

The most gifted son 183   Life in Dresden 187   Move to Halle 190   Braunschweig 197   Johann Nikolaus Forkel at Göttingen 199   Bach in Berlin 200   Notes to chapter 9 204

10 EMANUEL BACH IN HAMBURG

Music in a 'Democratical' Society 207   The oratorio cult 211   English interests 212   Picture collection 213   A many-sided musician 214   Reputation of Emanuel Bach 220   Notes to chapter 10 221

11 THE CLASSICAL BACHS

The Bückeburg tradition 223   The influence of Count Wilhelm at Bückeburg 224   Court music at Bückeburg 225   Friedrich Bach and Herder 227   A visit to the 'London' Bach 230   Competence of a Kapellmeister 231   Painters in the family 235   Johann Sebastian Bach II 238   Johann Ernst Bach of Eisenach 241   Notes to chapter 11 245

12 THE LONDON BACH

An Ode for the Queen's Nuptials 248   Early years in Prussia and Italy 250   The operatic situation in England 254   Concert promotion 259   A wide range of musical interests 264   Social contacts 268   Country excursions 270   Man and musician 271   Notes to chapter 12 273

13 END OF AN OLD, AND ESTABLISHMENT OF A NEW, TRADITION

The passing of the old order 275   Planting seed in alien soil 281   Forkel and Zelter 283   Samuel Wesley and the Bach tradition 290   Broadening of interest in England 292   Inauguration of Bach Societies 298   Notes to chapter 13 301

CONTENTS

Appendix 1 Johann Jakob Bach in Stockholm   305

Appendix 2 Works based on the theme BACH   307

Appendix 3 *Das angenehme Leipzig*   309

Appendix 4 Portraits by Gottlieb Friedrich Bach (1714–85) and Johann Philipp Bach (1752–1846) in the Schloss Elisabethenburg (City Museum), Meiningen   312

Bibliography   315

Index:
  People   329
  Places   339

Illustrations

Between pages 74 and 75

Hans Bach?, after a woodcut, 1617
  Deutsche Staatsbibliothek, Berlin
The Bach House, Eisenach, drawing by Hanns Bock
  Bachhaus, Eisenach
Receipt for payment of wages signed by Swedish Royal musicians, including Johann Jakob Bach, 20th July 1714
  Stockholms Slottsarkiv
Minute of Nedre Borgrätten, Stockholm, 12th July 1728, concerning the Estate of Johann Jakob Bach
  Stockholms Slottsarkiv
Lüneburg in the seventeenth century
Johann Ludwig Bach, portrait by G. F. Bach
  Deutsche Staatsbibliothek, Berlin
St Thomas's Church, Leipzig, with the school in the background, in the time of J. S. Bach
  Bacharchiv, Leipzig
Violin part of Handel's *Armida abbandonata*, copied by J. S. Bach
  Landes- und Hochschulbibliothek, Darmstadt
J. S. Bach's testimonial for J. A. Scheibe, 4th April 1731
  Stadtarchiv, Freiberg
Das angenehme Leipzig, 1727, opening pages of word-book
  Martin-Luther-Universität, Halle
Portrait of J. S. Bach, by E. G. Haussmann, 1746
  Museum für Geschichte der Stadt Leipzig
Death of J. S. Bach and names of his successors noted in a copy of the *Leipziger Adress-Post-und-Reise Calender*, 1750
  Museum für Geschichte der Stadt Leipzig

Between pages 170 and 171

School note-book embellished by its owner—W. F. Bach
  Bachhaus, Eisenach
List of instruments at the Marktkirche, Halle, in the time of W. F. Bach
  Marktkirche, Halle
Frederic the Great as Commander-in-Chief, from *Historische und geographische Nachricht von ... Dressden*, 1761
  British Museum

Frederic the Great playing the flute, copper engraving by Peter Haas

Bombardment of Dresden by the Prussians, 1760, from *Historische und geographische Nachricht*, 1761
  British Museum

W. F. Bach, pencil drawing by P. Gülle
  Staats- und Universitätsbibliothek, Hamburg

C. P. E. Bach, drawing by Andreas Stöttrup
  Staats-und Universitätsbibliothek, Hamburg

Ideale Landschaft, 1776, painting by J. S. Bach II
  Kunsthalle, Hamburg

Portrait of Johann Wilhelm Treiber, by G. F. Bach
  Staatliche Museen, Meiningen

Portrait of Major von Uglansky, by J. P. Bach
  Staatliche Museen, Meiningen

Portrait of Luise-Eleonore, Duchess of Sachsen-Meiningen, by J. P. Bach
  Staatliche Museen, Meiningen

Between pages 266 and 267

Silhouettes of Tobias Friedrich Bach II (1723–1805), Kantor in Erfurt, and his wife Sophia Christina

J. C. F. Bach, drawing by Friedrich Rehberg
  Niedersächsische Staatsarchiv, Bückeburg

Violin I part from Symphony in E flat by J. C. F. Bach (autograph)
  Niedersächsische Staatsarchiv, Bückeburg

Concerto in C minor by C. P. E. Bach, copied by J. C. F. Bach
  Landes- und Hochschulbibliothek, Darmstadt

J. N. Forkel, anonymous drawing
  Deutsche Staatsbibliothek, Berlin

K. F. Zelter, lithograph by Count Anton Radziwill
  Deutsche Staatsbibliothek, Berlin

A German copy (late eighteenth century) of an unaccompanied sonata by J. S. Bach, brought to England
  Henry Watson Library, Manchester

Signs of the English 'Bach Revival', 15th June 1840

Morning Hymn at Sebastian Bach's, by T. E. Rosenthal, Berlin, published in *Illustrated London News*, 1877.

Music Examples

Chapter 1

                                                Page

'Meister Vriderich von   'Nu merke'   13
Svnnenburc':

Chapter 2

Johann Walther:	*Mitten wir im Leben sind*	21
Heinrich Schütz:	*Selig sind die Töten*	22
Melchior Vulpius:	*Dein Zorn der trückt uns mit Gewalt*	23
Georg Neumark:	*Du Beherrscher unsrer Sinnen*	25
Melchior Franck:	(a) Galliard	27
	(b) Gesang	27
Johann Bach:	|*Weint nicht um meinen Tod*	32
Heinrich Bach:	*Ich danke dir, Gott*	36

Chapter 3

Johann Ahle:	*Merk auf mein Herz*	44
J. Christoph Bach:	(a) & (b) *Meine Freundin, du bist schön*	53
,, ,,	*Der Mensch vom Weibe geboren*	54
,, ,,	*Fürchte dich nicht*	55
,, ,,	*Warum betrübst du dich*	55
Georg Christoph Bach:	*Siehe wie fein*	58
Johann Michael Bach:	*Es ist ein grosser Gewinn*	58
,, ,,	*Halt, was du hast*	58
,, ,,	*Halt, was du hast*	59

Chapter 4

Johann Bernhard Bach:	(a) Ouverture in G minor	71
	(b) Ouverture in G minor	71
Georg Böhm:	Prelude and Fugue in A minor	74
J. G. Kühnhausen:	*Matthäus-Passion*	75

Chapter 5

| J. S. Bach: | Chorale prelude, *Christum wir sollen loben schon* | 103 |
| ,,   ,, | Fantasia and Fugue in F minor | 105 |

Chapter 6

J. Nikolaus Bach:	Mass in E minor	117–20
,, ,,	*Der Jenaische Wein- und Bierrufer*	121–2
J. Ludwig Bach:	*Das ist meine Freude*	127
,, ,,	*Siehe, ich will meinen Engel senden*	128

Chapter 7

Sebastian Knüpfer:	*Ach Herr, strafe micht*	133
Johann Kuhnau:	*Ich freue mich im Herrn*	134
J. S. Bach:	*Gieb dich zufrieden*	136
„ „	*Hercules auf dem Scheidewege*	147
„ „	*O Ewigkeit, du Donnerwort*	
	(Cantata 60)	149
J. Ernst Bach:	*Passionsoratorium*	149
J. S. Bach:	*Auf, schmetternde Töne der*	
	muntern Trompeten	152
'Sperontes':	*Mein Vergnügen*	154
Alessandro Poglietti:	Ricercar Quarti Toni	156

Chapter 8

C. P. E. Bach:	Fugue in A major	174
„ „	*Pastorella*—'Eilt, ihr Schäfer'	177

Chapter 9

W. F. Bach:	Clavier Sonata in D major	190
„ „	*Dies ist der Tag*	193
„ „	Fugue in F minor	202
„ „	Clavier Concerto in F minor	204

Chapter 10

C. P. E. Bach:	Variations on 'Was helfen mir	
	tausend Ducaten'	210
„ „	*Die Israeliten in der Wüste*	216–17
„ „	*Morgengesang am Schöpfungsfeste*	218
„ „	*Jehova herrscht* (Ps. 93)	219
„ „	*Jehova sprach* (Ps. 110)	219–20

Chapter 11

J. C. F. Bach:	*Die Kindheit Jesu*	229
„ „	*Angloise*, from *Nebenstunden*	232
„ „	*Ich bin ein teutsches Mädchen*	232
„ „	*Ino*	233
„ „	Symphony in E flat	233–4
J. E. Bach:	Psalm 8	242–3
„ „	*An die Geissigen*	243
„ „	*Die Unzufriedenheit*	244
„ „	Fantasie	244

Chapter 12

J. C. Bach:	*Ode on the Nuptials of Queen*	250
	Charlotte	
„ „	*Si nocte tenebrosa*	252
„ „	*Salve regina*	253
„ „	*Zanaida*	255
„ „	*Carattaco*	257
„ „	*La Clemenza di Scipione*	261
„ „	*Catone in Utica*	261

J. C. Bach: Sonata in C minor (Op. V)   264

     ,,   ,,   Dance for a Court ball   266

     ,,   ,,   *Blushing shame*   268

     ,,   ,,   *Let the solemn organ blow*   268

Chapter 13

W. F. E. Bach: Violin sonata in A major   277

     ,,   ,,   Violin sonata in B flat major   277

     ,,   ,,   Ballet pantomime   279

C. P. E. Bach?:   Fugue subject for organ trial 281

Thomas Adams: Fugue in D flat major   297

ACKNOWLEDGMENTS

Mr Bertil Broomé, Kungl. Krigsarkivet, Stockholm; Dr Dieter Brosius, Niedersächsisches Staatsarchiv, Bückeburg; Dr Hans Walter Crodel; Dr Harald Heckmann, Deutsches Musikgeschichtliches Archiv, Kassel; Frau Elisabeth Heinritz; Dr Alex Helmer and Mr Anders Lönn, Svenst Musikhistoriskt Arkiv, Stockholm; Dr Annemarie Hille and Herr Klaus Bulling, Universitätsbibliothek, Jena; Prof. Dr Georg Knepler, Musikwissenschaftliches Institut, Humboldt Universität, Berlin; Dr Günther Kraft, Bachhaus, Eisenach; Herr Eberhard Matthes, Stadtarchiv, Eisenach; Dr Werner Neumann, Bacharchiv, Leipzig; Dr Nissen, Stadtarchiv, Göttingen; Mr Ewald V. Nolte, Moravian Music Foundation, Winston-Salem, North Carolina; Dr Konrad Sasse; Prof. Dr Walter Siegmund-Schultze and Dr Bernard Baselt, Musikwissenschaftliches Institut, Martin-Luther-Universität, Halle; Frau Walther, Museum für Geschichte der Stadt Leipzig; Landes- und Hochschulbibliothek, Darmstadt; Deutsche Staatsbibliothek, Berlin; Universitätsbibliothek, Halle; Staats- und Universitätsbibliothek, Hamburg.

ABBREVIATIONS

ABA	Altbachisches Archiv
B & H	Breitkopf und Härtel
BG	Bachgesellschaft
BJB	Bach-Jahrbuch
BM	British Museum
BWV	Verzeichnis der Werke J. S. Bachs (W. Schmieder)
DDT	Denkmäler deutscher Tonkunst
Falck	Catalogue of works of Wilhelm Friedemann Bach (Martin Falck)
NBG	Neue Bachgesellschaft
PRMA	Proceedings of the Royal Musical Association
Wtq.	Thematic Catalogue of works of Carl Philipp Emanuel Bach (Alfred Wotquenne)

The
Bachs
1500 – 1850

'It is certainly more laudable to be supported by merit than Blood, such advantages fortunately mixed make a strong Cement for lasting Renown.'

The Earl of Clarendon, Minister at the Court of Poland, 1766.

I

Thuringia in the Sixteenth Century

LANDSCAPE AND ECONOMY

In Saxony it used to be said that King August 'the Strong', in more senses than one, was the father of his people. The most likely candidate for this title in neighbouring Thuringia might well appear to be the first to be identified of the most famous line of Bachs—the almost legendary Veit. It was believed by his descendants—including Johann Sebastian and Carl Philipp Emanuel—that Veit, a miller and/or baker by trade, came to Thuringia at some time during the sixteenth century from Hungarian territory, which he had been compelled to leave on religious grounds. This assumption, to which we will revert, now provides a whetstone for genealogically minded musicologists, who prove that the *Ursprung* and the earliest lexicographers were wrong or right according to their own national affiliations.[1] At this juncture the point of importance is that Veit settled in Thuringia, and that his descendants, to a man and a woman, were typical Thuringians.

It is said that genius is born and not made. To this a rider may be added: it is more helpful to a genius to be born in one place than another. Thuringia—where the natives were supposed 'to be born to music'[2]—provided a congenial environment for musicians. To this the careers of half a hundred, or more, Bachs bear witness. It is one thing to state a fact, but another to explain it.

The musicality of Thuringia can only be interpreted in relation to geographic, historic and social circumstances, and the particular genius of the famous Bachs only understood in the light of such interpretation. Thuringia is a region within, but never quite of, Germany; proud of its indigenous traditions and culture, and insulated against criticism and even ridicule from outside by a sturdy, virile provincialism. The sum of Thuringian characteristics may be descried in the personality of J. S. Bach.

Thuringia—the term has ethnic but not political significance[3]—stretches eastwards from Eisenach for eighty miles or so to the neighbourhood of Altenburg, in a sequence of wooded hills—sometimes rising to mountains of 3,000 feet—and valleys. A line running roughly from Mühlhausen through Sondershausen and along the course of the Unstrut river marks the northern edge, while the southern limit borders Bavaria. Across the middle of Thuringia runs the main route from Frankfurt, Kassel and the west, through Leipzig and Dresden, to Warsaw, Prague, Budapest and the east. The principal Thuringian towns lying about this route are Eisenach, Gotha, Erfurt and Weimar. A north–south route from the old Hanseatic ports to Nürnberg, München and Italy crosses Thuringia by way of Jena and Rudolstadt.

The landscape of the region has exerted a strong influence on natives and strangers alike and its romantic properties have determined the style of prose and poetry of those who have attempted its description.

> Terra Thuringorum nulli ubertate secunda
> Frugibus ac herbis luxuriare solet . . .

So wrote Jeremias Wittichius, public notary and 'poet laureate' of Ohrdruf in 1660.[4] A Swiss tourist of the year 1800 was enchanted by the invitation the landscape offered to the painter. 'Between the slopes of the hills', he noted, 'narrow, dark valleys fade into the depths of the woods. Here one remembers the adventures of medieval knights and brigands.' In those retreats, he added, all was fantasy. But in between the hills were many villages, surrounded with pastures and orchards, where it seemed that life was idyllic.[5]

Thuringia was not only beautiful. It was, when and where circumstances allowed, also once prosperous. The natural resources were many and varied. There were the rural industries of agriculture and forestry. From the trees were built picturesque black-and-white houses, annexes to castles, and town halls, many of which still stand. Wood-carvers adorned the churches and monasteries, and individual craftsmen made toys and household ornaments (especially in the township of Sonneberg) that attracted tourist custom at an early date. The hills gave granite, sandstone, limestone and slate for the building trade. They also held deposits of iron, copper and manganese ore, which by the sixteenth century were put to extensive industrial use in the neighbourhood of Schmalkalden, Saalfeld, Zella-Mehlis, Suhl and Ilmenau. In this region, before the Reformation, there was also a profitable trade in ornaments. Alabaster was quarried near Friedrichroda. Langewiesen and Gehren were centres of the pottery industry, Lauscha of glass manufacture.

During the Middle Ages the benefits of native industry were enjoyed by the Church, by the territorial rulers and also by the towns—in which mayors and councils were more effective than they were to be again for a long time. At the beginning of the sixteenth century, after the decline of French power and the disruption of the Italian cities and states by war, the German economic situation overall was the most stable in Europe. Some part of the national wealth had been invested in education—the University of Erfurt was founded in 1392—and its tendency was often towards the spirit of inquiry, if not scepticism.

POLITICAL AND RELIGIOUS BACKGROUND

Politically Germany was a patchwork of states, parcelled out among princes, dukes and counts, who, in theory at least, were subject to the authority of the Emperor. The most powerful of these were the seven Electors: the spiritual princes of Köln, Mainz and Trier; and the secular princes of Bohemia, Saxony, Brandenburg and the Palatinate. Each, to a greater or lesser extent, was an absentee landlord; the ruler of Erfurt, for instance, was the Archbishop of Mainz. There was, in addition, a multiplicity of inferior nobility. From the height of the Wartburg, above Eisenach, one now looks out over two German states. In the sixteenth century one could see the outstretched territories of, perhaps, a dozen rulers. Herein lay the roots of the tragedy of German history; but also (depending on one's point of view) of what often may be seen as tragi-comedy. For instance, Gräfenroda—where at an early date certain virile members of the Bach clan were to be found—was the property of the counts of Henneburg. But they, in debt, put the district and its inhabitants in pawn, the pawnbroker being the House of Schwarzburg. To confuse the position still further there were in Germany some eighty-five 'Imperial' cities, which, answerable only to the Emperor, enjoyed a relative independence in respect of local government. In Thuringia there were two such cities; Nordhausen and Mühlhausen. Mühlhausen, with its fourteen Gothic churches, became a particularly important cultural centre with a powerful civic, musical tradition. In due course J. S. Bach was to benefit from this tradition.

The problems of the German states and cities in the late fifteenth and early sixteenth centuries were those of Western Europe in general; but, because of an unco-ordinated political structure, their solution was even more difficult. As the population grew, so pressure on land increased. Partly because of the growth of trade incident on a larger population, and partly because of the surplus yield of the silver mines at Freiberg in Saxony, inflation began to get out of hand. The nobility solved their own difficulties in this respect by putting up rents (and by insisting on more work and the fulfilment of duties that had previously tended to be ignored). Not the least pressing of the landlords were the clergy, whose frequent nepotism, indolence and corruption were thought not to be endearing characteristics. The time was ripe for a show-down.

The leaders of revolt were Martin Luther (1483–1546) and Thomas Müntzer (1490–1525), both of whom campaigned from and within Thuringia.

Within a decade the preaching and writing of Luther, attracting humanists already alive to the philosophy of Erasmus, patriots who resented both imperial and papal pretensions, and those in all ranks of society whose sense of piety was affronted by the exercises and exactions of the Roman Church, had coalesced into a definable Lutheranism. The cause of what by now had become a crusade was furthered by the edict of the Diet of Worms, which denounced Lutheranism as heresy and Luther as a heretic. After preaching a sermon in St George's Church, Eisenach, on 2nd May 1521, Luther took refuge for a year in the Wartburg—the legendary source of German song. Almost at once he began his great work, the translation of the New Testament into the vernacular.[6] At the same time he busied himself in the translation and composition of hymns and in the shaping of a new liturgy. The 'German Mass' was published in Wittenberg in January 1526. Eight years later the Bible, as a whole, became available to Germans in their own language.

Meanwhile the spirit of reformation conjoined with that of revolution. Müntzer, sometime a student in Halle and evangelical minister in Zwickau, was strongly influenced by the post-Hussite philosophy of the Bohemian Brethren. As a peripatetic preacher he aroused enthusiasm in Saxony, Thuringia, Hesse and Bavaria. At a tempestuous time in the history of Thuringia, Müntzer came to Mühlhausen in 1525. He intended to establish this town as the stronghold of his cause. He was prepared to do so by force of arms.

In 1525 there was a general uprising of peasants all over Germany. They wished to overthrow all authority and to make themselves free . . . [From Hesse and Thuringia some 8,000 assembled at Frankenhausen, near Mühlhausen.] These men were rabble-rousers, thieves, robbers, murderers, despoilers of the land, and they were led by extraordinarily inept commanders. Their chief was Thomas Müntzer, a Master of Arts and a dispossessed minister. His second-in-command was Heinrich Pfeiffer, formerly a monk at Reisenstein . . .[7]

Outnumbered, ill-equipped and without any strategic plan of campaign, the peasants were quickly subdued by the troops of Braunschweig, Hesse and Saxony. The field of Frankenhausen was a disaster. Müntzer was taken prisoner on 16th May and executed eleven days later.

The Peasants' War was not only disastrous in a particular but also in a general sense. Luther, already under obligation to the Elector of Saxony (Frederick 'the Wise') for support and protection, opted for alliance between State and Church. Thus the Lutheran became the Established Church in those dominions where the ruler embraced that faith. In much of Hesse, Saxony and Thuringia the agreement regularizing this, arrived at during the protracted negotiations towards the Peace of Augsburg (1555), recognized a *fait accompli*; even in Catholic Erfurt the town council imposed restrictions on the Catholics. Those who gained most from the Peace of Augsburg were the aristocracy, who 'triumphed over the national as well as the imperial interest',[8] and settled down to the not uncongenial task of translating *Feudalismus* into *Absolutismus*.

One benefit of the Reformation was that churches in towns and villages, many of which had been finally Gothicized only on the eve of the Reformation, took on a new lease of life; not merely as places of worship, or of theological exposition, but also as community centres and as focal points for musical activity.

Another benefit of Lutheranism was that the principles of humanism in education, already developed in the civic schools established before the Reformation in some Thuringian towns, intensified. That this was so was due to Luther himself and to Melanchthon. More schools were founded—as at Mühlhausen in 1544—and the importance of a higher education was marked by the opening of the University of Jena (as a 'high school') on 19th March 1548 in the former home of the Dominicans; with departments of theology with philosophy, poetry with rhetoric and, soon afterwards, medicine and law.[9] Among early enrolments at Jena were those of Laurence and Wolfgang Bach (1552),[10] to remind us that at that time almost every other native of Thuringia bore this name.

These particular Bachs, however, were not of the main stream. Those who now seem of the most significance were then those of the least.

EMERGENT BACHS

The name Bach (= brook) was widespread and appeared in various countries in different forms during the fifteenth and sixteenth centuries. In the *Chronik der Bäckergenossenschaft* (1569) of Bratislava (Pressburg) there were entries to lend support to the theory that the most significant branch of the Bachs had originated in those parts: of bearers of the name Bach, there were mentioned Paul Pach, Andreas Bach, George Bach, Elias Bach, Paulus Paach, Georg Pach. The same names were to be found in the church records at Pressburg a hundred years later, as also in the Bohemian town of Hustomice pod Brdy: these Bachs, some Catholic, some Protestant, were occasionally described as German.[11]

But the largest colony of Bachs was settled in Thuringia. A selection of ecclesiastical entries is sufficient to show their persistence. Gunther Bache (mentioned in 1372) belonged to Georgenthal, and Hans Bach (1415) to Schmalkalden. Hans (Johannes, Johann) was a popular Christian name and occurred frequently, as in Ohrdruf (1472, 1473, 1490) and in Gräfenroda, near Arnstadt, where, in 1509, Hans Bach (*b.* 1480) was prosecuted by an ecclesiastical court of the Archdiocese of Mainz, at Erfurt, but defended by Count Günther of Schwarzburg.[12] In Ohrdruf at this time were also Kurt Bages and Matthäus Bach, and in Mechterstädt (1531) Hartung Bach.[13] Most of these Bachs were peasants, though some were miners. They were, and continued to be, prolific. Thus Wolf Bach, of Rockhausen near Arnstadt, fathered eleven children during the last quarter of the sixteenth century.[14]

At this point comes into view the one whose name is rather more than a mere shadow on the pages of history: Veit, the miller and/or baker of Wechmar. The trouble with him is to separate scanty fact from romantic legend. The *Ursprung* gives to Veit the honour of being the first of the apostolic line. It states his arrival in Thuringia from Hungary. It relates how he played the *cythringen* (a Thuringian type of zither) while he worked. Supposititiously it states that he learned how to keep time by disciplining his rhythm to that of the mill-wheel, in this way ensuring the gift of music for his descendants. The main part of this pious recollection is reasonable deduction: many Thuringians played the zither at that time and, whether millers or not, sired musical progeny. To be truthful, it was practically impossible to be an unmusical Thuringian. What may be accepted as historical—for to have invented it would have been pointless—is the reference to a Hungarian episode. (It should be added that Thuringia had suffered invasion by Magyars during the Middle Ages and that both place names and family names bore—and still bear—witness to the fact.)

Assuming that Veit was a Thuringian who migrated to Hungary (or to a Magyar community)—which still ought to remain an open question in spite of the general inclination to answer it in this way—it must be accepted that he may have had good reason. During the first part of the Luther-Müntzer Reformation many Thuringians were compelled to review their religious beliefs. After 1526 some, accepting the principles of the Czech Brethren, moved to the east. (There were German minorities, both Catholic and Protestant, in Transylvania, which even in troubled times enjoyed a degree of toleration.) It is possible that Veit Bach was among them. On the other hand, after the suppression of the peasants in 1525 there may have been political reasons for emigration. One Caspar Bach, together with Niclas Hoffman (another musical family), was reported to have been among the supporters of Müntzer; Hoffman was also connected with the Bohemian Brethren.[15] And why did Veit return to Thuringia? In 1548 there was a movement of persecuted Brethren from Bohemia. Some went to Poland, but for a German the obvious thing to do was to return whence he had come. Some such refugees were at this time housed in the quarters of the Kreuz Chor in Dresden. There may of course have been economic, social or family reasons for Veit's return.

Like most other Thuringian villages Wechmar, some two miles south of Gotha, had its quota of Bachs in the sixteenth century. There were, for instance, a Hans Bach, who was living there in 1561; 'Margarete Bach von Wechmar', whose wedding, in February 1564, was recorded in the Ohrdruf parish register:[16] and there was a regular procession of Veits. One, said to have come from 'Presswitz',[17] was documented in 1519; a second, living from 1535 to 1610, left Thuringia for Frankfurt (Oder) and, later, Berlin; a third was born in Oberkatz in 1579; a fourth married Margareta, widow of Klaus Volstein, in 1600; in the same year a Vitus Bach departed for Mellrichstadt; yet another Veit, whose profession, or trade, is unknown, died in Wechmar on 8th March 1619 and was buried on the same day.[18] The patron saint of Wechmar—adopted from the Benedictine mother-house of Corvey—was Vitus, who thus unwittingly strewed confusion into history. It was hitherto wrongly assumed that the original Veit of the *Ursprung* was he who was buried on 8th March 1619. It is now clear, however, that this Veit died before 1577,[19] which makes sense of the main part of his foregoing putative biography.

Veit I (in apposition to Veit II, *d.* 1619) had two sons for certain: Johannes (Hans), who was trained as a baker presumably to succeed to his father's business, and Lips, a carpet-maker. Both were noticed as householders in Wechmar in 1577—after the death of their father. It may be that Appolonia Bach, married in Ohrdruf in 1576, was a daughter, and Veit II another son of Veit I. What is certain is that Hans Bach I, living in the village when Veit I arrived (or returned), was not, as was formerly accepted, Veit's father. He may have been a brother or a cousin.

Young Hans (Johannes) inherited his father's musical inclinations to such a degree that he was given the opportunity of expert tuition. Since his aspirations went no further than the prospect of augmenting his earnings through proficiency in the field of popular music he was apprenticed to the *Stadtpfeifer* of Gotha. As was the practice, he lived for a year under the protection of his tutor in the Castle of Grimmenstein, which, notorious in the time of Johann Friedrich II (1555–67) as a refuge for brigands, was pulled down in 1567.[20] He married Anna Schmiedt, an innkeeper's daughter, and returned to Wechmar.[21] Among the children of Hans II, who died in 1626, were Johann (1604–73), Christoph (1613–61) and Heinrich (1615–92), who became musicians. Like all members of his craft Hans was often engaged to play in towns other than his own. He was reputed to have performed in Arnstadt, Erfurt, Eisenach, Suhl and Schmalkalden—all of them places in which the name Bach was to be more or less familiar in the years that were to come.

Meanwhile the Bachs were beginning to gain a more than precarious foothold in professional music in Gotha, where the establishment in 1565 of a separate court, independent of that of Weimar, gave incentive especially to secular musicians. Caspar Bach, of Wechmar (possibly a son of Hans I, and therefore a cousin of Johannes), at the beginning of the seventeenth century was one of the three-man team of town musicians who played from the towers of the town at stated hours, in church on festival occasions and for weddings and wherever otherwise required for ceremonial occasion or for entertainment.[22] Caspar left Gotha in 1620 for Arnstadt, where he followed his profession of *Hausmann*, and prepared his sons, Johannes (1602–32), Melchior (1603–34) and Nikol (1619–37), for the same career. The progeny of Lips the carpet-maker also showed a disposition towards music. Jonas (*b.* after 1567, date of death unknown) is said to have been sent to Italy to study music. He is also said to have been blind. It is possible that

another son of Lips also studied in Italy. Lips II (1590–1626), presumed
to have been the third of the 'drey Söhne' of Lips I, stayed in Wechmar,
modestly occupied as a *Spielmann*.[23]

By the beginning of the seventeenth century, then, there was a
network of musical Bachs in Thuringia. Professionally speaking,
however, they were near the foot of the ladder. A *Spielmann* belonged
to that ancient fraternity (described as 'Spellute' by the magistracy
of Zittau, Saxony, in 1393) of peripatetic musicians who, playing zink
(cornet), dulcian (the later bassoon), schalmei (shawm), pommer (or
bompart, the bass of the shawm family), krummhorn, recorder,
trumpet, bassoon or stringed instrument, wandered from village to
village, market to market. The *Hausmann* was on a slightly higher
grade, but inferior to the *Stadtpfeifer* (who, like the English wait, was
on the payroll of town and/or ruler). He in turn ranked lower than the
Court Trumpeter. At the top of the profession were the Kapellmeister,
the organist, the Kantor. These latter, if not overpaid, and often combining their musical duties with another occupation, were generally
regarded as men of learning, and in a society where education was
esteemed that counted for something. The first wave of Bachs had a
long way to go. But that their star began fitfully to shine during the
latter part of the sixteenth century was due, if indirectly, to the liberating influences of Lutheran humanism. One is not permitted to speculate.
If one were it might be urged that without Luther there would have
been no Bachs in the front ranks of music.

Music is (or was) essentially a communal art. Thuringia was (and is)
an aggregation of more or less self-sufficient communities. In villages
of a few hundred, and towns of a few thousand, inhabitants developed
their recreations and art forms from their own resources. Music, a
continuation of folk-song and dance on the one hand, and of the ancient
traditions of the Church on the other, flourished.

> Vox sacra ubique Dei viget, et lata Musica floret:
> Agricolae in pagis ore canora vibrant.
> Suaviter os cantat pueri, et delectat adulti:
> Organum et plectrum mulcat, et aede sonat.[24]

The fact that music belonged to the people—as it may be said to do in
Wales—was ever a source of pride to Thuringians.

> Because in these places [Gotha, etc.] the peasants understand
> instrumental music—not only stringed instruments of all kinds
> such as violins, viols, viols da gamba, 'clavzimbeln', spinets,
> 'zitrinchen', which are made in Grabsleben [a village near Gotha]

—one frequently hears works for organ, with so many forms and variations, often even in small hamlets, that one is amazed. In particular those who have made no small name for this province on account of its music are the Altenburg, Ahle, Briegel, Bach and other families.[25]

ASPECTS OF LUTHERANISM

Luther was both an idealist and a realist. He loved music for its own sake and in it found relief and inspiration, saying, 'Music is the best balm for a troubled heart. It makes the heart glad again, renews and quickens it.' Already in his youth music had its place in the curriculum of the Thuringian and Saxon schools as an adjunct to religious instruction. The works of the polyphonic masters were contained in manuscript collections to be found in the libraries of the principal ecclesiastical foundations,[26] and their performance was widespread. Luther had especial regard for the music of Josquin des Prés (c. 1445–1521) and Obrecht (c. 1450–1505). Of the former he spoke as follows: 'Sic deus praedicavit evangelium etiam per musicam, ut videtur in Josquin.' He resolved that what was good in the Catholic ritual should be retained: 'Nos interim omnia probabimus, quod bonum est tenebimus.' Luther had been well grounded in the theory and practice of music at Eisenach and at Erfurt. The university library at Erfurt possessed a number of medieval theoretical works. Luther's teacher, Nikolaus Marschalck, discussed music in his *Libellum de Orthographia* of 1501, and in the same year published a *Laus musarum* containing a four-part song, 'Mores amatoris', of his own composition. Other members of the university fraternity in Erfurt with especial interest in music were Conradus Muth (Mutianus Rufus), Eobanus Hesse—appointed Professor of Rhetoric and Poetry at Erfurt in 1517—and Johann Spangenberg, who published his *Quaestiones musicae in usum scholae Northusianae* in Nürnberg in 1536. In this environment Luther came to appreciate the intellectual properties of music and his esteem for composers was high. He was acquainted with Lucas Edenberger, musical adviser to Ernst, Duke of Saxony; Görg Planck, organist at Zeitz; Wolff Heintz, the famous organist at the church in the Market Place in Halle; Ludwig Senfl (c. 1490–1555), pupil of Isaac in Vienna and later musician at the Bavarian Court in München; and with Johann Walther (1496–1570). Walther, born at Kahla, in Thuringia, was Luther's closest associate among composers, and his counsel in the formulation of a broader musical culture was invaluable.

Luther himself played the lute and the recorder, and 'had a fine clear voice, both in singing and speaking'.[27] He was equally at home in the field of secular and church music and, remembering his own modest background, retained his affection for popular songs. From folk-music he learned the indissolubility of words and melody, and this affected not only his own style as poet but his whole philosophy of music in society. Music was an art. 'But Luther's was no modern concept of "art" as a phenomenon to which man should be receptive in museums, concerts, and so on: for him art was what man can himself do and produce.'[28] In 1523 he wrote to Georg Spalatin,[29] Counsellor to Frederick 'the Wise', of his intention to issue collections of 'German psalms for the people, so that the word of God might stay with the people through the medium of song'.

In 1523 Luther's principal concern was for the shaping of a liturgy, about which he wrote a letter to his friend Nikolaus Hausmann, minister at Zwickau, entitled *Formula Missae et Communionis*. For three years he laboured on this project, assisted by Johann Walther. Of the German Mass he wrote in 1524, 'text and music, accent and melody, and its general character must come directly from within the mother tongue; otherwise it is merely a copy—that is what asses do'. In January 1526 the *Deutsche Messe und Gottesdienst* with Luther's Preface and annotations was published in Wittenberg.

Two years before this publication the first fruits of Luther's and Walther's collaboration, *Geystliche Lieder, mit einer newen Vorrhede D. Mart. Luth.*, were published in Leipzig. This collection of 'spiritual songs' was set out in plain monody, for the 'chorales' (as they were now described) were essentially for congregational, unison, singing, in contrast to the motets which belonged to the more expert choir singers. *Ein feste Burg*, the foundation song of Lutheranism, was first issued in this anthology of 1524.

Luther's views on music came from his own experience. He could be sharply critical, as when Edenberger showed him a piece of clever canonic writing: 'Artis sat habet,' said Luther, 'sed caret suavitate.' He suggested to his friends what they might profitably treat as for choral use. Thus, on 4th October 1530, he asked Senfl to prepare for him a 'many-voiced' arrangement of *Ich lieg und schlafe*. Senfl in fact returned a setting of Ps. 118, v. 17, *Non moriar, sed vivam*. Most of all was Luther concerned for the place of music in education, and here again he worked from the particular to the general. On 26th August 1542 he wrote to Markus Crodel, master of the school at Torgau where

Walther was music teacher and where Luther's son was a pupil: '... wish Johann Walther well from me, and ask him to provide my son with instruction in music. I indeed must develop theologians, but I desire that also grammarians and musicians be trained among our people'.

Johann Sebastian Bach was, as is well known, a schoolmaster. He was a schoolmaster because Luther had designed his educational system in such a way that music could not be left out of the curriculum.[30] The system thus laid down lasted for about two hundred years. Bach was involved in it at its latter end when a new wave of educational reform was inexorably rising. It was unfortunate for Bach that he caught the full force of this wave. He was a conservative. What Luther had devised was good enough for him. We can see his point of view.

The teaching of music varied very much from town to town. In the smaller schools pupils learned their music by rote and did not go much further than the obligatory chorale. In larger schools—in Dresden, Leipzig, Torgau, Halle, Freiberg, Mühlhausen, for instance—the upper classes were expert sight-readers and instrumentalists. In a large establishment the Kantor, if he was fortunate, had the assistance of a Succentor, who took charge of the lower classes and directed choral performances when the Kantor—who often superintended the music of more than one church—was absent.

The focal point of musical performance was the *Kantorei*—the choir. Before the Reformation a *Kantorei* was attached to a monastery, to a Court chapel, or to a bishop's church. The most famous of the choirs in central Germany were those of St Thomas's Church, Leipzig, which was founded as a body of *Canonici* in 1213,[31] and the Kreuz Chor of Dresden, which was already in being at that time. The broad plan of Melanchthon, however, ensured that each town would have its own Kantorei, based on the *Chorus musicus*, for which the schools provided a steady supply of boys. As the boys matured they were promoted to be *Adjuvantes* (among whom were prefects responsible for some administrative duties), to help the masters with the tenor and bass parts. To be a member of such a choir was no sinecure. Each Sunday there were two motets to be sung, as also on Saturday, and at certain special Vespers. The choristers were employed for secular occasions too. At festival times they sang in the streets for the benefit of the townspeople, and sometimes gave cause for censure by unseemly behaviour. Particularly at Christmas, Easter and Whitsuntide, and on the Feast of St Gregory (12th March), they contributed hymns and songs to the dramas customarily performed at those times.

The stimulus given to general musical activity by the *Kantorei*, directed by a good Kantor, was great.

> The example of [former] monasteries and schools, the backward glance at the Mastersinger Guilds of Southern Germany, above all the fresh Protestant faith, so affected the laity, that in the year 1530, a new *Kantorei*, comprising scholars and citizens, came into being in Torgau, under the direction of the School Kantor [Johann Walther].[32]

NATIONALIST IMPULSES

The Reformation, and its consequences, turned the German-speaking people towards a new concept: that of a national homogeneity based on language. By his writing, and most of all by his translation of the Bible, Luther had raised the status of the German language, bringing it into the field of literature. At the same time he had given a new turn to German music by demonstrating that its true inspiration should be the language of the people. Yet, because of his regard for the musical accomplishments of the broader tradition, this principle was not permitted to provoke musical chauvinism. 'The age of Humanism', wrote Erich Wennig, 'brought together the artistic sensibilities of Germany and [the rest of the Holy Roman Empire] into a new expression. . . . Southern Germany was the point where influences from north and south coalesced.'[33]

The way in which these influences met is illustrated by the songbooks that were published during the Reformation and post-Reformation period. These books, which appeared in profusion, also testify to the broadly based *Kantorei* tradition, and to the fact that these bodies were 'not merely music societies but also fraternities, where were to be found the best elements of society'.[34] The choral society was not only an extension of the school choir, but also of the Meistersinger cult, which had spread from Nürnberg into Hesse, Thuringia and Saxony as late as 1500. Meistersinger songs, of which the words are in Thuringian dialect, are contained in the famous *Jenaer Liederhandschrift*[35] of the late fourteenth century, and from this type of song (see below) it is but a short step to the chorale—which had many roots.

Nu mer - ke, ho   und   e - dele man,   wer   dich   an   dy - me   ra - te

In Freiberg the existence of a Meistersinger guild was acknowledged in a statement of the town council as late as 24th September 1571: 'Singschule will ein Satler halden, man wilss ime uff negsten Dornstag zu halden vergunnen.'[36]

The *Kantorei* tradition, as established in the middle years of the sixteenth century, had a profound effect on music in Saxony and Thuringia, breeding a new race of composers. Composers whose competence was assured by wide experience of choral music, by practical undertakings with singers of average skill who were often amateur, and whose musical talent was supported by extensive reading in other fields—particularly those of the classics and of theology. These men had the advantage of working in a community in which music was respected, in which it was—as in few other communities—genuinely a way of life. They had the disadvantage of having to accommodate their ambitions to the decisions of town councillors, and sometimes also of aristocratic overlords. This tradition lasted for two hundred years, until the time of Johann Sebastian Bach, the general shape of whose career may be seen as emerging more than a hundred years before he was born.

Among this first generation of Lutheran Kantors were some whose influence overran the limits of their office. Joseph Schlegel (1529–93), for the last forty years of his life Kantor in Freiberg, was a fine organist, one of whose pieces was included in Hans Rühling's *Orgelbuch* of 1583. His *Te Deum*, published in 1568, was also designated as 'auff die orgel'. Schlegel, as will be shown, stands within the tradition of German Passion Music. He was succeeded in Freiberg by Salomon Künel, whose testimonials suggested that he had been an outstanding music student at the City School in Leipzig. He in turn was succeeded by Johannes Neuhass, a former pupil of Schlegel in Freiberg who had had his first experience of a Kantor's office in Dederau. In Magdeburg Gallus Dres(s)ler (1553–89) was for a time Kantor in the Cathedral School. A voluminous motet composer, Dresler's volume of *Sacrarum Cantionum* (1574) was among the volumes used at Jena in the last quarter of the century, and also at Weimar at the beginning of the seventeenth century, when the town (as opposed to the duke's) Kantor was the great Melchior Vulpius (*c.* 1560–1615). Interest in music as a philosophic study in the higher realms of education was now somewhat diminished, but (as a consequence of the curriculum in the schools and the general function of Kantors and organists in society) it began to figure among the practical exercises. In 1570 a *Societas musi-*

calis was established in the University of Jena. This, one of the oldest of such societies in Germany, experienced several deaths and rebirths.

A list of Thuringian musical dynasties given by Pfefferkorn puts at its head the family of Lindemann, which was connected with that of Martin Luther, whose mother was a Lindemann. Under Cyriakus Lindemann, Rektor from 1562 to 1568, the Grammar School of Gotha became famous. At the same time the performances of music of 'Josquinis, Clementis non papae, Orlandi und dergleichen Gesänge . . .'[37] also became famous. The Kantor, no doubt a relative of the Rektor, was Johannes Lindemann (*c.* 1550–*c.* 1634), *Musicus Gothanus Celeberrimus*, who in 1598 published an edition of *Fröhliche Madrigalia und Balletti auch andere liebliche Italienische Gesänglein zu Fünff Stimmen*. In Gotha, and through Lindemann, the first of the Bachs to be registered as musicians had opportunity to hear a wide variety of music.

The greatest of the Thuringian Kantors of that generation, however, was Joachim à Burgk (so named after the village near Magdeburg where he was born, his family name being Moller). Joachim à Burgk (1545–1610) was Kantor in the Grammar School (1563) of Mühlhausen, and organist of the Church of St Blasius—an office later filled by J. S. Bach. He also acted as secretary to various council committees and in due course became a town councillor. His second marriage (in 1583), to a councillor's daughter, brought him a substantial private income and ensured his place among the influential in the town. At least one of his pupils achieved distinction. This was Johannes Eccard (1553–1611), subsequently musician to the Fuggers in Augsburg, second Kapellmeister to the Margraf of Brandenburg-Ansbach, and Kapellmeister to the Elector of Brandenburg, in Berlin. Eccard's fame now rests on his *Geistliche Lieder* (1597), a summary of the great age of the Lutheran chorale. Eccard, however, first made his name in Mühlhausen, and in association with his teacher. Thus in 1576 there were published in Mühlhausen:

Odae Ludovici Helboldi, Latinae & Germanicae: Gregoriano scholasticorum festo, piae qū disciplinae auspicio, consecratae:

NEW GESAENGLEIN/AUSSER DER SCHÜLER Fest an S. Gregory tag/ gerichtet/nur in Vier stimmen Componiret/Durch Ioachimum à Burck, und Iohannem Eccardum = Mulhusinum,
and

Zwentzig Newe Christliche Gesaeng
. . . Iohannem Eccardum.

THE GERMAN PASSION

The importance of school music, indicated in the first of these titles, also explains the most significant work of à Burgk, his *Deutsche Passion*, printed in Erfurt in 1573. In his Preface to this work, the words coming from Luther's translation of St John's Gospel, à Burgk explained that hitherto the Passion setting generally used in Thuringia was that, in Latin, of Obrecht, but that, in his opinion, the time was ripe for a 'German Passion' for use in schools and churches. The need for a Passion in the vernacular is otherwise indicated by a copy of Obrecht's *St Matthew Passion*, to which Johann Steuerlein (1546– c. 1600) sometime secretary to the Court in Meiningen, and Poet Laureate, added a German text.[38]

At the beginning of the sixteenth century three types of *Passion* existed in Germany: one in plainsong, exemplified by the *Passio D. N. secundum quattuor evangelistas* in the university library, Ljubljana;[39] one in 'motet' style, as with Obrecht; and a dramatized version in the form of a mystery play. During the period of the Reformation the three types—which in any case overlapped—came closer together. From such association and assimilation emerged the 'oratorio' type of *Passion*, the settings of Scandello, Schütz, Sebastiani, Theile and Johann Sebastian Bach.

Before 1530 Johann Walther had prepared a plainsong version of the *Passion* according to St Matthew, with utterances of the crowd put into simple four-part harmony. A similar *Passion* was composed at about the same time by Sebald Heyden (1499–1561), of Nürnberg. In these, as in subsequent *Passions*, the interpolation of chorales by a congregation was anticipated. Walther's *Passion*, not unexpectedly, was widely used. Printed in the *Neu Leipziger Gesangbuch* of Gottfried Vopelius (1635–1715), Kantor of St Nicholas's Church, Leipzig, it was performed in that city until two years before Bach went to St Thomas's School.

The motet style of *Passion*, as developed by à Burgk after the model of Obrecht, was continued through the *Passio germanica Dom. n. Jesu Christi* of Joseph Schlegel,[40] the *Passio et Resurrectio* of Antonio Scandello (1517–80), the Italian Kapellmeister of the Electoral Court Chapel in Dresden, and the *Deutsche Passion*, after St John, of 1613, by the Freiberg Kantor, Christoph Demantius (1567–1643), into the *St Matthew Passion* of Schütz.

During this period the most popular form of representation of the *Passion* came to a climax, and was then more or less entirely extinguished. There was a long tradition of Christmas, Easter and Whitsun plays in Germany, as well as plays in celebration of St Gregory's Day. These plays were performed by citizens and their children, sometimes in pageant form through the streets (as in England,) sometimes on a particular site. In Freiberg, for instance, they were performed either outside the 'Golden Porch' of the cathedral, or in the Upper Market. These plays were arranged and supported by the town council and during their performance motets were sung by the cathedral choir.

Luther, afraid of unseemly laughter at such performances (as in England there was sometimes opportunity for merriment), urged the reconstitution of the traditional plays. Heathen elements were excluded from the Christmas Play, while Joachim Greff, minister at Zwickau, was encouraged to write an Easter Play less obscurantist than those that had been traditional. Greff's play, published in 1542, was in five acts and included songs and motets sung by the school choir and chorales sung by the people. Of these the principal was Luther's favourite chorale, *Christ ist erstanden*.

This kind of play, drawing together themes that were expressed not only in action, in poetry and in music, but also in the sculptures of many unknown masters, and the paintings of Cranach that were among the glories of the Saxon and Thuringian churches, brought to an end one tradition. But it was the beginning of a new tradition. The impulses inherent in the German mystery were transferred to the *Passion* in musical form. 'The Freiberg Play', wrote Wilhelm Creizenach, 'was not a conventional exposition of the Passion, but one of the great tragedies of the world, which in the last and most perfect period of medieval drama, must have had an overwhelming effect.'[41] The theme of suffering was to take on a new significance.

NOTES TO CHAPTER ONE

1. The *Ursprung der musicalisch-Bachischen Familie* (a genealogy), said by Carl Philipp Emanuel Bach to have been prepared by his father, was given to Johann Nikolaus Forkel in 1775. This *Ursprung*, of which two other copies exist, contained notes on fifty-three members of the family up to the year 1735 (5th September, the birthday of Johann Christian Bach). Johann Walther, a relative of Johann Sebastian and presumably acting on information received from him, stated in his *Musikalisches Lexicon* (1732): 'Die Bachische Familie soll aus Ungarn herstammen.' This statement was accepted by subsequent lexicographers until the present century.

2. Jacob Adlung, *Anleitung zu der musikalischen Gelahrtheit*, Erfurt, 1758, p. 107.

3. Thuringia was a 'Land' only during the period of the Weimar Republic after the First World War. For ecclesiastical purposes, the region is unified under the authority of the Evangelical Bishop of Thuringia.

4. *See* Joh. Christoph. Olearii: Hall. Sax., *Rerum Thuringicarum Syntagma, Allerhand denckwürdige Thüringische Historien und Chronicken*, Erfurt, 1703, p. 11.

5. *Briefe auf einer Reise durch Thüringen und Hessen; Geschrieben von einem wandernden Helvetier im Jahr 1800*, Altenburg/Erfurt, 1801, pp. 119–20, describing the journey from Gotha to Eisenach.

6. The New Testament, in German, was published in Wittenberg in September 1522, in an edition of, perhaps, 5,000. In December it was necessary to issue a second edition.

7. Olearius (*see* Note 4), p. 105, 'Plagen und traurige Zufälle'. Reisenstein = Reitzenstein, a village near Hof, in the north-east of Bavaria.

8. G. Droysen, *Das Zeitalter des Dreisigjährigen Krieges*, 2 vols., Berlin, 1888, I, p. 17.

9. During the plague years of 1527 and 1535 Wittenberg students had been evacuated to Jena. After the defeat of the Elector at Mühlberg in 1547 and the loss of Wittenberg it was necessary to set up a new Protestant university. Jena was chosen as the site. The university, as such, was instituted on 2nd February 1558, but the records of students date from ten years earlier.

10. *Die Matrikel der Universität Jena*, vol. I, 1548–1652, Jena, 1944, p. 9. In 1573 Bernhard Bach, of Wölfis, near Gotha, became a student, and in 1598 Melchior Bach, of Regenstauffen (Pal.).

11. Günther Kraft, *Entstehung und Ausbreitung des musikalischen Bach-Geschlechtes in Thüringen* (Doctoral Dissertation in the Martin Luther University, Halle-Wittenberg, 1964), p. 45. *See also* Ernest Zaversky, 'Zur angeblichen Pressburger Herkunft der Familie Bach', *BJB*, 53 Jg., Berlin, 1967.

12. *Bach in Thüringen*, Berlin, 1950, p. 162.

13. Kraft (*see* Note 11 above), pp. 41, 567a.

14. *Bach in Thüringen*, p. 178.

15. Kraft (*see* Note 11 above), p. 718.

16. In 1565 the parish registers recorded the marriage of Apollonia Bach; in 1570, that of Barbara Bach, of Wölfis; in 1576, the death of Anna Bach, and in 1579 that of Hans Bach, both of Erfurt.

17. Probably Presswitz, near Saalfeld; possibly Priessnitz, near Naumburg.

18. Kraft (*see* Note 11 above), pp. 521, 530, 544.

19. Kraft (*see* Note 11 above), p. 522.

20. Before the replacement of Grimmenstein by the Palace of Friedenstein (from 1643) the town hall of Gotha was adapted as a 'Residence'
for the use of Duke Ernst 'the Pious'. *See* A. Beck, *Geschichte des
gothaischen Landes*, 3 vols, Gotha, 1868–75, II, p. 3898.

21. Kraft (*see* Note 11 above), p. 523.

22. 'Scheidementel . . . het drey pfeiffer, Matz Ziseke, der Haussman
uf dem Neumarkts thorme, undt sein Bruder Liliax Ziske mit dem
Zincken [= English, 'cornet'] und Matz Ziseken Lehrknecht
Caspar [Bach] . . .', from Gotha Church Register, quoted by Kraft
(*see* Note 11 above), p. 525.

23. (*See* Note 22 above), p. 544.

24. Jer. Wittichius, in Olearius (*see* Note 4 above), p. 13.

25. *Merkwürdige und Auserlesene Geschichte von der berümten Landgrafschaft
Thüringen*, [Erfurt?] Anno 1685.

26. For example, the Masses of Lassus and Philippe de Monte in the
Library of the Gymnasium Albertinum, Freiberg (Saxony), and of
Josquin des Prés in the beautiful *Chorbuch Nr. 3* (copied in the Netherlands *c.* 1520 and once possessed by Frederick 'the Wise' of Saxony)
in the University Library, Jena.

27. Alberus, quoted in Hans Engel, *Musik in Thüringen*, Köln/Graz,
1966, p. 86.

28. Christhard Mahrenholz, *Luther und die Kirchen-Musik*, Kassel, 1937, p. 5.

29. Georg Spalatin, formerly Burckhardt (1482 or 4–1545) was a student
at Erfurt and a pupil of Marschalck, with whom he travelled to
Greece. A prominent humanist, Spalatin was first Master of the High
School (later University) of Wittenberg, and afterwards tutor and
secretary to Frederick 'the Wise'.

30. Cf. Johann Bugenhagen's *Braunschweigische Kirchenordnung* (1528) and
Wittenberger Kirchenordnung (1533) '. . . nach der für die erste Nach-
mittagsstunde die Musica mit der summa und secunda Classe . . .'

31. The Charter was given by the Emperor Otto IV: *see* 'Das Stift der
regulirten Chorherre zu St Thomas,' in K. C. E. Gretschel, *Kirchliche
Zustände Leipzigs*, Leipzig, 1839, p. 6 f.

32. Hermann Kretzschmar, 'Sachsen in der Musikgeschichte', in
Gesammelte Aufsätze über Musik, Leipzig, 1910, p. 249.

33. Erich Wennig, *Chronik des musikalischen Lebens der Stadt Jena*, Jena
[1943] I, p. 13.

34. Kretzschmar (*see* Note 32 above), p. 249.

35. University Library, Jena.

36. Walter Hermann, 'Geschichte der Schauspielkunst in Freiberg', in *Schriften zur Theaterwissenschaft . . . von der Theaterhochschule Leipzig*, Berlin, 1960, II, p. 524. A mining town, Freiberg also had a guild of singers from among the miners.

37. Saxon Church Order, quoted in Engel (*see* Note 27 above), p. 43.

38. London, British Museum, Add. MS. 34700.

39. Nuk. R. MS. 248.

40. Incomplete, in *Glashütter Motettensammlung*, No. 35. Landesbibliothek, Dresden.

41. *Geschichte des neueren Dramas*, Leipzig, 1903; *see* Hermann, Note 36 above, p. 507 *et seq.*

2

The Thirty Years War

A familiar picture is of the peasants and craftsmen of Thuringia and
Saxony, after the stern lesson of the Peasants' War of 1525, living in
blissful acceptance of that state to which it had pleased God, the local
duke and the town council to call them. The idea that Thuringia was a
centre of idyllic delight, however, was largely invented by patriotic
chroniclers, and poetasters, like Wittichius, who had read the *Eclogues*
and *Georgics* of Virgil. The story of the *Passion*, so familiar to Germans
of the sixteenth and seventeenth centuries, was not mythological, but a
statement, in mythic terms, of human experience. The music of the
period was a reflection of life as it was; it was also a reflection of life as
it might be. The first phase of the chorale kept the brevity of human
existence constantly before the people:

21

In this way, by motet treatment of a basic theme within the repertoire, Johann Walther set the idea before the faithful for contemplation. At the end, however, was the vision of eternal bliss, described below by Schütz, which in terms of music ran down through the German mystical tradition at least as far as the *Deutsches Requiem* of Brahms.

Some of the disasters that overtook the citizens of Thuringia and Saxony during this period could be accepted (or, at least, were accepted) as evidence of the displeasure of the Almighty. Among these were sudden storms and tempests, which whipped up the mountain streams and the rivers in the lowlands to destructive fury, and the epidemics that from time to time swept mercilessly through towns and villages. The calamitous storms of May and June 1613 were built into legend. Farther east:

> the water called the Ilme, which runneth by the gate, through Naumburg, and so to the Saale, rose so high the foure miles round in circuit, it over-whelmed and drowned all the villages and hamblets thereabouts. ... And about half a mile from Weinmar, in a small village, the water ran with so mighty a force, and such a stream, that it bare the bodies of the dead before it out of their graves in the Church-yard, and at Mulhausen and Solts[1] drowned all their cellers, and spoiled whatsoever was therein . . .[2]

Such misfortune came occasionally. The pest (bubonic plague) was a regular visitant. The timber and plaster houses of the small towns— some of which still remain as a delight to the eye—were an open invitation to disease. Huddled together in narrow streets and lanes, they were without sanitation and overcrowded; as well as human beings and domestic animals, rats—the germ-carriers—also found them habitable.

In Eisenach 2,500 inhabitants (half the population) were recorded as having died of the plague in 1577. In Arnstadt the death-roll for 1582 was 1,800; for 1611, 500; for 1625, 1,252. In the following year, on 21st September, Lips Bach of Wechmar was a victim of the plague. Throughout the seventeenth century the living mourned the many victims of plague and pestilence, and cried for deliverance:

The chorale-book of 1609[3] from which this is taken was in the possession of Jakob Bach, Kantor of Ruhla (see p. 123), in 1694.

Then there were the great fires. In Arnstadt there was a calamity of this kind on 7th August 1581, which reduced some 378 houses, the church of St Boniface, the town hall and some part of the castle to ashes. For many years afterwards a *Feuer-Predigt* was held, as commemoration and warning. But to small effect. The town was severely damaged by fire again in 1632, in 1670, when 163 houses were destroyed on Easter Day, and yet again in 1683, in which year the new church of St Boniface, having been seven years in the building, was consecrated. Sometimes such fires were due to plain carelessness, the notorious case being that of the absent-minded tobacco smoker of Eisenach, who, in 1635, managed not only to set his own house alight, but also those of his neighbours and the church of St James.[4]

INFLUX OF NEW IDEAS

Up to the end of the first quarter of the seventeenth century such disasters were conventionally dismissed as part of the inscrutable design of a beneficent God. While there was life there was occasion to enrich it, and in so doing to prove the invincibility of human nature. Humanism, though lacking dogmatic definition, was a powerful and persuasive creed. So much so that in smaller, provincial centres especially the authorities found it necessary from time to time to put a brake on its progress. Church music, always a matter of concern to dogmatists, became subject to restriction. In Eisenach, for instance, in 1626, the organist was instructed 'not to play many "strange" pieces' . . . and to concentrate on those 'that were not of a light nature, nor considered more suitable for dancing'.[5] This admonition is testimony to new impulses that were beginning to make themselves felt: impulses, both musical and otherwise, that came from Italy, France and England, and which added their inflections to German culture.

The nobility, intent on establishing their proper credentials, in the post-Luther epoch looked towards Italy for inspiration. The Elector of Saxony led the way, and in 1575 Giovanni Maria Nosseni (1544–1620) of Lugano was brought to Saxony to undertake 'all kinds of artistic work, as sculpture, painting and portraiture, store tables, alabaster sideboards, the devising of buildings, the invention of triumphal entries, mummeries and the like'.[6] Nosseni's masterpiece is the choir of Freiberg Cathedral, converted by him from Gothic to Baroque as an Electoral mausoleum. The free-flowing Italian style influenced Saxon sculptors and architects, in particular Sebastian Walther, and David and Michael Schwenke. In 1618 the palace at Weimar was refashioned, having been damaged by fire, by Giovanni Bonalino of Milan.

At this time intellectual life was stimulated by the establishment of academies, after the Florentine manner, by noblemen who had, after the custom of the times, gone to Italy as part of their upbringing. Ludwig of Anhalt-Köthen was the one to take the initiative. On visiting Weimar—on the melancholy occasion of his sister's funeral—he found enthusiastic Italophiles, and in conjunction with them established the so-called *Fruchtbringende Gesellschaft* in 1617. In the first place the aim was to fashion and promulgate a 'pure' form of the German language, which had already absorbed Spanish, Italian and French terms, particularly in the time of the Emperor Charles V; in the second to refine German manners and customs. Membership of the society initially was confined to members of the aristocracy, under whose patronage, however, writers and scholars of more modest social antecedents were encouraged. Within a century the idea of such a society had been adopted and enlarged by the intellectuals and bourgeoisie, with far-reaching effects in literature and music.[7]

With respect to the interfusion of literary and musical, secular and sacred ideas, the key figure of the *Fruchtbringende Gesellschaft* was Georg Neumark (1621–81), who was also its chronicler. Neumark, born in

Mühlhausen, eventually settled in Weimar, which became the centre of the society after the death of Ludwig of Köthen. Neumark's chorales were of a more flexible character than those of his predecessors and exerted a considerable influence. The best known, 'Wer nur den lieben Gott', is the basis of J. S. Bach's cantata of the same name. It is, however, in his secular pieces that Neumark demonstrates the manner in which disparate cultures were brought amicably together into the category of *Lied*:[8]

In respect of drama the Germans were from time to time entertained by troupes of English actors, who appeared in Dresden for the first time in 1586. Within a few years these companies, with between ten and eighteen players who stayed for two weeks or so in one place, were occasionally giving performances in German. In the first decade of the seventeenth century English actors were in Freiberg, Leipzig, Zittau, Dresden and at the Court of Moritz of Hesse, at Kassel, where the English company was an official part of the Court establishment.[9] In 1617 players from England appeared in Meissen. Nine years later 'Green's' players in Dresden were described as *Kursächsische Hof-komödianten*. This company remained in Germany for two years, and in 1628—the times being difficult—went home, on the way playing in Nürnberg, Frankfurt and Köln.[10] A considerable part of the repertoire of the English players, in German translation, is contained in two volumes of *Engelische Comedien und Tragedien*, published in 1620 and 1630. In some of these English 'jig' and German folk-comedy conventions met, to enrich the tradition of the *Singspiel*. The English actors presented something similar to *Singspiel*, for every performance (as in England) was relieved by relevant, and sometimes irrelevant, musical interludes. Of these a number are printed in the two volumes described above. Thus the travelling actors played their part in stimulating an interest in English music.

INFLUENCE ON MUSIC

During the first phase of the Reformation music in Thuringia and Saxony was mainly provincial in character. In the second phase, partly as a result of the strengthening of Lutheran orthodoxy (and the repulse

of 'Crypto-Calvinists' in Leipzig at the end of the sixteenth century[11]),
partly as a result of the influence of musicians of wider experience,
but most of all because of the anxiety of princes to expand their reputation for cultural initiative, this was less the case. Hans Leo Hassler
(1564–1612), of Nürnberg, was among the first German pupils of Andrea
Gabrieli, to whom he was sent at the expense of the city by the Councillors of Nürnberg. Hassler was a prolific composer—of masses,
motets, madrigals, chorale settings, organ music and instrumental
pieces. He acquired from Italian models a warmth of harmony and a
sense of spaciousness in design within which he accommodated the
German virtue of expressive simplicity. In 1596 he published his
*Neue teutsche Gesäng nach Art der welschen Madrigalien und Canzonetten
mit 4–8 Stimmen*, and five years later his *Lustgarten neuer teutscher
Gesäng*, comprising thirty-two German songs. The melody for 'Mein
Gemüt ist mir verwirret' in this collection was adapted to the sacred
words 'Herzlich tut mir verlangen' for *Harmoniae sacrae* (Görlitz,
1613), from which it was changed into the familiar form of the 'Passion' Chorale—'O Haupt voll Blut und Wunden'. In 1607 and 1608
Hassler issued two complementary anthologies of hymns: *Psalmen
und christliche Gesäng mit vier stimmen auf die Melodien fugweis componirt*,
and *Kirchengesänge, Psalmen und geistliche Lieder auf die gemeinen Melodien
mit vier Stimmen simpliciter gesezt*. Hassler was variously employed, or
patronized, by the Fugger family in Augsburg, by the Landgraf
Moritz of Hesse, by the Nürnberg authorities, the Emperor Rudolf (by
whom he was ennobled) and, in 1608, by the Elector of Saxony. He
was Court Organist in Dresden from 1608 until his death.

The example of Hassler was followed by two Saxon musicians in
particular, Melchior Franck (1572–1639) and Heinrich Schütz (1585–
1672), the one born in Zittau, the other in Köstritz, near Gera. Since
posterity is reluctant to allow the lustre of great masters to be dimmed
by the brightness of those contemporaries who in their lifetime at least
were admitted to the first rank, the importance of Franck, a pupil of
Hassler, has been insufficiently recognized. In so far as Thuringia was
concerned his significance was considerable. In 1603 he was appointed
by Casimir of Coburg to reorganize his musical establishment, which
he did to such effect that it became recognized as one of the most
effective in Germany. Franck remained in office at Coburg until his
death, thus serving that Court for thirty-six years. A prolific composer,
he distinguished himself in every field. To the churchgoer he was
known on the one hand as a skilful motet composer, and on the other

as the author of the magnificent melody to Johann Meyfart's (1590–1642)[12] famous hymn, *Jerusalem, du hochgebaute Stadt.* By the members of musical societies he was highly regarded for his many and lively part-songs. In the secular sphere he anticipated Telemann by often writing, on the one hand, what was vulgar and, on the other, what was sophisticated. Thus in 1602 he published *Musicalischer Bergkeyen, in welchem alleweg der Tenor zuvorderst intonirt, in contrapuncto colorato . . . gesezt.* In the next twenty years Franck issued many arrangements of folk-songs in quodlibet form, and of one of them, 'Kommt ihr G'spielen', he wrote that it was 'set in accordance with the old custom of Thuringia'. The titles of many of Franck's collections carry the enthusiasm of the *Fruchtbringende Gesellschaft*; e.g. the *Newe Pavanen, Galliarden und Intraden* for instruments of 1603, the *Deutsche Weltliche Gesäng und Täntze* of 1604 and *Viertzig newe deutzsche lustige musicalische Täntze*, some for voices and instruments, some for instruments alone, of 1623, which were published in Coburg. A galliard from the 1603 collection (which was prefaced by a flattering poem by Johann Faber, Rektor of the Coburg Gymnasium) indicates the developing influence of France:

an item from that of 1604 the growing inclination to idealize what was native and traditional:

Franck was also conspicuous in the field of musico-dramatic enter-tainment, for in 1630 he introduced *Interszenia*, songs with instrumental accompaniment particularly prescribed, between the acts of a Latin school play, *Von der Zerstörung Jerusalems*, played by the students of the Gymnasium Casimirianum in honour of the duke's birthday.

The expanded interest in instrumental music within polite society gave a lift to the fortunes of the hitherto relatively underprivileged *Spielmann* and *Hausmann*. Moreover instrumental music was taken more seriously in the field of education, while it began to play a new role in conjunction with the music of the liturgy. In this respect the consummation of new method is to be found in the works written by Schütz for performance in Dresden.

One point to be understood in relation to the musical tradition of middle Germany during the Renaissance and Baroque periods is the extent to which nepotism was practised. However undesirable in other fields, in that of music this proved the ideal instrument for building the great German tradition. In more ways than one this was a family tradition. Heinrich Schütz became a choirboy at Kassel, in the Chapel of Landgraf Moritz. The director of music, once the Landgraf's personal instructor, was Georg Otto (*c.* 1544–1617), a man of some influence. Born and brought up in Torgau, under the aegis of Walther, Otto registered his name with his own ruler[13] before taking up his appointment in Kassel. Heinrich Schütz spent nine years in Kassel before going to Marburg to study law (his father was a lawyer). After a year or so there he was sent to Venice, where he worked under Giovanni Gabrieli, whose influence is apparent in Schütz's first volume of madrigals (1611). Schütz then continued his legal studies in Leipzig, after which he was appointed organist to his old patron, who was less than pleased when Johann Georg, the Elector of Saxony, sought to transfer Schütz to Dresden. Although offered the place at Kassel left vacant by the death of Otto, Schütz finally accepted the Court office at Dresden in 1614. Here he was required to undertake the reconstitu-tion of the Chapel music.

There was at least something on which to build. For Samuel Rühling,[14] one of the Kantors, had already introduced music in the Venetian manner, and motets divided among two or three separate groups of singers were regularly practised. Schütz undertook the task of building up a worthy *ensemble*, both of voices and instruments, and he both engaged Italian performers and arranged for native members of the Chapel to go to Italy for further instruction. His own demonstration of the new style was contained in the collection of vivid and sonorous *concertato* settings, entitled *Psalmen Davids sammt etlichen Motetten und Concerten mit 8 und mehr Stimmen* (1619). Three years later he fell back on the local tradition in writing his *Historia der Auferstehung Jesu Christi*. In 1627 he collaborated with Martin Opitz in producing a 'pastoral tragi-comedy' for performance at Torgau on the occasion of the marriage of the Elector's daughter and the Margraf of Hesse-Darmstadt.

Meanwhile Samuel Scheidt (1587–1654), sometime pupil of Sweelinck, in Amsterdam, was popularizing the Venetian style in Halle, where he was organist at St Moritz's Church and also, as Kapellmeister to the Margraf of Brandenburg, at the Market Church.

Scheidt was a virtuoso in his own right, and his natural reluctance to suffer limitations on his imaginative processes and his experiences in northern Europe caused him to regard the local conventions of organ music with dissatisfaction. Merely to 'colour' chorale melodies, as was the custom, was to him a confession of inadequacy. Thus, although regarding the chorale as a convenient *terminus a quo*, he endeavoured to convey its spiritual content in independent forms—of fantasia, variation and fugue. In so searching for the truth he was indeed stating the faith of a Lutheran in a new way. But Scheidt was not limited. He was a collector of Dutch, English and French, as well as of German tunes, and the results of his studies in Amsterdam are recollected in variations on the 'Cantio Belgica', *Ach du feiner Reiter* (*Tab. Nov. I*, 10), the 'Cantilena Anglica', *Fortune, my foe* (*Tab. Nov. II*, 8), and the 'Cantio Gallica', *Est-ce Mars* (*Tab. Nov. I*, 11).

The first quarter of the seventeenth century thus was rich in achievement and in promise of further achievement. But then the process of artistic evolution was all but halted. Germany became a gigantic theatre of war.

WAR AND ITS CONSEQUENCES

The Thirty Years War was in the first place waged for the soul of Germany. The Jesuit-inspired Emperors Rudolf II and Ferdinand II, who had seen the onward march of the Counter-Reformation in the western and southern states of Germany, were intent on the extirpation of heresy in eastern and middle Germany. At the same time they were determined on the ultimate containment of Germany within the Hapsburg territories. In due course the Swedes, under Gustavus

Adolphus, were drawn into the war, in theory to defend Protestantism, in fact to obtain command of the Baltic and control its commerce. At a later stage the French joined in to check the pretensions of Austria.

Between 1618 and 1623 the war was marked by the positive campaigns of Tilly against Bohemia. The Elector of Saxony deemed it in his interest to ally himself with the Catholics. By 1625 the Protestants called for help from Christian, King of Denmark, and a campaign to halt the advance of the imperialists, now under the main command of Wallenstein, was commenced. In 1626 Saxony and Thuringia were drawn into the war, and on 27th August 1626 the Protestants suffered defeat from Tilly's forces at Lutter, some ten miles north-east of Mühlhausen.

From this time on, and for many years, Thuringia was occupied by foreign troops. In 1628 Wallenstein reached Thuringia, and in the next year decreed that all properties that had been conveyed to the Lutheran churches (or the princes) should revert to their former Catholic ownership. Not even the Catholic princes of Germany could stomach Wallenstein's pretensions, and France, alarmed by the changing balance of power in Europe, prepared to subsidize a Swedish invasion. In the summer of 1630 Gustavus Adolphus came to Thuringia with a large army of mercenaries. The Duke of Weimar, in a technical sense, was an ally of Gustavus Adolphus, but he deemed it prudent to preserve his privacy and thus retired to his seat at Lichtenberg, near Hof in southern Thuringia. The citizens of Eisenach were not pleased. The duke had left them, and Gustavus Adolphus as a token of friendship had impressed two hundred soldiers and fifty-four horses, and arranged a monthly contribution of 1,500 gulden from the town towards the costs of the war. So it was in all the other towns of Thuringia—which had already unwillingly given similar assistance to Tilly and Wallenstein. The situation grew steadily worse. 'Dear God,' said the Thuringians, 'preserve us from our friends. So far as our enemies are concerned we can look after ourselves.'[15]

In 1631 the city of Magdeburg, which had previously successfully resisted continual attacks by Wallenstein, declared for Gustavus Adolphus, and was promptly sacked by Tilly. The city was virtually erased and the great cathedral and the satellite churches lay in ruins. On 17th September, however, Tilly, with his headquarters at Mühlhausen, was brought to battle by the Swedish king and defeated at Breitenfeld, near Leipzig. Gustavus Adolphus left Leipzig and marched towards the west, resting at Halle.

His Majesty on the Sabbath day in the morning went to Church, to give thanks to God for his by-past victories, this church being the Bishop's Cathedrall seate, I did heare there sung the sweetest melodious musicke that could be heard, where I did also see the most beautiful women *Dutchland* could affoord.[16]

So a Scottish colonel paid tribute to the music still maintained by Samuel Scheidt (not in the 'cathedral', but the Market Church on this occasion). Since he also wrote appreciatively of the women of the town it is to be presumed that he, like most of his companions, also took full advantage of their attractions.

A year later Gustavus Adolphus, having secured Würzburg, Frankfurt and Mainz, retraced his steps to engage Wallenstein. In October 1632:

having left all behinde him in *Franconia* and *Schwabland* in good order, his Majesty in all haste to relieve the Duke of Saxon and his county, went from *Nurenberg* to Swinefort [Schweinfurt] and from there over *During Vault* [Thüringerwald] where he joyned his forces with Duke Barnard of *Wymar*, and then continued to march towards *Arnestat*, where he lay still two days, to refresh the Army wearied with hard marching; and from *Arnestat* he marched to the generall Rendez-vouz, being there appointed at *Erfort*, the Army being then eighteen thousand strong, under whom there was no other *Scots* Regiment but Colonel Lodowicke Lesley his Regiment.[17]

Armies of occupation, whether friendly or hostile, had their own methods of 'resting', as the inhabitants of Thuringia and Saxony knew only too well. Mühlhausen, for instance, having harboured Tilly, was punished by a looting operation, carefully organized by General Pappenheim. In the meantime Wallenstein had been plundering Leipzig, Merseburg, Weissenfels and Naumburg. At Lützen, by Leipzig, however, he was defeated by Gustavus Adolphus, who was killed in the battle.

For two years there were attempts to secure a peace settlement. In 1634 the Elector of Saxony and the Duke of Weimar were ready to cancel their Swedish alliance and to come to terms with Wallenstein. Bernard of Weimar, disillusioned by lack of personal success as a field commander, went to Eger to negotiate with Wallenstein, who, however, was murdered on 25th February 1634. None the less, general war weariness brought the Swedish general, Banér, into Germany to guarantee the adherence of the rulers of Weimar, Saxony, Brandenburg and Mecklenburg, to what in 1635 took shape as the Peace of Prague. But at that point the war took a new turn, with the forces arranged thus—Sweden, France and Holland, against Lutheran Germany, Austria and Spain. For thirteen more years the war dragged on. In the villages and towns of Germany murder, rape and pillage continued unchecked. The rate of mortality was higher than ever and, the birth-rate falling progressively behind the death-rate, the population dwindled. Often there were none to carry out essential services, and from time to time the inhabitants of the Thuringian hamlets fled to the hills for refuge.

On 16th June 1650 the Thirty Years War was formally ended by the peace treaty signed at Nürnberg:

> Wer hilft, nun Friede wird,
> Bei solcherlei Verwüsten,
> Sich wohl am ersten auf?
> Die Henker und Juristen!

'Who benefited most', asked Friedrich von Logan cynically, 'from all the devastation? The hangmen and the lawyers!' The effects of the war lasted for generations.

A WAR GENERATION OF BACHS

The first works, still extant, attributed to a member of the Bach family illustrate, both in words and music, the mood of the times. The first quotation gives a simple air that betrays its folk-song connections by reason of rhythm. The second shows a union of old and new, the texture and the figuration being controlled by the character of the text:[18]

Johann Bach (1604–73), the composer of these works, was the eldest son of Hans (II), and brother of Christoph (1613–61) and Heinrich (1615–92), who between them firmly established the family name in Erfurt and Arnstadt. As for other Bachs of the same generation one may perhaps read the misfortune of war behind the dates of birth and death. The three sons of Caspar Bach, 'Haussmann' of Arnstadt, all died young; Johannes, at the age of thirty, in 1632, Melchior, at the age of thirty-one, in 1634, and Nikol, at the age of eighteen, in 1637. Hans Bach, who died in 1626, and his wife, Catharina, who died in 1635, were both victims of plague.

The three sons of this marriage brought together the native traditions of sacred and secular music. Johann and Heinrich broke loose from the limitations of their father's calling and both achieved respectability by finding posts as church organists. Christoph, who remained a Court musician, was the grandfather of Johann Sebastian. Johann was apprenticed to Johann Christoph Hoffmann, of Suhl—an acquaintance of Johann's father, who had at various times undertaken engagements there as in other Thuringian towns. Hoffman was not only *Stadtpfeifer* but also—and probably more profitably—a dealer in firearms (in the manufacture of which Suhl had long been well known). There is no reason to suppose that Hoffman instructed Bach in the mysteries of this trade, but he was said to have been a good pupil and competent in vocal as well as instrumental music. Altogether he spent seven years with Hoffman, six as apprentice, one as assistant.[19] He made full use of all the opportunities available to him and—when eventually he was secure in his profession—in 1635 he married Hoffman's elder daughter Barbara. His youngest brother, Heinrich, who also worked for a time in Suhl, married the younger daughter Eva.

The times were unpropitious and it was not easy for musicians to obtain regular jobs. Johann spent some years after leaving Suhl in Schweinfurt, Wechmar and Arnstadt, before benefiting from the temporary relief from tension seemingly afforded by the Peace of Prague and accepting the direction of the town music in Erfurt. The city, impoverished by war and taxation, was still under Swedish occupation. Johann Bach took over a five-man *ensemble* (to which he appointed his brother Heinrich) which, according to ancient usage, served as the town watch, played 'tower-music' three times daily, was in attendance at civic functions and weddings as and when required. In addition to controlling this group Johann was also organist in the former church of the Dominicans (Predigerkirche), once the centre of the activities of 'Meister' Eckhard, and now Evangelical.

Life in Erfurt was not easy for Johann Bach. After two years of marriage his wife Barbara died. A year later he married again. His second wife was Hedwig Lämmerhirt, who belonged to another family well known in Thuringian church and musical life.[20] Of this marriage there survived four sons. As a composer Bach was over-shadowed in Erfurt by a relative of his second wife—Michael Altenburg (1584–1640), a pastor as well as a musician who, when driven from his parish of Grossen-Sömmerda by war and plague in 1637, found refuge in the city. He was minister of St Andrew's Church. As a composer of large-scale motets as well as of instrumental pieces, both for organ and for instruments, he was highly regarded throughout Thuringia (his works were readily published in Erfurt). But his wider fame was due to his composition of the music for *Verzage nicht, du Häuflein klein*, the battle-song of Gustavus Adolphus.

After the Peace of Prague in 1635 Catholic rights were restored in Erfurt, and the cathedral, which had been secularized by the Swedish king, reverted to the authority of Mainz. In 1656 the archbishop planned the return of Jesuits—but not even the Catholics approved of this and so the project was dropped. None the less the former ritual came back, and in the Church of the Ursulines High Mass was celebrated in the 1650s with a full panoply of strings and trumpets. In this decade it was hoped that a final peace had been achieved. But Erfurt suffered further distress and humiliation. Since the citizens were showing a marked inclination towards insubordination the Elector of Mainz, adding troops from France and Trier to his own, sent an expeditionary force to bring them into proper obedience. The town was besieged and then, on 5th October 1664, bombarded. After capitulation an army of occupation, with headquarters in the renovated

Petersberg, was installed, and two representatives of the Elector were put at the head of civic administration. It is perhaps not surprising that the only music by which Johann Bach is now known is conservative in style and pessimistic in tone.[21]

Johann had lifted himself up to a position of relative dignity. He also looked after the interests of his brothers, both of whom joined his staff in Erfurt. Christoph, who married Maria Magdelena Grabler—daughter of the *Stadtpfeifer* of Prettin, Saxony, who was Christoph's master— spent twelve years in Erfurt between 1642 and 1654, between terms of service at the Court in Weimar and in Arnstadt. Heinrich was seven years in Erfurt until appointed organist of the Oberkirche and also of the Church of Our Lady in Arnstadt. The latter, after the cathedral in Naumburg, is the most notable Thuringian example of the transition in architecture from Romanesque to Gothic. In Arnstadt the two brothers were sustained at the beginning by the reputation of old Caspar. And they were in a community where they knew many people. Christoph, the grandfather of Johann Sebastian, enjoyed his office as town musician only for seven or eight years. His widow survived him for less than a month. Their daughter Dorothea Maria (1643–79), severely men- tally retarded, became a burden on the rest of the family after her parents' death; one, however, that was carried with a due sense of responsibility.

Heinrich, who added the post of organist to the Court to his other commitments, became both a local and a family legend. It could hardly have been otherwise. He was in office for more than half a century, and when he died he was the subject of a touching funeral oration preached by Johann Christoph Olearius.[22] Heinrich was eulogized as a man of piety, whose favourite text was *Repleatur os meum laude tua*, and as the composer of chorales, motets, concertos (i.e. 'sacred' concertos), preludes, fugues and so on. Little of his music has survived.[23] But behind the exemplary record lie facts which throw the musical career into relief. As subject to a count Heinrich Bach, like others of his family, received his stipend when the count could afford to pay it. So it was that in 1644 Heinrich, without emolument for a year, had to humble himself and point out to his 'gracious lord' that he was not able to maintain his family. That this was the case he attributed to an 'extra- ordinary visitation from the dear Lord God'. Under such circumstances piety was strained. At the end of his life Heinrich, who died in poverty, went blind. He was cared for by his daughter Maria Katharina, wife of Christoph Herthum, who, among other appointments, held that of organist in the palace chapel in succession to his father-in-law.

Carl Philipp Emanuel, never backward in commending his ancestors, wrote of Heinrich that 'he was a good composer and of a lively
disposition'. From what remains it may only now be said that Heinrich
was a typical Thuringian small-town composer—with one eye on the
forward-looking masters of the age in which he lived. However, there
is perhaps a clue to personality within the cantata *Ich danke dir, Gott*:

The Bachs were a God-fearing family, and between them they
presented both the simplicities and complexities of their faith in
unambiguous terms. In this engaging manner therefore Heinrich
observed the wonder of creation, and in so doing gave brief evidence of
the liveliness of spirit on which Carl Philipp Emanuel commented.
Ich danke dir, Gott, a characteristic example of transitional music
—between motet and cantata—moving from the direct homophonic
manner of the past towards the florid, instrument-inspired techniques
of established German Baroque, was composed for performance on
the seventeenth Sunday after Trinity. Written for five-part chorus, two
violins, two violas and continuo, it is prefaced by a somewhat tentative
instrumental sinfonia of twenty-five bars.

The sons of Johann Bach were Johann Christian, Johann Egidius,
Johann Jakob and Johann Nikolaus (I); of Christoph, Georg Christoph, Johann Ambrosius and Johann Christoph; of Heinrich, Johann
Christoph, Johann Michael and Johann Günther. Since all (with the
possible exception of Johann Jakob) became musicians the statistical
chances of ultimately arriving at a talent that was more than ordinary
were good. But the Bachs were never unwilling to profit by the example
of others. By the end of the Thirty Years War there were a number of
composers of progressive views working in Thuringia. And away in
Dresden new splendours were being created.

NOTES TO CHAPTER TWO

1. Solz, near Meiningen; or Sollstedt, near Nordhausen; or Sollstedt,
   near Mühlhausen.

2. *A Wonderfull and most Lamentable Declaration of the great hurt done, &*
   mighty losse sustained by Fire that hapned; & mighty stormes of Winde,
   Thunder, Lightning, Haile & Raine, etc., London, 1613, pp. 1–4.

3. *Ein schön Geistlich Gesangbuch darinnen Kirchen Gesange und Geistliche Lieder/Dr. Martini Lutheri/und anderer frommen Christen/so in den Christlichen Gemeynden zu singen gebräuchlich/begriffen Mit vier/etliche mit fünff Stimmen/nicht allein auff eine/sondern dess mehrentheils auff zwey oder dreyer-ley Art/mit besondern Fleiss* contrapuncta *Weise gesezt/im Discant der Choral richtig behalten/und zum andern mal sehr vermehrt/und verbessert in Truck verfertiget Durch. Melchiorum Vulpium Cantorem zu Weymar,* 1609.

4. See *Alte Thüringische Chronicke . . .*, Frankfurt/Leipzig, 1715, pp. 13–21, 80–90 and 272 f.

5. *Regulierung und Reglementierung des Kirchengesangs,* 1626, copy in Bachhaus, Eisenach.

6. Contract of employment, quoted by Eberhard Hempel, *Baroque Art and Architecture in Central Europe,* London, 1965, p. 53.

7. *See* Ph. E. Bertram, *Geschichte des Hauses und Fürstenthums Anhalt,* 2 vols., Halle, 1780, II, pp. 736–41.

8. *Newe Musicalische Schäfferey, oder teutsche liebes beschreibung von der verliebten Nymfen Amanda und von ihrem lob-würdigem Schäffer Amandus,* Königsberg, 1641.

9. Engelbrecht, Ch., and others, *Theater in Kassel,* Kassel, 1959, pp. 6–12.

10. Hermann (*See* Chapter 1, Note 36 above), pp. 556–66.

11. *See* Ernst Kroker, *Leipzig,* Leipzig (1914?), pp. 59–60.

12. Meyfart was Professor of Theology at Erfurt. His *Das höllische Sodoma,* which ran through many editions in the seventeenth century, was one of many works published at this time in which the masochistic delight of the author in the prospective pains of hell (for unbelievers) gave pleasure to those readers who considered themselves as among the elect. (*See* p. 131.) Meyfart's *Christliche Erinnerung . . .* (1636) was among the works in the library of Johann Sebastian Bach.

13. *Melodiae Continentes Introitus totius anni praecipuos, Quinq vocibus compositos, & diligenter elaboratos, studio & opera,* Georgii Otthonis, Torgensis, Musici Salzensis (1574), a collection of works by Josquin, Clemens non papa, Créquillon, Matthieu le Maistre (Walther's successor as Music Director to the Saxon Chapel Royal) and Scandellus (who succeeded le Maistre) was dedicated to the Elector Augustus.

14. Samuel Rü(h)ling (*c.* 1586–1626) was the son of Hans Rü(h)ling, a Saxon organist whose *Tabulaturbuch auf Orgel und Instrument . . .* (1583), containing arrangements of Latin and German vocal pieces, is important in the field of German organ music. Samuel, poet and clergyman as well as musician, composed a number of works in eight and nine parts, and he was a close friend of Schütz.

15. Herbert Koch, *Geschichte der Stadt Jena,* Stuttgart, 1966, pp. 124–43.

16. *Monro, His Expedition with the worthy Scots Regiment (called MacKeyes Regiment) levied in August 1626. . . . Colonel Robert Monro,* London, 1637, Part II, p. 73.

17. *See* Note 16 above, p. 160.

18. *Unser Leben ist ein Schatten* and *Weint nicht um meinen Tod*, in copies dated 1696, were attributed to Georg Christoph Bach in the *Verzeichniss des musikalischen Nachlasses des verstorbenes Capellmeisters C. P. E. Bach*, Hamburg, 1790, p. 85. C. P. E. Bach inherited a large number of works by early members of the family, which he regarded with reverence and described collectively as the 'Old Bach Archives'. *Unser Leben* and *Sei nun wieder* were published by F. Naue, in Leipzig, in 1821, as by J. S. Bach.

19. Kraft (*see* Chapter 1, Note 11 above), p. 566a.

20. Johann Lämmerhirt was minister in Pfullendorf (1576–1613); another Johann Lämmerhirt, formerly a schoolmaster in Sonneborn, was minister in Grossen-Behringen (1626–35); and Antonin Lämmerhirt was minister in Herbsleben (1659–60); *see* A. Beck, *Geschichte des gotaischen Landes*, Gotha, 1868–75, 3 vols., III, pp. 308, 354. Johann Ambrosius Bach married a step-sister of Hedwig Lämmerhirt (*see* p. 65); Johann Heinrich Buttstett, organist in Erfurt, married a second cousin of Elisabeth, Martha Lämmerhirt; and a niece of Hedwig, Martha Dorothea Lämmerhirt, was the mother of J. G. Walther, thus conferring on him kinship with J. S. Bach.

21. Johann's known works are: (1) Aria à 4: *Weint nicht um meinen Tod* (*see* p. 32); (2) Double choir motet: *Sei nun wieder zu frieden*; (3) Choral motet: *Unser Leben ist ein Schatten;* pub. ABA, B & H Leipzig, ed. M. Schneider, 1935: there is one piece by J. M. Bach in the *Tabulaturbuch* in the Parish Archives at Elleben, near Osthausen (see *Johann Sebastian Bach in Thüringen*, p. 114, fn. 1).

22. *Leichenrede auf Heinrich Bach*, Arnstadt, 1692.

23. Cantatas: *Ich danke dir, Gott* (RD II), *Als der Tag der Pfingsten erfüllet war* (lost); Motet, *Nun ist alles überwunden* (RD I), dated Arnstadt, 6th July 1686; Chorale Preludes, *Christ lag in Todes banden; Erbarm dich mein* (Ritter, *Gesch. d. Orgelspiele*, Leipzig, 1884).

3

Middle German Baroque

THE POPULAR TRADITION

The chorale was in every sense the music of the German people, and its unifying effect was never more strongly felt than during the period of the Thirty Years War. It was, in truth, the focal point of social, spiritual and musical experience. The fact that it was so deeply embedded in the life of each community, and that its cultivation was the first duty of schoolmaster, Kantor, organist and minister, meant that new musical influences, as from Italy, were often noticed with some reluctance. Such influences were felt first in the courts, where Baroque was less a style than a way of life. In its various forms it appeared as a symbol of aristocracy. The people as a whole held firm to their own popular tradition.

The chorale also came to represent one aspect of an increasing sense of nationalism, otherwise stimulated by the insistence of educationalists that the German language should be the basis of instruction. Whereas formerly music textbooks had been written in Latin there was a growing tendency for them to be issued in the vernacular, and in the second half of the seventeenth century the standard work was Wolfgang Hase's *Gründliche Einführung in die edle Music oder Singe Kunst* (1657). During this period certain changes took place in respect of music in the schools. Some were necessitated by the stringencies of the times. Tenors and basses were often in short supply, and it became accepted practice for their absence to be compensated for, or their weakness masked, by instruments. In due course this expansion of resources made also for a more expressive type of music. It also entailed more work for the Kantor.

The Kantor was indeed kept permanently busy. Not only was he teacher, director of church (and a good deal of secular) music, moral preceptor and disciplinarian, but also librarian and copyist. In various ordinances he was expressly enjoined to be diligent in making copies of choir music.[1] Where the principles of Rattichius and Comenius were put into effect, however, he benefited from a reduction in his non-musical duties. New educational principles which were being adopted removed music instruction from the curriculum on the grounds that it was to be considered rather as recreation, and to accommodate new disciplines. It was this principle that in due course was to cause a feud between J. S. Bach and Johann Ernesti, the Rektor of St Thomas's School, in Leipzig. It is fair to add that in the seventeenth century the idea was implicit that the Kantor should thus be able more effectively to specialize. Although he was expected to do a good deal of his teaching out of school hours, he was able to choose the more, rather than the less, musical for instruction. He could in fact usually conscript boys—especially when he not only had to supply singers for a town church but also, as at Sondershausen, for a court chapel as well.[2] Here he was backed with the authority of the Kapellmeister, and the administration, of the Court.

During and after the Thirty Years War the Kantor faced fresh difficulties. Boys were not what they had been, so it seemed. In Erfurt in 1663, and again in Weimar in 1670, for example, there were heavy complaints about their going from church into tavern and thereafter making a nuisance of themselves in the streets.[3]

Yet there was much to set on the credit side. The engagement of instrumentalists, in the first place to support choirs reduced in numbers, led inevitably—since other influences affected this—to their retention. This being the case the status of the *Stadtpfeiferei* was improved since players belonging thereto were now given regular church engagements. This came about, in Dresden at all events, because of a reluctance on the part of members of the congregation to revert to unaccompanied motets that had hitherto been the rule. In 1652 the Dresden *Stadtpfeiferei* played in the Church of Our Lady and the old Dresden church on Sundays, and in St Sophia's Church on Mondays.[4]

Because of the years of intensive cultivation of music in schools there was a renewal of the full activity of the town *Kantoreien*. In some places Kantors had managed to keep going without interruption.[5] In others a fresh start was made. At Eilenburg, in Saxony, for example, Martin Rinckart (1586–1649), once a pupil at St Thomas's, Leipzig, and author of the poem 'Nun danket alle Gott,' founded a famous *Kantorei* in 1648. It was in keeping with the temper of the age that the officers of the society were given German titles, whereas previously they had been distinguished by Latin names.

In respect of programmes the *Kantoreien* varied. Some remained stolidly conservative, but occasionally there was an urge towards the 'new music'. So it was that Kantor Menzig of Wittenberg, whose preference was for 'grave authors and organ accompaniment', was gently retired in favour of a young organist, Lange, whose taste was in the direction of instrumental music, cantata-type works with dramatic texts, containing solos, duets and instrumental movements. Lange, however, was rather exceptional. The *Kantoreien*, which enjoyed a florescence during the last third of the seventeenth century, on the whole remained conservative. By the time Pietism on the one hand and the *Aufklärung* on the other had become dominant influences on thought the members of the *Kantoreien* were often too old and fixed in their ways to come to terms with fresh impulses. The final difficulty was that young people, with fresh interests of their own, were unwilling to become members.

As the *Kantorei* thus began to decline its place in the community was increasingly taken by the *Collegium Musicum* which, deriving in part from the *Kantorei* and in part from the 'Academic Concert' (as established at Jena, see p. 14), was less tied down by the Church tradition. Johann Schein acknowledged the existence of a music society among the Leipzig students in 1626 in the title of his *Studentenschmaus*. In 1654 Johann Rosenmüller, then organist at St Nicholas's Church, Leipzig, published a similar collection of *Studentenmusik*, and three years later Christian Dedekind's *Studentenleben* was issued in Erfurt. In a short time the student music societies were to develop into associations of a more public nature (see page 112).

It is clear that by deliberately encouraging extra-curricular music the educationalist had done the musical a good turn. This was also true of musico-dramatic functions. After the Thirty Years War the tradition of school drama was renewed and established also in the universities. Thus at Jena in 1668 the new Rector Magnificentissimus (the thirteen-year-old prince) was welcomed with a student performance of an *ad hoc* work for voices and instruments, entitled *Jenaische Wunsch und Freuden-Erschallen*, while in 1677 the director of the school staged *Comödie von der Auferstehung Christi, Drama et poema paschale in ovo poetico*, in the town hall. A keen advocate of musico-dramatic performances at Arnstadt was Adam Drese (1650–1704), Kapellmeister there from 1683 until his death. Supported by Duke Anton Günther II, Drese, who also had an orchestra at his disposal, not only produced such works at Arnstadt, but also in Weimar and Jena. Dramatic development in the country was once again stimulated by

visiting English players, as also by Italian actors and singers.[6] It was—
as tends to be after the upheaval of war—an age for youth, and the
enthusiasm of students for music in its many forms was decisive in
effecting the great modern (i.e. post 1700) tradition of music and music-
making in Germany.

The popular tradition of music was thus extended on the secular
side, and towards the end of the century came to terms with the other,
courtly, tradition. It is true that at all times the music of the Court
was more or less influential in the community, but immediately after
the Thirty Years War there was a divide between the popular and the
courtly. In the community as a whole music fulfilled one function; at
Court it fulfilled another.

THE ARISTOCRATIC TRADITION

After 1684, predictably, there was a wave of luxurious living in Germany. The aristocracy saw no reason why this shouldn't be so and,
according to custom, increased their revenues to keep up with the
standards to which they considered themselves entitled. The princes
also increased their armed forces; for the first time standing armies
needed to be maintained without, at least overt, foreign support.
Between 1650 and 1679 the land tax in Bavaria increased from 160,000
to 628,000 gulden; in the same period military expenditure in Saxony
went up from 80,000 to 400,000 thalers.[7] There was also a great renewal
of architectural activity. Between 1643 and 1654 Andreas Rudolf
designed the Friedenstein Palace to replace the ruinous Grimmenstein
Castle in Gotha. Between 1657 and 1678 Johann Richter built the
palace at Zeitz, and a few years later that at Weissenfels. In the plans
for these buildings there was a strong French influence. Schemes for
making Dresden into a worthy capital city were in preparation throughout the seventeenth century, but the masterpieces of Dresden architecture did not begin to appear until after the accession of August
'the Strong' in 1694, and the appointment of Marcus Dietze, Balthasar
Permoser and Mathaes Pöppelmann as the principal architects. In 1701
the Electress Sophie, in Berlin, cynically observed, 'c'est la mode que
les électeurs deviennent rois'.[8] Such aspiration inspired a general
intention to provide musical establishments of fitting quality and
strength.

In 1669 a French traveller, Samuel Chappuzeau, visited Dresden,
and reported of the Elector, Johann Georg II:

Il est splendide dans toutes ses actions, et il ne se peut rien voir de plus superbe que son équipage de chasse, ni de plus Royal que sa Musique, qui luy coûte bon, et qui est aussi une des plus belles de l'Europe. Elle est toute composée d'Italiens, gens bien faits, et qui font honneur au maître qu'ils servent . . .[9]

Chappuzeau also visited Jena, on the invitation of one of the duke's privy councillors, and there heard an entertainment that pleased him.

Durant le déjeuné les trompettes et les tymbales nous donnerent à l'autre bout de la caue, un agréable concert, qui ne pouvoit que charmer l'oreille, sous cette voûte, et ce fut Monsieur Pflugg qui voulut être luy même le tymbalier, pour se divertir, et faire admirer son adresse à la compagnie.[10]

CONFLUENCE OF TRADITIONS IN MÜHLHAUSEN

Of Thuringian composers of this transitional period the principal was Johann Rudolf Ahle (1625–73), of Mühlhausen, whose works had a strong influence on his provincial contemporaries and successors. Ahle, in a worldly sense, was a success, and his career presents a contrast to those of the majority of the Bachs, who were in the habit of arriving at barriers beyond which they found further progress impossible. Partly, one suspects, this was a matter of temperament.

Ahle, the son of a soap-maker, was fortunate in his parentage in so far as there were funds available for his education. He was a pupil of G. A. Fabricius at Göttingen, and afterwards a theological student at Erfurt. During his student days in Erfurt he took the Kantor's post at St Andrew's Church once held by Michael Altenburg. In 1649–50 he returned to Mühlhausen as 'civis ac musicus Mulhusinus' and four years later was appointed organist of the church of St Blasius (or *Untermarktkirche*). At a later stage of his career he became minister of St Nicholas's Church. He was also a town councillor and, after being chairman in turn of the Water, Market and Hunt Committees, was eventually chosen as mayor. In Mühlhausen they remembered with pride the years in which Joachim à Burgk had added lustre to the musical reputation of the town by his compositions. Ahle worthily followed in the same tradition. Like à Burgk he could be described as a progressive conservative. He was also a voluminous composer.

True to tradition Ahle added to, and made full use of, the existing chorale repertoire. His most famous and popular chorale melodies are those for 'Liebster Jesu, wir sind hier' and 'Morgenglanz der Ewigkeit'.

In these Ahle shows a tendency towards grace in melodic contour hitherto unusual in the chorale, and they stand in close relationship to secular song. Ahle was indeed an important figure in the development of song, and among his works are settings of poems by leading figures in the *Fruchtbringende Gesellschaft* tradition, who were also founders of similar, derivative, but more broadly based literary societies. Among them were Martin Opitz (known as 'Der Gekrönte'), Andreas Tscherning, Christian Brehme, Philipp Harsdörffer ('Der Spielende') and Philipp Zesen von Fürstenau ('Der Wolsetzende')[11]. In a dedication to Hartmann von Berlepsch ('Der Gebrauchte') Ahle explained how, when setting such lyrics, he deliberately avoided a severe style. 'I have', he said, 'aimed only at charm [of style], so that the beauty of the text can be better retained in simplicity.' Ahle also had the advantage of being able to work with a not inconsiderable poet in Mühlhausen, Ludwig Starck (*d.* 1681), sometime assistant director of the Gymnasium and minister of various churches in the neighbourhood.

Ahle's church music ranges over a wide area: from simply arranged chorales, through masses, magnificats and motets, to 'spiritual concertos' and 'spiritual dialogues' after the manner of Schütz.[12] He was a fine craftsman and handled both form and instrumentation with ease and originality. Sensitive to environment, he kept within the limits of general understanding and, in his church music, understood the sentiments that were evoked by familiar texts. In the first example below there is an intensity of expression that came by way of Lassus and Schütz:

in the second a naïvety that is most affecting within the context of Christmas:

The second excerpt, following an opening *Sinfonia*, belongs to what is in effect a church cantata with solo sections based on the chorale melody, separated by brief choral episodes. The chorale is presented in spacious manner as conclusion to the whole work. Ahle here uses six voices and four instruments, and a feature of the piece is the broad simplicity of the choral sections. Ahle appreciated that his choristers preferred to rehearse what was well within their capacity. These singers were amateurs, belonging to the *Musikalische Societät* (sometime known as the *Musikalisches Kränzchen*), founded in 1617, which comprised twenty-three members. Ahle was active on many fronts. A volume on the art of singing, written in Latin, *Compendium pro tonellis* (1654), ran into three editions, while to help to satisfy the increasing demand for purely instrumental music he issued, in Erfurt, in 1654 his *Dreyfach Zehn allerhand Sinfonien, Paduanen, Balletten, Allemanden,* etc.

Ahle's lively interests were communicated to his son, Johann Georg Ahle (1651–1706), who was his father's pupil and also his successor as organist of St Blasius. The younger Ahle, a pioneer of the *Aufklärung*, was rather more poet than composer and as such he was nominated by the Emperor, Leopold I, as successor to Georg Neumark, also of Mühlhausen, as Poet Laureate. Mühlhausen was not only a musical but also a theological centre, and during the time the younger Ahle was organist conflict between the Pietist and Orthodox branches of the Evangelical Church—of which the echoes still reverberated in the ears of J. S. Bach when he lived in the town—came to a head. The champions of the respective causes were, for the Pietists, Johann Adolf Frohne, and for the Orthodox, Johann Christian Eilmer, minister of St Mary's Church. J. G. Ahle was organist in this stimulating city until his death. He was succeeded by J. S. Bach.

Always understanding that there was a good deal of reciprocity between musicians of different callings it should now be noticed that those members of the Bach family who were born towards, or soon after, the end of the Thirty Years War divided into two groups. Some opted for the traditional vocation of *Stadtpfeifer*, some for the offices of organist or Kantor. Three of the four sons of Johann, and two of the three sons of Christoph, belonged to the first category (although one son of Johann was also an organist). On the other hand, all the three sons of Heinrich became organists, while a distant cousin in Ruhla, Jakob (1655–1718), became a Kantor. None showed much disposition to move far away from home.

SONS OF JOHANN BACH

The eldest son of Johann, Johann Christian I (1640–82), was trained by his father and served on his staff before taking up a similar appointment in Eisenach. In 1665 he obeyed a family convention by marrying into the profession, thus establishing a further bridgehead from which subsequent Bachs were to advance their professional prospects. Johann Christian's bride was Anna Margretha Schmidt, by whom he had two sons. Anna died in 1678, and on 1st June 1679 her widower married again. His second wife was a widow, Anna Dorothea Peter (or Petri). Johann Christian was now director of the town musicians in Erfurt, to which office he had been appointed in 1676. But he had not long in which to enjoy this dignity before he was counted among the victims of the plague which swept through the town in 1682–3. His youngest brother, Johann Nikolaus I (b. 1653), a gamba player in the Erfurt establishment who had only been a year married to Sabina Burgolt, also died during that epidemic. Since there were young children of these marriages there was a particular and pressing problem to be solved: that of upbringing and education. The problem was one that was to recur. Happily, the Bachs being close-knit, there were always relatives who were prepared to undertake responsibility.

Johann Egidius (1645–1716), second son of Johann, was a viola player in the Erfurt band, of which he became director after the death of his elder brother. At the same time he was organist of the Evangelical church of St Michael. Like Johann Christian he was twice married. His first wife was also his sister-in-law. The Schmidts having moved to Erfurt from Eisenach and Anna Margretha's sister Susanne being as yet a spinster, it was not unexpected that she should contract marriage within the musical profession and with a promising member of that profession. Susanne died in 1684 after ten years of marriage, leaving one son, Johann Bernard. Soon after Susanne's death Egidius married Judithe Katharina Syring, by whom he had one son, Johann Christoph III. Although much respected in Erfurt, Egidius Bach had the misfortune, at any rate during the earlier part of his career, to live in the shadow of a far more versatile and dominant personality, Johann Pachelbel (1653–1706), who was active in Thuringia for some fifteen years.

A southerner, imbued with the spirit of Italy and Austria, Pachelbel was more extrovert, and more opportunist, than the Thuringians among whom he lived. He certainly livened the community by his versatility both as organist and composer, and there were those among the Bachs who held him in high respect. In Saxony and Thuringia there were probably more organists per square mile than almost anywhere else in Europe, but, apart from Scheidt, few of marked initiative. Pachelbel's fluency of manner was an incentive and, since he was a popular teacher, he established, particularly in Erfurt, an important school of organists. Among his pupils the most significant was Johann Heinrich Buttstett (1667–1727), who succeeded him at the Predigerkirche.[13]

SONS OF CHRISTOPH BACH

Of the children of Christoph Bach of Arnstadt, the eldest son, Georg Christoph, became Kantor successively at Suhl, Themar and Schweinfurt—territory which had been well prepared by his uncles. His one extant composition is a cantata, *Siehe, wie fein und lieblich ist es*, for two tenors and bass, violin, three viols da gamba and continuo.[14]

Johann Christoph II (1645–93) remained with his father in Arnstadt, going on the Court pay-roll as a musician in 1671. Two years later he appeared in a situation of some delicacy, to extricate himself from which called for the kind of determination which was a family characteristic. He was landed in a breach of promise case. Having (as is said) carried on with the prettily named Anna Cunigunda Wiener, and having given and received rings as tokens of mutual affection, he was hard put to it to deny that his intentions, if honourable, were towards marriage. He did, however, deny it, before the Consistory Court in Arnstadt. As is frequent in such cases the defendant was fighting not so much against the plaintiff as against her mother, Anna Margaretha Wiener, and his weaponry was inadequate against a powerful opponent. Mrs Wiener was a widow and automatically attracted sympathy. The court found against Bach. Thereupon he appealed to the higher court in Weimar (the Schwarzburg jurisdiction was subordinate to that of the dukes of Saxony), and managed thereby to escape the consequences of his indiscretion. It was none the less a near escape. Johann Christoph did not marry until 1679, when he made a satisfactory match with Elisabeth Eisentraut, daughter of the town clerk of Ohrdruf.[15]

If Johann Christoph had acted indiscreetly in respect of Miss Wiener, his reputation was ultimately cleared by the redoubtable Spitta, who took advantage of the opportunity to issue a certificate of propriety for the whole family. 'It is', he wrote of Johann Christoph and Anna Cunigunda, beyond any manner of doubt that their relations were strictly pure and moral. . . . Moreover, I may here add with general satisfaction, that as regards the relations of the sexes, the strictest principles prevailed in the Bach family, and that in this particular they certainly distinguished themselves as in advance of their time . . .[16]

Whatever Spitta, who did not know him, wrote, the fact remains that Johann Christoph was not universally popular. Heinrich Gräser, director of the Court music at Arnstadt, took a poor view not only of him but also of the family as a whole. It may be that Gräser was a friend of the Wieners, or that he had heard of the recent expulsion of Johann Jakob Bach from the school in Eisenach because of alleged larceny; it may be that he himself was of a psychotic disposition. He was very firm in his opinion that the Bachs were 'pig-headed and stubborn', that they were 'inefficient rogues', and that their apprentices were invariably 'thieves and robbers'. Gräser kept up a steady stream of colourful abuse, laced with threats to the effect that he would notify the musicians of Naumburg and Leipzig of the vices and incompetencies of the Bachs. His particular butt was 'Hans Toffel',[17] who eventually was driven to appealing to his employer for protection and to the more prominent among his relatives for assistance in promoting his cause. Apart from litigation there was little peace among the lower grade musicians of Arnstadt for years, as was further evidenced by Johann Christoph when he complained of being cut out of free-lance work by Gräser. The reason lay deeper than mere dislike. The reigning count, Günther of Schwarzburg, paid his musicians irregularly (as Johann Christoph protested) with the result that extramural engagements were, even more than ever, a necessity.

In 1681, Count Günther, his temper shortening as the complaints of his musicians lengthened, dismissed the Bachs and, having done so, died. There was no music at his funeral, which meant another deprivation for musicians. His successor, Anton Günther, however, was of a more agreeable disposition, and in 1682 he confirmed the musicians in their previous offices. Johann Christoph, who had spent his period of suspension helping his uncle Heinrich, was therefore once again in regular employment. And conditions were much improved in that the new countess, daughter of Duke Anton Ulrich of Braunschweig-Wolfenbüttel, coming from a music-loving family, was herself an ardent music-lover. At her instigation the musical establishment was maintained at full strength, and sometimes augmented. On occasion the Kantors from Gehren and Breitenbach were brought in; as also

Johann Michael Bach, organist in Gehren, a useful bassoonist from Sondershausen, boys from the local grammar school and clerks, estate workers and musicians' apprentices.

In 1690 the Court singers were: Hans Dietrich Sturm (descant); Hans Erhardt Braun (alto); Clerks of the Chamber and Granary as first and second, and Hans Heinrich Longdius as third tenor, the Clerk of the Works and the Kantor as first and second basses. Adam Drese, who played viola da gamba, was leader of the instrumental music. He was assisted by Wentzing and Paul Gleitsmann, Grooms of the Chamber, who played violin, and violin, lute and viola da gamba respectively; Heindorff the Actuary, and Heindorff the town Kantor, violinists; Clerks of the Granary and the Kitchen (Christoph Herthum, see p. 35), harpsichord and violin, and harpsichord and double bass; Drese's son (or nephew), viola da gamba; a bassoonist and five trumpeters; Christoph Jäger, the principal trumpeter, also a violinist; two oboists, also competent violinists; Johann Christoph Bach and his apprentices, who supplied a complete string quartet; and old Heinrich Bach still, nominally at least, organist.

In this community Johann Christoph lived and worked, and if little regarded in his lifetime is recollected by the Arnstadters of today, since the house in which he lived, Kohlgasse 7, is now marked by a suitable inscription. Johann Christoph was twin brother of Johann Ambrosius (1645–95), who became famous, not on account of his own musical talents, which were not extraordinary, but those of his youngest son, which were. Ambrosius became an Eisenacher and as such will be discussed in the next chapter.

SONS OF HEINRICH BACH

The three sons of Heinrich, Johann Christoph I (1642–1703), Johann Michael (1648–94) and Johann Günther (1653–83), were by far the most distinguished representatives of their generation of Bachs, and in any country less well endowed with musical talent than Thuringia the first, at least, would occupy a high place. He was regarded with great respect by his young kinsman, Johann Sebastian, who was happy to use his works as models, and by Carl Philipp Emanuel.

> [Johann Christoph] was particularly happy in the invention of beautiful melodies, and in the Expression of his Text. . . . He was also an uncommon master of full Harmony, as is proved by a piece of Church Music, compos'd by him for Michaelmas-day, to the words, 'Es erhub sich ein Streit', etc., which has twenty-two

obligato parts, and yet is perfectly pure in respect to the Harmony
... C. Ph. Emanuel had a particular regard for him. It is still quite
fresh in my remembrance how good-naturedly the old man smiled
at me, at the most remarkable and hazardous passages, when he
once gave me the pleasure, in Hamburg, of letting me hear some
of those old pieces.[18]

These 'old pieces' were composed in Eisenach, where Johann
Christoph succeeded Andreas Osswald as organist of St George's
Church at the end of 1665.[19] He was also a cembalist at the Eisenach
Court, and after 1700 a 'Chamber Musician'. In 1667 he married Maria
Elisabeth Wedemann, whose father was the town clerk of Arnstadt,
and whose sister Katharina became the wife of Christoph's brother
Michael in 1675. So far as his ducal employer was concerned Johann
Christoph Bach was a trouble-maker. He was for ever sending complaints to the palace: that his salary was in arrears, that his emoluments
in kind were not forthcoming, that his housing was inadequate.
Christoph and his family eventually lived in that part of the old Domi-
nican monastery that had been taken over by the duke as a mint: the
building still stands. In pre-Reformation times this part of the conven-
tual buildings had been used as a hospital. In one of his letters of complaint to the duke, Johann Christoph, writing amid a general sickness
among the family, observed that his home had become a 'Lazaret'.
When Johann Christoph Bach died, in debt and embittered, his post
was offered to Johann Nikolaus Bach of St Michael's, Jena who, however, was too comfortably situated in the university city to wish to
leave it for the more enclosed atmosphere of Eisenach. Nevertheless
one Bach was followed by another, for what was refused by Johann
Nikolaus was accepted by Johann Bernard, son of Egidius (see page
112). The job offered one particular attraction: a 'beautiful and expensive' new organ with fifty-eight registers and four manuals, built by
Georg Christoph Sterzing, that had been begun according to Johann
Christoph's design in 1695 and completed in 1698.[20]

It has already been made clear that a Thuringian or a Saxon composer of the seventeenth century moved only as fast as his patrons
permitted or encouraged. On the one hand stood the prince, on the
other the community as a whole. French, Italian, even English,
influences were admitted into courtly music, but even there with
certain reservations; for the cult of what was German because it was
German acted as a brake on excessive stylistic novelty. In respect of
church music congregational conservatism combined with a realistic

appreciation of the capacity of the church choir to prevent too much innovation. When Johann Christoph Bach was a boy in Arnstadt the motets of Lassus, de Monte, Senfl, were in regular use; and in Eisenach polyphonic music of the sixteenth century was zealously rehearsed in the Grammar School. The principles of classical polyphony were maintained by Schütz, as also by the more familiar Ahle and Hammerschmidt. Andreas Hammerschmidt (1612–75), a Bohemian, was organist at St Peter's Church, Freiberg, and at Zittau, and his motets, 'sacred concertos' and dialogues were extremely popular in Saxony and Thuringia.

The two collections of *Geistliche Dialoge* of Hammerschmidt, containing 150 pieces for various groupings of voices with or without figured bass and/or instruments and published between 1639 and 1652, were before every provincial organist as a model. To discover Johann Christoph accommodating himself to the demands of the 'simple country-folk', for whom Hammerschmidt wrote so well,[21] one may turn to such motets as *Mit Weinen hebt sich's an*, which has something of the character of folk-song.

The guiding principles for the general run of composers (and every organist and Kantor was, *de facto*, a composer) were these: that the chorale should remain at the centre of any exercise; that polyphony should be controlled by practical considerations; that the significance of texts should be underlined by musical expression; that the use of instruments should be subject to their availability. Johann Christoph, and even more Johann Michael Bach, kept within the limits imposed by these principles. The former, perhaps, was more skilled in perceiving that within the prescribed area there was much room for initiative and imaginative interpretation of the accepted terms of reference. Carl Philipp Emanuel described Johann Christoph as a composer 'full of expression', and this, indeed, he was. The extension of vocabulary through a more evocative style of harmony that especially captivated Carl Philipp Emanuel is shown in the examples on page 53.

The boundaries of Johann Christoph's achievement are marked by the contrasted cantatas *Es erhub sich ein Streit im Himmel* (*Revelation of St John*, XII, 7–12), composed for Michaelmas, and the wedding piece, *Meine Freundin, du bist schön*, of which the text is taken from *The Song of Solomon*. The text of the former had previously been set by Hammerschmidt, and published in *Andern Theil geistlicher Gespräche über die Evangelia* (Dresden, 1656). Hammerschmidt employed trumpets, cornets and organ, and set the battle scene between Michael and Satan around the chord of C major. Bach, with double choir, two violins, four viols, basses, four trumpets, drums, and organ, follows the same procedure. And so, at a later date, does Handel—as in the 'battle' music of *Saul*, or the 'hailstones' chorus of *Israel in Egypt*. Concerning this point Spitta observes:

> Inasmuch as most of the composers of sacred music at the end of the seventeenth century display their harmonic simplicity even in their purely lyrical choral subjects, they must be regarded in this, as the forerunners of Handel, while Sebastian Bach achieved his style of choral treatment in a different way, by means, namely, of instrumental music.[22]

Like Hammerschmidt, Bach in setting his Michaelmas cantata was concerned to transfer the vivid imagery through sonority to vision:

> ... the composer evidently sought to make a picturesque impression of the scene as he imagined it, and, like the earlier German painters, filling in the details of their pictures . . . with the dresses, utensils, and paraphernalia of the everyday life of their time, Johann Christoph brings to bear the effects suggestive of warfare in contemporary mundane experience.[23]

Immediately, no doubt, Johann Christoph was stimulated towards a representation of the victory of the angels by the fine, gilded, sculpture of a Renaissance-style St George, carved by Hans Leonhardt, that stood near the entrance of his church. The spirit of Johann Christoph may be seen to have communicated itself to Sebastian and to have renewed itself in his *Es erhub sich ein Streit* cantata (No. 19) of 1726; especially in the opening chorus. If one goes along with Smend in accepting symbolic intentions, we may even suppose in the title, *Concerto à 14* (14 = BACH), there is a hidden reference to the older Bach.

Away from the splendid noises of Johann Christoph's cantata are the intimacies of *Meine Freundin, du bist schön*, for four solo and four chorus voices, violin, three viols, violone and cembalo. There is no doubt that Bach had observed the tendencies of Italian and French music, and sought to make use of them within the limits of function as understood in Eisenach. Italian influence, by way of Schütz, is apparent in the motet *Lieber Herr Gott* (1672)[24]—the text is non-biblical and a Lutheran prayer—the words of which were also set by Schütz (*Musicalia ad Chorum Sacrum*, Dresden, 1648, composed for St Thomas's, Leipzig). The motet *Der Gerechte, ob er gleich zu zeitlich stirbt* of 1676 (rearranged to form the first and last chorus of a cantata by Emanuel Bach a hundred years later) is related textually to Giovanni Gabrieli's *Sancta Maria succurre*. But the masterpiece of assimilation is the wedding cantata, *Meine Freundin, du bist schön,* which in its imaginative extension of a new vocabulary resembles the contemporary work of the English composer Matthew Locke. Bach, aware (see the first quotation given below) of the programme element inherent in the words, disciplines declamation to mood. His sensibility, however, is more strikingly shown in the final soprano air, written over a chaconne bass. A solo violin enhances the kind of truth to psychological condition which is Bach's particular achievement in this remarkable, and beautiful, work. The use of variation form to intensify the significance of the music reaches backwards to Cavalli and Monteverdi, sideways to Purcell and forward to Johann Sebastian. So too do the suggestive harmonic transitions.

Within the context of the Thuringian motet-cantata Bach liberated the solo voice, as may also be appreciated in the solo cantatas *Achs dass ich Wassers genug hätte* (alto, five str., cont.) and *Wie bist du denn, o Gott, im Zorn auf mich entbrannt* (bass, five str., cont.). He underwrote vocal with instrumental rhythms and inflected melodic contours with subtlety, influencing his nephew in both directions. A work which may be regarded as a bridge between old and new is the double-choir motet *Ich lasse dich nicht.*[25] The first part combines firmness and simplicity of melodic and harmonic structure, and is effectively—if somewhat repetitiously—based on the contrast between two choral groups. The next section is a strenuous contrapuntal embellishment of the chorale melody, and distinguished, on the one hand, by the energy of the accompanying rhythmic figuration and, on the other, by occasional acridity in the harmonic processes. Johann Christoph was an exponent of realism. This shows not only in figuration and harmonization, but also in instrumentation. In his cantata *Die Furcht des Herrn*, composed for a town council celebration, he conveyed the significant word of the title to his employers through the use of *tremolo* strings, *piano*, hoping, no doubt, that thus inspired they might be led at least to the threshold of wisdom. Johann Christoph, in that he considered both the means at his disposal and his music as he wrote it with critical care, was an intellectual composer. He was also a passionate composer and, as also in his daily life, he did not disguise his emotions. He was often pessimistic, obsessed with the brevity of human existence.

According to his creed he looked for relief to the Saviour whose image stood above the altar of St George's Church, expressing himself thus:

Here, in the disposition of the voices, the broken rhythm and invocatory repetitions of the accompanying voices, and the exploitation of harmonic expression, one may feel the climate of German Romanticism of later date. The characteristic moods of the nineteenth century were in fact based on the homophonic tradition of Thuringian and Saxon village church music of the sixteenth and seventeenth centuries.

Of Johann Christoph's organ music there survive only (44) *Choräle welche bey wärendem Gottesdienst zum Präambulieren gebrauchet werden können gesezt und herausgegeben von Johann Christoph Bachen Organ: in Eisenach.*[26] These represent the stock-in-trade of the Lutheran organist, either of that period or, indeed, of more recent times; introductory, or concluding, improvisations on chorales according to the canzona principle. Bach's pieces, by the standard of those of Pachelbel which in pattern they closely resemble, are unremarkable. He found it difficult to avoid the typical organist's cliché of tonic or dominant pedal, the recurrence of which tends to inhibit the contrapuntal movement. Nevertheless Johann Christoph kept an ear open for the striking figure—as in *Warum betrübst du dich mein Herz.*

As chamber musician at the Eisenach Court Bach is represented by two extant sets of variations for harpsichord: the first, in G major, on a Saraband, the second on an air—a kind of cradle-song—by Eberlin.[27] In these works the influence of Froberger and Buxtehude are joined together to foreshadow the more comprehensive manner of Johann Sebastian, who

> ... seems to have known and loved this little work [Variations on a Saraband]. In his A minor variations we find a good deal that is thought out in a similar way, and the beginning of the third Goldberg variation appears to be a further development of Johann Christoph Bach's fourth ...[28]

Johann Michael Bach in comparison with his elder brother has been somewhat undervalued.[29] This is for two reasons: first, because he held a modest office in comparison with that of his brother at Eisenach; and, secondly, because he handled the material of music with a generally lighter touch. Michael Bach may very well be regarded as the supreme village organist of all time. That he spent his working life as organist and parish clerk is the most eloquent testimony to the vigour of Thuringian musical life. Gehren, where he lived, is only marked on large-scale maps and then, in its hill-girt seclusion southeast of Ilmenau, it is not easy to find. Michael, taught in Arnstadt by his father and Kantor Jonas de Fletin (Heindorff's successor), was appointed to Gehren in 1673, being twenty-five at the time. He took the place of Johann Effler, who had removed to Erfurt. Two years later, on 27th December 1675, he married Katharina Wedemann (d. 1704). Except for the sixth and last—Johann Gottfried, born in 1690, who died when a year old—all their children were daughters. Since the eldest daughter, Friedelene Margaretha, was baptized on 20th October 1675 it is to be observed that either the Church records or Spitta (see page 48 *supra*) were in error. Anna Dorothea (b. 1677), the second daughter, married Hans Gregor Schneider, a master carpenter from Oberweissbach, in 1701. After Barbara Katharina (b. 1697) and Maria Sophia (b. 1682) came Maria Barbara (born 20th October 1684), who in due course made what was regarded as a not unsatisfactory marriage: she became the wife of her cousin, Johann Sebastian, three days before her twenty-third birthday. Maria Barbara's godmother was Sophie Dorothea Emmerling (also godmother to her god-daughter's son, Johann Gottfried Bernhard), who belonged to a well-known Thuringian family of musicians. It may of course be quite fortuitous, but Michael Bach, living in an environment where feminine influence was strong, composed in a style that might (in comparison with that of Christoph) be described as feminine. Alternatively it might be defined as more Italian. Either way the style is individual and remarkably polished, considering that Michael's immediate contact with the higher cultural values was only possible through his occasional engagements at the Court at Arnstadt (ten miles away).

Michael Bach was both fluent and lively. In general he simplified harmonic procedures in a manner that would have gained him credit half a century later, and he tightened rhythmic structures. In respect of melody, he cultivated shapely outlines and well-defined phrase units, while he had a sure and convincing technique in the arrangement of instrumental sonorities. He had something of Telemann's facility for writing music for which the performer is grateful. In Gehren presumably this was important. The principal characteristic of his music, then, is its clarity. Within the familiar territory of the chorale-motet this is demonstrated in the setting of the well-used text of 'I know that my Redeemer liveth'. Like Handel, Michael Bach imbued this setting with the feeling of life rather than of death; this is enhanced by the poised entry of the chorale 'Christus der ist mein Leben' at the seventeenth bar.

A similar tenderness pervades the Dialogue for four voices, strings and organ, *Liebster Jesu, hör mein Flehen*, which begins with a *Lied*-like tune that anticipates Carl Philipp Emanuel, and ends with the consoling chorale, 'Nun lob, mein Seel, den Herrn' (to the words 'wie sich ein Vater erbarmet'). In his cantatas for solo voice Michael Bach balances voice against instruments, and in those works he appears as master of a fully fledged Baroque style. The introductory symphonies (sonatas) to *Auf, lasst uns den Herrn loben* and *Ach bleib bei uns, Herr Jesu Christ* are notable in this respect.

The extent to which new conceptions of instrumental design and of the relationship between instrumental and vocal sonorities were affecting even the remotest parts is emphasized by the character of the only extant piece by Michael's cousin, Georg Christoph (1642–97). The eldest son of Christoph—and the only one successfully to be launched on a career before the death of his father—Georg Christoph went first to Suhl as schoolmaster and Kantor before settling at Themar, near Schweinfurt, as Kantor in 1668. The *Praeludium* to the Birthday Cantata of 1689,[30] *Siehe wie fein und lieblich ist* (chor., vl., 3 vle. da gamba, organ), is evidence of a lively and informed interest in current

Italian techniques such as also impressed Johann Michael in Gehren.

Johann Michael was a church musician, but in contrast to his elder brother he might appear to have been less committed to theological and more to aesthetic values. Thus in considering his works one is aware of a general sense of emancipation from the more binding conventions. The *Aufklärung* was beginning to affect music from one side as was Pietism from another. The former is inherent in the nature of Michael Bach's 'advanced' works—those in Italian style—in which the music, free from literary connotations, may be appreciated for its own sake.[31]

None the less this is but one side of a composer whose attitudes were effective influences on Johann Sebastian. Michael lived in the present, but respected the past. This is shown in his noblest work, the motet for two choirs, *Halt, was du hast*, of which the foundation is the chorale 'Jesu, meine Freude'. The motet is treated with great originality, within the form of dialogue between the two choirs. This method was used later by Johann Sebastian, as notably in *Singet dem Herrn* (where the chorale is as in Michael's *Liebster Jesu* as noted above).

The ending of *Halt, was du hast* is, in the accepted sense, Bachian; austere—with its false relation of C sharp and C natural—yet benedictory.

There is a sense of vision about this music: the sense that comes only when—as in Renaissance Italy in respect of painting—there are no frontiers between life and art, when the artist is at one with the citizen. This condition endured only a little while longer in Germany, but long enough to admit the greatest of all musicians. Johann Michael lived a quiet life in Gehren. His stipend was seventy-two gulden a year, supplemented with free firewood, allowances of corn and barley, a strip of pasture land and a free house. He was also permitted to brew three and a half barrels of beer annually. When not engaged in clerkly duties or in composing or performing music he made the instruments on which his music was played. One vocational contact resulted in a son-in-law who was a musician, the other in one who was a joiner. Michael Bach was well thought of in Thuringia—at least in the villages. Three of his motets[32] were copied for use in the village church of Udestedt, near Erfurt.[33]

Michael Bach's chorale preludes for organ closely resemble those of Johann Christoph and followed the pattern established by Pachelbel. One may endorse the observation of Adlung, that 'his chorales [i.e. preludes] do not have much significance today'.[34] Adlung, however, had not looked at the motets and cantatas, which are in a different class.

After Johann Michael's death the Bach tradition was carried on in Gehren by Johann Christoph IV (1673–1727), second son of Johann Christian (1640–82) of Erfurt. Christoph studied theology as well as music and came to Gehren, as Kantor, in 1698 after having been employed in a similar capacity in Niederzimmern near Erfurt and also in St Thomas's Church in Erfurt. Described as 'quarrelsome, obstinate, and haughty', he spent various periods in prison—a distinction shared with Johann Sebastian.[35]

The third son of Heinrich Bach, Johann Günther (1653–83), was appointed as deputy to his father in Arnstadt in 1682, which meant that he did virtually all the work. In the natural order of things he would have inherited the full title and emoluments of his father's office. But he predeceased him, leaving a young widow, Anna Margarethe, daughter of Mayor Kuel of Arnstadt. Within the year Anna Margarethe remarried, her second husband being an Arnstadt clergyman, Jakob Bartholomäus. By him she had a daughter, Christiana Maria. On 27th November 1694, Bartholomäus having died, Anna Margarethe contracted a second marriage within the Bach family by becoming the third wife of Johann Ambrosius Bach of Eisenach, fathe of Johann Sebastian. In the February following Johann Ambrosius died, and the unfortunate widow returned with her small daughter to Arnstadt. She had petitioned the Eisenach Council for leave to remain in the Eisenach house for six months, explaining that since she was proud to bear the name Bach she hoped she might find another eligible holder of the name. But the city fathers of Eisenach turned aside her request and demanded immediate evacuation of the premises.

NOTES TO CHAPTER THREE

1. As at Gotha (1641: and Nordhausen (1658): *see* J. Rautenstrauch, *Luther und die Pflege der kirchlichen Musik in Sachsen*, Leipzig, 1907.

2. F. W. Beinrath, *Musikgeschichte der Stadt Sondershausen*, Innsbruck, 1943, pp. 14–15.

3. Rautenstrauch (*see* Note 1 above), pp. 365–6.

4. H.L. Techritz, *Sächsische Stadtpfeifer*, Dresden, 1932, p. 4.

5. In 1647 Christoph Schulze, Kantor in Delitzsch, wrote to his colleague in Bitterfeld congratulating him on having kept the Church music as well as the *Kantorei* going through the 'recent troublous times which are so inimical to music'. *See* Werner (Note 15 below), pp. 10–11.

6. Wennig (*see* Chapter 1, Note 33 above), p. 39.

7. *See* Berthold Haendcke, *Deutsche Kultur in Zeitalter des 30jähr Krieges*, Leipzig, 1906, p. 255.

8. *Briefe der Königin Sophia Charlotte . . .*, ed. R. Doebner, Berlin, 1905 (K.-preuss. Staatsarchiv, vol. 79).

9. Samuel Chappuzeau, *L'Allemagne, ou Rélation nouvelle/de toutes les Cours de l'Empire*, Paris, 1673; quoted by A. Pirro, 'Remarques de quelques voyageurs, sur la musique en Allemagne et dans les pays du nord, de 1634 à 1700', in *Riemann-Festschrift*, Leipzig, 1909, p. 233.

10. Pirro (*see* Note 9 above), pp. 302–3.

11. *See* Ph. E. Bertram, *Geschichte des Hauses und Fürstenthums Anhalt*, 2 vols., Halle, 1780, II, p. 742.

12. See *Erster Theil geistlicher Dialogen . . .* for Sundays and Festivals, for 2, 3, 4 or more voices, published in Erfurt by Friedrich Melchior Dedekind, in 1648, and *Neu-gepflantzter Thüringischen Lust-Garten . . .* 3, 4, 5, 6, 7, 8, 10 and more voices, with and without instruments . . . and without continuo, published in Mühlhausen by Johann Hütern, 1657. There were supplementary volumes. Works by Ahle are to be found in DDT V, 1901.

13. Buttstett composed chorale preludes of different kinds, canzonas in the manner of Frescobaldi, suites modelled on those of Froberger, Masses both for Catholic and Lutheran use (cf. J. S. Bach, *see* p. 146), and other works. His championship of traditional solemnization evoked the displeasure of Mattheson. He was one of the teachers of Johann Gottfried Walther (1684–1748) (*see* p. 92).

14. ABA, ed. M. Schneider, Leipzig, 1935.

15. Eisentraut was a well-known name in music in Saxony and Thuringia during the sixteenth and seventeenth centuries, especially in Halle, Eisleben and Zeitz: *see* Serauky, *Musikgeschichte der Stadt Halle*, and A. Werner, *Städtische u. Fürstliche Musikpflege in Zeitz*, Bückeburg, 1922.

16. J. A. P. Spitta, *Joh. Seb. Bach* (1951 ed.), I, pp. 162–3.

17. Dialect form of Johann Christoph.

18. J. N. Forkel, *Life of John Sebastian Bach*, English transl. pub. T. Boosey, London, 1820, p. 3.

19. Osswald was probably related to Katherine Osswald, who married Wolf Eisentraut of Halle, and to Johann Osswald, town musician of Erfurt (previously of Weimar) who married Hedwig Martha Bach in 1684. Kraft (*see* Chapter 1, Note 11 above), p. 211.

20. C. W. Schumacher, *Merkwürdigkeiten der Stadt Eisenach und Bezirkes*, Eisenach, 1777, p. 74.

21. Johann Beer, of Weissenfels, *Musikalische Diskursen* (1719), *see* E. Müller, *Musikgeschichte von Freiberg*, Freiberg, 1939, p. 83.

22. Spitta (*see* Note 16 above), p. 48.

23. C. H. H. Parry, 'The Beginning of German Music', *O.H.M.*, London, 1902, III, p. 444.

24. Date given in ABA (pp. 83–5, *Verzeichniss des musikalischen Nach-lasses des . . . Capellmeisters C. P. E. Bach*), p. 84.

25. Formerly ascribed to J. S. Bach, and published with his harmonization of the chorale, 'Dir Jesu, Gottes Sohn, sei Preis'.

26. Ed. Martin Fischer, Bärenreiter Verlag, Kassel, 1929.

27. *Sarabande mit 12 Variationen*, ed. Riemann, pub. Leipzig 1892: *Aria Eberliniana*, NBG, 39, II.

28. Spitta (*see* Note 16 above), I, pp. 128–9.

29. *See* Parry (Note 23 above), pp. 450–1.

30. *Verzeichniss des . . . C. P. E. Bach*, p. 85.

31. *Es ist ein grosser Gewinn, wer gottselig ist*, for soprano, violino piccolo, 'Quart Violino nur di grosso grande' (in c′g′d″a″), ripieno str., and continuo.

32. *Nun treten wir ins neue Jahr*, 8-part; *Ehre sei Gott in der Höhe*, 8-part; *Fürchtet euch nicht*, 8-part: *see* F. Krummacher, 'Motetten und Kantaten der Bachzeit in Udestedt, Thüringen', in *Die Musikforschung*, XIX, 4, 1966, p. 402 f.

33. Tobias Friedrich Bach was Kantor in Udestedt from 1722–1768 (*see* p. 137).

34. Adlung (*see* Chapter 1, Note 2 above), p. 69.

35. Spitta (*see* Note 16 above), I, p. 22.

4

Johann Ambrosius Bach of Eisenach

COURT LIFE IN EISENACH

When, in disgruntlement, Heinrich Gräser made life difficult for
Johann Christoph Bach in Arnstadt he was protesting against the
nepotic principle that brought so many Bachs into positions of moderate
prominence within his own profession. In building on their family
connections the Bachs were doing no more than following the example
of their superiors. For, from the beginning of the seventeenth century
at least, the governance of regions under the general overlordship of
the House of Weimar depended on the number of male relatives of the
duke who needed to be established in positions of authority, to which
their noble birth alone was entitlement.

In 1672 a new disposition of the family properties brought Johann
Georg I from Marksuhl to Eisenach. Eisenach then became the seat of
an independent duchy—of Sachsen-Eisenach—and the town thereby
again acquired the dignity of a 'Residenzstadt'.[1] It held this status
until 1741, when, on the death of a duke without issue, it was returned
to Weimar.

The setting up of this state was the circumstance which drew members of the Bach family to it in the first place; the manner in which it
was organized was the cause of some of them—as well as of other
independent-minded citizens—wishing to leave it. In all, the state
of Eisenach formed less than a thousandth part of the empire, but
within its limits was concentrated the full force of absolutism. The
social inequities of the system have been veiled by an opaque screen of
romanticism that has been frequently lowered before them.

Eisenach was a small town, enclosed by walls and protected by
watch-towers. In 1670 there were about five thousand inhabitants. This
population grew to about seven thousand by the end of the century.
To a considerable extent this was due to the demands of the Court for
an ever increasing, but largely unproductive, labour force. The town
council of this period, called together no more than four or five times

a year, had become a rubber-stamp for the duke, against whose exactions in the way of taxation occasional feeble voices were raised, but to no effect. Any who protested or were late in paying their dues were quickly persuaded by the duke's soldiers to restrain their tongues, or repair their tardiness. The council had theduty, however, to appoint the town officials. In 1679–80 these included a doctor, an organist (Johann Christoph Bach), a Stadtpfeifer (Johann Ambrosius Bach), a carpenter, a butcher, two attendants (for waiting at municipal functions), two midwives, a keeper of the town clocks, several care-takers for the watch-towers, a roof-repairer, a grave-digger, a fire prevention officer and three shepherds.[2]

Those who had marketable goods possessed their own horses, and sometimes wagons. Citizens possessing neither needed to hitch-hike if and when they wished to travel. In the year 1700 communications were somewhat improved by the introduction of the Imperial Post to Eisenach, but conveyance by the postal wagons was limited to women with children and to the sick. So far as the outside world was concerned a certain amount of information was available through the *Erfurter Zeitung* and the *Franckfurter Zeitung*, first published in 1675.[3]

Above this little community was the superstructure of state govern-ment. However Lilliputian the domains of the duke it was essential to maintain the full panoply of power. Thus Eisenach was administered by four Departments of State: the Privy Council—which made its presence felt by meeting in the town hall, the senior Consistory, the Rent Office, and the Council for War, Home Affairs, Taxation and Mining. The household of the Court itself had a separate adminis-tration, which, after Johann Wilhelm as a young man had paid a visit to the Court of Louis XIV, grew out of all proportion. Eisenach, he considered, should become a 'little Paris'. (It was not the only German town with this aspiration.) Therefore by 1708 there were at the new palace, in its terraced gardens splendid with statuary: a Lord Marshal; a parasitic cohort of 'cavaliers' and ladies-in-waiting; a sizable body of pages under the direction of a page-master; a French elocution teacher, whose duties were as important as they were onerous—taking into account the Thuringian dialect also privately used by the nobility; male and female servants; kitchen staff; officers of the chapel, and musicians; and a company of gardeners and huntsmen, the latter superintended by the master of the hunt, who had charge of eighty-two horses and all the coaches, conveyances and other equipment necessary for the hunt. In front of the palace was permanently stationed a 'corps de garde', which made its presence audible through the frequent sounding of fifes and beating of drums.

The wise musicians were those who stayed briefly in Eisenach, picking up experience of Court requirements and credit for pursuing the fashions of the day sufficient to give them *entrée* into more significant establishments. As has been stated Pachelbel was among this number. So too were Daniel Eberlin (a friend of Johann Christoph Bach[4]), who spent three periods as director of sacred music with the Court (the last between 1685 and 1692), and Johann Valentin Meder (1649–1719), a Thuringian by birth and sometime Court musician in Gotha as well as Eisenach.

The musicians of Eisenach, when a 'Residenzstadt', who were held in highest esteem, were Panteleon Hebenstreit (1669–1750) and Georg Philipp Telemann (1681–1767), sophisticated, well versed in French culture and the principles of French music, and unwilling to tie themselves for any length of time to a minor, provincial Court. In this environment the Bachs were not among the trend-setters.

JOHANN AMBROSIUS BACH, CITIZEN OF EISENACH

Johann Ambrosius Bach—the name Ambrosius being that of his godfather, Ambrosius Margraff—learned the violin and viola from his father. After a peripatetic period he returned to Erfurt in 1665, being drawn there by reason of the departure of his cousin, Johann Christian, for Eisenach. Two years later he became an official member of the town music. A year later he married Elisabeth Lämmerhirt (see p. 38, n. 20), whose father was a furrier and a town councillor in Erfurt. Elisabeth was a year older than Ambrosius. In 1669 a son, Johann Rudolf, who died shortly after his birth, was born. On 16th June 1671 Johann Christoph was born, his godfather being Christoph Herthum, who had married Heinrich Bach's daughter and was Court and town organist and, additionally, a book-keeper in the Court catering department in Arnstadt (see page 49). Later that year Ambrosius moved to Eisenach— Johann Christian having returned to the senior post in Erfurt—where his contract from the town council was ratified on 12th October.

The town musicians of Eisenach lived in the streets about the 'Frauenplan' (the church of Our Lady had been finally destroyed during the Reformation). When Johann Ambrosius arrived—with a mother-in-law and a mentally defective sister among his responsibilities—he found a housing shortage, and until he was able to buy a home of his own he was ineligible for citizenship. He at first rented a property (Rittergasse 11) from Balthasar Schneider, the duke's head forester. The relationship between landlord and tenant was amicable and Schneider was godfather to the first of Ambrosius's children born in Eisenach. This was Johann Balthasar (*b.* 6th March 1673) who, according to convention, bore the name of his godfather. After three years Ambrosius bought a house immediately at the back of that in Rittergasse on the Frauenplan and facing the town brewery. On 4th April 1674, among those of other newcomers to Eisenach, his name was entered in the *Bürgerbuch*: 'Joh. Ambr. Bach erwirbt mit Frau und Kindern das Bürgerrecht'.

On 5th February 1675 a son, Johann Jonas (his godfather being Jonas Mehler, a nail-maker), was christened. After him came Maria Salome (*b.* 1677), Johanna Juditha (*b.* 1680), Johann Jakob (*b.* 1682) and Johann Sebastian (*b.* 1685). Maria Salome was the god-daughter of that Maria Salome who, as the widow Petri, married Caspar Läm-merhirt, furrier, in 1674, until when she had lived a stone's throw from the Bachs in Fleischgasse (now Lutherstrasse). Much liked by the younger members of the family, Maria Lämmerhirt is immortalized in Johann Sebastian's *Hochzeits-Quodlibet*. Johanna Juditha was sponsored at baptism by the wife of Georg Chrisoph Bach of Themar and also Johann Pachelbel, then organist at Erfurt. Johann Jakob's godfather, Johann Jacob Schön, was a stonemason, while the godfathers of the youngest son were Sebastian Nagel, a musician at Gotha, and Johann Georg Kochen, a ducal forester in Eisenach. These friends of the parents indicate the social circle in which Ambrosius and his family moved.

Ambrosius was not only town musician but also Court trumpeter, and his membership of the duke's staff was an impediment when, in 1684, he proposed moving back to Erfurt. He petitioned the council for release from his contract on the grounds that the cost of living was cheaper in Erfurt than in Eisenach, and observed that he had six children and that there was another on the way. As previously mentioned the town council were impotent to grant such requests without reference to the palace, and when they had received their instruction they notified Ambrosius that the duke 'was unwilling to release him from his service'. So Ambrosius stayed, and Johann Sebastian was born in Eisenach on 21st March 1685, and christened in St George's Church two days later.

The young Bachs lived in a town of which the charm may very well impress us more than them. From their father's home, having picked their way through the livestock outside the front door, and through citizens collecting their beer from the brewery, they could lose themselves within five minutes in the woods that covered the paths to the Wartburg. But the idyllic surroundings were slender compensation for the misfortunes that afflicted them. They were brought up against the grim realities of life very early, some of them so early that they hardly had time to recognize them as such. Jonas died when he was ten, Juditha when she was six and Balthasar, an apprentice of his father, and lately appointed trumpeter at Köthen, when he was eighteen. Their grandmother, Eva Barbara Lämmerhirt, had died in 1673 in the house in Rittergasse. Their aunt, Dorothea Maria, died on 7th February 1679: a merciful release, as is said, and she was honoured with a splendid funeral sermon preached by Valentin Schrön. The preacher did not neglect to pay tribute to the Bachs in general and to Johann Ambrosius in particular.[5]

The children were brought up in overcrowded conditions, for their father's apprentices also lived in the house. During the day, and presumably into the night, there was a constant stream of music, to which in due course they were expected to contribute their share. This after all was the family way of life, and in time to come there would at least be jobs for the boys. More than formerly a grammar school education was regarded in the last decade of the seventeenth century as a necessary preliminary to a satisfactory musical career, and the Bachs of Ambrosius's generation upheld the principle that their sons should have the opportunities that had often been denied to them. The Grammar School in Eisenach was, as has been said, well known in Thuringia—and beyond. Before Johann Sebastian became a pupil various members of the clan had been at school there. Jakob from Grossenbehringen and Johann Jakob from Erfurt were the first. In 1671 another Jakob, in the 'Tertia' class, was withdrawn under a cloud, having been suspected of theft. Johann Christoph of Eisenach sent his sons to the school. Johann Nikolaus progressed satisfactorily from the 'Quarta', which he entered in 1678, to the 'Prima', whence he proceeded to the University of Jena in 1690.[6] His brother Johann Christoph (V), who was born in 1676, entered the 'Sexta' in 1684 and left from the 'Secunda' in 1693. The older Eisenach Bachs overlapped Ambrosius's sons. Christoph and Balthasar entered the school in 1681, Jonas in 1686 (the year in which he died) and Jakob in 1690. He was the only one still in the school when Johann Sebastian was enrolled in the 'Quinta' in 1693.

The Eisenach Grammar School may have had a good reputation, but the conditions were far from ideal. The pupils—previously given elementary instruction in a 'Deutsche Schule'—were packed into two small rooms that were freezing in winter and stiflingly hot in summer. In the 'Quinta' and 'Sexta' classes the number of pupils ranged between seventy and one hundred. The task of the teachers, however, was somewhat lightened in one way by frequent absences on account of sickness. In his first year in the school, for instance, Sebastian missed fifty-nine school periods,[7] and in the following year one hundred and three. The teaching hours were from 6 to 9 a.m. in summer and from 7 to 10 a.m. in winter, with afternoon classes from 1 to 3 p.m. Wednesday and Saturday afternoons were free, but there was religious instruction on Sunday mornings. There was of course also religious instruction on every other day of the week. The boys were taught the Catechism and the Psalms, and 'Dicta Scripturae Sacrae', as well as choice extracts from native theologians, were instilled into them. They were taught Greek and Latin, and after 1690 Hebrew was in the curriculum. German grammar was compulsory (although indifferently taught), and as the boys progressed up the school they were introduced to logic and rhetoric. After 1690 arithmetic was taken more seriously and history was added to the general scheme. The teaching was superintended by the Rektor (Borstelmann, followed by Zeidler, in Sebastian's time) and the Usher (Hesselbarth). It was fortunate that the most able teacher in the school was the Kantor of St George's, Andreas Dedekind, who had succeeded Andreas Schmidt in 1690.

Dedekind's choir was brought up on a well-balanced diet: of traditional material by Walther, Musa, Josquin, Isaac, Stoltzer, Renerus, Senfl and Obrecht (among others) in the *Kantoreibuch*, that belonged to the school, copied by Kantor Wolfgang Zeuner more than a century earlier; and the chorales in Melchior Vulpius's *Gesangbuch* of 1609, that was still widely used in Thuringia;[8] of newer cantata-motet music available from many local and contemporary composers, of whom the most convenient was Johann Christoph Bach, of St George's; and of secular songs. The choristers sang in the town at New Year for the benefit of the citizens, and at various times throughout the year for their own benefit, in the neighbouring villages.

In the Easter record of 1693 Sebastian was forty-seventh in his class, one place above Johann Jakob. Since the latter was three years older, the hit-and-miss character of the general teaching is obvious. After a year Sebastian improved his place in class, moving up to fourteenth, whereupon he was transferred to the 'Quarta', where he was listed as twenty-third and Johann Jakob as twenty-fifth.

In the early summer of 1694 Sebastian's mother died; she was buried on 3rd May in the cemetery beside the Kreuzkirche, of which the duke had laid the foundation stone in 1692. Less than a year after the death of Maria Elisabeth, and three months after his third marriage (see page 60), Johann Ambrosius also died.

JOHANN CHRISTOPH BACH, GUARDIAN OF JOHANN SEBASTIAN

Of Ambrosius's children Johann Christoph was already launched on his career, and Maria Salome was old enough to look after herself. But the two youngest boys were but thirteen and ten respectively, and their upbringing presented a problem. In times when such situations were not uncommon, and when large households were not considered irregular, the problem was usually soluble. Johann Christoph, an Erfurter by birth, had left Eisenach when Sebastian was a year old, to take lessons from Pachelbel in organ and harpsichord in Erfurt. He lived here for three years, during the last of which he was organist at St Thomas's Church. Since, however, the organ was indifferent and the stipend inadequate Johann Christoph looked towards Arnstadt in the hope of succeeding to some part of Heinrich Bach's duties. For a few months he played the organ in Arnstadt, but, a vacancy occurring in Ohrdruf in 1690, he put in an application for that. Having satisfied the Consistory of his competence, and having arranged for the teaching in the school (for which he said he had no inclination) to be taken on by Johann Günther Schneider, he assumed his post at St. Michael's Church. In 1694 Johann Christoph Bach married Johanna Dorothea, of Hof. When Johann Ambrosius Bach died in Eisenach, Johanna Dorothea, in Ohrdruf, was five months pregnant. Nevertheless she agreed to take in her husband's schoolboy brothers: so Jakob and Sebastian came to Ohrdruf.[9]

The extent to which musical genius is inherent is a matter for speculation. About the influences of environment there is more positive evidence. In respect of Johann Sebastian Bach the fact that he was brought up in Ohrdruf and not in Eisenach was decisive. That he became the kind of musician he was was, in the first place, due to the encouragement of his eldest brother—a shrewd and well-balanced man who was highly esteemed both as man and musician in Ohrdruf. He was the only organist in the history of Ohrdruf of whom it was written (in the church register) that he was *optimus artifex*.

MORE BACHS IN EISENACH

It is possible that when orphaned Johann Sebastian might have been entrusted to the care of Johann Christoph (I) of St George's. That he was not was probably due to Johann Christoph's poverty, ill-health and the demands of his own small children. If Johann Sebastian had remained in Eisenach the kind of career he might have followed may be surmised from those of Johann Bernhard Bach (1676–1749), son of Egidius; Georg Philipp Telemann (1681–1767); and Pantaleon Hebenstreit (1667–1750), each of whom, to a greater or lesser degree, adjusted his creative talent to the Francophile atmosphere of the Eisenach Court. Hebenstreit, a native of Eisleben, was a violinist and a dancing master, and the inventor of a particular kind of dulcimer. As a performer on the 'Pantaleon', as it was called at the suggestion of Louis XIV, he was acclaimed in Paris and Dresden. In 1706 he came to Eisenach as dancing master and director of music to the Court. In his latter capacity he built up an excellent orchestra, of which Telemann became leader in 1707. Seven years later, Hebenstreit being promoted to Dresden, he became director of music. While cantatas, whether secular or sacred, were expected to be in either the 'German' or the 'Italian' manner (according to Telemann's autobiography), the guiding principle for instrumental music was that of the French overture. Johann Bernhard Bach—a friend of Telemann and, since he was cembalist in the Court orchestra since 1703, also a colleague—was an elegant practitioner in this field. Indeed it is virtually only as such that he is known to posterity.

Johann Bernhard's first appointment as organist was in the Kaufmannskirche in Erfurt. Thence he moved north to Magdeburg (an unusual destination for a Thuringian Bach) where he remained until 1703. Then, after the refusal of his Jena kinsman Johann Nikolaus, he was elected to succeed Johann Christoph at St George's Church. At the same time he joined the Court establishment. Johann Bernhard was one of the most agreeable of the Bachs. Contented with his life in Eisenach he gave general satisfaction, so that in 1723 Duke Johann Wilhelm raised his salary, and in 1741, when the Eisenach Court was discontinued, he was permitted to go on drawing a pension. Bernhard was godfather to one of Johann Sebastian's sons, and Johann Sebastian performed a like service for Bernhard. Bernhard, whose suites were copied by Sebastian for the benefit of his pupils and also for concert use in Leipzig, wrote in the French manner, but with a distinctive, and German, accent.[10] Thus the opening of his *Ouverture in G minor* (vli. concertante, vl.1, 2, rip., vla., continuo) is Handelian:

The unexpected *Fantaisie* that follows the conventional *Air*, *Rondeau* and *Louré*, however, has an austerity in its textural patterns that is—in a general sense—familiarly Bachian.

The eldest son of Bernhard Bach, Johann Ernst (1722–77), became a scholar of St Thomas's school in Leipzig, and while there lived with and was taught by Johann Sebastian. A man of parts, Johann Ernst held a juridical post in Eisenach and Weimar and also those of organist and Kantor in succession to his father. As a composer he is discussed on pages 242–4.

On his death the Eisenach appointments were bestowed on his eldest son, Johann Georg (1751–97). (The other sons, whose Christian names indicate the sentimental attachment within the family to those of the more illustrious, were Carl Philipp (*b.* 1754), J. Theodor Friedrich (*b.*1755), J. August Jakob (*b.* 1763), J. Christian Gottlieb (*b.* 1763) and J. Christian (*b.* 1766). The last musical member of this line was Philipp Ernst Christian Bach (*d.* 1840) who, while never organist in the town, was well known as such in the surrounding villages. By profession he was a local government officer and, if known to history at all, is so through the pen of a young Englishman, Edward Holmes, who visited Eisenach in 1827 and described his meeting with 'the only one of the *auld* original stock left in the town' in his *Ramble*.

IN OHRDRUF

By being taken away from Eisenach as a small boy Johann Sebastian was withdrawn from a climate that in the end might well have proved relaxing. He was by temperament built to accomplish his aims the hard way. But, as we see, he had no option: in 1695 he was on his own.

Like the other Thuringian towns Ohrdruf had had to pick itself up from the calamities of the Thirty Years War. When Ernst I, 'the Pious', became Duke of Sachsen-Gotha and Altenburg in 1640,[11] the general situation within his little realm was discouraging. Many ministers and schoolmasters—their houses often burned down—had become soldiers because of the irregularity of their stipends. Those who had no taste for military adventure and whose houses were intact took in paying guests, especially 'actors, clowns, dancing masters, ape- and bear-leaders'. Performances by such artists were given in the churches.[12]

Recognizing that education and a regular church life were essential to the well-being of a society, the duke set about the task of reclamation and reconstruction. In the first year of his reign he established a book printer in Gotha, Peter Schmid of Schleusingen, and dignity began to return to the state. Schools and churches were renovated, and in 1666 the issue of the first Gotha *Gesangbuch* brought the two into an harmonious relationship again. One of the focal points of a renewed intellectual life in the duchy was the Grammar School in Ohrdruf, for which (as for other schools) a new curriculum had been ordained in 1660. From 1675 to 1696 the school was under the control of the Superintendent of St Michael's Church, Melchior Kromayer. He was succeeded by his son, Johann Abraham, who was in office until 1733. The general scheme at Ohrdruf was similar to that at Eisenach, with much insistence on classical and religious instruction. The school examinations took place in the second part of July each year. In respect of religious instruction the boys returned to their classrooms on Sunday mornings to be examined in the sermon to which they were supposed to have listened.[13] The character of Lutheranism in Ohrdruf —important in respect of Bach's development and future views—was orthodox and strongly anti-Pietist.

As a pupil in this school Sebastian had daily Latin and German lessons in the 'Quarta' (in 1702 this subject was commenced in the 'Quinta') as well as an hour of Greek each week. Music lessons, at the customary hour after midday, were given four times a week. For the first two years of Sebastian's school days these were a terrifying prospect. The Kantor was Johann Heinrich Arnold, formerly Kantor in Breitenbach, whose conduct was such that even the official school register named him as 'a menace to the school, a scandal to the church, and a cancer in the community'.[14] In 1697, to the relief of his colleagues and the delight of his pupils, he was dismissed. The young Bachs must have been particularly relieved at Arnold's departure, for he had a family connection in that he was godfather to Maria Sophia, Johann Michael's fourth daughter, in Gehren.

When Sebastian first went to the Grammar School in Ohrdruf he was accompanied by his brother Jakob, who left in 1696 to be apprenticed to his father's successor in Eisenach. From his record in the Grammar School in Eisenach it would seem that Jakob was academically undistinguished, but the Bachs tended to leave school at fourteen, since funds for their maintenance as students were slender. Sebastian moved up the school satisfactorily, and in 1698 caught up with his Arnstadt cousin, Johann Ernst, in the 'Secunda'. Ernst departed during the next year and Sebastian was promoted to the 'Prima' in which, at the beginning of 1700, he was placed tenth in a class of fifteen. At this point, however, he was withdrawn from the school. It was noted that he left for 'Lüneburgum ob defectum hospitiorum . . . d. 15 Martii, 1700'.[15] The domestic situation with Johann Christoph and Johanna Dorothea (with two small children of their own and another on the way) was such that it was desirable that Sebastian should find lodging elsewhere. His passport was his voice.

At Ohrdruf he was a member of the *Chorus Musicus*, a body of twenty to twenty-five singers. (As such he had been able to contribute his share to the household exchequer.[16]) And he was among the more dependable performers. At that time, when civic music was a matter of prestige, talent spotters, scouts and agents were active in the transfer market. Thuringia was—and for a long time remained—a happy hunting-ground for choristers, a fair number of whom were taken into the choir of the Ritterakademie (formerly Michaeliskloster) attached to St Michael's Church in Lüneburg.[17] Elias Herda, the Kantor of Ohrdruf after Arnold, was a former pupil of the Lüneburg school, and it was on his recommendation that Sebastian and his class-mate Georg Erdmann (who later followed a diplomatic career) were accepted as scholars and as members of the *Mettenchor*, a select group of twelve to fifteen singers (including soloists) drawn from the *Chorus Symphoniacus* of about twenty-five singers, who were normally directed by a Prefect.

LÜNEBURG AND THE COURT OF CELLE

Sebastian set out for the unfamiliar north with the intensive training of the tyrannical Arnold and the gentler Herda to sustain him. He had

naturally benefited from the advice of his brother Johann Christoph
(who became a member of the Ohrdruf Grammar School staff in 1700).
Subtracting the fantasy later retailed by Forkel that he sampled forbidden fruit by moonlight in despite of a jealous-minded elder brother,
it may be accepted from the first biography that (among others) he had
studied the keyboard works of Froberger, Johann Caspar Fischer,
Kerl Pachelbel, Buxtehude, Nikolaus Bruhns and Georg Böhm
(1661–1733). The last—a Thuringian educated in Gotha and Jena—
was the son of an organist, and in 1693 he emigrated to Hamburg.
From there he moved to Lüneburg in 1698 as organist of St John's
Church, which had its own *Kantorei*. It was clearly congenial to the
young Bach to find a fellow countryman in a position of authority in a
new environment, and it is clear that Böhm (one of whose minuets was
copied into the Anna Magdalena *Clavierbüchlein*) was an influential
figure in his musical development. The rhetoric of Böhm's preludes
and the taut arguments of his fugues were among the inspirations of
Bach's organ works as this example shows:

Lüneburg, an old Hanseatic town and a centre of the salt trade, had
diminished in commercial significance since the Thirty Years War.
But when Sebastian Bach arrived there it appeared an impressive
place by reason of its spacious planning, the distinguished character of
the late Gothic and Renaissance houses (still there) on the *Am Sande*,

Hans Bach?, after a wood-cut, 1617

The Bach House, Eisenach, drawing by Hanns Bock

Right: Receipt for payment of wages signed by Swedish Royal musicians, including Johann Jakob Bach, 20th July 1714

Far right: Minute of Nedre Borgrätten, Stockholm, 12th July 1728, concerning the Estate of Johann Jakob Bach

Lüneburg in the seven-
teenth century

Above: Johann Ludwig Bach, portrait by G. F. Bach

Above right: St Thomas's Church, Leipzig, with the School in the background, in the time of J. S. Bach

Right: Violin part of Handel's *Armida abbandonata*, copied by J. S. Bach

Far right: J. S. Bach's testimonial for J. A. Scheibe, 4th April 1731

Das
Angenehme
Leipzig!

In einem
Musicalischen Dramate
aufgeführet.

Von dem
bey
Herrn Gottfried Zimmermann
florirenden
COLLEGIO MUSICO
In Leipzig.

ANNO MDCCXXVII.

DRAMA PER MUSICA.
Chor der vier Jahrs-Zeiten.

ARIA.

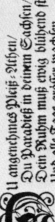

U angenehmes Pleiß-Athen/
Du Paradieß in deinem Sachsen/
Dein Ruhm muß ewig blühend stehn
Und alle Tage grösser wachsen.
Aller Zeiten Müh und Fleiß/
Sorgen wie sie deinen Preiß
Schöner machen und erhöhn.   Da Capo.

Der Frühling.

Recit. Ich will mir nichts als Leipzig dich erwehlen.
Du bist der Platz,
Wo meiner Lieblichkeiten Schatz
Am häuffigsten soll liegen.

Ergö=

):(2

Das angenehme Leipzig, 1727,
opening pages
of word-book

Portrait of J. S. Bach, by E. G. Haussmann, 1746

Rector.

Herr M. Johann August Ernesti, P. P. E.

Con-Rector.

Herr M. Conrad Benedict Hülse. +

Cantor.

Herr Johann Sebastian Bach, Königl. Pohln. und Chur-
fürstl. Sächs. wie auch Fürstl. Anhalt-Cöthnischer
Capell-Meister. +

Tertius.

Herr M. Abraham Krügel.

Quartus.

Herr M. Gabriel Matthesius.

Baccalaureus Funerum.

Herr M. George Irmler.

Collegen.

Herr Johann Friedrich Breunigk.
Herr N. N. Meyer.

Schul-Medicus.

Herr D. Anton Wilhelm Platz.

Nota. Ausser diesen öffentlichen befinden sich auch in
und vor der Stadt viele Privat-Schulen, allwo die
Jugend beyderley Geschlechts im Christenthum und
andern nöthigen Stücken unterrichtet wird. Ueber
diese Privat-Schulen haben die vier untersten Herren
Geistlichen des Ministerii die Inspection und Visitation,
nach den vier Stadt-Vierteln eingetheilet, und darf
niemand eine solche Privat-Schule anstellen, als bis
er von einem dieser Herren Inspectoren ein Testimo-
nium Habilitatis bey E. E. Hochw. Rath produciret,
und um die Concession, Schule zu halten, schrifftlich
angehalten, auch die Concession dazu würcklich in
Schrifften erhalten hat.

Sechste Abtheilung.

Von der sämmtl. Bürgerschafft.

I. Abschnitt.

Von Handlungs-Verwandten.

I. Von Buchhändlern, nach Alphabetischer Ordnung.

Herr Arckstee und Merkus.
  • Blochberger, Michael.   Herr

Death of J. S. Bach and names of his successors noted in a copy of the
Leipziger Adress-Post-und-Reise Calender, 1750

the group of buildings around the town hall which included the newly built residence of Eléonore d'Olbreuze (now housing the department of Justice) and the three great Gothic churches of St Nicholas, St John and St Michael. Of these St John's, double-aisled and splendidly sonorous, had a famous altar-piece from the Hamburg school of Heinrich Bornemann. St Michael's Church stands in a tree-lined close which today is named Johann Sebastian Bach Platz. It is a spacious building (which has now undergone complete restoration) with high windows, making walls of glass through which light streams into the interior. In Bach's day there was in the church a comprehensive library of music which had been carefully kept and recently brought up to date by the Thuringian-born Kantor Friedrich Emanuel Praetorius (1623–1695). The fact of copies of works by Heinrich and Johann Christoph Bach and other Thuringian composers being in the library may be explained by the antecedents and regional loyalty of Praetorius. Gratifying as it was to Sebastian to find the family name in the catalogue, it was more exhilarating to have the opportunity of seeing works by the then distinguished Kantors of Leipzig (see pages 133–5) as well as by the great seventeenth-century Italian masters. There were also represented in the library Thomas Selle (1599–1663), Kantor in Hamburg, and Christian Flor (1626–97),[18] sometime Kantor in Lüneburg. Both composers had added to the repertoire of Passion settings, and one of Selle's two settings of the St John narrative is distinguished by the orchestration, which differentiates character by tone colour. During Bach's time in Lüneburg the town Kantor in Celle was Johann Georg Kühnhausen (d. 1714), and it is more than probable that the young student had opportunity to hear his *St Matthew Passion*,[19] from which this effective crowd scene comes.

The contact between Lüneburg and Celle was close, for since 1665 the town had been under the protection of the dukes of Celle, whose Court was a centre of French culture. That it was so was in spite of the males of the ducal family. Christian Ludwig, elder son of Duke Georg, 'was a drunkard and a despot. He lowered himself to the extent of fighting with the bourgeois in the public thoroughfares as well as in his own residence . . . [and] he retained his rude unpolished manners to the last.'[20] His brother, Georg Wilhelm, was little better, but redeemed by a sense of generosity—'especially perhaps to impoverished German nobles'.[21] Georg Wilhelm, however, refined his manners somewhat by residence in France, whence he brought a mistress, Eléonore Desonier d'Olbreuze. This lady was given the designation of 'friend' to the duke and the title of Mme d'Harbourg, a title previously borne by the less regular ladies of the House of Braunschweig. In 1676 the duke legitimized his 'friend' by marriage and also their daughter Sophia Dorothea, the future unfortunate wife of George I of England.

In return for exchanging the pleasures, and respectability, of France for the austerities and embarrassments of northern Germany, Eléonore insisted on being surrounded with sufficient of her countrymen to recall the former and to mitigate the latter. An Huguenot, the duchess gave sanctuary to refugees from France, as at the same time did the Great Elector, Friedrich Wilhelm, of Brandenburg, and the musical establishment at Celle was almost entirely composed of Frenchmen.

Sebastian spent three years in Lüneburg. During this period—his voice not having changed into anything particularly pleasing—he continued his general studies, assisted in the musical affairs of St Michael's, and took every opportunity to broaden his musical outlook. There is no doubt that he visited Celle from time to time. The southern gateway to the Lüneburger Heide, Celle is a beautiful town, crowned by the castle that rises nobly above its park and water-courses. The Gothic chapel of the castle, with Renaissance additions, is the very essence of the transition from *Gottgläubigkeit* to *Ichzeit* discussed in relation to music on page 143. In Bach's day large-scale performances of church music, however, were given not in the castle chapel but in the town church that lay just below the castle. Musical interest in the residence was concentrated within the theatre which, built in 1674 and decorated by Giuseppe Arighini of Brescia, is the oldest surviving theatre in Germany. Although Bach heard performances in Celle he had frequent opportunity to encounter the Celle Court musicians in Lüneburg, where they were frequently required to attend to play in the new palace of the duchess. French influence was all-pervasive, and a taste in French music was inculcated into the young aristocrats from Celle who were students at the Lüneburg *Ritterakademie*. French music was also in vogue in Hannover and Hamburg, to which city Bach was drawn particularly by the reputation of the famous, near-legendary Johann Adam Reinken (1623–1722), who had been organist of St Catharine's Church for almost half a century.

RETURN TO THURINGIA

Fortified by his experiences in the north, but pulled by affection for his homeland, Sebastian returned to Thuringia, and in 1703, for a brief period, played the violin in the orchestra of Duke Johann Ernst at Weimar. Since Johann Effler was Court organist and Johann Samuel Drese was Kappelmeister—both of whom were well acquainted with the Bach family—it is unlikely that Bach had much difficulty in obtaining at least temporary employment. Whether he found conditions entirely congenial is another matter, for he was also engaged as Court 'lackey'. Meanwhile in Arnstadt a new organ had been installed in the church of St Boniface—itself a replacement of that destroyed in the fire of 1581. The organ, built by Johann Friedrich Wender of Mühlhausen, was a two-manual instrument (with pedals) with twenty-three speaking-stops.[22] According to custom the organ was approved by an independent expert before Wender was paid, and it was Johann Sebastian Bach who was called in to certify the work. Lately unsuccessful in an application for the organist's place at Sangerhausen, which was given to Johann Augustin Kobelius (1674–1731), Bach took advantage of the trip to Arnstadt to prove that he was not only a good judge of an organ but also the only man capable permanently of satisfying the requirements of the Arnstadt Consistory. Having given a recital on the new organ to display its and his qualities, and having made his position clear in respect of the appointment, Bach received a letter confirming his election to the organist's place on 9th August 1703. Not yet nineteen, he was nicely settled, with an annual salary of fifty florins and an allowance of thirty thalers for board and lodging.

The appointment at Arnstadt was at the instance of the count, Anton Günther, and it may well be that he was prodded into supporting a bright young man who had some experience of the cultural climate of Lüneburg and Celle by his countess. As a daughter of Duke Anton Ulrich of Braunschweig-Wolfenbüttel, who was himself the author of various libretti for operas (including those set by Löwe), Auguste Dorothea had close family connections with Celle and Hannover. To keep up with her relations she built her own theatre at Augustenburg.

The Arnstadt musico-dramatic performances depended on the local Rektor, Johann Friedrich Treiber, who was the only available librettist. In 1705 two works by Treiber were presented: *Der Carneval* and *Die Klugkeit der Obrigkeit in Adordnung des Bierbrauens*. The music of these works—characterized by an admixture of classical nomenclature and low, topical comedy in Thuringian dialect—is lost. The composer may have been Treiber's son, Johann Philipp; on the other hand it is not impossible that it may have been Bach, some part of whose salary was derived from the local tax on beer. It is not without interest that a better known (and extant) work of similar nature, based on an alcoholic theme, was composed somewhat later by Johann Nikolaus Bach, the teacher of the younger Treiber at Jena (see page 113). What part Bach played in the Court music is not recorded, but that he visited the palace is testified by the occasion of the disreputable incident described below.

He stayed in Arnstadt for rather less than three years; on the whole rather turbulent years. Lack of sympathy between generations is not only a phenomenon of the twentieth century. The young Sebastian Bach, inspired by his brief acquaintance with the wider world and endowed with a certain arrogance, was, his employers were to discover, an awkward customer to handle. The Arnstadt years are marked therefore with notices of Consistorial disapproval. One of the difficulties with which Bach was faced when he took up his appointment was that, there being no Kantor in the new church, he was expected to undertake the Kantoral as well as the organist's duties. Not only was he slack in this respect (he claimed that he was only engaged to direct chorale and not 'figured music' performance), but he was frequently at cross purposes with his student choristers. This was made apparent when, in August 1705, Bach brought a dispute with one Geyersbach before the Consistory court. On his way back from the palace—presumably from a playing engagement—he and Geyersbach, having called each other rude names, brawled, and the disorder was only ended by the intervention of other students. Bach, who was in the company of his girl friend, had gone so far as to draw a dagger. A month or so later, having asked his cousin Johann Ernst to deputize for him, and having received permission for a month's leave of absence, he disappeared to Lübeck.[23]

The reason for this long, much romanticized, expedition[24] was the music of St Mary's Church, directed by the venerable Buxtehude. On the one hand there was the organ playing of Buxtehude himself, on the other the famous *Abendmusik* performances directed by him on the five Sundays before Christmas. These performances, which had already been flourishing for half a century, were unique. They were instituted by the merchants of Lübeck and, although held in the church, were extraliturgical. Although generally religious in character the works performed were not exclusively so, as evidenced, for instance, by the *Winterlied* of 1700. Bach must have heard four or five sessions of *Abendmusik* in St Mary's, and possibly others in neighbouring churches. It is likely that he was present on 2nd December 1705 when—with the church draped with banners and adorned with imperial coats-of-arms, the choristers all in black and instruments muted—an 'extraordinary' *Abendmusik* took place in honour of the Emperor, Leopold I, who had died on 5th May.[25] Apart from the quality of the music Bach was no doubt impressed by the respect in which organists were held on the Baltic coast.

It was otherwise in Thuringia. In February 1706 Bach was once more called up before the Consistory to explain his four months' absence. His answer—that he had been improving his skills—was not good enough for his employers, who went on to list other sins of commission and omission. He played the chorales extravagantly, to the confusion of the faithful; when the superintendent asked him to abbreviate his voluntaries he cut them too short; there was no improvement in his attitude to the 'figured music'. At the end of the year the Consistory came back to this matter, and also asked by what right he had invited a girl (presumed to have been Maria Barbara) into the organ loft during divine service. It is difficult not to feel some sympathy for the Consistory.

Arnstadt and Sebastian Bach were incompatible, but the latter had the sense to realize the fact and to look elsewhere for more congenial conditions of employment. The death of the much respected Johann Georg Ahle left a vacancy at the church of St Blasius in Mühlhausen. Bach applied for the post and was appointed, his place in Arnstadt being filled by Johann Ernst Bach. In 1728 Johann Ernst, who led a blameless and undistinguished life, became organist of the Church of Our Lady and also the Oberkirche.

Appointed to Mühlhausen on 15th June 1707, Bach took the first step towards 'settling down'. On 17th October he married Maria Barbara (daughter of Johann Michael of Gehren), who was a year older than himself. Thereupon he appears to have devoted himself wholeheartedly to his duties. Helped by a pupil—Johann Martin Schubart[26]—he copied music for the use of the church. In honour of the joint mayors (Adolf Strecher and Georg Adam Steinbach) and the annual reconstitution of the town council he composed (and himself probably engraved) a celebratory motet (Cantata 71) which was performed on 4th February 1708. (This, published in Mühlhausen, was one of the only two cantatas published during Bach's lifetime.) He advised the reconstruction and enlargement of his organ—the specification he proposed being patterned after that drawn up by Johann Christoph for St George's, Eisenach—and was happy that the work was entrusted to the local builder, Wender. But he suffered discontents.

Mühlhausen, as has been seen, was a centre for theological disputation, and when Bach arrived there the conflict between Orthodoxy and Pietism was fierce. The Pietists were not only opposed to elaborate church music, they objected to most forms of music. August Hermann Francke, the founder of Pietism, fulminated from the new University of Halle (1694).[27] Gottfried Vockerodt, Rector at Jena, and related to Councillor Vockerodt of Mühlhausen, added his pen to the good cause of piety and purity.[28] Vockerodt referred disparagingly to the 'contemporary *hyporchematicus* style', to the 'so-called *Stylo Phantastico*' peculiar to 'Sonatas, Toccatas, and Ricercari'.[29] Stage productions tending to the encouragement of transvestism particularly upset his equilibrium. 'It is known', he wrote, 'that men have to put on women's clothes in theatrical performances.' This, he added while turning the reader to the *Book of Deuteronomy* (XXII, 5), was expressly forbidden by God.[30] The minister of Bach's church, Johann Adolf Frohne, had Pietist inclinations, and it was not much help to Bach that Johann Christian Eilmar, minister of St Mary's, was Orthodox. He began to think again of moving. By good fortune Effler of Weimar, an acquaintance of many Bachs, was contemplating retirement. Bach was not slow to accept an offer of an engagement at Weimar where, promised the full emoluments of the office, he could perform all the duties of Court Organist as well as those of chamber musician, while Effler (who died in 1711) remained titular organist. At Mühlhausen the new organist was Johann Friedrich Bach (1682–1730), third son of Johann Christoph of Eisenach. Friedrich Bach was not only organist but also organ builder. As a teacher he was gratefully remembered by Heinrich Nikolaus Gerber, of Sondershausen, father of the lexicographer. Gerber was a pupil at the Grammar School in Mühlhausen, from where he went to Leipzig University and to lessons from Sebastian Bach.

EMIGRANTS

The fertility of the German musical dynasties meant that there was a surplus of labour on the market. It is not surprising, then, that there was a tendency towards emigration. For the adventurous there were new worlds to conquer overseas. There were, for example, opportunities in Sweden and England.

The power of Sweden as a first-class European military force was established by Gustavus, Adolphus. For almost a century after his death Swedish imperialism was a decisive factor in the realignment of the balance of power, at any rate in northern and eastern Europe. For it was the threatened domination of Poland by the Swedes that led to the development of strong militaristic and nationalistic tendencies within Prussia and Saxony. During the seventeenth and eighteenth centuries it may be said that as a rule where there was power there was also culture; the converse, however, was not necessarily valid. Before her abdication and spectacular exile in Rome, Queen Christina established standards of culture in Stockholm that were maintained across the reigns of Charles X, XI and XII. Of the Bachs (a line rather remote from the main stream) who lived in Molsdorf, a village between Erfurt and Arnstadt, one Nikol was conscripted into Swedish service during the Thirty Years War. He was stabbed to death in a brawl in 1646 (as Geyersbach might have been almost sixty years later). Johann, also of Molsdorf, was said to have become a musician on the staff of General Karl Gustaf Wrangel, commander of the 'Dalregementet' (1638–45) and commander-in-chief (1646–8). If this was the case the date of Johann Bach's enlistment would seem to be established by an entry in the *Fürstlicher Sächsischer Geschichts-Calendar . . ., 1601–97* (Leipzig, 1697) for October, 1646: 'In diesem Monat *marchirte* die Swedische Armee unter Wrangeln durch Thüringen an die Weser; welcher die Käyserl. und Chur-Bäyerische aus Böhmen folgte/durch Meissen und Thüringen/ hielten bey Arnstadt *General Rendezvous . . .*; folgends gieng der *March* auff Gotha/ Eisenach/ und in Hessen.' ('The Swedish army, under Wrangel, marched through Thuringia to the Weser during this month. The Imperial and Bavarian Electoral army followed from Bohemia, and a general rendezvous was held near Arnstadt . . .; afterwards the march proceeded into Hesse by way of Gotha and Eisenach.')

In or about 1704 Sebastian Bach's brother Jakob, now out of his apprenticeship in Eisenach, announced that he was joining the forces of Charles XII of Sweden, who at that time was campaigning in Poland in an effort to dislodge the Elector of Saxony from his throne. Sebastian proceeded to give his brother a proper send-off with a flourish; with the familiar Kuhnauesque programme fancy of the

Capriccio sopra la lontananza del suo fratello dilettisimo. Kuhnau's so-
called 'Biblical Sonatas' were published in 1700. In his preface he
rightly disclaimed credit for originality in respect of descriptive music,
referring the reader to the 'Batailles, Wasserfällen, Tombeaux' of
Froberger and other 'excellent composers'. In the same fanciful
mood of the capriccio and at about the same time Sebastian also composed the sonata in D major, of which the last movement is a fugue
based on a 'Thema all'imitatio Gallina Cucca', inspired by a capriccio
on a 'hannen und henner geschrey' by the Viennese composer Alessandro Poglietti, a composer whom Kuhnau also, no doubt, had had in
mind. Poglietti was killed during the siege of Vienna by the Turks in
1683. One of the main tasks of Christendom for the next thirty years
was the containment of the Turks. In prosecuting this task Christendom was more or less united.

A Thuringian of military age, particularly if living under the rule
of a 'Reichsfürst', then stood a good chance of conscription. Friedrich I
of Sachsen-Gotha, for example, provided one horse and two foot regiments (2,000 men in all) for the Elector Johann George III of Saxony in
1689, and a regiment of dragoons (800–1,000 men) for the imperial campaign against the Turks in Hungary. Friedrich II provided even more
men for the Emperor, who promised to maintain the Gotha troops as
though they were his own. In 1703 some of these troops, led by Johann
Wilhelm, the duke's brother, saw service in Holland and England.[31]
Johann Jakob Bach was thoroughly caught up in the military machine.
For after taking part in the battle of Poltava (28th June 1709), in
which the Swedes were routed by the Russians, he accompanied
Charles XII to Turkey, where both became prisoners-of-war. Bach,
however, was not lacking in resourcefulness. He managed to find his
way to Constantinople where he met Buffardin, the flautist, who was
in the company of the French ambassador. Thus a Bach was able to
have flute lessons from a Frenchman in Turkey. After his return,
Johann Jakob went to Stockholm, where his name first appeared in the
royal accounts, as a musician, in 1713. His annual stipend, like those of
his colleagues often tardily paid, was 300 dalers—less 1 per cent
income tax. Bach was twice married. His first wife, Susanna Maria, died
in 1719, leaving a two-year-old daughter (who died in youth); his
second wife, Magdalena Norell, who bore no children, outlived him.
Bach died on 16th April 1722. On 21st January 1723, the king,
Friedrich I, confirmed the conveyance to the distinguished musician,
Johann Heinrich Roman, of Bach's salary.[32] At about this time Johann

Michael (*b.* 1685), fourth and youngest son of Johann Christoph Bach, of Eisenach, a contemporary of Johann Sebastian at the grammar school there, and who became an organ-builder, was also supposed to have been in Scandinavia. The *Ursprung* stated that he went 'to the Northlands and never returned, so that no more is known about him'. There is no evidence in Sweden, however, to suggest that he settled there.

There was an increasing tendency to consider the allurements of London, where middle-class enthusiasm had established a tradition of public concerts that afforded considerable opportunity to the enterprising. There were German musicians in London in Purcell's day. The number increased when the consort of Queen Anne, Prince George of Denmark, expressed a preference for their talents. At some uncertain date the German community in London was joined by Johann Christoph Bach (1676–*c.* 1730), second son of Johann Christoph of Eisenach. Another alumnus of the Grammar School, Johann Christoph V (see page 67), became a harpsichord teacher and manufacturer. He worked in Erfurt, in Hamburg, in Rotterdam and finally in London.[33] In the *Catalogue of Musical Instruments* belonging to Handel's sometime patron, the Duke of Chandos, made by Pepusch on 23rd August 1720, item thirteen is a 'harpsichord, two rows of keys'. This may reasonably be identified with the instrument 'bought by Chandos in 1720 for £572 from Johann Christoph Bach, probably the one who is supposed to have died in London in 1740, a cousin of Johann Sebastian's first wife and a music teacher in England'.[34]

In the long run, however, the Thuringian composer who travelled least travelled farthest. Johann Sebastian Bach went to Weimar in the late summer of 1708 content that there was a new organ, built by Johann Conrad Weishaupt, of Seeburgen, in the palace chapel, and that he would be earning nearly twice as much as in Mühlhausen— 150 gulden a year.

NOTES TO CHAPTER FOUR

1. Duke Johann Georg III (*b.* 9th July 1566, in Grimmenstein) built palaces in Marksühl (1588) and Eisenach (1597). In 1628 Duke Johann Ernst III restored the Wartburg and made it a residence.

2. Karl Schrader, 'Die Fürstlich-Sächsische Residenzstadt Eisenach, 1672–1741', in *Beiträge zur Geschichte Eisenachs*, Nr. XXIX, Eisenach, 1929, pp. 47, 57, 83.

3. *See* Note 2 above, p. 17.

4. *See* reference to *Aria Eberliniana*, p. 56.

5. The sermon was printed by Johan David Kohl, Court printer, at Eisenach soon after Dorothea Maria's funeral. There is a copy in the Landesbibliothek, Gotha.

6. Johann Nikolaus left school in 1689. ('. . . hat sich verabschiedet, um nach Jena zu gehen', *Matrikel der Eisenacher Lateinschule*), (1690–1707), and matriculated at Jena on 12th May 1690 (*Die Matrikel der Universität Jena* II, 1652–1723, Weimar, 1961–   ).

7. 'Joh. Seb. Bach besucht 1694 die Quinta und versäumt 59 Stunden.' *Matrikel der Eisenacher Lateinschule*.

8. The copy that was once the property of Jakob Bach of Ruhla, and bears his inscription, is now in the possession of the Bachhaus.

9. A brief autobiography of Johann Christoph Bach, dated 29th December 1700 was written into the *Ohrdrufer Personal-Chronik für Pfarrer, Kantoren, Lehrer*, etc. This is published in Conrad Freyse, *Die Ohrdrufer Bache in der Silhouette*, Eisenach/Kassel, 1957, pp. 83–4. This also contains similar autobiographies by Tobias Friedrich, Johann Bernhard, Johann Christoph and Johann Andreas, sons of Johann Christoph.

10. C. P. E. Bach possessed overtures in E flat, G major, D major and two in G minor, by Johann Bernhard (*Verzeichniss*, etc., p. 83).

11. Gotha became an independent duchy in 1640 and remained such until 1825.

12. A. Beck, *Geschichte des gothaischen Landes*, Gotha, 1868–75 I, p. 332.

13. '. . . dass Sonntags zu Mittage die kinder in allen Classen müssen in die Schule kommen, da sie aus der Predigt examiniret werden und andere gute Übungen treiben'. School rule, quoted in F. Thomas, *Einige Ergebnisse über Johann Sebastian Bachs Ohrdrufer Schulzeit*, Ohrdruf, 1900, p. 5.

14. 'In der Schule ist der Gotlose *Cantor Arnold* (*pestis scholae, scandalum ecclesiae et carcinoma civitatis*) durch Urtheil *removiret* . . .' School register, quoted by Thomas (*see* Note 13 above), p. 9.

15. *See* Note 13 above, p. 15.

16. In 1699, for example, the following sums were distributed among the members of the *Chorus Musicus*: New Year, 64 Thaler, 17

Groschen, 6th March, 57 Th., 13 Gr., 7 Pfennig; 3rd July, 74 Th., 6 Gr., 3 Pf.; 2nd October, 52 Th., 11 Gr., 8 Pf. (*See* Thomas, Note 13, p. 5.)

17. Johann Nikolaus Forkel, a Thuringian, became a chorister at Lüneburg in 1766, and Thuringian names are frequent in the Lüneburg register throughout the eighteenth century.

18. *See* P. Epstein, 'Ein unbekanntes Passionsoratorium von Chr. Flor (1667)', *BJB*, 1930, p. 56.

19. *See* A. Adrio, 'Die Matthäus-Passion von J. G. Kühnhausen', in *Festschrift: Arnold Schering zum 60 Geburtstag*, Berlin, 1937, p. 24 f.

20. Viscont Horric de Beaucaire, *A Mésalliance in the House of Brunswick*, London, 1886, p. 18.

21. *See* Note 20 above.

22. The console is now exhibited in the museum in Arnstadt.

23. Documents relating to Arnstadt are accessible in *The Bach Reader*, ed. Hans David and Arthur Mendel, New York, 1945, 1967.

24. E.g. Hans Franck, *Die Pilgerfahrt nach Lübeck, eine Bach-Novelle*, Berlin, 1959.

25. *See* Oskar Sohngen, 'Die Lübecker Abendmusik als Kirchengeschichtliches und theologisches Problem', in *Musik und Kirche*, Jg. 27, Nr 4, Kassel, 1957, p. 161 f.

26. Schubart (1690–1721) came from Geraburg, near Ilmenau: in 1717 he succeeded Bach as Court organist in Weimar.

27. E.g. in his preface to the pamphlet . . . *Erklärung der Frage: was von dem weltüblichen täntzen zu halten sey?*, Halle, 1696. Cf. 'Francke, a minister of their [Pietist] sect, established by his own industry a college at Halle. This was a nursery for young divines . . . who formed a sect of rigid Lutherans. . . . These are Protestant Jansenists, who are distinguished from the rest by their mystical severities.' *Memoirs of the House of Brandenburg*, London, 1757, p. 285.

28. Vockerodt, *Misbrauch der freyen Künste/in sonderheit Der Music . . . was nach D. Luthers und anderen Evangelischen Theologorum und Politicorum Meinung von Opern und Komödien zu halten sey?*, Frankfurt, 1697.

29. *See* Note 28 above, p. 41.

30. *See* Note 28 above, p. 140.

31. *See* Note 12 above, p. 355.

32. *See* Appendix I.

33. J. G. Walther, *Musicalisches Lexicon*, 1732. *See* also J. Hawkins, *History of Music*, 1875 ed., p. 852.

34. O. E. Deutsch, *Handel, a Documentary Biography*, London, 1955, p. 110; *see also* C. H. Collins Baker and Muriel I. Baker, *The Life and Circumstances of James Brydges, First Duke of Chandos, Patron of the Liberal Arts*, London, 1940, p. 131.

5

Court Musician

During the lifetime of Johann Sebastian Bach the principle of absolutism in monarchic government reached its climax. During the lifetime of his sons the validity of the principle was both assailed and reduced. Within his own field Bach was something of an absolutist. His sons and, indeed, some of his relatives who were his contemporaries, were not. These contrasts derived partly from personality and partly from environment, and are to be recognized within the territory of music in details of style. Stylistic changes within German music took place partly under the influence of Court fashion, but partly in reaction against aristocratic attitudes. Telemann, it will be remembered, left the confines of Court life with the remark that he who wished for security should live in a republic. The attitude is reflected in the character of his works. Telemann, who became a man of some substance, was exceptional; he managed to make a profit out of an ideal.

As Bach came to maturity so too did two German states: Prussia and Saxony. The former, raised to a major power by the Great Elector, Friedrich Wilhelm, became a kingdom in 1701, Friedrich Wilhelm's son thereby becoming Friedrich I. The significance of Saxony increased when Friedrich August II (1670–1733), 'August the Strong', acquired the crown of Poland as a result of bare-faced horse-dealing, which in due course involved his acceptance of Catholicism. 'La Saxe', remarked Friedrich II with an avaricious eye on the Electorate,

> est une des provinces les plus opulentes de l'Allemagne: elle doit cet avantage à la bonté de son sol, et à l'industrie de ses sujets, qui rendent leurs fabriques florissantes. Le souverain en retirait 6,000,000 de revenue, dont on decomptuit 1,500,000 écus employés à l'acquit des dettes auxquelles les deux élections de Pologne avaient donné lieu.[1]

The Courts of Berlin and Dresden (united in an uneasy political alliance in 1692) first brought together the various strains in German thought and tradition and then gave them fresh purpose. Berlin made a virtue out of native tendencies towards Puritanism and austerity; Dresden capitalized on the romantic *Doppelgänger* within the German soul. Berlin refined aspects of life and thought by constant references to French philosophy and behaviour; Dresden prospered under the warming influence of Italy. Music in Berlin was preferred to show a due respect for 'science'—so it was that fugal form was regarded with especial favour for many years to come (see page 299); a circumstance beneficial to the posthumous reputation of J. S. Bach. In Dresden the exhilaration of instrumental music and the graces of the solo concerto and of Italian opera were more welcome.

Berlin was governed by reason, and in the spirit of the *Aufklärung*. In this connection the King of Prussia was happy that, by the Peace of Westphalia, Halle had been annexed to Brandenburg, for the University of Halle was a principal centre of enlightenment. Christian Thomasius, Rektor of the university, promoted the claim of scientific thought and native culture. In his hand 'the victory flag of the mother tongue fluttered over the grammar schools'.[2] Thomasius was a humanist, and believed that intellectual inquiry should lead to social reforms.

> Of all the learned men that have adorned Germany, Leibnitz and Thomasius did the greatest service to the human understanding, by pointing out the right road which reason ought to pursue to come after truth. They opposed prejudices of every kind. . . .[3]

John Toland, the English scholar who was a guest at the philosophic discussions encouraged by Sophie Charlotte, Queen of Prussia, was enthusiastic over every aspect of Prussian development. The roads were in excellent order and well signposted, the public conveyances were frequent, the postal service was regular, the towns were well ordered and the churches and churchyards neat and tidy; while the enthusiasm of the king for architecture was evident in new and fine buildings, mostly designed by Andreas Schlüter and Jean de Bodt.[4] Like many others, Toland was captivated by the intellectual brilliance of Sophie Charlotte, whose

> favorit Diversion is Music, and one must judg as well of it as her Majesty (which is not easily done) to love it with a Passion equal to her's. She plays to Perfection on the Harpsichord, which she practices every day: she sings finely, and the famous Bononcini, one of the greatest Masters alive, told me, that her Compositions are most exact. . . .

During the reign of August the Strong Dresden was transformed
into one of the most beautiful of the cities of Europe. Taking advantage of its situation on the banks of the broad Elbe and of the monarch's
love of open space and ceremonial splendour, Mathaeus Pöppelmann and
Balthasar Permoser, the principal architects and sculptors, built palaces
and pavilions around parks and gardens that were of an almost unique
elegance. August, a full-blooded hedonist, but also a forceful ruler,
was typical of his age and class in his range of interests. These covered
buildings, gardens both for humans and animals, and interior decoration; and uncovered a sequence of mistresses, the conquest of whom
earned for the monarch the envious esteem of his subjects. He was
devoted to ballet and masquerade, and, not surprisingly, musicians
were attracted to Dresden by the prospect of full employment.

Jean Baptiste Volumier (c. 1670–1728) came by way of Berlin and
was leader of the orchestra in 1709. In due course he became acquainted
with Sebastian Bach and one of his staunch supporters. Georg Pisendel
(1687–1755), a pupil of both Corelli and Vivaldi and a virtuoso violinist
and able composer in his own right, was appointed director of music
in 1712. Having seen operas by Antonio Lotti (c. 1667–1740) in Venice
in that year August persuaded him also to visit Dresden, where he
produced operas between 1717 and 1719. By 1727 there were some 120
musicians attached to the Saxon Court, each earning an enormous
salary. A castrato (such as Senesino) could demand anything from
7,000 to 9,000 thalers. A Kapellmeister was worth 1,200. Orchestral
players were paid between 200 and 300, with an exceptional player
rising to 500.

THE COURTS OF WEIMAR

Berlin and Dresden were centres of power; Weimar, on the other hand,
was not. The splendours of the ducal Court there were not the outward
sign of a hidden force, but existed for themselves alone. Up to a point
such a duchy was a cloud-cuckoo-land. Like many others it survived
for a long time. In favour of the system, it may be said that it supported
such as J. S. Bach (whose independent attitudes, however, earned for
him a period of imprisonment at the duke's behest) and Wolfgang von
Goethe. There is, however, much that could be said against the system.

The ruling Duke of Sachsen-Weimar at the time of Bach's first
arrival in the town (once the 'Residenz-Stadt' of Friedrich 'the
Benevolent') was Wilhelm Ernst, who had succeeded to his title in

1683. By a long-standing family contract Wilhelm Ernst was obliged to acknowledge his younger brother (Johann Ernst, who maintained a separate establishment) as joint administrator. His relationship with Johann Ernst, happily married to the lively Sophie Auguste of Anhalt-Zeitz, was cool. To some extent this coolness came from the fact of Wilhelm Ernst's unhappy experience of marriage. His wife, Charlotte Marie, of Sachsen-Jena (*b.* 1669), had been unable to bear children, and after seven years the duke divorced her. She died in 1703. The division within the ducal family continued, however, beyond her death and even that of Johann Ernst in 1707, and his sons, Ernst August and Johann Ernst, were never on cordial terms with their uncle.

Wilhelm Ernst sought refuge from his private griefs in intellectual and artistic pursuits. He was of a Puritan disposition, but, deploring extremes, advocated religious tolerance. He was insistent on the values of education and, while Bach was among his servants, provided a new building for the grammar school (an institution with a strong dramatic tradition). In the early years of his reign a new organ, decorated by the Weimar painter Rentsch, was installed in the church of St Peter and Paul (now known as the 'Herder' Church), and he undertook the restoration of St James's Church. Wilhelm Ernst enjoyed superintending the layout of his gardens; he acquired books and coins to add to an already fine collection; and he loved music. This was a taste shared with his brother, who was perhaps better informed. Wilhelm Ernst instituted the first opera house, as such, in Thuringia,[5] and he assembled round him men of 'taste'. Weimar had of course had an independent cultural tradition—Lucas Cranach (whose altar-piece stands in the 'Herder' Church) had lived and worked here after 1552.[6]

CITIZENS OF WEIMAR

Until 1705 the arbiter of courtly taste had been Johann Paul von Westhof (son of a Swedish officer of Gustavus Adolphus), who had trained as a chamber musician in Dresden, and been employed there as teacher 'in linguis exoticis' to the sons of Johann Georg III. From there he returned to Sweden to join the army and fight against the Turks in Hungary, toured as virtuoso violinist in Italy, France, Austria, Holland and England, and became Professor of Modern Languages at Wittenberg. In 1698 he arrived in Weimar as Court Secretary. The duties of this office—which gave him the privilege of eating at the Court

Marshal's table[7]—he combined with those of orchestral supervisor. At the High Table an elevated standard of conversation was maintained by other leading courtiers. These included Baron Wilhelm Ferdinand von Lyncker, formerly Professor at Jena, his fellow privy councillors Friedrich Gotthilf and Friedrich Gottlob Marschall, Moritz Gerhard von Lilienheim, Vice-Chancellor from 1694 to 1701, and Gottfried Christian Rappold, Vice-Chancellor from 1708 to 1711. The Court establishments of Weimar—the dukes continually picking up hints from Dresden—were expensive. The people of Weimar paid for them. The extent to which daily life was regulated by decree is shown by the precise formulae published in 1702, which covered every contingency from birth to death. Even the fees for music at weddings were laid down,[8] as also the exercise of, and restraints on, the activity of the pigs of the city.[9]

Within his own circle Bach had congenial company. He may or may not have arrived in Weimar before his distant cousin, Nikolaus Ephraim (1690–1760), third son of Jakob Bach, of Ruhla, left, but certainly he would have heard of him. Nikolaus came to Weimar in 1704 as apprentice to Georg Kessler, Court Painter to Duke Johann, Ernst. Also gifted musically, Nikolaus was appointed to the staff of the Abbess Elisabeth Ernestine Antonia, sister to the Duke of Saxe-Meiningen, at Gandersheim. It may well appear that he was the staff, for he served as organist, cup-bearer, head butler, accounts keeper, instructor of novices in music and painting, and became Keeper of Pictures and Statues, and Composer, at a yearly salary of twenty thalers, with a food allowance, two liveries, travelling coats and winter stockings. Nikolaus Ephraim remained at Gandersheim for the rest of his life.[10] In 1702 Salomo Franck (1659–1725) was appointed consistorial secretary, librarian and museum curator. Franck, whose tendency towards puritanism and mysticism was one cause of his appointment, came back to Weimar, where he was born, after having held official appointments in Arnstadt and Jena. Respected as poet and hymn-writer, he composed the libretti (excepting one) for all Bach's Weimar church cantatas. In 1712 Johann Georg Kiesewetter, formerly master at Ohrdruf, became Rektor of the grammar school and was joined by Johann Matthias Gessner (Co-Rektor) in 1715. Bach was on friendly terms with both, and the latter was an important influence on Bach's subsequent career in Leipzig (see pages 141–2).

The town Kantor, Georg Theodor Reineccius (1660–1726), an industrious and typically Thuringian motet-cantata composer, who was at Eisleben before coming to Weimar in 1687, and author of the libretti of an annual cycle of cantatas (from 1700), was godfather to one of Bach's children. At the town church the organist was Bach's cousin Johann Gottfried Walther (1684–1748), whose mother was a Lämmerhirt (see p. 38, n.20). Walther, at first intended for the law, was a pupil in Erfurt of Buttstett, Johann Bernhard Bach and Johann Andreas Kauffmann, and he came to Weimar in 1707, with excellent credentials after a period of service as organist of St Thomas's Church, Erfurt. Like Bach he was engaged as music teacher in the household of Johann Ernst. Having a larger organ (two manuals, pedals, twenty registers) at his disposal than Bach it is presumed that Bach from time to time took advantage of the fact. Walther's is one of the important names in German musical history, for he was the first to compile a systematic biographical and bibliographical dictionary of music. The *Musikalisches Lexicon*, which was issued as a try-out in a limited edition at Erfurt in 1728, is one of the foundations of musicology.

J. S. BACH ACHIEVES PROMINENCE

Six children were born to Maria Barbara Bach in Weimar, and their respective godparents are an index to family friendships and cordial associations with the socially superior. Catharina Dorothea (1708–74) was sponsored by Martha Catharina Lämmerhirt, widow of Tobias Lämmerhirt of Erfurt (who left the Bachs a legacy and for whose obsequies Sebastian may have composed the *Actus tragicus*,[11] which represents his noblest example in the conservative Thuringian tradition of cantata with arioso rather than recitative and aria), and Johanna Dorothea Bach of Ohrdruf. Wilhelm Friedemann (1710–84) had as godparents Baron von Lyncker, of the Weimar Privy Council, Anna Dorothea Hagedorn, wife of a Mühlhausen lawyer, and Friedemann Weckbach, a lawyer, also of Mühlhausen. In 1713 twins—Maria Sophia and Johann Christoph—were born, the one dying at birth, the other, whose godfather was Reineccius, a few days later. In 1714 Carl Philipp Emanuel was born. He was named after Adam Emanuel Weltzig, Master of the Pages and Musician, of Weissenfels, and Georg Philipp Telemann. The last of the children to be born in Weimar was Johann Gottfried Bernhard (1715–39), named after Johann Bernhard Bach, of Eisenach.

During the Weimar period Bach arrived at maturity and gained a more than local reputation. His problem was to balance his prescribed duties with his personal inclinations, his executant with his creative functions, and—within the latter—his own with his patron's inclinations. In addition to playing when required (under orders from Kapellmeister Drese), Bach probably gave lessons to Johann Ernst, and certainly to Ernst August. The former, from whom six violin concertos in Italian style were published by Telemann in 1718, was a violinist and harpsichordist. A memorial of Bach's teaching of Ernst August exists in the form of a *Canon à 4, perpetuus*,[12] the inscription to which suggests a more than formal relationship between musician and princeling. In Friedrich Smend's interpretation of the cryptographic content of this canon,[13] references to the fact of Bach's playing the viola (defined by the initial notes of each of the four staves, when adjustments of clef have been made), and to his own name and to that of Walther (by means of transmutation of letters into figures and by computation of the latter), are exposed. The significance attached to the possible information conveyed by such means is less than that of Bach's dedication to the principle of productive fission contained within the scholastic conventions of counterpoint, which were part of his heritage and reached their culmination in the *Art of Fugue*. Cryptographical issues, however, are side issues and, except in learned society, were of less consequence to Bach than the musical possibilities opened up by their consideration.

Bach was required to travel with his master's retinue when the duke made a 'progress'. At the end of 1714 the Court travelled to Kassel, and Bach took the opportunity of playing the organ in St Martin's Church at the invitation of Carl Möller, the Court and church organist.[14] A little more than a year later Ernst August, being contracted to marry the widowed sister of Duke Leopold of Anhalt-Köthen, was obliged to travel to Nienburg—ten miles from Köthen, on the Saale—for the nuptials on 24th January 1716. The Weimar musicians were in attendance as also at Weissenfels in the next month. Wilhelm Ernst then was a guest of Christian of Sachsen-Weissenfels, and as the latter celebrated his birthday during the visit there was opportunity for a gala occasion. Bach composed his secular cantata, *Was mir behagt*, for this festivity. For various reasons Bach should have been regarded as indispensable at Weimar. He was thorough in carrying out his commitments, which, on account of the inability of the assistant Kapellmeister, the younger Drese, to do so, included the composition of church cantatas, and he was standing high in his profession. He was also likely at any time to be enticed elsewhere. In 1714 (to eliminate this possibility) he was up-graded to the rank of Konzertmeister, with the responsibility of providing one new work each month. In 1716 on the death of J. S. Drese he might reasonably have expected promotion to the office of Kapellmeister. He was in for a disappointment: Drese's son got the job. More of a duke's man (who had been sent to Italy at the duke's expense), Johann Wilhelm Drese was more predictable and less troublesome than the prickly Bach who, in any case, was inclined to visit the *Rotes Schloss*—the home of the other branch of the ducal family—far too often for the duke's liking.

Although Bach was not infrequently away from Weimar on the duke's business he was often an absentee on account of his own. As an organist he was much in demand both for giving opinions on and inaugurating new instruments by the outstanding builders of the period—Schröter, Scherer, Schrittger, Compenius, Gottfried Silbermann and Christoph Cunzius of Halberstadt. In 1712 Cunzius was engaged on a new organ for St Mary's Church, in Halle. In August of that year Zachau, the great organist of that church and once Handel's teacher, died. The appointment to succeed Zachau was an important one. The church committee took their time and, after asking J. P. Krieger of Weissenfels, and J. Kuhnau of Leipzig (two of the best musicians in the country) to act as referees, drew up a short list consisting of Kirchhoff of Quedlinburg, Haussmann of Schafstädt, Hoffmann of Leipzig and Lippe of Mansfeld. Before a final decision was made there appeared on the scene J. S. Bach of Weimar.

With an idea that Cunzius's organ would be one which would give him more opportunity than those at his disposal at Weimar, with the knowledge that a civic post might well offer more independence, and (thinking on the civilized atmosphere of Jena where his cousin Nikolaus was employed) with the prospect of a close association with a new and lively university, Bach offered himself as candidate. After submitting himself to the customary test, and having performed the cantata *Ich hatte viel Bekümmernis* (No. 21, notable for its references to Handel's *Almira*), and the claims of the other candidates having been reconsidered, Bach was offered a contract. Having examined it he turned it down.[15] When, soon afterwards, the Halle committee heard that Bach's Weimar salary had been raised they were not pleased—and wrote to say so. In general Bach is given credit for not having used the Halle offer as an offensive weapon in Weimar. One may of course never be sure, but if he had he was, according to the rules of the game, hardly acting with impropriety.

However, since Kirchhoff, who received the Halle appointment, gave satisfaction the Halle people let their anger cool and, recognizing that Bach was a man of distinction in his own field, called him in, with Kuhnau and Christian Friedrich Rolle (*d.* 1751), the Kantor of Quedlinburg, to examine the new organ—a large instrument with forty-seven registers for the three manuals and eighteen for the pedals. The examining body were well wined and dined; when the immortal Bach added his signature to the document of ratification he managed to splash ink on to the paper. In the same year he was in Erfurt approving Schröter's new organ in the Augustiner church in Erfurt.

In 1717, at the invitation of Volumier, Bach paid his first official visit to Dresden to justify his own reputation and to uphold the honour of Germany by taking part in a keyboard contest with the Frenchman Louis Marchand. Bach admired Marchand as a composer, but as a performer he was prepared to back his own chances in any competition that might be organized (at the home of Count Joachim Friedrich von Flemming, commandant of the city)[16]. According to the legend Marchand failed to turn up at the prescribed place and time. Thus Bach was acknowledged to be the champion organist of Europe!

At this time Bach had accepted appointment as Kapellmeister at Köthen, but, Wilhelm Ernst refusing to accept his resignation, he was in a state of uncertainty. At the beginning of December Bach, after spending a month in preventive detention, having been summarily convicted of 'obstinacy', was given permission to go.

As has been noted Bach was also engaged in teaching. Traditionally this was part of his calling, but he was better at it than most. Through his pupils he disseminated standards of technical thoroughness that continue to characterize German music. Among his Weimar pupils were Johann Caspar Vogler (1696–1763), formerly a schoolboy in Arnstadt, who succeeded Schubart of Weimar (of which he eventually became mayor)[17]; Johann Tobias Krebs (1690–1762), who used to come over to Weimar from Buttstett twice a week for lessons from Walther and (in harpsichord playing) from Bach; Johann Gottfried Ziegler (*c.* 1706–47) of Halle; and two Bachs. Johann Lorenz (1695–1773), elder son of Johann Valentin, Kantor of Schweinfurt,[18] was one. When qualified he went to Lahm, in Bavaria, where he found occupation as organist and Kantor. The other was Johann Bernhard (1700–43), second son of Johann Christoph of Ohrdruf. Bernhard was a favourite pupil of his uncle, whom he accompanied to Köthen before returning to Ohrdruf to take over his father's duties as organist at St Michael's Church.[19] Bernhard is of considerable importance in that he was the principal copyist of the so-called 'Andreas Bach Book' and the 'Möller MS'.[20] Out of fifty-six keyboard works in the former and fifty-one in the latter there were respectively fifteen and eleven by Sebastian Bach, and of them the majority were not preserved elsewhere.

The reasons for Bach's departure from Weimar should be clear. He had suffered an affront when Drese was preferred for the senior post in the musical establishment—an affront which was harder to stomach in view of the easy progress of another Bach at another court (see page 123 ff.). He was irked by the squabbles between the two branches of the ducal house, and by the limitations imposed on his personal activities. One suspects that his reprehensible 'obstinacy', punished on the one occasion, was but a last straw. Further, his Lordship of Köthen had turned up with an offer of a better contract, with a guaranteed income of 400 thalers a year as against 250 at Weimar.

PROGRESSIVE GOVERNMENT IN KÖTHEN

Bach was a patriotic Thuringian, but his early travels had taught him what Niedt had trenchantly observed; that within the field of Thuringian music there was a strong strain of conservatism. This was especially true of church music. Farther north newer impulses were admitted and encouraged, and for a man of ambition there was more opportunity to expand his creative capacities. There was a great deal to be said in favour of Köthen. The idea, formerly expressed with some force,[21] that Bach was in some way guilty of impiety in moving to a centre of the Reformed (i.e. Calvinist) Church is untenable. Like all the members of his clan he was a professional musician, total and undivided, impartially prepared to function on behalf of Church and State. It was of course a basic fact of life that Church and State were indivisible, and one from which it was not possible to escape. According to his upbringing Bach was an orthodox Lutheran. He had read (and continued to read) theological works. In so doing he was continuing his further education along the lines prescribed in his school days. It is dangerous to attempt to define the character of Bach's views on religion in any kind of detail. The most that may be presumed is that he was, in general, not intolerant. It was in fact becoming fashionable to preach tolerance, not least in Berlin, and Köthen and Halle.

The cultural tradition of the House of Anhalt-Köthen was an honourable one, and Duke Leopold, Bach's employer, was a worthy protector of the tradition. Born in 1694, Leopold succeeded to his inheritance through the death of his father in 1704 when he was a minor. Thus, until he came of age and took over the government of his realm on 28th December 1715, his mother, the Dowager Duchess Agnes Gisella, acted as regent—with the consent of, and to some extent under the influence of, the King of Prussia. (Reasons of state increased the political dependency of small and impotent states, just as they impelled Berlin and Dresden to strengthen their control within their zones of interest.) Leopold, therefore, was sent away to school in Berlin and, with other young aristocrats, was a pupil of the royal Academy in Berlin. One consequence of his Berlin education was Leopold's appointment of Augustinus Reinhard Stricker, a musician of some importance at the Prussian Court, as Kapellmeister at Köthen in 1714. Leopold was a composition pupil of Johann David Heinichen and a proficient performer on several instruments. Under Stricker's direction he kept a band of eighteen players.

The resignation of Stricker in 1717 gave Leopold the opportunity to engage J. S. Bach, whose musical abilities he admired and in whom he discovered a congenial temperament. Bach was well content with his situation at Köthen—which was as comfortable as that of his distant cousin Ludwig at Meiningen—until it was disturbed by the consequences of Leopold's marriage at the end of 1721.

At Köthen Bach was mainly required to stimulate concert life. Rehearsals in the first instance were held on the premises of a shopkeeper in the town, later in Bach's own house. His resident forces were from time to time increased by visiting artistes, mostly from neighbouring courts. On festival occasions he produced honorific works for birthdays: *Durchlaucht'ster Leopold* (1717); *Der Himmel dacht auf Anhalts Ruhm und Glück*, text by Chr. Fr. Hunold (known as 'Menantes') (1718); *Heut ist gewiss ein guter Tag* (1721), of which the music is lost; and, for the New Year: *Die Zeit, die Tag und Jahre macht* (or *Mit Gnaden bekröne*, Cantata 134a, 1719); *Dich loben die lieblichen Strahlen der Sonne* (1720, music lost). Church cantatas, as such, were outside the main line of duty, but there were occasions when Bach was able to remain in touch with this form of composition, sometimes by composing new cantatas, sometimes by reviving old ones. Cantata 61, *Nun komm der Heiden Heiland*, for example, was performed in Leipzig, probably during Advent, 1717.

At this time Bach was invited to go to Leipzig, at Kuhnau's instigation, to examine the new organ in the university (St Paul's) church.[22] Although Bach was not normally required to function as organist at Köthen, he managed to keep his hand in. There were convenient organs in the (Reformed) St James's Church and in the new church, known by her name, built by the Dowager Duchess Agnes, and there were not infrequent invitations to perform on instruments in other places. Bach's most notable organ-playing expedition was to Hamburg in 1720 where he was a candidate for the appointment at St James's Church (in which there was a famous organ built by Arp Schnitger), vacant on the death of Heinrich Friese. Although unsuccessful in his application (because, it was suggested, he was unwilling to follow the convention of making a donation to the church funds), he was happy again to meet Reinken—now nearly a hundred years old—and to play before that master at St Katherine's. Having heard Bach extemporize on *An Wasserflüssen Babylon*, Reinken observed that until that moment he had thought the art of extemporization dead. 'But', he was reported to have said to Bach, 'I see it still lives in you.' At this time, and in subtle tribute to Reinken, Bach composed and first played the Fantasia and Fugue in G minor, the subject of which was derived from a Dutch folk-song. The subject also resembles that of the fugal movement in the fifth sonata of Reinken's *Hortus musicus*. Another famous organ work appears to be owed to an excursion to Weissenfels; this is the Toccata and Fugue in F major.

Kapellmeister Bach was one of the chief ornaments of the Köthen Court, and as such he was from time to time given leave of absence to compose for and/or to perform at other courts. In August 1725 he stayed for a week in the 'Blue Angel' in Schleiz, where his former pupil, J. S. Koch, was Kantor, on the invitation of Heinrich XI, Count of Reuss-Schleiz.[23] In the following year he completed a commission for the Margraf Christian Ludwig of Brandenburg, dating his Dedication (in French) of the 'Brandenburg' Concertos, 24th March. In 1722 he composed a Birthday Cantata (unspecified) for Duke Johann August of Anhalt-Zerbst. Visits to Zerbst and Weissenfels, celebrated through Kapellmeister J. P. Krieger and for its connection with the youthful Handel, are indicated by the circumstances of Bach's private life.

In the early summer of 1718 Duke Leopold travelled to Carlsbad (now Karlovy Vary) to take a cure. He was accompanied by six of his music staff, including the Kapellmeister. In November he showed his favour to Bach by acting as godfather to the last of the children of Sebastian and Maria Barbara—Leopold Augustus who, however, died less than a year later. In the summer of 1720 the duke again went to Carlsbad with Bach among his retinue. In July Bach returned home to find that his wife had died and that she had been buried. He was left with four children, the eldest of them, Catharina Dorothea, twelve years old. Friedemann was ten, Carl Philipp Emanuel was six and Gottfried Bernhard just five. The premature death of the mother of a young family was no uncommon occurrence in the Bach clan. The effect on the children of the loss of their mother, and the subsequent complication of a stepmother, may in this instance only be guessed at. It is, however, not impossible to determine in these circumstances part of the cause for the later psychological difficulties of Friedemann and Gottfried Bernhard. On 12th February of the same year Bach himself was further subdued by the death of his eldest brother, Johann Christoph, at Ohrdruf.

It was almost immediately after the death of Maria Barbara that Bach sought the post of organist in Hamburg. He may very well have wished for a change of environment, and the submission of the Brandenburg Concertos and the visit to Schleiz too may have been supported by an exploratory intention. However, at the beginning of December 1721 he had reconstituted his household by remarriage. His second wife, Anna Magdalena Wülcken, a soprano singer at the Court of Zerbst, was the twenty-year-old daughter of Johann Caspar Wülcken, formerly trumpeter at Zeitz, and since 1719 at Weissenfels. Anna Magdalena—on both sides she was of Thuringian and musical descent—had visited Köthen in her professional capacity in the autumn of 1720. She retained her post at Zerbst after her marriage. With her earnings (half those of her husband) and money from a legacy from the estate of Tobias Lämmerhirt's widow (she died just before Bach's second marriage) the Bachs were relatively well off.

Six months after Bach's second marriage the death of Kuhnau took place in Leipzig. Thus became vacant one of the most sought-after positions in the whole of Germany. It is not unlikely that Bach would have submitted his name in any case. That he was by now somewhat disenchanted by Köthen encouraged him to make strenuous efforts to obtain the cantorship of St Thomas's. Duke Leopold had married his cousin, Friederica Henriette, of Anhalt-Bernburg in the middle of December 1721, 'and it seemed thereafter that the said prince's inclination for music had somewhat cooled, especially as the new princess appeared to be an amusa'.[24]

THE COMPOSER'S VOCATION

At the age of thirty-seven Bach was at the height of his powers, a master in almost every branch of his craft, and already the outstanding German composer of his age. That he was probably one of the best living organists in the country was acknowledged at least in Thuringia, Saxony and Prussia. His compositions, however, were known only to relatively few, so that in 1723 they were more acceptable as a long-rather than as a short-term investment. Sebastian Bach perhaps was one of the few among the greater musicians who, believing in the lasting virtues of his own genius, was not disinclined to leave his creative works to the judgment of posterity. He lived to some extent, and in more than one sense, 'in the futurity of his art', as Edward Holmes eloquently wrote. This is much more than a matter of technical innovation, in which respect the contributions to musical vocabulary and form are frequently exaggerated; it is a matter of faith. Bach was a Thuringian, and as such the last of the great Bachs to be aware of his roots in Thuringian soil, and he inherited the simple mystical canons of belief that were peculiar to his race.

The basis of this belief was that the craftsman's work had its own sanctity. The craft to which one was dedicated, and to which all one's early training had been directed, was an end in itself, to be accomplished to the best of one's ability and for the general benefit. The Kantor created music for specific social purposes—civic, ecclesiastical, and educational—and did so in the spirit of the many anonymous stone-masons, and carvers in wood and stone, who had adorned the public buildings of town and village. The Kantor–composer, more often than not, was content to accept at least a partial anonymity. Behind this acceptance lay the tenets of the faith, as it was preached weekly by the pastors of the Lutheran Church on the basis of the twenty-one Articles of the Confession of Augsburg. Such preaching—an inescapable factor in the life of Bach—encouraged a vision of infinity, of the relationship of the present with the past and with the future—of the present world with the two possible worlds to come. Under the influence of the *Auf-klärung*, and amid the clash of theological disputants in the Orthodox–Pietist controversy, old views were assailed, but (as the orders for, and the sermons preached on, particular church occasions show) speculation was not indulged in by the majority.

The attitude to life (and to death) of the rank and file of Thuringians and Saxons, among whom Bach moved, was Christian. Whether this is a matter for present praise or censure (the preaching of some eminent theologians of the period on the related subjects of sin and its penalties was pretty horrifying) is irrelevant, the fact is undeniable. The principles of Lutheran Christianity—which found their most eloquent expressions in terms of music in the Baroque period—were built into the patterns of society and into the structure of personality. Thus J. S. Bach, as all Bachs who were his contemporaries, held a point of view that in modern terms is unintelligible. He did not question the eighteenth Article of Faith that, while admitting the existence of man's free will, limited its range of freedom by stating that nothing could be effectively performed except through the grace of the Holy Spirit. Bach was a religious man (as we say) because he could not have been otherwise, and his religious self was his whole self. This means that whatever he did was done as a religious man, that to him there was no separation of functions. The orchestral suite in essence was no less religious than the church cantata.

The general view was a medieval one. Bach's progressiveness consisted often in his capacity to look backwards, and if he is regarded (as he was) as the last of the 'Gothic' composers, the summation of an attitude rather than of an era, that is neither irregular nor improper. He was of course also the beginning of a new dispensation but that is another matter. At this juncture it is important to set aside the various contentions that have rumbled round the market-places of musicology concerning what in Bach belongs to the Church and what to the world. As a composer and as a man Bach was a Christian believer to the extent that all his work, whether nominally secular or sacred, was an expression of his integrated personality. Therefore two points of recent debate may be disposed of. First, that when Bach made use of apparently secular motivs in church cantatas he was guilty of some kind of impropriety; secondly, that he adopted one spiritual approach in Weimar, another in Köthen, and yet another in Leipzig. Although the technical nature of his vocations altered somewhat according to environmental changes, the intrinsic values within his music remained constant. The labels attached to Bach by a sequence of chroniclers of Romantic disposition—'the Archcantor', the 'Spielmann of God', even 'the fifth Evangelist', and so on, have been removed by Friedrich Blume in his presentation of an 'Outline of a new image of Bach'.[25] This was necessary, but true objectivity yet demands that the Christian (as distinct from the ecclesiastical) foundation of Bach's art shall not be denied.[26]

The Weimar period was that in which Bach established himself as an organ virtuoso. So it is that to this period belong a large number of his important works for the instrument. They were recognized as such as far away as Hamburg where the busy Mattheson was able to write in his *Das beschützte Orchestre*, of 1717, that he had 'seen things by the famous organist of Weimar, Herr Joh. Sebastian Bach, both for the church [chorale type works?] and for the fist [*sic*, possibly more virtuoso compositions] that are certainly such as must make one esteem the man highly'. As is possibly indicated by Mattheson, there are two main categories of works particularly associated with the liturgy and therefore based on chorales; and of those not so committed. The chorale-motivated organ works of Bach were a summary of general practice ranging from the partitas, intended more for private than public use,[27] through the short, but functional, preludes, such as belong to the *Orgelbüchlein* (1717), to extended preludes in which the individual lines of chorale melody are separated by more or less rhetorical interludial sections. The chorale was, as has been already stated, the centre of Lutheran devotion. To this extent compositions based on chorales were intended as expository, this intention being accomplished by means of established symbolic devices. The chorale was also the basis of musical instruction, and how to treat a chorale was the foundation of the young Thuringian and Saxon composer's technique of composition. Bach himself, like Buttstett and Johann Walther, and the other prominent church musicians of Thuringia, was schooled in the methods of Johann Christoph and Johann Michael Bach, Pachelbel, Böhm,[28] and so on, and his own essays—especially in the *Orgelbüchlein*—were the material on which his pupils were instructed.

The chorale prelude was the last genuine tribute to the spirit of medieval polyphony, in that it preserved the primacy of a presanctified *cantus firmus*. Any variation on the *cantus firmus* by means of 'contrapunctus fractus und floridus', or by any other means, was dedicated to the purpose of underlining the significance of the particular associations of the *cantus firmus*. The chorale prelude as played in its general context, before the singing of a chorale, was meant, as Georg Friedrich Kauffmann specified,[29] to enable properly devotional singing. With one look over his shoulder Kauffmann—a pupil of Buttstett and, Alberti's successor as Kapellmeister at Merseburg—contrasted the correctly restrained chorale prelude which would bring tears to the eyes with the 'strange fantasies' that were sometimes to be heard. In point of fact Kauffmann's compositions in this province are merely dull, and his versions of the chorales themselves grotesquely and extravagantly overdecorated.

In all there remain from Bach some 150 organ works based on chorales, of which the greater number were composed before he went to Leipzig. The scope of these works is indicated by the fact that they range textually from two to six parts, and are comprised in half a dozen formal categories. These are (1) simple congregational settings (Arnstadt), (2) partitas, (3) fughettas, (4) choral fantasias, (5) short preludes in which line follows line as in the *Orgelbüchlein*, (6) extended preludes, as in the Eighteen Chorales composed about 1715 and revised about 1750.

These works—of which the influence extended to the church cantatas and the Passions—were the point at which harmonic and contrapuntal processes merged to provide the vitality of Bachian counterpoint. This counterpoint, not at first designed as an end in itself, stands as one of the most intensely expressive phenomena in the Western musical tradition. The extent to which it transcends mere realism is shown in *Christum wir sollen loben schon*, a reflection on the Mystical Adoration. The *cantus firmus*, unusually, is given in the alto part. The manner in which all else devolves from this theme gives an irrefrangible unity. The literary background to the art of Bach has been emphasized, but not those related elements that stimulated the eye—the sculptures of Thuringia and Saxony. The development of sculptural techniques towards emotionally expressive ends is shown in thousands of examples, once familiar to Bach, from the Romanesque to the Baroque periods; from the geometric division of the *Rankentympanon* at St Mary's, Mühlhausen, to the heavy commentary of the memorial to Johann III in the town church in Weimar. It is perhaps in relation to the sculptor's art that the moulding of the figures of *Christum wir sollen loben schon* into a co-ordinated texture of counterpoint may best be appreciated.

At a somewhat later stage a similar feat of contrapuntal dexterity on a chorale theme by Bach drew a critical observation from a writer who was by no means sure that musical geometry (as he called it) was conducive to the proper mood on the part of the listener.[30] The world of the organist for the most part is a private world and the chorale preludes, standing testimony to the art of improvisation, are the index to Bach's intimate relationship with the faith of his fathers. They also represent the doctrine of accomplishment as an offering to God. The science of Bach's composition springs from older sources than those created by the optimistic pioneers of the *Aufklärung*.

While at Weimar Bach had opportunity to display himself more publicly as an organ virtuoso, and the major works written during that period prove that the high regard in which he was held by his colleagues was not misplaced. Nearly three-quarters of the works for organ, exclusive of those of the chorale prelude type, are wholly or in first form assigned to the Weimar–Köthen period. They include the Fantasia and Fugue in G minor (BWV 542), the Preludes and Fugues in G major (BWV 550), A minor (BWV 543), F minor (BWV 534) and C minor (BWV 546); the Toccatas and Fugues in F major (BWV 540), C major (BWV 564) and the so-called 'Dorian' (BWV 538); the Pastorale in F major (BWV 590), and movements in the old Allabreve and Canzona style that Bach discontinued after Weimar. The elements out of which these works were constructed were various, being taken from the common pool as and when required. He raided the whole standard repository of techniques established by Pachelbel, Buxtehude, Reinken and Böhm in particular, and borrowed fugue subjects from many sources—from Corelli, André Raison, Pachelbel and even from folk-song (as has been shown). The results of a close study of an enthusiasm for Italian models, ranging from Frescobaldi (*Fiori musicali*) to the more recent scores of Legrenzi, Corelli, Albinoni and Vivaldi, are evident in many ways; in the concerto arrangements undertaken in partnership with Duke Johann Ernst, in the suave mellifluity and

beguiling imagery of the *Pastorale*, in the three-movement structure of
the Toccata and Fugue in C. In one way or another many of these
works are symbolically referential—obviously as in the case of the
Pastorale and the G minor Fantasia and Fugue, otherwise less patently.
We have Mattheson's word for it that the character of keys was
significant, so that that of F minor, for instance, exposed 'anxiety and
despair'. This concept is implied at least in the Fantasia and Fugue in
F minor (BWV 534), especially in the convolutions of tonality in the
Fugue which, however, display Bach's propensity for logic and a
desire to carry a process through to a logical conclusion:

More than any other part of his music, even taking into account
the '48', the organ works of Bach maintained and extended the inherent and distinctive qualities of German music. This part of the
tradition remained firm. Generations of organists and Kantors were
brought up to continue this particular part of the tradition. Often they
were no more than relatively successful, and sometimes a good deal
less—simply because Bach brought that side of native music to its
peak point. This was recognized in the indelibility of his organ works,
on which the so-called 'revival' of the nineteenth century centred
much more than on Mendelssohn's more spectacular representation
of the *St Matthew Passion*. The organ works had not been forgotten,
except by those who had forgotten to look for music in church.

It was while he was at Weimar that Bach evolved the pattern of
church cantata that is the particular contribution of the German
Lutheran Church to church music as a whole. The cantata sprang from
two roots; from the indigenous motet, securely based on the chorale
cantus firmus, and the Italian cantata, characterized by contrasted use of
recitative and *da capo* aria. So far as Bach was concerned the catalytic

agent was the new style of libretto written by Erdmann Neumeister (1671–1756). A native of Weissenfels, a friend of Johann Philipp Krieger (1649–1725)—the progressive and prolific Kapellmeister of Weissenfels—and pastor of St James's Church, Hamburg, when Bach made his application there, Neumeister's cantata plan was a counter-blast to the provocations of the Pietists. As he said in the Preface to his *Neue Geistliche Gedichte* (Eisenach, 1718), 'music had a particular power, through a reasonable and Christian [type of] harmony to revivify the spirit.' The plan of the cantata consisted of aria 1—recitative, chorus to a biblical text, recitative—aria 2, concluding chorale. Neumeister inherited the characteristics of German baroque verse and his lines contain many, and sometimes far-fetched, allusions. Such allusions none the less were an inspiration to a number of composers, including Krieger, Telemann, Christoph Graupner and Bach himself. The Neumeister cantata texts were issued in four sets, in 1704, 1708, 1711 and 1714. Bach set five of Neumeister's texts (Cantatas 18, 61, 59, 28 and 24—the last two in Leipzig), but his preference was for those of Salomo Franck. No doubt this preference was a matter of convenience, Franck being on the spot to remind the composer of the availability of convenient libretti. Franck was a well-read and inventive author, whose vocabulary and imagery were inspired by such previous poets as Hoffmanswaldau, Rist and Fleming; he was particularly partial to the transposition of the love duet into one between the Saviour and the Soul.[31]

Bach seized the Baroque imagery of his librettists and applied to the cantata the techniques of symbolization endemic in his organ works. There was more to it than this, but it was the sheer concentration on the inner content of the cantatas within the context of Lutheranism that gave to them their particular variety and intensity. Krieger and Graupner tossed off more than a thousand cantatas apiece, but neither composer—nor for that matter Telemann,[32] whose record in this field was relatively modest—was committed to the extent that Bach was. The contrast between Bach and them, or between him and his cousin Johann Ludwig, at Meiningen (see pages 123–8) was considerable. But it was Bach, the conservative, who prevailed in the end. The greater part of Bach's church cantata output, however, belonged to the Leipzig period.

The Köthen phase of Bach's life was complementary to that of Weimar, and it is to be noted that his most distinguished contemporary relatives, content to remain occupied in one environment, lacked the stimulus that such contrasts induced. Sebastian Bach's temperamental restlessness was part of his genius. In Weimar he concentrated on organ music and cantatas—though not entirely neglecting other forms of composition—but it was in Köthen that he explored the fuller possibilities of cembalo and chamber music. At Weimar, deep in his Italian scores, he made keyboard arrangements of Vivaldi concertos and wrote fugues on subjects by Albinoni. A miscellany of other keyboard pieces belongs to this period, but at Köthen the 'English' and 'French' suites, the Chromatic Fantasia and Fugue, and the first book of the *Wohltemperirtes Klavier* were composed. The last-named was the consequence of Bach's function as teacher, as also were the two- and three-part Inventions that formed part of the anthology of pieces carefully assembled for the benefit of Wilhelm Friedemann. The more extensive works were intended as fulfilment of the duties of a Kapell-meister. So too were the solo sonatas (suites, partitas) for violin, violoncello and flute; the sonatas (suites) for flute and cembalo, viol da gamba and cembalo, and violin and cembalo; the concertos for violin, one for two violins; the overtures for orchestra. The Branden-burg Concertos were an extension of the Kapellmeister function, but intended more particularly as a possible means toward promotion.

With hindsight we recognize the works of the Köthen interlude as among the major contributions to the literature of music. To those who were living in 1723, however, they were either unknown or unremarkable. When, in writing his dedication to the Margraf of Brandenburg, Bach referred to his 'insignificant talents', he may well have done so in a wry humour. The significant talents, as people then recognized them, belonged to the Muffats, Graupners, Kuhnaus, Fischers, Matthesons and Telemanns of the world. These, like the two Bachs who follow in the next chapter, understood the eighteenth century. Even then Sebastian Bach stood outside time.

NOTES TO CHAPTER FIVE

1. *Mémoires de Frédéric II, Roi de Prusse*, ed. E. Boutarie & E. Campardon, Paris, 1866, 2 vols., I, p. 46.

2. Item X of the Statutes of the Royal Prussian Academy (1705) reads: 'There will be also taught . . . all the languages which are at present the most in use; as Latin, French, Italian, Spanish, English, and even the German shall be taught there in all its Purity, to which particular application will be made at Meals'. John Toland, *An Account of the Courts of Prussia and Hanover*, 3rd ed., London, 1706, p. 24.

3. Thomasius, *Memoirs of the House of Brandenburg*, London, 1757, p. 284.

4. Toland (*see* Note 2 above), p. 8.

5. In the Wilhelmsburg, the palace built between 1651–4 on the ruins of the Hornstein, and destroyed by fire in 1774.

6. His house stands in the market-place, near the site of the house occupied by Bach. The latter, adjoining the present Park Hotel, was destroyed during the Second World War.

7. Telemann, also a Court Secretary, enjoyed a similar privilege at Eisenach. The Bachs never reached such eminence.

8. *Statuta des Fürstl.-Sachss. Residentz-Stadt Weimar*, Joh. Andreas Muller, 1702, Clause XVI.

9. *See* Note 8 above, Clause XXIV.

10. Spitta (*see* Note 16, Chapter 3), p. 11.

11. Church Cantata 106, *Gottes Zeit ist die allerbeste Zeit*, André Pirro, *J. S. Bach*, 4th ed., Paris, 1913, I, p. 87; *see also* Blume, *Syntagma Musicologicum*, p. 368.

12. See *The Bach Reader*, p. 64.

13. Friedrich Smend, *J. S. Bach, Kirchen–Kantaten*, Berlin, 1947, p. 9.

14. The organ in St Martin's at this time was the one installed during the reign of Landgraf Moritz by Hans Scherer of Hamburg, in 1610. Between 1730 and 1732 this was replaced by an instrument by Nikolaus Becker, of Mühlhausen. On 21st September 1732 Bach, accompanied by Anna Magdalena, arrived in Kassel (staying at the inn 'Zur Stadt Stockholm') to approve the work. After his examination he gave a memorable recital which was picturesquely described by Constantin Bellermann (*Programma in quo Parnassus Musarum* etc., Minden, 1743, p. 39).

15. Committee resolution of St Mary's Church, Halle, 1st March 1714. The successful candidate was Kirchhoff, on whose death in 1746 Wilhelm Friedemann Bach was elected organist (*see* p. 191).

16. Count von Flemming was also acquainted with Handel, whom he described as 'a little mad'.

17. A chorale prelude, by Vogler, *Jesu Leiden*, was until 1904 ascribed to Bach (*see* Chapter 1, Note 27, Engel, p. 225).

18. Johann Valentin inherited his Schweinfurt appointment from his father, Georg Christoph (*see* p. 57).

19. See Freyse, *Die Ohrdrufer Bache*, p. 85.

20. The first book was so-called because it was eventually the property of Johann Andreas Bach (1713–79), youngest son of Johann Christoph, and organist in Ohrdruf. The second MS. at one time belonged to an 'Org. Möller'. Regarding these MSS. *see BJB* (1912), Werner Wolffheim, and *BJB* (1954), Alfred Dürr. Dürr establishes the authenticity of Johann Bernhard Bach as copyist.

21. Cf. C. S. Terry: 'In such a mood he now shook the dust of Weimar from his feet, surrendered the declared object of his life, and divorced his art from the exalted purpose to which he had dedicated it.' *Bach*, p. 116.

22. The organ was built by Johann Scheibe; the church was sacrificed to town-planning in 1968.

23. R. Hansel, in *Schleizer Zeitung*, No. 286, 1942, quoted in 'Johann Sebastian Bach's Reisen im Thüringer Land' (H. Löffler), *Bach in Thüringen*, p. 87.

24. Letter from Bach to Georg Erdmann, Leipzig, 28th October 1730.

25. 'Umrisse eines neuen Bach-Bildes', a lecture delivered at the Bach Festival at Mainz, 1st June 1962, published in *Syntagma Musicologicum*, p. 466–79. The dialectical position of this essay, particularly in respect of the arguments of A. Dürr and F. Smend, is discussed in W. Blankenburg 'Zwölf Jahre Bachforschung', *Acta Musicologica*, XXXVII, 1965, p. 118 f.

26. The point is firmly put by Wilhelm Schäfer, the poet, in which he contrasts the *Gottgläubigkeit* of the Middle Ages (and Bach) with the *Ichzeit* that distinguishes modern concepts. (*Johann Sebastian Bach: eine Rede*, München, 1935.)

27. That there was a domestic market for chorale preludes in general is attested by Georg Friedrich Kauffmann (1679–1735) in the Preface to the 'Geneigter und Music-liebender Leser' of his collection of such preludes in *Harmonische Seelen-Lust*, Leipzig (1736).

28. See *Choralevorspiele alter Meister . . .*, ed. K. Straube, Leipzig (1907).

29. Kauffmann, *see* Note 27 above.

30. Writing on the canonic variations on *Vom Himmel hoch*, M. Schmidt commented: '. . . ich kann mich nicht überreden, dass die schwerste geometrische Demonstration ein viel tieferes und weitläuftiges Nachdenken erfordert haben muss', *Musiko-Theologie*, Bayreuth, 1754, quoted by Adlung, *Anleitung* (1758), p. 692.

31. Franck supplied Bach with the libretti of Cantatas 31, 70, 72, 80a, 132, 147, 152, 155, 161, 162, 163, 164, 165, 168, 185, 186, and probably 12, 21 and 182.

32. The appealing *Ich weiss, dass mein Erlöser lebt* (listed as Cantata 160), with a text by Neumeister, is now attributed to Telemann.

6

Enlightenment at Jena and Meiningen

LIBERAL STUDIES IN A THURINGIAN UNIVERSITY

The three Estates of German music during the period of the late Baroque were the municipality, the Court and the university. In each case there was responsibility for both secular and sacred music—even if in respect of the latter within a Reformed community (as at Köthen) this was exercised sparingly. That lines of communication existed between the three Estates goes without saying, but differences of function were beginning to clarify. The effect of the *Aufklärung* on an innate respect for, and love of, music was indicating a new direction for music, particularly within the field of academic study. On the one hand there was a growing tendency to examine music and musical phenomena in the light of, and according to the principles of, contemporary scholarship; on the other, steps were being taken to widen its social scope. In both cases the result was to diminish the influence of theological dogma and speculation. At the beginning of the eighteenth century the University of Jena was distinguished for a progressive attitude towards music; at the end of the century the focal point was Göttingen. At Jena the guiding hand was that of Johann Nikolaus Bach, at Göttingen that of another Thuringian, Johann Nikolaus Forkel.

Nikolaus Bach came to Jena as a student in 1690. He remained in that city until his death in 1753.[1] Active in all kinds of music both in town and university, and highly respected as scholar and citizen, his influence was considerable. During his early years in Jena Nikolaus enjoyed the opportunity of travelling to Italy.[2] He went in the company of a university friend, Georg Bertuch (1668–1738), who, however, since he had found employment as Master of the Pages to a young Danish nobleman, did not come back. Bertuch was also a musician, but ended his career in Denmark holding the rank of major-general. Another student who visited Italy was Johann Georg Wentzel, who superintended the revived Collegium Musicum in Jena, and who performed his Passion—*Der Gottliebenden Seelen Wallfahrt zum Creutz und Grab Christi*—in the University Church in 1693. Wentzel was a typical Jena student of that period, competent not only in music but also in medicine and theology.

The organist of the town church—St Michael's—at this time was Johann Magnus Knüpfer, son of a famous Kantor of St Thomas's, Leipzig. Nikolaus Bach was a pupil of Knüpfer and in 1696 succeeded him at St Michael's; also taking over the supervision of the musical instruction of the students. In 1697 he married Anna Amalia Baurath, daughter of a Jena goldsmith, who died in 1713. In that year Bach married again, his second wife, Anna Sibilla Lange, being the daughter of the Pastor of Isserstedt. Of the six children of the first marriage only one, the second daughter, Maria Elisabeth (1700–1740), survived infancy. The three daughters of the second marriage, after waiting an unusually long time, all made matches that were eminently satisfactory —Anna Catharina (*b.* 1715) married an electoral tax examiner, Johann Gottfried Thieme, in 1758; Dorothea Magdalena (1719–99), a lawyer, Friedeman Wilhelm Stock, also in the civil service of Saxony, in 1753; and Johanna Maria (*b.* 1721), the theologian and musician Johann Heinrich Möller, a pupil of her father, in 1757. The only son of the second marriage, Johann Christian (*b.* 1717), who was a student of philosophy, died in 1738. On the female side, at least, the Bachs were moving up in the social scale, and invading the increasingly significant sector of officialdom.

Nikolaus Bach was not only a musician, but expert in the mechanics of musical instruments. This of course was not unusual in the family, but Nikolaus was equally competent in matters both of theory and of practice. He had plenty of opportunity to make use of his dual competence. Between 1704 and 1712 a new organ, by Georg Christoph Sterzing of Eisenach,[3] was installed in St Michael's Church. The building of this instrument was long drawn out, partly because of difficulties between the builder and the town council, and partly on account of Bach's insistence on having an adequacy of reeds at his disposal. Like his cousin Johann Sebastian he had a zest for colourful registration. In the end he had one of the best instruments in Thuringia—with three manuals and forty-four registers. This proved a good investment (the cost was 3,500 thalers), for after restoration in 1798 it remained in use until the beginning of the twentieth century. The organ in the University Church, restored by the local builder Zacharias Thayssner[4] between 1701 and 1704, was, however, less satisfactory. Neglected for some years it was in a deplorable condition in 1719 when Nikolaus Bach was appointed University Organist, and he refused to take up this additional appointment unless an extensive overhaul was undertaken.[5] He was, however, happy in his Jena assignments, and when offered a post elsewhere on one occasion he declined. This was in 1704, when he was asked to succeed to his father's office in Eisenach. That he refused to return to his native town (he went so far as to undertake the trial and he then created a fine impression by his playing) was undoubtedly due to the engaging qualities of his Jena acquaintances. His colleagues were stimulating and sympathetic; he had many promising pupils; and he was not obliged to temper his inclinations to the whims of a gaggle of Court functionaries. Bernhard Bach, who did accept the post at Eisenach, was a close friend of Nikolaus, and, accepting the office of godfather, gave his name to one of the sons of the latter; one, alas, who died in infancy.

In 1653 an important addition to the teaching strength of the University of Jena was made when Erhard Weigel became Professor of Mathematics. Weigel, who probably studied music with Samuel Scheidt in Halle, wrote many books and was still active when Nikolaus Bach arrived in Jena. Weigel preached the doctrine of learning through doing, and emphasized the value of the arts in a literal education. He placed music high on the list of priorities, defining it as the 'common voice of many different kinds of people in the community'. When Nikolaus Bach lived in Jena he was supported by many colleagues in the university who were keen musicians, and Professors Wedel, Russ and Hallbauer were close friends—each acting as godfather to a child at some time or other—while he was well acquainted with Professors Slevogt and Schellhammer.[6]

One consequence of professorial enthusiasm for music was the renewal of regular concert activity under the aegis of the university. The *Akademisches Konzert*, alive at the end of the sixteenth century (see page 14), was reconstituted under the leadership of Nikolaus Bach in 1733. Ten years later (when a similar society was established in the University of Leipzig) Johann Christoph Mylius, director of the university library (*f.* 1711) wrote:

> Previously the public concerts of the Collegium Musicum of Jena University took place in 'The Rose' on Fridays, but now they are, as formerly was the case, on Wednesdays at 8 p.m. Members of the audience are charged 2 groschen each, out of which the expenses are discharged. What remains over, when it has reached a

certain sum, is shared between the ordinary members of the Society[7].

There were at that time twenty-four members, which number was increased to thirty to thirty-six for special occasions, and especially at Passiontide. The leader of the orchestra in 1743 was Christian Siegmund Apel, of Eisenberg. It was for this society that Nikolaus Bach composed his entertainment, *Der Jenaische Wein- und Bierrufer* (see page 120).

JOHANN NIKOLAUS BACH AS A TEACHER

Nikolaus Bach's greatest contribution to the musical traditions of Germany was made by way of his teaching. Not only did he train a number of able musicians, but, and this perhaps was more important, he enthused many who were destined for other professions. Through his pupils he spread a zest for music among the middle classes. One of his earliest pupils was Abraham Pfuhl of Nürnberg (1681–1723), who became Kantor in Fürth, and later a well-known teacher of singing and keyboard instruments in Nürnberg. Johann Georg Neidhart (1685–1739), to become Kapellmeister to the Prussian Court at Königsberg, was a pupil of Nikolaus Bach at about the same time. In 1706, while still a student, Neidhart published a 704-page treatise on the monochord. Maintaining the scientific traditions of his university he issued a further essay on acoustics in 1724.

Johann Philipp Treiber, son of the Rektor of Arnstadt, was an assistant in the Faculty of Philosophy at Jena, and he took advantage of Nikolaus Bach's wide experience to improve his own not inconsiderable musical capacity. In 1702 he published a work which, on the vocal side, anticipated some part of the purpose of the *Wohltemperirtes Klavier*. This was his *Sonderbare Invention, eine einzige Arie aus allen Tönen und Akkorden Takten und Mensuren zu komponieren*. Two years later, in Arnstadt, where he was for the time being helping his father, he published *Der akkurate Organist im Generalbass*. Johann Stengel (b. 1689), a former pupil of the Grammar School in Gotha, a law student at Jena until 1709, also had lessons from Bach. He returned to Gotha where he was engaged as a singer in the Court. Listed as a soprano,[8] he would appear to have been a rare phenomenon in German musical life. He was also the author of the libretto of Gottfried Stoelzel's *Das mit Gotha ämulirende Altenburg* . . . (1722), a dramatic entertainment designed for the opera house lately built in the gardens of the Duke of Gotha's residence at Altenburg.

Contemporaries of Stengel at Jena were Philipp Samuel Alt (*b.* 1689), son of the Court Kantor at Weimar, and Friedrich Reutz (1689–1744), of Augsburg. The former, a pupil of J. S. Drese, G. C. Strattner and Samuel Heintze, before receiving tuition from Bach, returned to Weimar where he combined a legal appointment with that of organist in the Jacobikirche. Reutz, who became a pastor in Augsburg, was described by Gerber as a well-known dilettante of music. Another amateur who passed through Bach's hands was Johann Adam Bernhard, a lawyer, whose *Kurzgefassten cürieusen Historie der Gelehrten* (Frankfurt/Main, 1718) unusually included musicians among the learned men of the time.

There were Jena students who passed from one Bach to another. Among them were Johann Sebastian Koch (*b.* 1689) and Jakob Adlung (1699–1762). Koch, Choir Prefect at Mühlhausen under J. S. Bach, matriculated at Jena in 1711, and after graduation settled down as Kantor in Schleiz.[9] A native of Bindersleben, near Erfurt, Adlung, a pupil of Johann Walther, was acquainted with the Erfurt Bachs before entering the University of Jena. He returned to Erfurt as Buttstett's successor at the Predigerkirche. He was also a teacher at the Grammar School in Erfurt and, as writer, is a valuable guide to Thuringian musical life of the eighteenth century. His *Musica mechanica organoedi*, dating from 1726 but issued and edited by J. F. Agricola in Berlin in 1768, is an exhaustive treatise on organ building in the Bach era, while the *Anleitung zu der musikalischen Gelahrtheit* (1758) is an engaging book of a more general nature. The introduction to the latter was contributed by Johann Ernst Bach of Eisenach. Adlung was grateful to Nikolaus Bach (and he said so) for permission to practise on the organ at St Michael's. Generous in his references to Nikolaus[10] Adlung noted his excellence as organ builder and his original ideas in respect of incipient pianoforte mechanisms. Bach, who derived his interest in this field from his uncle, Johann Michael, was a keen experimenter. His greatest success was his *Lautenklavier*—lute tone stimulated by pianoforte action.[11] Instruments of this kind were marketed by him at sixty thalers apiece. A similar instrument, a *lautenclavicymbl*, was built also by Zacharias Hildebrand before 1740. This was said, by Agricola, to have been on the suggestion of J. S. Bach; but it seems likely that the hint was taken from Johann Nikolaus Bach.

Two students of Jena in particular benefited from Bach's skill in technical matters. Christoph Gottlieb Schröter (1699–1782), a former chorister of the Kreuz Chor, in Dresden, and sometime a pupil of Lotti, developed an early interest in keyboard instruments. Inspired, as he said, by Hebenstreit's 'Pantaleon', he deposited models of a combined harpsichord–clavichord action at Dresden in 1721 and laid claim to have been in fact the inventor of the piano action. Although his claim is disallowed (in favour of Cristofori), there is no doubt, since he exerted influence on Gottfried Silbermann, that he merits a place of honour in the history of the pianoforte. He went to Jena in 1724 and remained there for two years, having had the good fortune in the preceding years to have been taken to Holland and England by a patron. Schröter, enjoying a status equivalent to that of a modern research assistant, exercised an influence not only on musical studies in Jena, but also further afield. Following the example of Heinrich Bokemeyer at Helmstedt (who had done pioneer work at the beginning of the century) he demonstrated the physical properties of music by publicly conducted experiments. Ten years later Christoph Mizler, influenced by Schröter, announced to the students of Leipzig University that his lectures would cover the theoretical aspects of music in every field.[12] From Jena Schröter went to Minden as organist, and then, in the same capacity, to Nordhausen. He also added to the considerable store of existing theoretical works. Bernard Hoffmann (b. 1710), a former scholar of J. W. Drese, studied mathematics and architecture, and combined his polymath interests in the best tradition of Weigel. He was a composer, but also an authority on the tuning and construction of instruments.

Nikolaus Bach's concern for the lute is reflected in Ernst Gottlieb Baron's (1646–1760) *Untersuchung der Laute* (Nürnberg, 1727). A brilliant performer, Baron was in Jena in 1720. Seven years later, after touring with great success, he became lutenist at Gotha, and in 1732 he joined the Court band at Eisenach. His later years were spent in Berlin, in the service of the Prussian Court.

Christian Gotthilf Jacobi of Magdeburg (1696–1750), who held posts in Magdeburg and was well known in middle Germany both as piano and organ virtuoso, was a Jena student during the time of J. N. Bach. So too was Caspar Reutz who later paid this tribute to him: 'Acquaintance with the fine organist, Bach, in Jena, was advantageous to me, and, on account of my love of music, caused a congenial change of course.'[13] In 1739 Johann Gottfried Bach (1715–39), the third surviving son of Johann Sebastian, arrived in Jena somewhat unexpectedly and enrolled as a law student in the university on 28th January 1739. A young man of talent but of unstable habits, he had run into debt in

Mühlhausen and Sangerhausen (he was, for brief periods, organist in those towns). Four months after his arrival in Jena he died of typhoid fever, thus preventing the embarrassment that almost certainly he would have created for Johann Nikolaus.

Taking into account the general professional expectations of the Bachs, Johann Nikolaus was successful in his career. He achieved a position of some importance in one of the most important Thuringian towns. He was respected and befriended by some of the principal figures in German intellectual life. A many-sided man he exercised a quiet but beneficial influence on the future of German music through his teaching, especially in respect of those for whom music was a recreation. He was active until his eighty-first year, when his future son-in-law (and successor), Möller, undertook his duties. In Jena the present Bach Strasse is in honour not of Johann Sebastian but of Johann Nikolaus—'der Jenaer Bach'.

JOHANN NIKOLAUS BACH AS A COMPOSER

Whether Bach was an unwilling composer, or (as is more likely) merely careless with his manuscripts, is not known. Of his works three only are extant: a chorale prelude, *Nun freut Euch, liebe Christen*, of no great distinction; a Lutheran Mass; and a 'cantate en burlesque'—*Der Jenaische Wein- und Bierrufer*. The two latter works give some indication of Bach's wide range of interests—from somewhere near the sublime to topical comedy.

The Mass, probably composed in 1716,[14] for four-part choir with an additional 'ripieno soprano' and accompaniment for two violins, two violas and continuo, consists of Kyrie and Gloria. This was in accordance with Lutheran practice. It may be surmised that the work was written for some exceptional occasion in Jena. It is characterized by fluent manipulation of a strongly Italian technique which, however, is given German nationality by the incorporation of the melody of the chorale 'Allein Gott in der Höh sei Ehr' (sung by the 'ripieno soprano' group) in the Gloria. 'We have the good fortune', wrote Adlung, 'to live in a century in which the majority of the sciences and arts have reached a standard of excellence never before attained. One might say of music that it has now almost arrived at the very summit of beauty.'[15] The Mass by Nikolaus Bach, euphonious, deft in counterpoint, assured in harmony, represents the kind of style which Adlung had in mind. The music is 'scientific'; by its contrasts and allusions it is emotionally affecting. These factors—taking into account

the Italian quality that was attractive to the progressive, and the chorale
that stirred deep-seated local pride—must have ensured its appreciation
in Jena at least. Since Johann Sebastian[16] similarly introduced a chorale
into a similar situation in a Mass it may be supposed that the work in
question was also known beyond Jena.

It is naturally instructive to compare J. N. with J. S. Bach, and it may
be felt that if the latter had followed his cousin's example more closely
he would have produced a work rather more acceptable to the Elector
of Saxony than the *Mass in B Minor*. As has frequently been pointed
out, J. S. Bach was a terminal point in the development of music.
So far as J. N. was concerned the German tradition passed through
him and, having adapted itself to changes of taste and outlook,
emerged on the other side. The same of course is true of Telemann,
and of Sebastian's sons. The opening bars of the Kyrie of the Mass in
E Minor (after six bars of instrumental introduction) could hold their
place in the approved ecclesiastical style of half a century later.

The Gloria begins with a flourish transferred from the idiom of the
violin, but within which is the outline of Decius's original chorale.

It may also be observed that the chorale itself is a version of the Gloria and that the melody has a certain jubilation that Nikolaus Bach restates according to the temper of his own environment. The opening figure is maintained until at bar thirty it is replaced by one of cognate melodic origin which serves as a fitting preface to the chorale theme.

The chorale pattern is rarely out of mind and is implied in a section which, in a very general way, may seem to anticipate the attitude of J. S. Bach in treating the same text.

Nikolaus Bach, in the proper sense, was an effective composer. The 'sins of the world' may or may not have disturbed him deeply. None the less he exposed their presence in a passage of which the harmony, tilted towards Mozart, compels sympathy, if avoiding the sense of tragedy. The telling passage preludes the image of the saving 'Lamb of God'.

The Jena church register for 1724 recorded the name and occupation of one Johann Michael Vater. He lived in St John's Tower—of which he was the caretaker and from which he kept watch over the town by night. He was also responsible for informing the customers in The Rose (almost next door to St John's Tower) when fresh casks of wine or beer were being broached; hence he held the title of 'Wein- und Bierrufer'. To these duties were added that of organ-blower. A well-known figure in Jena, he was acquainted with Nikolaus Bach through one, at least, of his offices. Inevitably he was also known to the members of the Collegium Musicum. Thus Nikolaus Bach had the happy notion of investing Johann Michael Vater with a little immortality as the hero of a comic cantata. *Der Jenaische Wein- und Bierrufer* lies well within the category of sociable music of more or less dramatic character that, whether as *Singpsiel, dramma per musica* or cantata, was popular on all levels of society. Nikolaus Bach's essay in this *genre* is a clean-cut piece of work, simple in outline, warm-hearted, sentimental, patently eligible for comic exposition and moving in the direction of bourgeois humour later exploited by Nicolai and Lortzing.

The *dramatis personae* of the piece in addition to the hero (who as Johannes is undisguised) are two newly arrived students, Peter and Clemens (alto and tenor), and the innkeeper (of The Rose) who, being nearest to villainy and for the sake of *ensemble*, is a bass. The story, enclosed by eulogies to Jena, is simple: the innkeeper provokes the students to disagreement with Johannes, but the contention, hardly serious, is happily resolved within the space of half an hour.

Bach is something of a minor master of understatement. Panegyrics to Jena were two a penny. So, in the opening duet, the composer plays it cool. None the less he gives his students some kind of canonic academic dress:

That they are at first smooth in approach and fashionably mannered is indicated by the consecutive thirds (to which Nikolaus Bach was addicted) and by their knowledge of the French language:

In such a work (intended for private use) characterization is largely left to the performers. However, the principal songs of Johannes are not without pathos on the one hand and dignity on the other. Bach laughed with, and not at, his anti-hero, as these two arias show:

Not far away in one direction is the world of folk-song; nor in another the popular songs (which led to the 'Lied' of the Romantics) of C.P.E., Johann Ernst and Johann Christoph Friedrich Bach, that were published in weekly numbers towards the end of the century. Nor, for that matter, is Nikolaus's cantata far distant from the 'Coffee' and 'Peasant' cantatas of his cousin.

The difference between talent and genius is a slender one. So it is that a number of works by his relatives could at one time be confidently ascribed to, and accepted as by, Sebastian Bach. That such works were not regarded as among the most notable makes no odds; the fact remains that there was a middle ground on which the great and the less-than-great composer could meet. The question as to what constitutes genius, however, remains. It becomes increasingly clear that this quality stems partly from a particularly patterned temperament and partly from the reaction of this temperament to changing circumstances. The latter more often than not are seen to be proportioned in favour of the unfavourable. Of the Bachs of his generation Nikolaus is perhaps to be envied. Under the prevailing conditions of the age in which he lived he enjoyed a considerable independence. So far as may be judged—especially from his career in the one place—he was not discontented with his lot. The same is true of Johann Ludwig Bach, who was the principal musician member of the so-called 'Meiningen line', and a number of whose cantatas were once erroneously added to the catalogue of those of Sebastian.

MUSICIANS AT MEININGEN

The 'Meiningen line' deserves some special notice, for here, to a marked degree, another strain of artistic capability developed. Ludwig was the eldest son of Jakob, the able Kantor of Ruhla,[17] who in turn was the son of a farmer named Wendel presumed to have been of the stock of Lips, the carpet-maker. This descent is markedly different from that of the other 'lines', being less strongly associated with professional music. That the family was musical is not in dispute; but its members recognized that there were other directions in which to explore. Jakob, educated at the grammar schools in Eisenach (see p. 67), Gotha and Mühlhausen, and a soldier in Eisenach between 1674 and 1676, was very much a professional schoolmaster. He taught in Thal (1676–9), Steinbach, near Bad Liebenstein (1679–90) and Wasungen (1690–4) before settling finally in Ruhla. Jakob Bach was three times married. His first wife was Anna Margarethe Schmied of Gotha, by whom he had one son, Johann Ludwig (who was born in Wolfsbehringen, where his father's parents lived). Nikolaus Ephraim (1690–1760), already noted on page 91, was the son of the second wife (Dorothea Katharina). After Dorothea's death in 1697 Jakob married Christiane Regina Vogeler, daughter of the town musician, Michael Vogeler, of Hirschfeld. From this union came Georg Michael Bach, who was born on 23rd September 1703. Michael, whose godfather was Kantor Andreas Dedekind of Eisenach, studied at the universities of Helmstedt and Halle, matriculating at the latter in theology in 1731. A year later, following a probationary period in the same capacity at neighbouring Neumarkt, he was appointed Kantor of St Ulrich's Church in the city. In 1733 Bach married Elisabeth Schleyer, by whom he had four sons. Of these Johann Christian (b. 23rd July 1743) became the best known, achieving some eminence as a keyboard player and collecting the title of the *Hallische Klavierbach*. Johann Christian paid due regard to the fame of Johann Sebastian, of whose works he was an ardent copyist. Michael Bach remained in Halle until his death in 1777 and was there during the period of Wilhelm Friedemann Bach's office at the Market Church (see page 191).

In the Meiningen branch of the Bachs there was a strongly marked talent for painting, which has already been noticed in connection with the career of Nikolaus Ephraim. With successive generations this talent increased, remaining in evidence until the twentieth century, and to such a degree that in one or two cases it ultimately overpowered that in music.

Meiningen, tucked away in the south-western corner of the Thüringer Wald, lay in a kind of paradisial seclusion in the time of the Bachs. But its cultural traditions were established first by the counts of Henneberg, and then after 1680, when it became an independent duchy and the seat of the dukes, were further developed by the House of Saxe-Meiningen. As far back as the late sixteenth century there had been a preference at Meiningen for musicians who were more than musicians. Thus Johann Steuerlein (see page 16) was not only musician to the Court, but also secretary and official poet.

In the great age of patronage progress in the arts depended not so much on the patrons themselves as on their wives. So it was in this case. Bernhard I was married to the widowed Duchess of Mecklenburg-Schwerin, a daughter of Anton Ulrich of Braunschweig, who was not only well known for his proficiency in the fine arts but also those of nepotism. The Duchess of Saxe-Meiningen, accustomed to the joys of Braunschweig, encouraged her husband to bring his Court entertainments towards the same standard. In 1702 Georg Caspar Schürmann (1672–1751) was temporarily transferred from the Braunschweig-Wolfenbüttel Court to Meiningen, with the task of establishing opera there. Schürmann, once a singer in the Hamburg Opera, was an important figure in the early history of opera in Germany, being among the first to set German libretti. At Meiningen he was in a particularly favourable situation. Not only had he come with the best credentials, but he was, by marriage, related to the ducal House. His wife, Philippine Elisabeth Cäsar, was the sister of the Duchess Sophie Charlotte (wife of Anton Ulrich of Meiningen, who had married 'out of his class') In 1703 Schürmann's *Opfer der Zeiten der wahren Tugend gewidmet* was the first of a series of operas at Meiningen composed and directed by him. In this year Johann Ludwig Bach (1677–1731) took over from Schürmann his Kantor's duties. At the same time he was appointed Master of the Pages.

JOHANN LUDWIG BACH, A STYLIST

Johann Ludwig, whose early professional experience of music had been in Bad Salzungen, became a member of the chapel choir in Meiningen in 1699. He was at that time friendly with Ernst Ludwig, heir to the duchy, who was a man of taste. When he was seventeen years old Ernst Ludwig compiled a collection of French and German songs. He was also a composer of church music. In 1706 he succeeded to the title and promptly made certain changes at Court. Some of these were enforced. The Court Kapellmeister, named Dedekind, had also died recently, and Schürmann was required back at Wolfenbüttel. The new duke had a high regard for Ludwig Bach, who had for some time been acting as drawing-master to his children. Therefore he released him from general teaching duties and put him in complete charge of the chapel music. For Bach this was ideal. His inclinations were towards church music, and he would have time for his artistic pursuits. In 1711 he married Marie Johanne, daughter of the architect Samuel Rust. The two sons of this marriage, Samuel Anton (1713–81) and Gottlieb Friedrich (1714–85) born and brought up in Meiningen, spent their lives in the service of the Court. The elder, who studied in Leipzig from 1732 and when there was one of Sebastian Bach's house-guests, became in turn Secretary for War(!), Chamber Registrar and Secretary to the Rent Office—which offices he held together with that of organist. The younger, also on the pay-roll as an organist and from whom a cello sonata is extant, became more important as Court Painter. In this connection he is discussed at a later point in this book (pages 235–6). Among his portraits, however, was one of his father, which was in the possession of Carl Philipp Emanuel Bach before passing into the collection kept in by the Royal Library in Berlin.

No man was more respectful of family tradition than J. S. Bach. It is therefore not surprising that he collected the music of his Meiningen cousin, Johann Ludwig. It is perhaps surprising that he made copies of so many works, for out of eighteen church cantatas known to have been taken from the Meiningen into the Leipzig repertoire seventeen were copied by Sebastian himself. Of these thirteen were performed in St Thomas's Church, Leipzig, in 1726. That they were so performed is an additional indication of the high opinion in which their composer was held.

The contrast between Ludwig's style and that of Sebastian—despite their common heritage—is considerable. By the standards of the age in which he lived, that of the former was agreeably determined by undiminished mellifluences introduced from the south, and by the circumstances of life at the Elisabethenburg Palace in Meiningen. One of the most charming buildings of its kind in Germany, this encouraged a particular and civilized outlook. Thus that music which was composed here has the clarity, precision and painterly quality that is otherwise to be appreciated in the portraits executed by the painter members of the Meiningen branch of the Bachs. So far as Ludwig Bach was concerned, music was intended to affect the emotions, but feelings were only to be invaded with a sense of delicacy to which the more northerly based Bachs were unaccustomed. Like that of the Jena Bach—whose E minor Mass, possibly composed at Meiningen, was attributed to Ludwig by Spitta—Ludwig's music is transitional, moving away from the conservative practices of the older Thuringians.

Ludwig, however, was a master of choral effects in the grand manner of the Thuringian motet composers, even though he was sparing in his use of chorale motivs. His motets *Uns ist ein Kind geboren*, *Unsere Trübsal* and *Das ist meine Freude* are independent of this aid, although the first is based on the familiar third tone melody of the *Magnificat*. The second and third of these motets are effectively programmatic. In *Unsere Trübsal* (six voices, skilfully disposed so as to suggest two four-part groups) the idea of 'affliction' is conveyed through diminished-seventh chord units, whereas that of 'eternity' is stretched out melismatically. In these, as in other respects, the composer appears to anticipate the Austrian school, particularly Michael Haydn. In the third of Ludwig's motets there is more than a hint of the intention of Sebastian's *Singet dem Herrn*. The ear catches the similarity in dramatically separated chords, and in the counterpoint that flows through the voices of the one choir over the harmonic interjections of the other. A little short-winded, and too readily dependent on successions of glittering Italian thirds, *Das ist meine Freude* is an engaging portico to the larger structure of Sebastian's motet. The fugato that begins in the fourth bar of the following quotation also serves as the coda of the work—both choirs now being united:

Like that of Nikolaus, the vocal writing of Ludwig Bach is affected by instrumental idiom. Both in his cantatas and his one extant overture he may be seen to have handled instruments with facility and felicity—though without marked originality. The *Ouvertüren-Suite* in G major, composed in February 1715, is akin to, but more elegant, more ballet-like, than the G minor Ouvertüre of Johann Bernhard Bach.

In his cantatas Ludwig was content to aim at the maximum of effect with minimal means. Ten of the seventeen works in this form were written for four voices, strings and continuo. To this slender orchestration oboes were added in five cantatas, and in one the score was further amplified by the introduction of flutes. Only in the cantata for the sixth Sunday after Trinity, *Ich will meinen Geist in euch geben*, is a larger body of performers required. Here trumpets and horns are added. Ludwig took note of any dramatic implications within the texts he set and indicated them by judicious placing of sonorities—as, for example, in the opening statement of *Wie lieblich sind auf den Bergen*, for three voices, in the sections showing the contrasts between darkness and light (truly 'painterly') in *Mache dich auff werde Licht*, and in the symbolism of the warring elements in *Gott ist unser Zuversicht*. In general, however, the music of the cantatas is of an even tenor and a tendency towards brevity of utterance sometimes suggests a sense of naïvety. This is aptly demonstrated in the first part of *Siehe, ich will meine Engel senden*.

The finest, and most characteristic, work of Ludwig Bach is the *Trauermusik*, composed in 1724 in memory of the recently deceased Duke Ernst Ludwig. The duke himself had prepared the text of his Funeral Music from Psalm 116, 16–19. This work, between cantata and motet, is an example of Ludwig's virtuosity in so far as sonorities were concerned. It was composed for two choirs, the one accompanied by strings and continuo, the other by a variety of instrumentation. The accompaniment for the second choir comprises: for the first section, woodwind, strings, continuo; for the second, the strings are omitted; for the third three muted trumpets and drums are added to woodwind and continuo. The vocal writing, which is mostly homophonic, has a Handelian directness and culminates in a splendid valediction. As the soul of the departed duke finally enters heaven it is greeted by jubilant Hallelujas floated by the one choir over a chorale joyously intoned by the other. This is Melchior Franck's superb *Jerusalem, du hochgebaute Stadt*, which had previously been sung on the anxious approach to the heavenly Jerusalem. So far as Ludwig Bach was concerned, the heavenly Jerusalem lay somewhere across the stream behind the Schloss Elisabethenburg, in the Thuringian hills.

NOTES TO CHAPTER SIX

1. The name Bach was by no means unfamiliar in the university: Johann August Bach, Vindelicor = Augusta Vindelicorum = Augsburg (1672); Johann Poppo Bach and Johann Stephans Bach,

Ilmenau (1697); Johann Christoph Bach, Eisenach, and Johann Georg Bach, Ilmenau (both in 1696); Johann Friedrich Bach, Eisenach (1707); Johann Cizens., Misn = Meissen (1709); Johann Paul Bach, Westheimens, Franconia (1710); and Johann Christoph Bach, Thuringia (1721), are all registered in the Matriculation list.

2. Walther, *see* Chapter 4, Note 33 above, p. 90.

3. Sterzing also built the organs at St Peter's, Erfurt, in 1707, and at St George's, Eisenach, in 1707.

4. '1701 und folgende Jahre wird die Orgel in der Collegenkirche repariret, verbessert, und die Defecte suppliciret durch Zacharias Thayssner . . .' Martin Schmeizel, *Jenaische Städte- und Universitäts-Chronik*, Devrient, Jena, 1908, p. 188.

5. See *Bach in Thüringen*, p. 141 f., where the contract between Bach and the university in respect of his appointment as university organist is also given.

6. *See* Günther Kraft, 'Thuringische-Sächsische Quellen zur musik-physiologischen Forschung des 17 und 18 Jahrhunderts', *Bericht über den Köln Kongress:* 1958, p. 166.

7. *Das in dem Jahre 1743 Blühende Jena*, Jena, 1743, pp. 289–90.

8. Wennig (*see* Chapter 7, Note 33 above), p. 81.

9. Walther, *Lexicon*, 1732.

10. *Adlung, Musica mechanica organoedi*, Berlin ed. 1768, I, pp. 174, 244, II, p. 37; *Anleitung zur musikalischen Gelahrtheit*, 1758, pp. 311, 555, 575, 706.

11. *See* H. David and A. Mendel (Chapter 4, Note 23), p. 259.

12. L. C. Mizler, *Musikalische Bibliothek*, Leipzig, 1738.

13. J. W. Marpurg, *Historisch-kritische Beiträge*, 1754, p. 357.

14. One copy of the Mass, formerly in the possession of Breitkopf und Härtel, Leipzig, was dated 16th September 1716, and said to have been written at Meiningen; a second copy, in the former Prussian State Library, Berlin, was dated 1734.

15. Adlung, *Anleitung* (*see* Note 10 above), p. 9.

16. Short Mass in F.

17. Teacher of Kapellmeister Johann Theodorich Römhild, of Merse-burg: Gerber, *Lexicon*, Leipzig, 1792, Pt 2, Col. 309.

7

Leipzig

THE CITY AND ITS KANTORS

Extra Lipsiam non est vita;
Si est vita, non est ita.

During the period of the *Aufklärung* Leipzig became the most lively
and enterprising city in Middle Germany, a centre of cultural and
commercial development in which the foundations of an independent
bourgeois tradition were greatly fortified. The extent to which culture
and commerce were conjoined is epitomized by Dr W. Schöne who,
commenting on the appointment of J. S. Bach to the St Thomas
Kantorate, observed that 'thereby the City of the Trade Fair also became
the City of Music'.[1]

After the Thirty Years War Leipzig had rapidly recovered its
former prosperity. The fair, established in the Middle Ages and
reconfirmed in its privileges by the Emperor at the beginning of the
sixteenth century, was once again the chief market for the exchange
of goods between east and west, north and south, and an attraction
for visitors from all parts of Europe. It was a stimulus to local
patriotism (the devotion of Leipzigers to their dialect, their traditions
and the condition of their city was intense) and also to the exchange
of points of view. During the last forty years of the seventeenth century
there was a general urge to project the city into the eighteenth century.
Thus it was that in 1660 the first daily newspaper in Germany—the
Leipziger Zeitung—was issued there, and publishing became a major
industry. In 1677 the city library was founded. Freedom of speech and
of opinion, thus given opportunity for expression and reception, was
of course a vital if implicit principle of the *Aufklärung*.

Since progress in general is achieved spasmodically, and as the
consequence of opposition to vested interests and stubborn prejudices,
it should at once be stated that there were reactionary forces in Leipzig
with a not inconsiderable influence. The sternest conservatives were
the ministers of the Lutheran Church. Unimpeachable in orthodoxy,

they made life as difficult as possible both for members of the Reformed Church and also for the Pietists. As refugees poured out of France after the Revocation of the Edict of Nantes they were welcomed in Leipzig, as in Prussia and its dependencies, for various reasons; but not least because of their technical know-how. Since, however, their religious views were heterodox by orthodox Lutheran standards they were not permitted to be registered as full citizens. Nor were Catholics.[2] The adoption of Catholicism by the Elector of Saxony—who maintained military forces and courts of law in Leipzig—was seen as a disagreeable act of political necessity, and few Saxons were disposed to follow the example of August in this particular. Even in Dresden the majority of courtiers remained Protestant.

On account of the theological climate in Leipzig, Christian Thomasius, who was born and educated in the city, preferred to leave and to attach himself to the University of Halle. Lutheran piety was no doubt an admirable virtue, but it had its unamiable side. Joachim Boeldicke, for example, writing of the 'eternal torments of the damned', opined that it was logical to expect that 'the happiness of the elect will be greatly heightened and intensified by the contemplation of their sufferings'.[3] Bach was an orthodox Lutheran. As a composer he did not neglect to draw attention to the discomforts likely to be endured by the sinner.

The theological faculty at Leipzig was a powerful corporation, but the university was more indebted to its professors in other departments for its progressive image. Otto Mencke (d. 1707), a jurist, was the founder of the first journal of criticism in Leipzig—the *Acta eruditorum* (f. 1682). His son, Johann Burckhardt Mencke, who had visited Holland, France and England, and was a Fellow of the Royal Society in London, held the Chair of History at the time of Bach's arrival in Leipzig. A strong supporter of the *Görlitz poetische Gesellschaft*[4] and of Johann Christoph Gottsched, who became Professor of Philosophy, Mencke was the first great teacher of modern history in Germany. Johann Heinrich Ernesti, who was Professor of Poetry as well as Rektor of the Thomasschule, was among Mencke's distinguished colleagues. Ernesti, who belonged to a family eminent in Thuringia and well known to Bach, was the author of a history of the Kantors in the Thomasschule in the seventeenth century.

The line of Kantors was a distinguished one, and on the death of Kuhnau—who was not only a musician but also well acquainted with Hebrew, Greek, Latin and mathematics, as well as being a trained

lawyer—the city councillors were determined, if possible, to appoint
a successor who would not lessen the respect in which the office
was held. At the same time they were not disposed to be imprudent
in the matter of emolument. The first applications were from J. F.
Fasch of Zerbst; G. B. Schott, organist of the New Church, Leipzig;
C. F. Rolle of Quedlinburg; Georg Lembke of Taucha; Johann
Martin Steindorff of Zwickau; and Telemann. As was predictable the
spirits of the council rose when they saw the prospect of the engaging
and famous Telemann returning to the city in which he had first commanded attention. But (to cut a long story short) Telemann was not
disposed to undervalue his gifts. He played off the actual against the
potential and, having persuaded Hamburg to raise his salary, declined
the Leipzig post. At the next round the council considered the other
candidates named, together with Georg Friedrich Kaufmann, a former
pupil of Buttstett and court and cathedral organist at Merseburg, and
A. C. Tufen of Braunschweig.

At this juncture the fact that the Kantor would be expected to
teach subjects other than music was a deterrent to some. Telemann
himself had laid down from the start that he would not engage in the
duties of a mere usher. Fasch was the next to withdraw on these
grounds. At this point Bach—at first put off from applying by the
candidature of Telemann—submitted his name. So too did Telemann's
friend Christoph Graupner, a former Thomaner and a pupil of Schelle
and Kuhnau, and now Kapellmeister at Darmstadt. Graupner had
played the cembalo at Hamburg under Keiser and was a friend of
Heinichen of Dresden, who supported him in his Leipzig application.
At the second round Graupner was the choice of the Leipzig Council.
This having been announced, the Count of Hesse-Darmstadt responded by refusing to allow Graupner to resign on the one hand, and
by putting up his salary on the other. With a graceful gesture Graupner,
in informing the council of the situation, commended Bach to them
with the opinion that he was 'as effective on the organ as he was in
respect of church music and instrumental works' and that he would
'perform the duties required of him with honesty and thoroughness'.[5]
Bach therefore, who had nursed his chances by the presentation of the
Cantata *Jesu nahm zu sich die Zwölfe* (No. 22) on Quinquagesima Sunday
and the *St John Passion* on Good Friday, was somewhat reluctantly
elected to Kuhnau's place.

At this point the character of the post as developed by his more
recent predecessors may be defined.

Sebastian Knüpfer (1638–76), who succeeded Tobias Michael in 1657, engaged in the whole musical life of the city and was out-standingly successful in enthusing the students of the university. As a composer he won renown on account of his Coronation (of the Emperor) and Peace motets of 1658, and he added funeral motets and church cantatas to the repertoire of St Thomas's. A typical Middle-German composer of the period he developed a style distinguished by its emotional insights. In the melodic convolutions, and harmonic intensity, of *Ach Herr, strafe mich nicht* (Ps. 6), for instance, a type of expressionism characteristic of Sebastian Bach is already evident.

As heir to the Schütz tradition, Knüpfer was a master of choral-instrumental sonorities. A splendid example of his mastery of a festal idiom is the cantata *Machet die Tore weit* (Ps. 24), for five-part chorus, brass and strings. The treatment of the phrase 'Who is the King of Glory?' in this work clearly demonstrates that its efficacy was not lost on Handel when he came to set the same words.

After Knüpfer came Johann Schelle (1648–1710), who superintended the affairs of St Thomas's during a period of rapid musical expansion which was coincident with a surge of intellectual energy on the broad front already indicated. Required to produce large-scale works for the principal festivals in the Church Calendar, Schelle takes a prominent place in the St Thomas tradition by reason of his *Actus Musicus auf Weyh-Nachten*, a 'Christmas Oratorio' in three parts. Schelle's setting of this work, of which the text is a lyrical expression of the Lucan narrative, comprises introductory sonatas for instruments to each Part and one interpolated *Sonata pastorella*, recitative secco for the plain narrative, lyrical *arioso* solos, motet-style choruses for angels and shepherds, and chorales. The latter, after Leipzig use and taken from the *Cantional* (1627) of Schein, and the *Neu Leipziger Gesangbuch* (1682) of Gottfried Vopelius, play a prominent part in the structure of the work. The particular emphasis on the Luther hymn 'Vom Himmel hoch' (Schelle uses it as a 'motto' theme), is paralleled by the use of the same chorale in his *Christmas Oratorio* by Bach, whose composition was certainly stimulated by Schelle's example. This in turn stemmed from the Schütz precedent.[6] Among Schelle's other works (no longer existing) were 'histories' for Passion[7]- and for Whitsuntide.

Schelle's obligations included the provision of music for secular civic festivities and the Arcadian quality aimed at by the (unknown) librettists of occasional works is indicated by the titles of three (lost) pieces for which he wrote the music: *Auf ihr Musen an der Pleisse*, *Auf, Musen, springt und lacht* and *Auf, Leipzig, küsse dein Gelücke*.[8] Similar titles occur in the Bach canon (see pages 151–2).

Schelle was a versatile musician. His successor Kuhnau, in the tradition of Schein and Calvisius, was a many-sided man. An ex-chorister of the Dresden Kreuz Chor he studied languages (for a time he was a teacher of French) and law as well as music. Unlike some who studied but never practised law Kuhnau did both. In 1684 he was appointed organist at St Thomas's, which office he combined with that of advocate. In both faculties Leipzig offered exceptional facilities. Nor was he only thus far versatile. He was a satirist both in verse and prose, and his novel, *Der musikalische Quacksalber* (1700), placed him in the forefront of Saxon writers—not least of all on account of his vigorous patriotism. A distaste and lack of respect for overvalued Italian immigrant musicians was not disguised—even though as a composer he was by no means indifferent to Italian virtues, as is shown both in the limpid lines of his most engaging vocal melodies, and in the form and content of his most famous keyboard works. Thus he transmutes a characteristic German word—*fröhlich*—into Italian musical terminology:

Kuhnau, if not the founder, was the first to organize the university *Collegium Musicum* with some efficiency, and regular concerts under his sponsorship started in 1688. In 1701—the year in which Kuhnau became Kantor—another Collegium Musicum was begun by Telemann, whose acquaintance with Kuhnau was to prove something of a liability to the latter. During the last twenty years of his life Kuhnau was frequently ill (he suffered from consumption) and in 1703 was somewhat put out to discover that the council, anticipating that he appeared not to have long for this world, had come to an arrangement with Telemann (whose successes included works at the Opera House) that he should now regard himself as heir apparent.

Had Kuhnau died according to the council's reckoning the history of music would have been very different. As it was he survived long enough to celebrate the peace treaty between Saxony and Sweden in 1706, the tercentenary of the University of Leipzig in 1709 and the bicentenary of the Reformation in 1717 in musical works, and of course to become an occasional co-adjudicator with J. S. Bach in respect of organ installations.

HOUSEHOLD AFFAIRS

To be the Kantor of St Thomas's School in 1723 therefore required a wide spread of qualities: pedagogic efficiency, and an appreciation of the values of a new philosophy of education; a capacity for musical direction and organization; fluency in composition, but preferably in a recognizably contemporary idiom; a sense of diplomacy; and a conviction that all was for the best in the best of all possible worlds. For Bach the situation was one of challenge; but being the man he was he met opposition head on. He had therefore more than a fair share of disappointment and disillusionment. This he bore sustained by the simple faith of his fathers. He was the last of the Bachs truly to live according to the heroic precepts of the Reformation.

Bach was a family man. One of the attractions of Leipzig so far as he was concerned was the opportunity available there for the education of his sons. So far as musical education was concerned Bach was, in his opinion, the best tutor for his children—and Wilhelm Friedemann already had his *Clavierbüchlein* and the first book of *Das Wohltemperirte Clavier* on which to work—but, with an eye on the future, he recognized the advantages that would accrue from a higher general education. There was also the matter of Anna Magdalena.

In some ways the wives of great men are more important than the great men themselves; if only because theirs is the ability to help or hinder, make or mar. About Anna Magdalena too little is known, but it may be suspected that she, the lively little soprano, was by no means averse from moving into the metropolitan society of the 'city on the Pleisse'. There is no doubt that Bach loved her deeply, and the songs of the *Notenbüchlein*, tender and intimate, and combining the impulses of sacred and profane love, are as moving as any of their kind. Of these songs the three settings of Paul Gerhardt's *Gib dich zufrieden* are the most touching, not least because of the complete fusion of words and music. Towards Anna Magdalena Sebastian was both teacher—hence her *Clavierbüchlein* and indeed her *Notenbüchlein*—and lover. But the shape of the Gerhardt settings, in which the chorale tradition is embedded, suggests that unity of spiritual and worldly love of which another side is to be seen in the church cantatas and *Passions*. From such a song as this, from the *Notenbüchlein*, Carl Philipp Emanuel learned much about the art of the Lied.

But Anna Magdalena had her sorrows. In nineteen years she bore thirteen children. Of these seven died in early childhood, and one, Gottfried Heinrich (1724–63), was mentally defective. Of those who did survive, Elisabetha Juliane Friederica (1728–81) became the wife of Bach's pupil, Johann Christoph Altnikol, organist at Naumburg, while Johann Christoph Friedrich (1732–1803) and Johann Christian (1735–82) followed their father's profession with some success. The other daughters of this marriage—Johanne Carolina (1737–81) and Regine Susanna (1742–1809)—remained unmarried.

The household was augmented, according to custom, by paying guests, of whom a number were members of the Bach clan. Bach's connection with his brother's family in Ohrdruf was particularly close. In 1724 Johann Christoph's fourth son, Johann Heinrich (1707–83), left the Grammar School in Ohrdruf to study music in

Leipzig. There, a pupil of his uncle, he remained for some few years before returning home. In 1735 he was appointed Kantor to the Count Hohenlohe, in Oehringen (Württemberg), and also Preceptor in the 'German School'. Johann Heinrich Bach, described as a 'particularly gifted musician', appears to have lived happily ever afterwards; but his compositions (if any) are lost. In 1732 Tobias Friedrich Bach (1695–1768), the eldest of Johann Christoph's children and by now well settled in Udestedt as Kantor (he was Kantor from 1722 to 1768), invited Wilhelm Friedemann Bach 'Studiosus, . . . des Johann Sebastian Bachens, hochberühmten Musicus und Cantoris zu Leipzig an St Thomas Sohn', to act as godfather to his second daughter, Dorothea Wilhelmine.[9] Bach himself had opportunity to keep in touch with his Thuringian relations and friends when tours of inspection took him into those parts. In 1724 or 1726, or both, he was in Gera to approve Georg Fincke's new organ—with twenty-eight registers and three manuals—in the church of St John the Baptist; in 1728 he was in Erfurt (on this occasion he met Adlung); in 1735 he visited Mühlhausen to improve the chances of Johann Gottfried Bernhard in his application for the post of organist; unnoted, but certain, is a sad journey to Jena in 1739 on the death of Johann Gottfried; in September of the same year he visited Altenburg to survey the new palace organ, and he took the opportunity of visiting his former pupil Koch, to whose new-born daughter he was godfather. This visit had been anticipated, for Bach had given notice to Koch in January 1739 that the third part of the *Clavierübung* was expected to be published in time for the Easter Fair and that in due course he would bring a copy to Ronneburg (in the hope of obtaining subscribers).

Bach did not write this letter himself. It was written by his new secretary, Johann Elias Bach (1705–55). Elias Bach, son of Johann Valentin Bach of Schweinfurt, arrived in Leipzig as a theology student in 1738. He lived with the Bachs and agreed to take on secretarial duties for the overworked Kantor and also to act as tutor to the boys. From his surviving letters emerge the only intimate details of life in the household.[10] In all, Johann Elias spent five years with the Bachs, and his letter of 7th November 1742, written from Zöschau, is a testimony to the kindliness and generosity of the master to those who were within the family circle.

'I will not forget', wrote Elias,

> the great kindness I enjoyed for several years in his household, but will on the contrary always remember it with grateful feelings,

and will, if possible, show myself grateful therefore in deeds; and to the same end I will not cease to pray the Almighty daily in warm entreaty for the welfare of Your Honour's whole highly cherished household, and particularly to beg fervently for the lasting health of Your Honour . . .[11]

So much for the private Bach. If his first loyalty was to God, then running close was his loyalty to the name of Bach, which was the source of his concern not only for the future of his own children but also of his nephews and nieces, their children and their children's children.

THE TRIALS OF A SCHOOLMASTER

We move away from the private to the public life, but some part of the latter was an extension of the former. As a schoolmaster, especially in St Thomas's School, where most of the boys came from modest if not penurious backgrounds, Bach often stood *in loco parentis*. A large number of pupils passed through his hands, and of these there were many (including private pupils and university students) who were to venerate his name and protect his fame. As has already been suggested, the generally accepted thesis that he was 'forgotten' and then 'rediscovered' is not quite the truth. Neither he nor his music was ever completely forgotten.

Apart from members of his own family, Bach's pupils in Leipzig included Johann Friedrich Agricola (1720–74); Johann Christoph Altnikol (1719–59), his future son-in-law; Heinrich Nicolaus Gerber (1702–75); Johann Gottlieb Goldberg (1727–56)—also a pupil of Wilhclm Friedemann Bach in Dresden—for whom the 'Goldberg' Variations were written in 1742; Gottfried August Homilius (1714–85); Johann Philipp Kirnberger (1721–83); Johann Christian Kittel (1732–1809); Johann Ludwig Krebs (1713–83), son of a former pupil, Johann Tobias; Lorenz Christoph Mizler (1711–78), who was a philosophy student at Leipzig University; Johann Gottfried Müthel (1718–88), who, however, arriving in Leipzig in the last few months of Bach's life, learned the precepts of the master at second-hand, from Altnikol, in Naumburg; Christoph Nichelmann (1717–62); Peter Schiemert, a native of Siebenburgen, in Transylvania, and later organist in Bucharest; Christian Friedrich Schemelli (*b.* 1713); Johann Jakob Schmidt, (1707–68); Johann Schneider (1702–87); and Christoph Transchel (1721–1800). In one way or another all of these achieved at least moderate distinction in one or more fields. Agricola, who was also a pupil of Hasse and Graun, and whose works ranged from church cantatas to operas, and took in theoretical writings, became director of the music in the Prussian Chapel Royal in Berlin. Nichelmann—whose works alternated with those of Carl Philipp Emanuel in the weekly Saturday issues of the *Musikalisches Allerley* and were of similar nature—was also in the service of the Prussian Court, as cembalist, from 1744. In 1751 Kirnberger joined the establishment of Frederic the Great as violinist, but in 1758 he was appointed Kapellmeister to Princess Amalia (1723–87), the youngest sister of Frederic the Great. The princess was an accomplished and serious musician, playing the organ, the cembalo, the violin, and the flute, and having some talent for composition. Kirnberger—a composer of broad tastes and equally at home in the severer forms of fugue as in the newer sphere of sonata —exercised a considerable influence on the princess, who kept his portrait, painted by the Court Painter Ch. F. R. Lisiewsky (1725–94) in the organ room of her establishment in the Wilhelmstrasse, Berlin. She also had a portrait, by the same artist, of J. S. Bach hanging beside that of his sometime pupil. Kirnberger helped to build the famous music collection of this princess, and in it were many works representative of the Bach family as a whole (see page 180).

Müthel (whose piano music was appreciated in polite society in England) became an organist in Riga, whereas Gerber, who had gone to Leipzig to study law but capitulated to his inclinations to practise music as a profession, returned to native soil in Sondershausen.[12] His son, Ernst Ludwig Gerber (1746–1819), the celebrated lexicographer, became one of the agents who conveyed a faith in the old, Bachian, traditions of German music into the nineteenth century.

Schneider succeeded Johann Gottlieb Görner as organist of St Nicholas's Church, Leipzig, in 1729, when Görner took Christian Gräbner's place (which he had held since 1701) at St Thomas's. Kittel, an Erfurter, returned to Erfurt to maintain the old Thuringian traditions of organ playing and composition into the nineteenth century. Schmidt, also a pupil of Johann Peter Kellner (see page 140), succeeded his father, Johann Schmidt (1674–1746), as organist of Zella-Mehlis. Johann Georg Schübler, organist and music publisher (who issued the 'Schübler' chorale preludes of Bach) like his brother, Johann Heinrich Schübler (1728–68), also had lessons from Bach. Another Zella-Mehlis pupil was Johann Georg Zang, sometime Chancellor of the Court at Coburg.[13]

Homilius and Johann Ludwig Krebs perhaps were the two pupils who most proudly displayed their loyalty to their master in their organ works. The former, organist of the Church of Our Lady, in Dresden, handled the chorale prelude with notable skill, maintaining the statutory principles, but presenting them with grace and fragrant charm, reflecting something perhaps of the character of his city. Characteristic examples of this style are the near rococo prelude in *Sei Lob und Ehr*[14] and the trios *Erbarm dich mein* and *O grosser Gott*.[15] Krebs, finally Court Organist at Zeitz, was celebrated through Saxony, and the splendour of his *Praeludium cum Fuga pro Organo pleno* in C major which Count Johann Moritz von Brühl (?) brought to England is a testimony both to his quality of playing and to his absorption of Bach's creative processes.[16] The Prelude, with fine flourishes, ambitious pedal solo and piled-up chordal clusters, is succeeded by a vivid 12/8 fugue that looks back to the Weimar of Bach and forward to the Weimar of Liszt. Krebs also left a memorial to his master in the form of a fugue on B A C H.[17] The passage of this atonal incipit through a variety of works, from the eighteenth to the twentieth century, is an index to the changing attitudes to harmonic behaviour, in which the motiv itself has played a stimulating role (see Appendix 2).

The pedagogic influence of Bach was also absorbed indirectly. Among those who were not pupils, but clearly wished that they had had that opportunity, were Georg Andreas Sorge (1736–78), by whom there are extant three fugues on B A C H.[18] Of these one is unusual in being a high-spirited frolic. Sorge, an organist at Lobenstein, was a theoretician whose views on acoustics brought him into conflict with Marpurg and Quantz. In 1745 Sorge dedicated the third part of his *Clavierübung in 3 Tln. zu je 6 nach ital. gusto gesetzten Sonatinen* to Bach, and two years later he was elected a member (No. 15) of Mizler's Musical Society (see page 157). Johann Peter Kellner (1705–72), proud to relate in old age how he had known both Handel and Bach, also recalled how when the latter had visited his church at Gräfenroda he had extemporized on the B A C H motiv. Among Kellner's works for organ are a fine near-Dorian *Präludium und Fugue*, with a great pedal solo recollecting that of Bach's Toccata in F, a stern double fugue in D minor, and two trios.[19]

A long list of testimonials, carefully composed and always to the point, further extend our respect for Bach's sense of reponsibility towards his pupils and for the maintenance of high standards in his profession. Apart from his own sons, those who carried documents of recommendation when in search of employment included: George

Gottfried Wagner, who was successful in his application for the Kantorate of Plauen where he served for thirty years; Christoph Gottlob Wecker, who none the less did not receive the appointment he sought at Chemnitz; Carl Gotthelf Gerlach, 'von H. Bachen recomendiret' in respect of his successful submission to succeed Georg Balthasar Schott as organist of the 'New' church in Leipzig; Altnikol at Naumburg; and Johann Adolph Scheibe (1708–76). Scheibe's letter of recommendation, to the town council of Freiberg, being unfranked, was clearly taken by Scheibe in person—but to no avail. The competitors for the post of cathedral organist (the organ being Gottfried Silbermann's masterpiece) were three Bach students—Scheibe, Freudenberg and Th. Gerlach—and Johann Christoph Erselius, a Court musician from Dresden. The last, later described as an outstanding player by Agricola and composer of a fugue in B flat formerly ascribed to Bach,[20] was selected. Like other performers whose ambitions suffered frustration, Scheibe made a name for himself as a critic. As such he was not always awed by reputation or seniority, as his references to J. S. Bach show.

If Bach had not gained some reputation as a composer it is clear that he would have done more than most men do simply in a lifetime of teaching. One stands back before the prodigious energy that was invested in this one branch of his career. It was—taking the long view —a sound investment, for finally it was out of the reputation of the 'learned' Bach that the greater reputation as the greatest of German musicians grew. But it was precisely this sense of dedication that led him into conflict with his educational superiors.

As Kantor of St Thomas's School Bach had the status of an assistant master—with some responsibility also for the domestic life of the boarders. He taught Latin and gave some religious instruction. When he was appointed his Rektor was Johann Heinrich Ernesti, with whom—despite Ernesti's lax control of the school—he was on excellent terms. Ernesti was godparent to Gottfried Heinrich Bach, his wife to Regine Susanna. On Ernesti's death Bach composed the eight-part, commemorative, motet *Der Geist hilft unsrer Schwachheit auf*. The next Rektor after Ernesti was Bach's old friend of Weimar, Johann Matthias Gessner. Sometime a student at Jena (and presumably acquainted with Nikolaus Bach), Gessner published a thesis on philological problems there in 1714 and a pedagogic work, *Institutiones rei scholasticae*, in the following year. Before coming to Leipzig he was for a year Rektor in Ansbach. An admirable and experienced administrator with a keen perception of the nature of a modern education, and a man of tact, he improved the conditions of St Thomas's School. What is more, he had a strong feeling for the educational value of music. His affection for Bach led him by diplomatic intervention to erase some of the contentions that arose between Bach and other authorities in Leipzig—notably the city council. He also reduced Bach's general teaching commitments.

Gessner's predecessor had held his Rektorship in conjunction with the Chair of Poetry in the university. This not being allowed in Gessner's case, he migrated to the newly founded University of Göttingen as Professor of Poetry. He remained in Göttingen until his death in 1761, and helped to found both the university library (of which he was the first librarian) and the 'Teutsche Gesellschaft zu Göttingen'. Gessner, a man of the greatest talent, was remembered as a prophet of the age of Winckelmann, Lessing and Goethe.

On 18th November 1734 Johann August Ernesti (1707–81), a Thuringian born near Erfurt, was installed as Rektor of St Thomas's School. Having but lately studied philology, philosophy, theology and mathematics at Leipzig University, Ernesti was a modernist. His new broom methods were distasteful to Bach in every way, particularly because he found that through their application his own status was impaired and his authority reduced. The dissension between Rektor and Kantor came to a head in 1736 over the right to appoint choir prefects, and the controversy that this involved dragged on for a long time, involving in the end not only the city but also the Electoral authorities.

The pity of this dispute was that it was unnecessary. Gessner had been as humanistically inclined as Ernesti but less dogmatic. With a genuine zeal for educational reform and much to support his propositions to effect such reform Ernesti combined a degree of dogmatism unacceptable to an older man of marked distinction in his own faculty. His reputation ultimately stood so high, however, that it was the magnetic force that attracted Goethe to Leipzig in 1763.

To meet the requirements of the era of Enlightenment the school curriculum—intended to build the 'whole man', *mens, animus, ingenium*, and so on—was extensive. It embraced Latin, Greek (but less than formerly), philology, mathematics, scientific studies and history, as well as other disciplines within the general category of philosophy, and there was scarcely room for music.[21] In 1755 Ernesti (Professor of Philology at the university since 1742) detailed his system in an essay,

'Initia doctrinae solidioris', contributed to the *Encyclopädie der Schulwissenschaften*, which was the basis of the Saxon School Ordinance of 1773. Ernesti had a few words to say about dancing-masters and writing-masters in his essay, but none concerning music. He was, in short, anti-music. To boys who proposed music as a possible career he was abusive and is reported to have had one phrase of dismissal: 'Do you too want to play the fiddle in a public house?' But there was much more to it than this. The previously privileged position of music in the school curriculum had been suffering erosion over a period of years.[22] Extra-curricular developments, however, had somewhat disguised this process. *Collegia musica* had been, and were, flourishing and a vigorous concert life had developed (not least in Leipzig). These institutions, however, assailed the prerogatives of church music, which increasingly was thrust into second place. By the diehards this tendency was abhorred and, as late as 1782, Johann Samuel Petri (1704–93; from 1762 a music teacher in Halle, where he was a friend and admirer of Wilhelm Friedemann Bach), described the submission of church cantatas and so on to symphony, concerto and opera, as a 'great catastrophe'.[23] The truth is that society had become secularized. Ernesti's reforms, desirable in themselves and in accord with progressive ideas, were symptomatic of this secularization. In Ernesti—who retired from St Thomas's in 1759 to take the Chair of Theology at the university—we see the emergence of the 'Ichzeit', and the submersion of the 'Gottgläubigkeit'. Where Bach stood in this respect has already been stated.

MUSIC AND THE CHURCH

Midway between the mystique of Catholicism and the stringencies of Calvinism the Lutheran Church, like the Church of England, was very much institutionalized, to the extent that it played a significant part in civic affairs (whether the citizens continued to take interest in theological arguments is an open question), and reflected many facets of civic life and organization. In the period in which Bach was Kantor at St Thomas's School the significance of the Church as an institution was emphasized by bicentennial occasions. In 1717 the proclamation of Luther's Theses was celebrated, and the enthusiasm for the essentially German aspect of the Reformation carried on across two decades, until on 25th August 1739 the University of Leipzig organized a festival occasion in St Paul's, the University Church. Bach of course was not in Leipzig in 1717, but in 1739 the music for the university celebration was composed not by him but by Johann Gottlieb Görner.[24] That this was the case was due to a feud of long standing that bedevilled Bach's relationships within the ecclesiastical domain.

According to contract, Bach as Kantor was also Director of Music (but not organist) at St Thomas's, St Nicholas's, St Peter's and the New (St Matthew's) churches. The principal choral services—at which cantatas, masses, motets, *Passion* settings, and Magnificats were performed—took place in the two principal churches, St Thomas's and St Nicholas's, where the Kantor himself was directly responsible for the provision of music and also the maintenance of instruments. The chorale singing in the lesser churches was entrusted to small groups of the less experienced of the choristers under the control of prefects. The duties of the Kantor also embraced the superintendence of the music for funerals and weddings—on which occasions it was important not only that the choristers should sound but also look well. The principle was as in Weimar: the prosperous entered on matrimony, or departed from this world, with musical honours that reflected their social and financial standing. The rich enjoyed a full choir and 'figured' music; the less prosperous made do with half a choir and familiar chorales. *Jesu, meine Freude*, a motet with musical references back to Johann Michael Bach, was composed for the funeral of Johanna Maria Kees, stepmother (not wife as hitherto suggested) of Johann Jakob Kees, Postmaster of Leipzig since 1712, in July 1723.[25] *Der Geist hilft unsrer Schwachheit auf* was for the funeral of Johann Heinrich Ernesti in 1729. For what specific occasions the other four extant motets were composed is uncertain.

Although attendance at weddings and funerals helped to supplement Bach's stipend, his main duties concerned the normal liturgy. In respect of the composition of church cantatas, and *Passions*, he was liable to be pushed in one direction by the progressive element in Leipzig, including Gottsched, and his other librettists, Christian Friedrich Henrici (1700–64), known as 'Picander', and Mariane von Ziegler (1695–1752),[26] and to be restrained by the conservatives. It was easier in Hamburg, where the situation regarding church music was summarized, with a sense of disbelief at such impropriety, by an Englishman, Thomas Lediard, who, writing of the period 1727–9, said:

> They allow of Church Music, both Vocal and Instrumentall, and have a very good Band, paid by the Public, which performs

in all the Churches by Turns: But what is very remarkable, the same Persons are employ'd in the Church, and in the opera, and I have seen the same singer, after having sung in the character of *Jesus Christ* in the Church, act the Part of *Pluto*, in the Evening, in the Opera.[27]

On a famous occasion, Bach was arraigned for giving way to Italian tendencies. 'God save us, my children,' an old lady is reported to have said of the *St Matthew Passion*. 'It is just as though one were at a comic opera.'[28]

Since the alleged comment referred to the complexities of Bach's chorale treatment (which quite defeated congregational attempts to join in) it was wide of the mark. Bach of course did not have the operatic resources available in Hamburg at his disposal (as to what he might have done if he had gone to Hamburg is an interesting speculation) and had to work with and within the traditions of the choristers of St Thomas's and a more or less *ad hoc* orchestra collected from the permanent body of *Stadtpfeiferei* (trumpet, oboe, violin), from the professionals listed under the head of *Kunstgeiger* (oboe, violin, bassoon and another trumpet), from students of the university, and instrumentally proficient pupils of St Thomas's School.[29] This variable ensemble, whatever its enthusiasm, had its limitations—which Bach angrily pointed out in a memorandum to the city council on 23rd August 1730.[30] During the first part of his Kantorate Bach kept up a running battle with Görner, which serves to show still further his obstinacy and his regard for what he considered to be his prerogatives, as also the fact that there were those in Leipzig who were by no means committed to the opinion that he was the best of the city's church musicians. Görner himself certainly did not think so.

In brief, the *casus belli* was the direction of the music of the university church. When Kuhnau was Kantor he had at first controlled the music of this establishment, but when regular Sunday services were instituted in 1710 a suggestion was made, which Kuhnau resisted, that these should be directed by another. Since Kuhnau offered to officiate without increase of salary he was permitted to retain control, but after Telemann's refusal of a Leipzig appointment Görner was appointed as director of the university church music. Bach complained that the appointment was unconstitutional and, having his complaint dismissed by the university, took it to the Elector, from whom he received a response in the form of a compromise. This action was spread over three years. In May 1727 the Elector visited Leipzig, where he heard a birthday cantata, *Entfernet euch, ihr heitern Sterne,* composed by Bach. In September the Electress—the long-suffering Christiane Eberhardine who had been sent to August II as wife and diplomatic bargain by the Elector of Prussia—died. Gottsched wrote the text of a *Trauerode,* which Bach set to music. But since the Funeral Oration around which the Ode was to be set was to be delivered in the university church, the question of prerogatives arose once again. It was determined that Bach's music should be performed so long as Görner was in charge of the performance. Bach objected and his objection was sustained. The performance of this funeral music 'in the Italian style' was directed by Bach from the harpsichord, as was noticed in *Das thränende Leipzig.* Görner, however, persuaded the university to allow a document to be presented to Bach, in which he was to disclaim any further rights regarding the university church. Bach, otherwise nettled by Görner's poaching of players for his Collegium Musicum, refused to sign. But, looking to the bicentenary function of 1739 (page 143 *supra*), it would seem that in the long run Görner won his point.

Yet it was precisely in the years in which the Bach-Görner conflict was at its height that the former composed by far the largest part of his church music. The *St John Passion,* of which the text was partly taken from the popular libretto of Barthold Heinrich Brockes (1680–1747),[31] was apparently written in anticipation of his appointment to Leipzig for performance at St Thomas's Church on 26th March 1723.[32] Later in that year the magnificent and Italianate *Magnificat* was composed. Within a period of three years the majority of the extant church cantatas were completed, while the 'Sanctus' of the *Mass in B Minor* at least—as an independent work suitable for liturgical use—was written probably in 1724.[33] In 1725 Picander published a *Passion* after the manner of Brockes, and it is likely that this was set by Bach but that the setting has not survived. Three years later the same librettist prepared the book of the *St Matthew Passion,* which was first performed on 15th April 1729. Some part of this work provided the basis for the *Trauer-Musik* performed at Köthen in memory of Prince Leopold— from whom Bach had continued to hold the titular office of Kapell- meister. That there should be borrowing from *Passion* music for funeral music (or vice versa) raises no kind of question of propriety. But Bach did not confine himself to drawing only from one depart- ment. His borrowings from, and parodies on, secular works were frequent. Apart from individual cantata movements the greater part of the *Easter* (*c.* 1735) *Ascension* (*c.* 1735) and *Christmas* (1734) Oratorios (so called) are transcriptions of pre-existing secular works; while the 'Osanna' of the Mass in B Minor is a 'parody' of the cantata *Preise dein Glücke, gesegnetes Sachsen,* composed in 1734 in honour of the accession of the new Elector, August III, to the throne of Poland. The occasion was hardly worthy of the music. August III slipped onto the Polish throne, despite the election having shown Stanislas Leczinski the successful candidate, through the combined machinations and temporary support of Prussia and Austria. The result was the aggressive War of Polish Succession, a prelude to a depressing and humiliating era in Saxon history.

The subject of Bach's parody practice has replaced that of Handel's borrowings. In the case of the latter it was the ethics of the practice that came under scrutiny. So far as Bach is concerned, since the case is one of self-parody, it is the matter of propriety. Was it, for example, proper to adapt Herculean motivs into the musical apparatus of Christology in this way?

Part of the answer, as in the case of Handel, and most other composers of that age, lies in the exigencies of time. The pressure on a composer was extreme, and without recourse to existing material (whether his own or from another) the execution of commissions was often difficult. If, as C. P. E. Bach said, Johann Sebastian completed five cycles of church cantatas, and even if, as is now accepted, this should be reduced to three, the scale of the undertaking, as executed by Bach, was immense. Part of the answer, however, lies in the unwillingness of Bach at any rate to make a mental separation between secular and sacred, and part in the implications of imagery and symbolism in the religious poetry of the era. The 'new' poets, Neumeister, Franck, Brockes, Picander and, even more, Mariane von Ziegler, underwrote their spiritual verses with a good deal of worldly feeling, with the plain, and often stated, intention of stimulating emotional reactions in their readers and audiences. In so doing they took the church cantata in the direction of opera which, in common with his contemporaries, Bach was doing in another way, by means of recitative and *da capo* aria. Indeed in many instances—notably by patently erotic allusions not far to seek in the church cantatas—they went well beyond the emotional frontiers of stylized opera. Christian Friedrich Hunold defended the general principle of secularization by affirming that by such means people were enabled to recognize in their hearts what were known to be aspects of spiritual truths.[34] In Bach's youth the preponderance of weight had been on the didactic side of the motet-cantata. When he reached maturity, although the didactic element remained, the strongest aspect of the cantata was its appeal through the senses. Bach went along with this to the extent of missing no opportunity to convey verbal through musical imagery; but a sense of dedication to the principles of musical 'science'—especially to the traditions of counterpoint—and his obligation to a choral foundation, prevented him from going as far in the direction of a popular style as, for instance, Telemann did. Many of the cantatas, and much of the *St Matthew Passion*, appear as extended chorale preludes, of which the purpose has already been made clear. (The most complete example of a cantata as a transmutation of chorale prelude perhaps is No. 93—*Wer nur den lieben Gott lässt walten*.) In respect of cantata for solo voice, or otherwise not incorporating chorales, the attitude of the composer remains the same, and the spiritual connotations of the text are explored in depth.

For Bach the cantata, and the extended cantata that was the *Passion*, rooted in the chorale and choral tradition, was an integral part of the liturgy. And the liturgy, greater than itself, was the Faith. The fact that Bach took liberties with Mariane von Ziegler's texts and desecularized them to conform with doctrine reinforces the point.[35] During Bach's lifetime music and liturgy parted company—the aims of the one not being those of the other. However, in his church music (and the significance of the accident of 'parody' here disintegrates) the subject and the object (the worshipper) are seen as one. The attitude, inherited from predecessors at St Thomas's, from his Thuringian forbears, from Schütz, derived from the theme of suffering, shown in its most intense form in Cantata 60, *O Ewigkeit, du Donnerwort*.

The result of the *Aufklärung* was to diminish such involvement as J. S. Bach proposed. The *Passion* tradition passed through the hands of younger Bachs. In those of Johann Ernst of Eisenach it was moulded into this seductive form.

This, touching rather than moving, belongs to the new thought and, despite its occasional reminiscences (e.g. bar 6) has little in common with the world of J. S. Bach.

CIVIC AND UNIVERSITY AFFAIRS

The Kantor of St Thomas's was traditionally expected to be a man of parts, and his obligations, symbolizing the close connections between the ecclesiastical and the civic establishments, included the provision of music for many occasions other than those of the church. These fall under three main heads: university, civic and royal. From the time of his appointment Bach was continuously involved in work connected with such occasions, and in its execution, as often as not, reliant on the resources of the Collegium Musicum instituted by Telemann in 1701.

Six years after coming to Leipzig, Bach took over the direction of this society from Georg Balthasar Schott, who retired to the post of town Kantor in Gotha. Concerts of the Collegium Musicum took place on Friday evenings in Zimmermann's Coffee House, but when the fair was in being there were additional programmes on Tuesdays. In winter performances were held between eight and ten o'clock; in summer, transferred to the garden, between four and six. The duties of direction thus were onerous, and conscientiously to fulfil them Bach reduced his commitment to church music to the extent of largely abstaining from church cantata composition. He was in charge of the Collegium Musicum from 1729 until the summer of 1737, and then again from the start of the 1739 season until 1740. In that year Bach's former pupil, Johann Gotthelf Gerlach, organist of the New Church, became director of the Collegium. Three years later the formerly competitive societies—Bach's and Görner's—were united and the machinery was set in motion by which, through the exertions of other Bach pupils, Harrer and Doles, the Gewandhaus tradition was eventually established by Johann Adam Hiller (1728–1804) in 1781.

The secular works of Sebastian Bach's Collegium Musicum period fall into two groups: those which were occasional, and referential, and those—almost entirely instrumental works—which were at least intended as entertainment. For the former Bach was indebted particularly to Picander, but also to Gottsched, both for recommendations and for libretti. In general the secular cantatas, sometimes defined as *Drama per Musica* (of which the pattern and character was detailed by Scheibe in the *Critischer Musikus*, pages 540 ff.), tended towards opera, but, like Handelian oratorio, lacking costume, actions and *mise en scène*. True to the fancies of Baroque literature the characters were allegorical or mythological.

On 3rd August 1725 *Der zufriedengestellte Aeolus* was performed at the instance of the pupils of Professor August Friedrich Müller and in his honour. Sixteen months later *Vereinigte Zwietracht* (with borrowings from the first Brandenburg Concerto) celebrated the promotion of Gottlieb Kortthe to the Professorship of Law. This cantata was refurbished in 1734 for performance on the name-day of August III. Other university personalities commemorated by Bach in cantatas included Professors Rivinus (1732) and Gessner (1733). Royal cantatas clustered together in 1733–4, at which time Bach (who had acquired an honorific appointment as Kapellmeister to the Court of Weissenfels in 1731—which lapsed in 1736) was intent on acquiring a title from the Saxon Court. It was of course a propitious moment to make application—on the accession of a new monarch—but it was not until 1739 that he became 'Composer and Kapellmeister to the Elector-King in Leipzig'. The eight or nine cantata-type works that Bach composed for royal occasions to advance his claims were of course supported by the submission of the *Mass in B Minor* ('Kyrie' and 'Gloria')[36] in 1733. At this time he also used his influence to ensure the selection of Wilhelm Friedemann as organist of St Sophia's Church in Dresden (see page 187).

The texts of the ceremonial cantatas for royal delectation are for the most part of passing interest. Not so those that were of more circumscribed, Leipzig, interest, which act as commentaries both on locality and even personality, in the same way that gratulatory cantatas had done for a long time in the Thuringian and Saxon Courts. The 'Coffee Cantata', *Schweigt stille, plaudert nicht*, in manner not far removed from Johann Nikolaus Bach's entertainment at Jena, composed about 1732 and, apparently, with Bach's daughter, Elisabeth ('Lieschen') in mind as soloist, is a charming, if belated, skit on a bourgeois fashion. In the *Streit zwischen Phoebus und Pan* the gracefulness of the music is laced with astringency of satire—Midas being Beckmesserized as the pedant critic. That the object of ridicule was, as Spitta opined, Scheibe, is unlikely, since Bach at this period was doing his best to promote Scheibe's advancement (see page 141). This work was performed at a Collegium Musicum meeting in 1731. In the Peasant Cantata, composed for Carl Heinrich von Dieskau in 1742, Bach happily fell back on an established bucolic tradition—textually by way of dialect, and musically by way of folk-song and quodlibet practice—to provide a landscape peopled not by Arcadians but by Saxons.

A good Leipziger of Bach's time liked to delude himself that Leipzig was the next best place to (if not better than) heaven (see the reference at the foot of the page), and was wont both to take his leisure by and sentimentally to reflect on the waters of the Pleisse—a modest river that has long since disappeared from view. The 'little waves' of the Pleisse —smaller than those of the sea as pictured in a comparable recitative, 'Mein Wandel aus der Welt', in Cantata 56—were shown in *Vereinigte Zwietracht* and again in *Auf, schmetternde Töne*, a cantata for August III hurriedly knocked up from the former in 1734:

On 5th February 1728 the apotheosis of Leipzig as *Vergnügte Pleissen-Stadt* occurred in a delicate musical offering at the wedding celebrations of a citizen of Leipzig, Johann Heinrich Wolff, and a citizeness from Zittau, Fräulein Hempel. The latter town lying on the Neisse, that river too was within the story. In *Angenehmes Widerau* (1737) Johann Christian von Hennicke was welcomed to his inheritance of the family estate, with greetings from Time, Good Fortune, Fate and—the River Elster. For all the works of this type, Picander was the general librettist. When altered for a civic occasion, with Apollo and Mercury replacing the spirits of the rivers, the cantata took on a text likely to appeal to the governors of the city:

> Angenehmes Pleiss-Athen
> Wie die Diamenten dauern
> Also werden deine Mauern
> Unbeweglich feste stehn.
> Angenehmes Pleiss-Athen
> Weltberühmtes Pleiss-Athen
> Wer dich höret, wer dich nennt
> Wer dich liebet, wer dich kennt
> Wird dein Lob noch mehr erhöhn
> Weltberühmtes Pleiss-Athen.

With this may be composed:

> Du angenehmes Pleiss-Athen/
> Du Paradies in deinem Sachsen/

Dein Ruhm muss ewig blühend stehn
Und alle Tage grösser wachsen.
Aller Zeiten Müh und Fleiss/
Sorgen wie sie deinen Preiss
Schöner machen und erhöhn.

The latter stanza, the words of a *da capo* aria, is the opening of a *Drama per Musica*, entitled *Das angenehme Leipzig, in einem Musicalischer Dramate aufgeführet von dem bey Herrn Zimmermann florirenden Collegio Musico. In Leipzig Anno MDCCXXVII*.[37]

That Bach, who was involved in other cognate undertakings at about this time, was the composer of this work is open to little doubt. That the score does not exist—although the music may well have been absorbed into church cantatas—is not surprising. To have no music for this libretti is, however, regrettable, for of all the secular cantatas of the period this is the one which, from the literary point of view, is the most charming and the most topical (see Appendix 3).

As a great composer, and a man of strong individuality, Bach stood firm on principle. In so doing he remained independent of trends of intellectual fashion of which he disapproved. He was clear on the necessity for taking a firm stand on questions of doctrine, and averse from sacrificing tenets in which he believed to the vaguer precepts of enlightenment and humanism that were gaining currency—and not only in Germany. To this extent he was unshakably conservative. On the other hand he was indifferent neither to certain aspects of aesthetic philosophy nor to the efforts of Picander and Gottsched, among others, to enliven the life of the Leipzigers with elegant and diverting entertainment. The true function of all art was clear cut. It was laid out by Gottsched in *Oden der Deutschen Gesellschaft in Leipzig* (1728), reinforced in *Versuch einer critischen Dichtkunst* (1742), and realized in relation to music by an anonymous aesthetician in or about the year of Bach's death:

In so far as its imperfections allow, art in all its works shall imitate Nature. Music, therefore, must observe this rule of Nature, and endeavour to concern itself with every possible variation [within nature] by means of its sonorities, tones, and structures.

Which carries us to the conclusion that

The intention of music is to move the hearts of men towards gladness or sorrow through what is either pleasant or unpleasant.[38]

As has been seen Bach would not have dissented from this exposition in general—but he would naturally have qualified the 'intention'. The pseudo-philosophy, however, was so far as music was concerned an acknowledgment of a state of change within music that had been going on for a long time and which nothing, or nobody, not even J. S. Bach, could prevent. The true music of the Enlightenment, emblematic of that elegance which the Germans sought to import from France, was represented by the whimsicalities of the minuet-, bourrée-, march-, polonaise-songs of J. S. Scholze, or 'Sperontes'. From this point there is a direct line to Mozart's *Bastien und Bastienne*.

The *Singende Muse an der Pleisse*, of which this is No. 50, appeared in 1736, in which year Bach was editing and contributing to Georg Christian Schemelli's (*b.* 1678) *Musicalisches Gesangbuch*.[39] The pretty strains of Sperontes were popularized not only by the *Singende Muse*, but also by the porcelain-fragile shepherds and shepherdesses of *Das Kätzen, ein Schäferspiel* (1746) and *Das Strumpfband* (1748). Scheibe and J. F. Doles went off in this direction with *Neue Freymäurerelieder* (1749) and *Neue Lieder nebst ihren Melodien componirt* (1750) respectively. And before J. S. Bach was dead Johann Ernst of Eisenach had justified himself on the same band-waggon with his *Sammlung auserlesener Fabeln mit darzu verfertigen Melodeyen* (1749?), in which one of the poets represented is Christian Gellert (1715–69), one of the brightest sons of the Enlightenment and of Goethe's 'German Parnassus'. When Goethe arrived in Leipzig he found that all was 'Galanterie', and that 'the waters of Gottsched had swamped the German world with a veritable deluge, which threatened to rise up even above the highest mountains.'[40] It was a far cry from the Thuringian ways of the late seventeenth century to the brave new world of the 'Poeten nach der Mode' who were the arbiters of Leipzig taste in the last days of Sebastian Bach.

THE STATURE OF BACH OF LEIPZIG

The difference between the reputation that Bach enjoyed in his lifetime and that which accumulated posthumously is one of the remarkable phenomena in the history of music. This difference, having been accepted, immediately enables us to bring him back into some sort of relationship with the other Bachs. The fact that the family was long established in the field of music, increasingly widely dispersed, and enjoyed a built-in reputation for sound musicianship was, of course, a convenient launching-pad for any reputation, and by recognizing by how much the talent of one Bach outstripped that of another the casual critic had a ready calculator to hand. The Ohrdruf Bachs had sunk back into relative obscurity and, while performing useful functions and living contented and respectable lives, were isolated in what had now become a Thuringian backwater.[41] As for Ludwig of Meiningen and Nikolaus of Jena, both respected and virtuous, they had none of Sebastian's musical versatility nor his absolute dedication. This was obvious, at any rate in Leipzig and Dresden, in which cities, as later in Berlin, Bach was also benefiting from the rapid progress of his sons. The palpable genius, properly attuned to the ethos of the age of Gottsched, of Wilhelm Friedemann and Carl Philipp Emanuel reflected back to enlarge the genius of their father. By the 1740s there was no doubt as to which of the branches of the Bach clan conveyed the true tradition. The mark of approval was stamped on this branch by the invitation from the King of Prussia to J. S. Bach to visit Potsdam in 1747. 'Old Bach' was welcomed by the king as a master of the science of music, as the most redoubtable exponent of intellectual method, as evidenced shortly afterwards in the *Musikalisches Opfer*—a cycle of canons, fugues and ricercari, based on the *Thema Regium*; and as an executant. In the former capacity Bach was the *summa summarum* of the distinctive German tradition. The visit to Potsdam therefore was an end, but it was also a beginning. It was in 1753, three years only after Bach's death, that a civil servant in Berlin, Friedrich Wilhelm Marpurg (1718–95), emphasized the durable virtues of Bach's contrapuntal, scientific, techniques in his *Abhandlung von der Fuge*[42]—which was dedicated to Telemann.

During the period in which the Collegium Musicum in Leipzig occupied his immediate attention Bach composed (or rearranged) the main body of his clavier concertos, in which the energies of Vivaldian Baroque were transferred through the finger-work of the great master of the keyboard, cross-references (in slow movements) to the expressionism of the cantata, and fuller structural proportions, from the private to the public province. From these works Carl Philipp Emanuel and Wilhelm Friedemann moved into the classical field with concertos of their own. In 1731 the first part of the *Clavierübung* (six partitas in six different keys) was published. The second part, comprising orchestral forms reduced to keyboard proportions in an Italian concerto and a French overture, was issued in 1735. The third part, of the 'Cathechism' chorale preludes for organ, appeared four years later, while the fourth and final section of this comprehensive undertaking, with the 'Goldberg' variations, was published in 1742. In 1744 the second part of *Das wohltemperirte Clavier* was completed. Apart from the early Mühlhausen cantata, *Gott is mein König*, the only works published by Bach during his lifetime were instrumental. In addition to the *Clavierübung* these works comprised the canonic variations on *Vom Himmel hoch*—a particular exercise designed for the academicians of Mizler's Society (see page 157), the 'Schübler' chorale preludes (1746)—arrangements of cantata movements, and the *Musikalisches Opfer. Die Kunst der Fuge* was published posthumously.

Some of Bach's greatest organ works belong to the Leipzig period—symbols of his continuing activity as travelling virtuoso. They include the six trio sonatas, in the manner of Corelli, which were designed for Wilhelm Friedemann, and which were patterns for Wilhelm Friedemann's trios for organ; and the great architectural masterpieces of the preludes and fugues in C major (BWV 547), E minor (BWV 548), B minor (BWV 544) and E flat major (BWV 552). The last, much loved in England on account of the fortuitous relationship between the subject and the opening phrase of William Croft's 'St Anne' hymn tune, would seem to have been inspired by one of those motivs put to common use in the Baroque period and to be discovered in a *Ricercar Quarti Toni* by Poglietti.

At the end of his life, in conjunction with Altnikol (who wrote the last three examples from his father-in-law's dictation), Bach revised earlier works into the 'Eighteen Chorale Preludes'.

We thus see a pattern in Bach's Leipzig years: of an intensive six-year period of church music composition; followed by rather more than a decade of instrumental virtuoso, 'scientific' and pedagogic effort; and a final phase of, so to speak, recapitulation, in which more than forty church cantatas were executed, chorale preludes of more than liturgical dimension and design revised and the two great 'Prussian' works accomplished. The *Art of Fugue* broke off in Contrapunctus XIX at a place that carried suitably romantic overtones. 'The composer died', wrote Carl Philipp Emanuel, 'at the point at which the name B A C H was introduced into a countersubject.'

The name of Bach signified different things to different people among Johann Sebastian's contemporaries. In official circles, among the administrators of state, city, university and St Thomas's School it often seemed to spell trouble. The heirs to these authorities have spent two centuries in atonement for former neglect. Among those who led musical critical fashion Bach was a problematic figure. Mattheson and Scheibe applauded the keyboard works and, together with Mizler, were amazed by his contrapuntal virtuosity; but both were quick on the draw when faced with a luxuriance of ornamentation and complexities of part-writing and declamation that ran counter to the ideals of the *Aufklärung*. Mattheson and Scheibe suffered from a complaint that has infected later generations of critics: they were unable to comprehend a talent that refused to be confined within the limits of a modish scale of values.[43]

None the less there were those in Leipzig who had no reservations concerning Bach's stature. One, surprisingly perhaps, was Gottsched, who wrote with pride about the trinity of Telemann, Handel and Bach as early as 1728 in *Der Biedermann*.[44] Nine years later Johann Abraham Birnbaum, a teacher of rhetoric in Leipzig University, and a competent musical amateur, published a pamphlet in defence of Bach and in answer to Scheibe. This disputation, in which Mizler joined, continued for two years. In 1747 Mizler otherwise showed his regard for Bach by inviting him to become a member of his 'Correspondierende Societät der musikalischen Wissenschaften', founded in 1738.[45] In accordance with the conventions of similar societies in other branches of learning a classical flavour was imported by nomenclature. Mizler chose for himself the academic name of Pythagoras. In acknowledgment of his election to Mizler's select society Bach contrived a puzzle canon which, in incorporating the theme of a chaconne by Handel, also annotated the regard in which he held his great contemporary. At this

time, and in conformity with the custom of the society, Elias Gottlieb
Haussmann painted Bach's portrait.

The limitations imposed on Bach's fame during his lifetime by the
circumstances of his life, the paucity of his published works and the
general character of his music in relation to the climate of the age are
illustrated by the manner in which he was, outside Leipzig and Thuringia, often ignored.

Bach died on 28th July 1750—the *Spenersche Zeitung* of 3rd August
attributing his death to the incompetence of John Taylor, the English
eye surgeon who had unsuccessfully operated on Bach's cataract (?) in
the previous January. He was buried in the churchyard of St John's
Church. In 1894 his remains were reinterred within that church, where
they stayed until, after the destruction of the building during the
Second World War, they were taken to St Thomas's. A week after
Bach's death candidates for the succession were interviewed. They were
Carl Philipp Emanuel Bach; Johann Trier, student of music and theo-
logy; Görner, already organist of St Thomas's; Harrer, whose candi-
dature was strongly supported by Count von Brühl, the Saxon First
Minister; August Friedrich Graun of Merseburg; and Krebs, from
Zeitz. The interviewing committee agreed with Mayor Stieglitz that
what was wanted in Leipzig was a Kantor and not a Kapellmeister.
Harrer was the successful candidate.

It was eight years after Bach's death that the first effective shots were
fired in what was to become a general campaign to regard Bach not as
one of the greatest of German musicians but as the greatest. The
faithful Thuringian Jacob Adlung wrote in his *Anleitung* of 'our
great Bach . . . [whose] ashes I venerate', and of how 'through his
powers he held not only Germany but also Europe in wonderment'.
Finally, said Adlung, 'there has been only one Bach in the world'.[46]
A conclusion that would have been contested by the sons of the said
Bach.

NOTES TO CHAPTER SEVEN

1. 'Leipzig einst und jetzt', in *Leipzig in Wort und Bild*, Leipzig, 1928,
   p. 10.

2. Civic disabilities were removed from the Catholics in 1807, from the
   Calvinists in 1811.

3. *See* James Mew, *Some Aspects of Hell* (*Ancient & Modern*), London,
   1903, p. 312.

4. Mencke composed poems under the name of 'Philander von der Linde', and stimulated non-aristocratic literary and poetry societies after the pattern of the *Fruchtbringende Gesellschaft*. The influence on German literary development was considerable. In 1717 a *Deutsch-übende Gesellschaft* was established in Leipzig, the model for similar bodies in Königsberg, Göttingen and other towns. Henrici, Bach's librettist, was an adherent of this movement.

5. Letter of 4th May 1723.

6. *See* Bernd Baselt, *Der 'Actus Musicus auf Weyh-Nachten' des Leipziger Thomaskantors Johann Schelle*, Wissenschaftliche Zeitschrift der Martin-Luther Universität Halle-Wittenberg, Heft, 5, 1965.

7. The most famous extant *Passion* setting of this era is the *Matthäus Passion* of Johann Theile (1646–1724). This work published in Lübeck in 1673, was widely used.

8. *Leipziger Verzeichnis*, 1712; these works were described respectively as Aria à 13, à 26, and à 10.

9. Tobias Friedrich's wife was Susanne Elisabeth, younger daughter of the Kantor in Orlishausen, near Sömmerda, whose name was Wölckens (or Wölchner, in the Udestedt Church Register)—a relative of Anna Magdalena Bach.

10. See *The Bach Reader* (Chapter 4, Note 23), pp. 162 f.

11. *See* Chapter 4, Note 23, p. 171.

12. When a pupil at the Grammar School in Mühlhausen, Gerber had become acquainted with Johann Friedrich Bach; *see* Beinrath (Chapter 3, Note 2), p. 57.

13. *See* W. Schumann, 'Bach-Erinnerungen aus Zella-Mehlis', *Bach in Thüringen*, 1950, pp. 90–1.

14. *Die Orgel* (pub. Kistner und Siegel, Lippstadt): *Werke alter Meister, Reihe II*, 1, No. 6.

15. *Die Orgel; Werke alter Meister, Reihe II*, 2, Nos. 5, 6.

16. BM. Add. MS. 32075, where are also a toccata, some chorale fugues, by Krebs, a cembalo sonata by Kirnberger, and a 'Solo per il Cembalo Clavier', by Kirnberger.

17. Liturgical Music Press Inc., ed. Norman Hennefield, New York, 1944.

18. BM. Add. MS., 31307. These fugues are listed in Gerber (*see also* p. 247, n.20).

19. *Die Orgel; Werke alter Meister*, No. 7.

20. See *Ernst Müller, Musikgeschichte von Freiberg*, Freiberg, 1939, pp. 78–9, and BG vol. 42, p. 298.

21. *See* G. Schünemann, *Geschichte der deutschen Schulmusik*, Leipzig, 1928, pp. 226–8.

22. The manner in which music had been dethroned in the grammar schools over the years was deplored by Adlung, who observed that in Erfurt there was hardly any time left in the curriculum for the theory of music. (*Anleitung*, pp. 106–7.)

23. *Anleitung zur praktischen Musik*, Leipzig, 1782.

24. See *Kirkliche Zustände Leipzigs* (1839), p. 293.

25. 'Am 29. Juni 1723 starb nach längerem Leid seine Stiefmutter Johanna Maria geb. Rappold, die zuletzt im Hause des Buchhändlers Gleditzsch gewohnt hatte. Erst am 18. Juli fand die übliche Trauerfeier statt, und der im Mai dieses Jahres nach Leipzig gekommen Thomaskantor Joh. Sebastian Bach konnte bis dahin auf bestellung des Hof- und Justizrates aus der Vollwebung des Liedes: "Jesu, meine Freude" mit dem für diesen Tag bestimmten Text Röm. 8, 1–6 die schönste seiner Motetten: "Jesu meine Freude" schaffen.' Kurt Krebs, *Das Kursächsische Postwesen zur Zeit der Oberpostmeister Johann Jakob Kees I und II*, Leipzig/Berlin, 1914, p. 125.

26. C. P. E. Bach composed songs on poems from Mariane von Ziegler's *Vermischtte Schriften*, 1739 (*see* p. 177), as also did Haydn (No. 7 of *XII Lieder*, Vienna, 1782).

27. *The German Spy: In Familiar letters home . . . written by a Gentleman on his Travels to his Friend in England. . . .* Thomas Lediard, London, 1738, p. 241. Lediard's son, also Thomas, was among the English students at Leipzig University in Bach's time. He matriculated on 21st March 1737.

28. Christian Gerber, quoted in David and Mendel, *op. cit.*, p. 229.

29. The *Stadtpfeifer* in 1732 were Gottfried Reiche, Johann Cornelius Gentzmer and Johann Caspar Gleditsch; the *Kunstgeiger* were Heinrich Christian Beyn, Johann Gottfried Kornagel and Johann Friedrich Caroli. They all lived in Stadt-Pfeiffer-Gässgen.

30. Terry (*see* Chapter 5, Note 21 above), pp. 201 f.

31. Also set by Handel (1716) and Telemann (1722).

32. Concerning the possibility of the *St John Passion* having, in fact, been performed in 1724 rather than 1723 *see* W. Blankenberg (Chapter 5, Note 25 above), p. 107.

33. See Note 32 above, p. 109, for new chronology of the composition and assembly of the *Mass in B Minor*.

34. W. Flemming, *Oratorium und Festspiele*, Leipzig, 1933, pp. 19–20.

35. For discussion of this point see Wolfgang Herbst, 'Der Endzweck; Ein Vergleich zwischen Joh. Seb. Bach und Chr. Mariane v. Ziegler', in *Musik und Kirche*, 30 Jg., vol. 5, 1960, pp. 248 f.

36. The whole of the Mass, as is now known, was finalized in or about 1748. *See* Blankenberg (Chapter 5, Note 25 above).

37. Universitätsbibliothek, Halle, Yc 4414/Q/V./ The whole text is given in translation in Appendix 3.

38. *Einige zum allgemeinen Nutzen deutlicher gemachte Musikalische Erwegungs—und andere eingerichtete Uibungs-Wahrheiten . . . von einem Freunde dieser Wissenschaft.* Leipzig, n.d. (1750?), pp. 49, 60.

39. Schemelli was Kantor of Zeitz and his son, Christian Friedrich, for whom Bach wrote a testimonial in 1740, was a pupil at St Thomas's School from 1731–4.

40. Johann Wolfgang von Goethe, *Dichtung und Wahrheit*, Leipzig, Insel Verlag, 1958, II, 6, p. 262.

41. Johann Christoph Bach (1671–1721) had nine children. The eldest, Tobias Friedrich (1695–1768) sometime organist in Ohrdruf, Kantor at the Court of Gandersheim (Braunschweig) and organist at Pferdingsleben, was Kantor at Udestedt from 1721 until his death. The second son, Johann Bernhard (1700–43), a pupil of Johann Sebastian, lived in Ohrdruf but occupied no significant position. The third son, Johann Christoph (1702–56), studied theology at Jena, and succeeded Elias Herda (formerly of Lüneburg) as Kantor in Ohrdruf in 1728. Johann Heinrich (1707–83), also a pupil of Johann Sebastian, was a teacher at Oehringen, while the youngest son of the family, Johann Andreas (1713–79), was also organist in Ohrdruf. The twin brother of Andreas, Johann Sebastian, who took his name from his godfather, died two days after birth. The surviving members of the family were fertile, even by Bach standards. It is only to be remarked that the great-great-grandson of Johann Christoph—Hermann Julius Bach (*b.* 19th April 1853)—renewed the Hungarian connection of the family by becoming part owner of a pencil factory in Budapest in 1892. Kraft (*see* Chapter 1, Note 11 above), p. 20.

42. References to *Die Kunst der Fuge*, I, p. 130, II, pp. 28, 35, 37; to the *Inventions*, I, p. 94; to the *Musikalisches Opfer* II, p. 123; and to the double fugal methods of Kuhnau and J. S. Bach, I, p. 133.

43. Documents available in David and Mendel (*see* Chapter 4, Note 23 above), pp. 226 f, are not repeated here.

44. *Der Biedermann*, 1728, den 20 December.

45. *See* C. F. Cramer, *Magazin der Musik*, Hamburg, 1783, pp. 177–8. In 1755 Leopold Mozart, of Salzburg, was elected to membership of the society.

46. Adlung (*see* Chapter 1, Note 2 above), pp. 14, 690 and 692.

8

Frederic the Great

The death of Johann Sebastian Bach marked the end of an era in more senses than one. In general a medieval concept of the purpose of music was concluded—with an emendation of attitude to its functional and structural properties. In particular the ancient, and homely, character of Thuringian and provincial Saxon music was, for the most part, pushed into a backwater. During the second half of the eighteenth century there were significant members of the Bach clan active in Thuringia, but less renowned for their musical than for their artistic talent. That Bachs were distinguished in fields other than that of music has been conspicuously ignored; such neglect (even among German scholars) is not only unjust to men of outstanding skill, but an impediment to understanding the pattern of the new age in German culture.

At the beginning of the eighteenth century ambitious Bachs had looked towards Saxony for inspiration—to the capital city of Dresden, and then to Leipzig, the nexus of trade and culture. Many Bachs of the post-Johann-Sebastian era looked to Berlin. The capital of Prussia not only offered opportunity; in an age of war it also promised some security, in the sense that a sort of insurance appeared available through putting one's money on the odds-on favourite—Frederic II. Security is one thing and freedom another. Although any modern idea of freedom (if such there be) was unthinkable in the eighteenth century, there were—apart from the philosophers—degrees of freedom within different social systems. For those who entertained notions of a wider freedom the republic of Hamburg was a principal attraction in Germany; while across the sea the libertarian principles thought to be endemic in the British way of life often called. The sons of Sebastian Bach therefore severally operated, in Dresden—briefly, in Berlin, in the tiny duchy of Bückeburg, in Hamburg and in London. The careers of Friedemann, Carl Philipp Emanuel, Johann Christoph Friedrich and Johann Christian reflect the passage of events that so radically altered the balance of power within Germany and within Europe, and that heralded the shape of modern times.

Quite properly the sons of Bach are written of as pioneers of a new kind of music, although it is sometimes overlooked that they were not the only ones. (At the same time their alleged disrespect for their father's music is more than somewhat exaggerated). The new kind of music, however, was activated by many factors, of which the most were in origin extra-musical. In a general sense the sons of Bach were able, well-informed men with wide experience, and with many contacts and interests beyond the limited sphere of professional music. The passing of the old dispensation meant that the musician-craftsman of the familiar Thuringian-Saxon order was outmoded. The writing had of course been on the wall for some considerable time, as witness the suave progress of Telemann or, for that matter, of the expatriate Handel. The force behind change, the architect of the new age, was Frederic the Great. And it happened that Frederic was a passionate lover of music.

The son of Frederic William I and Sophia Dorothea (issue of the ill-starred marriage of George I of Hanover and England with Sophia Dorothea of Celle), Frederic inherited the qualities and defects of his parents in more or less equal proportion. The ensuing dialectic between the warring elements could have led to the madhouse. In fact its conclusion was the emergence of a type of statesman later to become increasingly familiar in German history: the absolute, professional, autocrat. Steeled by early adversity—the relationship with his uncouth father was traumatic in the extreme—Frederic sought refuge in philosophy (he was friend and patron of Voltaire) and in the fine arts. His first music tutor was Gottlieb Hayne (1684–c.1758), cathedral organist in Berlin, whose conservative methods left their mark on the prince. But neither philosophy nor the refinements of culture were ends in themselves; they were means whereby the state of Prussia (backed up by the first-class military organization that he inherited) should be taken into a leading place at the conference tables of Europe. As crown prince, Frederic rusticated himself to an establishment at Rheinsberg, a little way north of Berlin, where he lived from 1736 to 1740. On his personal staff were two former *alumni* of the Dresden Kreuz Chor—the brothers Johann Gottlieb (1703–71) and Karl Heinrich Graun (1704–59). The former, at one time a pupil of Georg Pisendel, was the virtual founder of the Berlin orchestral tradition. The latter stimulated Frederic's interest in opera and, what in the long run was more important, his zeal for choral music. Also among the prince's retinue at Rheinsberg was the Bohemian composer Franz Benda (1709–86).

On the death of his father, early in 1740, Frederic succeeded to the Crown of Prussia. Five months after his accession Frederic, hitherto an unknown piece on the diplomatic chess-board, but not to remain so for long, commenced his prepared policy of territorial aggrandisement by going to war with Maria Theresa of Austria. To strengthen his frontiers and his economy Frederic intended the annexation of Silesia, the diminution of the power of Austria and Saxony, and the domination of Poland and Bohemia. Intermittently Europe was at war between 1740 and 1748, the Treaty of Aix-la-Chapelle, which concluded that period, being celebrated by Handel in his *Fireworks Music*. Frederic emerged from his first ordeal by fire greatly strengthened, having had the satisfaction of punishing the vacillating Saxons—for shifting their alliance from Prussia to Austria—by defeating their army at Kesseldorf outside Dresden in 1745. In 1756 war broke out again. Apprehensive of encirclement and of the intentions of the French, the Russians and the Austrians, Frederic, having faked a case against the Saxons, swept into Saxony in the late summer, half destroyed Dresden and set German against German in a private war that was part of a continental conflict. After many vicissitudes and a display of military genius that was to become a legend Frederic emerged from the Seven Years War with his country beyond dispute the most powerful and efficient in Europe and—in the end—at no greater expense than the loss of any reputation for integrity that he might ever have possessed. However, in an age in which morality in international affairs was non-existent, it is doubtful whether Frederic was any less moral in respect of European politics than any other ruler. His crime was to have been successful.

In the present context the relationship between Prussia and Saxony alone is significant. The polarity between Dresden and Berlin has already been noted. Frederic not only demanded the submission of Saxony for patent reasons of state, but also because of his envy of the cultural hegemony of the southern capital. Besides, those with long memories in Berlin had not forgotten the snub rendered to Frederic's grandfather when the Saxon Elector withheld recognition of his title of king.

Indolent, amiable, immoral and artistically perceptive, August III, of Poland and Saxony, won his cultural spurs with relative ease.

Affairs of state he left to his leading Minister, Heinrich von Brühl.

Musical life in Dresden was much influenced by August's consort, the Austrian archduchess Maria Josepha, who was a pupil of Giuseppe Porsile and a strong advocate of the cause of Italian music against French. The great name in Dresden was that of Hasse, whose wife Faustina was one of the stars in the Italianate operas he so effectively composed and/or directed. The orchestra was an orchestra of virtuosi, led by Pisendel, and counting among its members the flautists Quantz and Buffardin, the oboist Besozzi, the lutenist Sylvius Leopold Weiss and the violinist and early symphonist Johann Neruda. From 1733 until 1746 Wilhelm Friedemann Bach lived in Dresden. Music prospered, not only under royal patronage but also that of the aristocracy, among whom Count Algarotti—a Paduan and later a friend of Frederic the Great—and von Brühl, who maintained his own musical establishment, were conspicuous. The cultural life of Dresden continued over the misadventures of the Saxon army during the Silesian Wars. And then, suddenly, in 1756,

> before hostilities began, all Saxony was over-run by Frederic's troops. The electorate was ravaged, the capital bombarded and plundered, the King of Poland driven from his hereditary dominion to take refuge at Warsaw, and his army ignominiously made prisoners of war at Pirna.[1]

Dresden suffered many calamities during the Seven Years War. There were great fires that destroyed many houses in 1758 and 1759 (including the home of Eva Christina Schubart, wife of one of the Court musicians). Between 12th and 30th July 1760 the Prussians ravaged the city, of which the garrison was strengthened by the troops of Haydn's employer, Nicholas Esterházy, and of the Duke of Saxe-Gotha, and by 1,184 Croat mercenaries. Most of the famous buildings of the city were damaged, more than five hundred houses were demolished, eighty private citizens lost their lives and many others fled the country. Among these were musicians and musical instrument makers. The cause of all this was Frederic of Prussia.

THE ENLIGHTENED DESPOT

For better or worse Frederic the Great was a despot, but, as was said in mitigation, an 'enlightened despot'. In this role he granted religious toleration even when such tolerance was unfamiliar; he maintained the relatively high standards of social organization that already obtained in Prussia; he planned progressively in the field of education; he took in hand the development of Berlin, to make it at least an impressive capital city; and he sponsored literary, scientific and musical initiative. Isolated by the inflexibilities of his own temperament, by estrangement from his wife and by the nature of his office, Frederic found in music a therapy. His zeal outran his executant competence, and his performances on the flute, while applauded by a steady circle of sycophants, were often likely to drive his private musicians to despair. He was also a composer. But his views on the general place of the arts in society showed little of the wider aspirations of more advanced students of the *Aufklärung*.

'Let us be frank,' he wrote,

> the arts and philosophy are the property of the few. The great mass of the people and the common herd of the nobility remain what nature made them, namely evil animals.[2]

At Sans Souci—the residence commenced by von Knobelsdorff and continued by Johann Boumann (1706–76), with the sculptor Johann August Nahl in regular attendance—the king established his cultural headquarters. Here, amid a conjunction of baroque styles derived from Italian, French, Dutch and English models, unique in their restlessness and symbolic of Frederic's acquisitiveness in the aesthetic province, a new age of German music was inaugurated. The king was enthusiastic rather than efficient, but from his enthusiasm there ultimately emerged the antithesis to his philosophical proposition quoted above.

> . . . At six the concert commenced, and lasted one hour. Frederic assisted on the flute; and it may be believed that, if he happened to break the time, his fault was repaired by those who accompanied him, or that they imparted to themselves the blame. However, by degrees, as he lost his teeth, he acquired a lisp that was extremely unfavourable to the sounds of his flute.[3]

For almost thirty years, during which Johann Joachim Quantz provided flute concertos at the rate of one a month, the second son of Sebastian Bach was Frederic's regular accompanist. Quantz had been Frederic's flute tutor since 1728 when he had visited Berlin with the Saxon Court and been engaged as Frederic's teacher by the Queen of Prussia.

EMANUEL BACH AT THE PRUSSIAN COURT

Carl Philipp Emanuel Bach (1714–88), a pupil of the Thomasschule, naturally learned music from his father, but without the intention of pursuing it as a career. Because he was left-handed he was excused from studying string technique—as his elder brother Friedemann had done—and was dedicated to the keyboard. Paternal ambition stretched beyond music, and Emanuel enrolled in the University of Leipzig to study law—the foundation course for any public office. Commended by Ernesti for his competence, Emanuel transferred to the University of Frankfurt/Oder in 1734. It so happened that Frankfurt/Oder—a small Prussian city on the Polish frontier—was in need of such a one as Emanuel, since the existing musical academy was temporarily leaderless. Emanuel, a fine performer, already skilled in composition and acquainted with the many musicians of his father's acquaintance, was immediately drafted. For four years he took a leading part in the concert life of Frankfurt, at the end of which the opportunity of travelling in the company of a young aristocrat presented itself. In fact Emanuel got no further than Rheinsberg, where he was brought to the notice of the crown prince as a promising prospect for the future of Prussian music.

There was no doubt a certain amount of influence brought to bear at this point, not only from the Grauns (Gottlieb had been Friedemann Bach's teacher in Merseburg), but also from the virtuoso lutenist Sylvius Weiss (1686–1750), an acquaintance both of Sebastian and Friedemann Bach[4] and one of the instructors of Frederic when he was crown prince. Emanuel Bach was added to the strength of the Rheinsberg staff and, two years later, in 1740, he had the honour (which he sufficiently regarded to note it in his brief autobiography) of accompanying Frederic in his first performance on the flute after becoming king. At this point Frederic, with his hands on the treasury, was able to increase his musical staff to which, among others from Dresden, Quantz was added. Pieces for flute were of course *de rigueur*. Emanuel Bach did his stint, but not to the extent of Quantz, who was writing his three hundredth flute concerto at the time of his death.

A year after the king's accession Emanuel Bach was visited by his father. In 1744 Emanuel married Johanna Maria Dannemann (*b.* 1724), daughter of a Berlin wine merchant, at the Petrikirche. A year later their first son, Johann Adam, was born, to be followed by a daughter, Anna Karoline Philippine, in 1747, and a second son, Johann Sebastian,

in 1748. The naming of Johann Sebastian after his illustrious grandfather was stimulated by the celebrated visit of the old man to Berlin
and Potsdam in the early summer of 1747. He was accompanied by
Wilhelm Friedemann, recently appointed Kantor in the Market
Church in Halle.

In the Hamburg newspaper *Relations-Courier* of 16th May a notice
concerning the elder Bach's visit to Potsdam—only a few days after
Frederic had moved into the newly completed *Sans Souci*—appeared,
with the date-line 'Berlin, 11th May 1747'.[5]

This visit would have taken place sooner but for the fact that while
Prussia and Saxony were at war permission for Saxons to travel in
Prussia was restricted; even in the Age of Reason German families
suffered division on account of the crassness of their rulers. By 1747,
however, normality temporarily prevailed, and a frequent post-coach
service from Leipzig to Berlin (by way of Düben, Wittenberg, Treuen-
briezen, Beelitz and Potsdam), at a cost of three thalers, made the
excursion reasonably comfortable and not too expensive. Three years
later, on the death of his father, Emanuel took the coach in the opposite direction to register his claims to the succession to the Leipzig
Kantorate. Other candidates were Emanuel's old friend Krebs and
August Friedrich Graun (1699–1765), elder brother of the two Berlin
Grauns and Kantor at Merseburg since 1729. But the post was filled,
by the intervention of the Saxon minister, von Brühl, by Johann
Gottlieb Harrer (1703–55).

The fact that Emanuel was not entirely content with his Prussian
appointment is indicated by his attempts to vacate it in 1750 and again
in 1753 for posts which, superficially at least, were less obviously
attractive. There was in Zittau, it is true, a Silbermann organ, but the
town was remote and without special distinction. None the less on the
death of Krause, Kantor at St John's Church, Emanuel filed his
application. So too did his brother Friedemann, and his brother-in-law
Altnikol, of Naumburg, as well as the persistent Krebs. In the event,
although the committee at Zittau were flattered by the interest of two
Bachs, and accepted their candidature as prestigious, they opted for
Johann Trier (1716–90). A student of theology at Leipzig who matriculated in 1741, Trier became a pupil of J. S. Bach and in 1746 made
himself useful by directing concerts at Bach's Collegium Musicum.
For the next two years he played the violin and cembalo in the *Grosses
Concert* (the next stage beyond the Collegium Musicum towards the
Gewandhaus Concerts), and in 1750 he was among the unsuccessful

candidates for the St Thomas Kantorate. Trier's moment of triumph came when he was preferred to two Bachs for the organist's post at Zittau.[6] One benefit came to Emanuel, however, through his polite demonstration of discontent; the king put up his stipend—which is more than happened to the luckless Friedemann at Halle. None the less he continued to find the conditions of Court music somewhat irksome, not least the royal incapacity for precision in time-keeping as he pursued his daily excursions through the wide ranges of the flute music provided for him by Quantz and others. In 1756 Frederic found a more understanding accompanist in the person of Carl Friedrich Fasch (1736–1800), a lad of twenty who came into the royal presence with the eagerness that Emanuel Bach had displayed almost twenty years before.

Emanuel's life in Berlin, however, was more seriously disturbed than by mere professional annoyances. For during the Seven Years War, when the military fortunes of the king were at their lowest point and the very survival of his kingdom in doubt, Berlin was in danger of invasion by the Russians. In August 1758, with many towns and villages in Prussia lying in ruins, it was thought expedient by Emanuel Bach to evacuate himself and his family to Zerbst, in Saxony, where they stayed for a month. During this month Frederic fought the fiercest battle of his career at Zorndorf, near Küstrin, to hold the Russians. The Bachs lodged with Johann Friedrich Fasch, the local Kapellmeister, who was the father of Emanuel's colleague. In the July following Emanuel served in the Berlin militia, hastily called up as a last defence for the city. On 12th August 1759 the Prussians were beaten at Kunersdorf, but the Russians failed to follow up their victory. So much were the times out of joint, and so long did it take for a semblance of normality to return to the sphere of culture, that it was impossible for Emanuel to do anything about moving to another sphere of activity. It was not until 1767 that he saw an opportunity of establishing himself elsewhere. On 15th June of that year his godfather Telemann died.

On 20th October 1767 the committee responsible for filling Telemann's place in Hamburg met, and voted on the four candidates: Rolle of Magdeburg; Hermann Raupach (1728–c.1786), son of a Hamburg musician, and at this moment away in Paris; Johann Christoph Friedrich Bach (1732–95) half-brother of Emanuel, now Kapellmeister in Bückeburg; and Emanuel himself. Raupach and the Bückeburg Bach received ten votes each, Rolle and Emanuel each seventeen.

On a second ballot, taken on 3rd November 1767, the last-named had twelve votes to Rolle's eleven. Neither Raupach—who went on to establish himself as opera director in St Petersburg—nor the Bückeburg Bach—who happily remained in that place for the rest of his life—gained a single vote.[7] So Emanuel just made it and, at the age of fifty-three, began a new and ambitious chapter in his life. In his autobiography he rather sadly complained of the principal regret of his life. 'My service in Prussia', he observed, 'never allowed me time to travel abroad. . . .'[8] In fact Emanuel found no opportunity to go out of Germany when he lived in Hamburg but at least contact with foreign visitors was easier there than it had been in Berlin.

THE INTELLECTUALS OF BERLIN

The place occupied by Emanuel Bach among the progressive thinkers of Berlin is indicated by Johann Wilhelm Ludwig Gleim (1719–1803), who detailed Ramler, Lessing, Sulzer, Agricola, Krause, Bach and the Grauns among the most prominent. Musicians were not only tolerated but welcomed as members of what became a regular club. In a letter to Gleim, Ramler particularly named Quantz, Agricola, Nichelmann and 'our dear father Krause'.[9] Those who were interested in the arts and in philosophy met together almost daily—'sometimes on land, sometimes on water'. 'What pleasure it was', Gleim continued, 'to vie with the swans in swimming on the Spree, and to lose oneself, in this company and among a thousand young women, in the Tiergarten.'[10]

Frederic the Great set out to be an all-round man, and he surrounded himself with those who shared his ideals in this direction. Ramler's 'dear father Krause' was an outstanding example. Christian Gottfried Krause (1719–70), the son of a town musician in Silesia, entered the University of Frankfurt/Oder in 1741 to study law. This he did with success, but, musically gifted, he followed Johann Gottlieb Janitsch (1708–63)—later double-bass player and composer for the Court balls of Frederic, and founder of a Berlin music club—and Emanuel Bach in running the public concerts in Frankfurt. Unlike Bach, however, Krause wisely stuck to law and, after being on the staff of General von Rothenburg, practised as an advocate in Berlin. There, supported by five domestic servants, he kept open house, and his music salon became famous. In 1748 Krause discussed the principal musical problems of the day in his *Lettre à Mr le Marquis de B. sur la différence entre la*

School note-book embellished by its owner—W. F. Bach

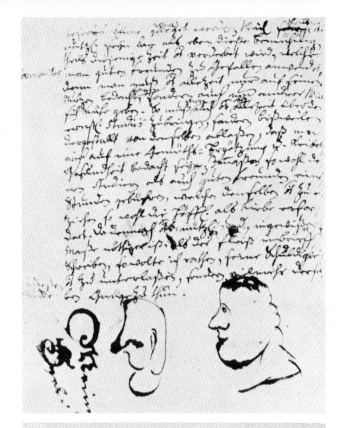

List of instruments at the Marktkirche, Halle, in the time of W. F. Bach

Frederic the Great as Commander-in-Chief, from *Historische und geographische Nachricht von ... Dressden, 1761*

Frederic the Great playing the flute, copper engraving by Peter Haas

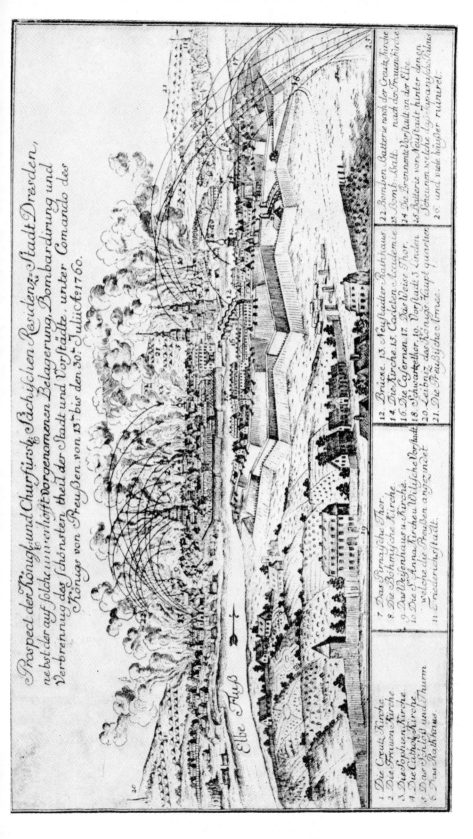

Bombardment of Dresden by the Prussians, 1760, from *Historische und geographische Nachricht, 1761*

W. F. Bach, pencil drawing by P. Gülle

C. P. E. Bach, drawing by Andreas Stöttrup

Ideale Landschaft,
1776, painting by
J. S. Bach II

Portrait of Johann Wilhelm Treiber, by G. F. Bach

Portrait of Major von Uglansky, by J. P. Bach

Portrait of Luise-Eleonore, Duchess of Sachsen-Meiningen, by J. P. Bach

musique italienne et française (Berlin). During the Seven Years War Krause, principally aided by Quantz, continued to give concerts at his house, and it is probable that a number of Bach's works of this period were there performed for the first time.

Gleim, a native of Halberstadt and a graduate of the University of Halle, where he was a member of a talented group (see page 191), came to Potsdam as a private tutor in 1740. Known to posterity through his racy account of his first meeting with Goethe in 1776, Gleim was a most influential figure in helping to liberate German literature from a too subservient attitude to French influences. Although he returned to his native town, on the edge of the Harz country, in 1747 Gleim retained influence in Berlin. A perfervid supporter of the warrior king, he was highly respected as a purveyor of war poems, and in this may be seen as a precursor of a later unhappy tradition.

If Gleim and Krause were relatively liberal, then Johann Georg Sulzer (1720–79), the twenty-fifth (!) child of a town councillor in Winterthur, Switzerland, was conservative. Trained as a minister he went to a teaching post in Berlin, by way of a private tutorship in Magdeburg, in 1747. His constricting moral principles as applied to aesthetics marked him out as a hard-liner, and brought him into dialectical conflict with Moses Mendelssohn, Friedrich Nicolai and Lessing, who, like Ramler, was sometime a teacher in the so-called *Kadettenanstalt* in Berlin. He left Berlin in 1763, having achieved membership of the revitalized *Académie des Sciences et Belles-Lettres* in 1750, and having done the basic work on his encyclopedic *Allgemeine Theorie der schönen Künste* (published in Leipzig, 1771–4)—a composite work from many hands.

The constant theme of this company was the nature and function of the arts, their relation to philosophy and (through consideration of indigenous literary values) their national significance. The unspoken aim of the dialectic of the period was to establish a distinctive German style, both in literature and music.

MUSICAL LIFE IN BERLIN

During his Berlin years Emanuel had the pleasure of the companionship of many old friends; some indeed were pupils of his father, and—as has already been suggested (see pages 138–9)—by no means unmindful of the debt owed to Sebastian. Kirnberger, a Court violinist, was appointed to the Household of the Princess Anna Amalia in 1758, by which appointment he was enabled to exercise a strong influence on the musical life of the city. In 1750 Agricola was given a place as court composer, and nine years later he succeeded Karl Heinrich Graun as director of the court music. Christoph Nichelmann (1717–62), not only a student of J. S. Bach in Leipzig but also of Keiser, Telemann and Mattheson in Hamburg, was, like Emanuel, cembalist to Frederic the Great. Marpurg was also in and out of Berlin.

Like Emanuel Bach, Marpurg was a polymath, only more so. In so far as he was a musician (and he was much else besides) his enthusiasm was tilted away from composition (although he was not quite negligible as a composer) towards pedagogic and critical literature. He was indeed one of the founders of a distinctively critical music literature as well as being a considerable popularizer of music. As editor of anthologies of popular music he contributed much to the consolidation of amateur taste. Somewhere behind Marpurg's belletristic writings lay the influence of Gottsched, whose Biedermann style carried through with the entertaining *Kritische Briefe über die Tonkunst, mit kleinen Clavierstücken und Singoden, begleitet von einer musikalischen Gesellschaft in Berlin*, issued by Friedrich Birnstiel from 1759. One of these letters, addressed to Emanuel Bach on 14th July 1759, was a satirical essay on the theoretical aberrations of Georg Sorge (see page 304 n.59).

Bach himself moved easily in this talented company. As harpsichordist and pianist he was recognized as possessing exceptional gifts; he was the outstanding performer in Germany, and his manner of performance enshrined the attitudes of his contemporaries. Emanuel wished to expand his knowledge of the world, but like his father his opportunities for displaying his executant skills were limited. In the long run, however, that was probably not disadvantageous to the emancipation (as it seemed) of German musical thought. The operative vogue words of the time were *Ausdruck* (expression) and *Empfindung* (feeling).[11] These were words that signified less to Sebastian Bach than to his sons—even though they were in the intellectual air of Leipzig during the period of his Kantorate. Emanuel gave them musical substance, not so much by the general character of his playing as by the manner in which he played his own compositions. These were the crux of the matter, and they opened the eyes especially of the young Haydn, as well as those of Mozart and Beethoven. What is more, the perceptive in other lands recognized their character, as is shown by the enthusiasm of the music-loving English poet, Thomas Gray. Emanuel Bach began to become a familiar name to the more cultivated and

British music-lovers surprisingly early, for a set of Concertos for Harpsichord or Organ (Wtq. 11, 14, 25) was published by John Walsh in or about 1750. The composer was described as 'Sign. Bach (of Berlin)'. The six sonatas of Op. II (Wtq. 51) were published by Walsh in 1763, and twelve years later were reissued by Longman, Lukey. In the 1770s other works by Emanuel were published by the firms of Bremner and Welcker.

As an employee of Frederic the Great, Emanuel was able to take occasional leave of absence, which enabled him to make excursions at least to other German towns. In 1751 he visited the poet Gleim in Halberstadt and also Johann Mattheson in Hamburg. This visit—in the company of an Italian violinist named Pio and a Swedish glocken-spiel player named Seliger—was described with much enthusiasm by Mattheson, who found their conversation enlivening. In the following year Emanuel was in the land of his remoter ancestors, for he visited Gotha. The Kapellmeister at that time (preferred to Agricola for the post) was Georg Benda, brother of Franz, one of Emanuel's Berlin colleagues. In 1754 there was occasion to go to Kassel, where Bach's portrait was painted by Johann Friedrich Reifenstein (1709–93). With a particular interest in painting, Bach would have been stimulated by Reifenstein—a friend of Winckelmann—whose zeal for the antique led him to join the large German artist colony in Rome, where he died. Reifenstein, who was also acquainted with Goethe, was one of those who helped to create the climate in which Bach's second son showed such promise as a painter.

Emanuel was a man of charm, intelligence and some passion. His performance at the keyboard represented very much an extension of his personality. In that lay its significance. 'Music', he said, 'must, above all, move the heart.'[12] Charles Burney visited Emanuel in Hamburg in 1773 and eloquently described how Emanuel effected this aim at the keyboard.[13]

As a composer Emanuel Bach was various. Like any other musician with a similar background—a background, that is, of solid profes-sionalism—he was adaptable. Although (according to Burney) he affected to despise the pedantry of 'learned music', and particularly canons, he was in no way indifferent to the emotional and structural properties inherent in counterpoint. Nor did he consider a student properly equipped until he had learned the approved, traditional techniques. So he demonstrated by his fugal compositions, of which several were published by Marpurg as lucid guides to proper procedure.

It is apparent, however, that Emanuel's attitude to contrapuntal balance was not that of his father. There is a general tendency towards smoothness of texture, a concession—implicit rather than explicit—to the claims of harmony. This is shown by the canonic episode from the A major fugue, published (with annotations) in Marpurg's *Raccolta delle più nuove Composizioni di Cembalo di differenti Maestri ed Autori per l'anno 1757* (Leipzig) and also in Clementi's *Practical Harmony*, London, 1810 (I, page 110).

At the other extreme lies the fantasia type of figuration that distinguishes the vigorous two-part fugue in D minor published in *Clavierstücke verschiedener Art* (Erste Sammlung) of 1763 and the stormy *Allegro di molto* C minor fugue of the same collection. Both of these were also republished by Clementi, and may be recognized as authentic vehicles of the *Sturm und Drang* mood. Emanuel's restlessness of temperament is well revealed in his not infrequent spasms of impatience within contrapuntal textures. It is not difficult to see how such works held particular appeal for Beethoven in his youth.

The German tradition of counterpoint, although removed from the central area of musical composition, was zealously preserved for church use, and cultivated by Emanuel when, in Hamburg, his commitments more frequently led him in this direction. In youth, however, and through his middle years in Berlin, he was fascinated by the emancipatory impulses inherent in the Francophilia that inspired the melodies of Sperontes, the regard for tone-colour that motivated the flute sonatas of Quantz, and the free movement within the keyboard writing of such transitional composers as Johann Paul Kunzen (1696–1757); Johann Nikolaus Tischer (1706–70), a pupil of Sebastian and organist at Schmalkalden; and Michael Scheuerstuhl (1705–70). These three composers (as also J. S. Bach) were in large measure responsible for domesticating the Italian concerto in Germany by composing such concertos for clavier solo. Scheuerstuhl, a *Mädchenschulmeister* at Wilhelmsdorf, was a notable exponent of *galant* method, and his *Sechs ganz Neue Galanterie-Stück oder sogenannte Murcki aufs Clavier* (Nürnberg, 1737) was a considerable aid to legitimizing charm—a quality in which, according to Frederic the Great, German culture was singularly lacking. The *Mädchenschulmeister* had an eye on the *Mädchen* for whom he was responsible, and saw the prospect of a wider market when such pupils discovered that practice at the keyboard could be less of a duty and more of an entertainment. No composer was more inclined to be 'with it' than Emanuel Bach (the gay side of whose nature was attested by Gleim), and his cultivation of the amateur was one reason for his stylistic development. Simplification was not merely an end to be pushed for aesthetic reasons; it was—when more and more young ladies were taking to the keyboard—of practical signi-ficance. In modern times we might speak of the 'liberalization' of music that took place in Germany during the reign of Frederic II (often, to be truthful, against the wishes of the monarch, whose musical tastes stayed in the groove of his own self-esteem), and Emanuel Bach was one of the liberalizers.

Throughout his Berlin years he wrote a mass of minor clavier (and other pieces) for amateur use; sometimes recalling the techniques and styles of his father, of his godfather and even of the distant Handel (in suites entitled sonatas), but more often the manner of Rameau. Towards the end of the Seven Years War the times were propitious for an all-out attack on the potential market. Even in 1760 (when Berlin was occupied for a time by Russians and Austrians), and until 1763, Birnstiel issued his *Musikalisches Allerley von verschiedenen Tonkünstlern*. Published weekly— each section appearing on Saturday at a cost of one groschen—this anthology contained odes, airs, polonaises, minuets, marches, fugues, sonatas, symphonies and so-called 'characteristic pieces', some arranged for duet, some for trio, after 'German, Italian and French taste'. Emanuel obliged with a piece a week more or less, of which a large number were more French than the French. In this respect one may note, for example, *La Complaisante* (20th December 1760) and *La Capricieuse* (27th December 1760) for ease and insouciance; or the more determinedly expressive *La Xenophon* in C sharp major (6th December 1760) with its companion, contrasting, piece *La Sybille* in C sharp minor. On 23rd–30th May 1761 Bach published a grave set of dances—Courante, Sarabande, Minuet, 1, 2, and 3, and Gigue—and two months later he provided a new-style sonata, in three movements, after the Italian manner. The figuration and plan of the first movement is recognizably 'classical', the slow movement a characteristic aria for keyboard. The sonata pattern was exhibited by other contributors: by Rolle of Magdeburg, Müller, the Court organist in Dessau, and Cramer, the Court musician of Gotha, a *Claviersymfonie* by whom was published on 11th April 1761. Nor were other composers backward in exploiting the 'expressiveness' of which Emanuel was an acknow-ledged master. One of the most interesting works published in the *Musikalisches Allerley* was the *Enharmonische Claviersonate* of Gottfried Heinrich Stoelzel (1690–1749). A man of enormous energy and wide experience, Stoelzel was Kapellmeister at Gotha for thirty years until his death. The *Enharmonische Sonate*, a study in chromatic harmony, which Emanuel Bach may have picked up when in Gotha in 1754, promised a limitless broadening of harmonic horizons and infinite possibilities of *Empfindung* and *Ausdruck*, and pointed, across the classical era that was to come, to the Romantic period. Chronology is not the best guide to musical thought. For Romanticism, or expres-sionism, was implicit in the whole German attitude to life; in the period of Emanuel Bach, and under the force of his personality, it began to appear in music in specific form.

MATTERS OF STYLE

The last section of the second part of the *Versuch über die wahre Art das Clavier zu spielen* (1762) deals with the subject of the 'Free Fantasia', and the effective word is 'freedom'. The manner of free expression is shown in the brief *Fantasia in D major*, given as an example; even more in the *G minor Fantasia*, printed in the *Musikalisches Vielerley* (Hamburg 1770).[14] From the latter model sprang the patterns that informed the improvisatory fantasies of Haydn, Mozart and Beethoven. When Burney visited Berlin he was not enamoured of the 'scientific' musicians, observing that:

> from all the learned and operose calculations of professed mathematicians, not a single piece of practical music has ever been produced, that is supportable to the ears of persons of taste; so true it is, that the operations of cool and deliberate reflection, have less power over our feelings, than those of passion and enthusiasm.[15]

Correctly stretching back this zest for theory to cover Emanuel's residence in Berlin he commented that:

> although Bach's style did not insinuate itself into the favour it deserved at the court of Berlin, it has been imitated and adopted by the performers upon keyed instruments in every other part of Germany.[16]

It is then hardly surprising that Emanuel's Romantic feelings intensified when he left Berlin, and that his Hamburg works range even more widely.

The ideal of classicism was balance. As the German composer—even of the late Baroque saw it—this hinged on a confluence of French, Italian and native idioms and practices, on a happy marriage of song and dance, on a perfect equipoise of melody and harmony. As early as 1723 the cry of the young, as stated by a fictitious composer of the new age in Tosi's *Art of Florid Song*, was 'We hate melancholy'. The consequence was, as stated by Szabolcsi, melody that was 'delicate, tender, nicely modulated and clear—like the dance'.[17] Emanuel Bach followed the fashion of the day from the outset of his career as a composer and, particularly in his song settings, arrived at a pretty rococo staging-post. So, in a pastorella to words by his father's friend, Mariane von Ziegler, he decorated the salon with a casual, and affecting, elegance.

Published in Gräfe's *Sammlung, III* (1741), this piece was reissued in 1762 by Arnold Werner (printed by Johann Gottlieb Immanuel Breitkopf) in a set of Emanuel's *Oden mit Melodien*. The clarity of melodic outline that distinguishes this set was a feature of Emanuel's song style. In due course, however, he deepened the significance of vocal melody by providing a new relationship with keyboard accompaniment, after the principles declared by Krause and his fraternity.

Because he was a master of keyboard effect he saw the possibilities inherent in an interdependence between vocal line and instrumental textures that were more than a support on the one hand or a foil on the other, and he went a long way towards establishing the essential character of German Lied. In so doing he also went a long way towards the ratification of the German sonata-symphony-concerto form, that complex of song and dance, of rationalism and imagination. The direction that Emanuel took was dictated by the nature of the cultural activity which both surrounded and involved him in Berlin and Potsdam.

Up to the time of his departure from Berlin Emanuel Bach had composed a quite formidable body of works. Of these many—dances, brief instrumental pieces, some slender chamber music—were ephemeral, comprising teaching material and casual offerings to amateurs. Others, more substantial, were composed under contract or in response to commissions. A third category represented music that Emanuel wanted to compose. To this he referred in his autobiography as 'the few pieces I wrote for my own pleasure', which was annotated further by mention of 'some trios, solos and concertos, that I wrote in all freedom, and for my own use'. Composers at all times had written for their own pleasure, but Bach's deliberate conjunction of freedom and pleasure coincided with an upsurge of libertarian philosophy, of which he may or may not have been aware. This philosophy centres on the theme of the liberty of the individual. The major works of Jean Jacques Rousseau, culminating in *La Nouvelle Héloïse* (1761) and *Du Contrat Social* (1762) were published during the severe years of the Seven Years War, when Berliners in particular were aware of the major disadvantages that could stem from a dictatorial regimen. Burney refused to attempt an analysis of the origins of Bach's style, contenting himself with the ascription of its singular excellences 'to nature alone', which—psychologically speaking—seems fair enough. The master of the free fantasia believed in the efficacy of improvisation in catalysing the musician's ideas; and many of his ideas came direct from the fingers at the keyboard. In this Emanuel Bach may be seen as a precursor of Robert Schumann. In round figures, and excluding miscellaneous pieces, Bach left Berlin with more than a hundred clavier sonatas or sonatinas, seven sonatas for organ, nine symphonies, two sonatinas for two claviers and orchestra and more than thirty clavier concertos.

Of the Berlin sonatas the first published set of six, of 1742, were dedicated to the king. Three years later a second set of six were dedicated to a pupil and friend, Karl Eugen, Duke of Württemberg. In 1760 a third set was inscribed to Princess Amalia, to whom Bach, as the other Berlin musicians, was greatly indebted—not least of all for her genuine understanding of their aims. The most important of the works of this period were the clavier concertos, and the so-called sonatinas for clavier and orchestra; first, because idiomatically they showed Emanuel's talents comprehensively; second, because more than any other works of the period they effectively conveyed music across the bridge from baroque to classical, with a promise of further developments.

Emanuel composed some concertos in Leipzig and some in Frankfurt/Oder in which, in some particulars, he reserved the right to call on his father's experience as, for instance, when in the concerto of 1737 he based the slow movement on a *ciaccona* bass motiv. But his inspiration was fundamentally harmonic, so that fertilization of melody by the triad formula became a commonplace. Formally Emanuel's concerti were founded on rondo principle, with alternating *tutti* and *solo* episodes. He was responsible for the rondo assuming independence and significance as a formal procedure, and in his slow movements in rondo form he produced 'echte Sturm—und Drangwerke'.[18] The concertos were in three movements, usually *allegro–adagio–allegro*, and modestly scored with accompaniment for strings. A number were alternatively available for some instrument other than clavier (or organ, which was occasionally prescribed), most often, and for obvious reasons, the flute. The D major Concerto (Wtq. 27), with optional parts for flutes, oboes, trumpets or horns and drums, was exceptional, and it can only be surmised that in this year of 1750 there was some particular reason for presenting a concerto in more or less ceremonial manner. The sonatinas for clavier and orchestra belong to the closing years of the Seven Years War, when a satisfactory conclusion to this was first in sight and then consummated. These three works are all designed for fuller orchestral resources, wind instruments being incorporated in each score. In his later Hamburg concertos Emanuel included wind as a matter of course. The sonatinas are otherwise important in that they are based on sonata form as such, and show the influence of the procedures of the south German school, especially of Wagenseil, who was Emanuel's almost exact contemporary. In the sonatinas Emanuel also introduces the minuet, a type of movement that does not occur in his symphonies, and only once in a concerto—one of the concertos of the Hamburg period (Wtq. 43, No. 4 in C minor).

C. P. E. Bach—thanks to Haydn and Mozart and the testimony of many other writers—is shown to stand out as a major influence on the course of musical composition. In fact he was a member of a school—rather more than that perhaps, of a closely knit community of artists and writers of different kinds. He was also a member of a closely knit family group. The school existed because of the conditions of time and place; because of the king who would be a philosopher. So far as the family was concerned each musician member made his own distinctive mark, as also did some who were not primarily musicians. The work of any one member of the family may only properly be understood in relation to that of the others. Those of this generation combined in exposing new paths to follow. Classicism in music was formulated not so much by C. P. E. Bach as by C. P. E. Bach, Brothers & Co. The family pattern, with its many involutions, is the theme of the next four chapters, from which C. P. E. Bach will rarely long be absent. His brothers, half-brothers and cousins acknowledged him, in matters of music at all events, as the head of the family, and his accomplishments and opinions were generally heeded by all. But deference to his judgments and respect for his talents were no impediments to individual development. The independence of the Bachs was notorious. It was as strong as ever in the generation of Emanuel. How it showed depended partly on personality but also on environment.

When the time came for Emanuel to leave Berlin the king was not altogether pleased. He disliked change within his establishment, and Bach, if not honoured as posterity considers he should have been, was an ornament to the Court. Moreover, estranged from Voltaire and full of grief on account of the death of his favourite nephew, Prince Henry, he was in low spirits. His permission for Emanuel to leave was grudging and delayed. Princess Amalia was also sad at his departure. For Amalia music was a chief consolation in life. Embittered by a broken romance with Baron Trenck, an aide-de-camp to the king, discouraged from matrimony by her brother's concern for her receiving the emoluments of the abbey of Quedlinburg (which post, although nominal, was best served by celibacy), she lived out her emotions through music. Her generosity to musicians was considerable and she collected together a great library—towards which the Quedlinburg stipend of £5,000 a year was a great help. On Emanuel's departure to

Hamburg she honoured him with the title of *Kapellmeister von Haus aus* (Director of Music *in absentia*).

As to Emanuel's brothers: the youngest, Johann Christian, was music master to the Queen of England, and the outstanding composer resident in London; Johann Christoph Friedrich was happily stationed in Bückeburg; while Wilhelm Friedemann, out of regular work, was living in Halle and hoping for something to turn up. In Weimar Johann Ernst Bach (1722–77), lawyer and civil servant as well as a composer of substantial gifts, was Kapellmeister. In Ohrdruf Bachs proliferated, the daughters and grand-daughters of Johann Christoph (1671–1721) often marrying pastors and schoolmasters, the sons and grandsons often serving modestly as Kantors. In Meiningen the two younger sons of Johann Ludwig were distinguishing themselves more as painters than as musicians. The area of the influence of the family was wide.

NOTES TO CHAPTER EIGHT

1. N. W. Wraxall, *Memoirs of the Courts of Berlin, Dresden, Warsaw and Vienna*, 1777–9, London, 1799, 2 vols. II, p. 152.

2. Quoted in G. P. Gooch, *Frederick the Great*, Hamden (Conn.), 1947, p. 190.

3. Dieudonné Thiébault, *Original Anecdotes of Frederic the Second*, London, 1805, 2 vols., I, p. 137.

4. Weiss was a member of the Dresden musical establishment during the time of Friedemann Bach's residence in the city. In the summer of 1739, together with Friedemann, he visited Sebastian—who had a particular interest in the lute—in Leipzig.

5. *See* Heinz Becker, 'Die Fröhe Hamburgische Tagespresse als Musikgeschichtliche Quelle', in *Beiträge zur Hamburgischen Musikgeschichte*, Hamburg, 1956, pp. 44–5.

6. *See* Heinrich Miesner, *Philipp Emanuel Bach in Hamburg*, Berlin, 1929, p. 116, and Martin Falck, *Wilhelm Friedemann Bach*, Lindau, 1956 edition, pp. 34–5.

7. Miesner (Note 6 above), p. 117.

8. Ludwig Nohl, *Musiker-Briefe* . . . , Leipzig (1867). p. 60.

9. Quoted by Walter Haacke, *Die Söhne Bachs*, 1962, pp. 12–13.

10. *See* Note 9 above.

11. *See* C. P. E. Bach, *Versuch über die wahre Art, das Clavier zu spielen*, I, Berlin, 1753, p. 122 f.

12. Nohl (*see* Note 8 above), p. 62.

13. Charles Burney, *The Present State of Music in Germany*, etc., 2nd ed., II, pp. 270–1.

14. Also in Clementi, *Practical Harmony*, I, p. 117 f.

15. Burney (*see* Note 13 above), II, p. 225.

16. Burney (*see* Note 13 above), p. 273.

17. Bence Szabolcsi, *Bausteine zu einer Geschichte der Melodie*, Budapest, 1959, p. 124.

18. Hans Engel, *Die Entwicklung des deutschen Klavierkonzertes von Mozart bis Liszt*, Leipzig, 1927, p. 4.

9

The Halle Bach

THE MOST GIFTED SON

The burden of being a son of Johann Sebastian Bach, so it would seem, weighed more heavily on Wilhelm Friedemann than on his brothers. The most gifted of the sons—according to his father's reckoning and, perhaps, according to the character and scope of his works—he was the least able to accommodate himself to social stresses. As a boy he promised great things. As organist in Dresden, generally acknowledged as a fine player, he hoped for, but did not get, a place at Court. He moved to Halle, lived there through the Seven Years War, quarrelled with authority and, after twenty years as Music Director of the Market Church, suddenly and impulsively resigned his office. For the remainder of his life he lived on the outskirts of official music, first in Braunschweig and then in Berlin. Throughout his life he was recognized as a musician of talent, and accorded the first place in Germany as an organist. Yet he dragged out his last years in poverty, and five years after him his widow also went to a pauper's grave.

Success breeds legends. So too does failure. Most particularly in the case of the unfulfilled genius, the great man *manqué*. The career of Friedemann Bach gave rise to many legends, some of which were given currency by Johann Friedrich Reichardt (1752–1814) and subsequently enlarged.

> One does not wonder about his fate when one has learned the kind of his disposition. All his penury was caused by his coarseness, his obstinate artist's pride, his extreme absentmindedness, and the sulky, quarrelsome characteristics that showed when he was drunk and took away from him any right to remain in proper society.[1]

Since this stood on German authority it is not surprising that English lexicographers seized on the case.

> [He] led a strolling, desultory life, until he died in distress and misery at Berlin. Thus ended a man, whom his contemporaries

acknowledged to be the most ingenious fugue and general organ player, and one of the first musical savants of the age. But his eccentricities, intemperance and absence of mind were also extravagantly great, and many amusing instances thereof are recorded.[2]

Against many legends that set out to expose the deficiencies in Friedemann's character may be placed the one attempt to explain such as there were. A study of a case history in terms of psychology must take background into account. Within the Bach family there was an established record of mental instability (which, considering the size of the family, is hardly surprising). This has been summarized in this manner:

> A musically gifted son of Johann Sebastian Bach [by Anna Magdalena], Gottfried Heinrich (1724–63), became progressively insane through hebephrenia (schizophrenia); Friedemann, otherwise a musician of genius, was a—probably schizoid—psychopath. A sister of [J. S.] Bach's father died at the age of twenty-six, her mind gradually destroyed either through schizophrenia or imbecility. H. Lämmerhirt[3] mentioned the mystical undercurrent in [J. S.] Bach's character. His mother's family had a tendency to religious fanaticism and the cult of sectarianism. In all probability Bach himself may be seen as a carrier of a (compensatory) hereditary schizoid disposition.[4]

To this list of psychological casualties there should be added Johann Gottfried Bernhard, the third son of Sebastian by Maria Barbara, whose instability of temperament has already been noticed (see page 115).

The subject of abnormalities of genius still attracts the consideration of the psychologically expert (as well as inexpert), and the closeness of genius to madness still tends to be a tenet of belief. Certainly there were frequent deviations from the norm within the family, and the collision of the positive and negative factors in the family tradition in Friedemann certainly resulted in an inconveniently unco-ordinated personality. But his genius was considerable, arguably more than Emanuel's, and his contribution to the tradition of German music hardly less than that of his more competent brother.

The eldest son of a large family, as has already been seen, is in a vulnerable position within the family. In general he bears the greatest hopes of his mother, and also—more than likely—of his father. He is the one who is aware of domestic tensions, the one expected to take on particular functions in case of emergency. He is also liable to be called upon to control and to superintend his younger brothers and sisters. In the eighteenth century the family ties for a child were almost exclusive. The home was the undisputed centre of his existence. Wilhelm Friedemann Bach was born in Weimar, the second child of Sebastian and Maria Barbara. Catharina Dorothea, the first-born, was two years older than Friedemann. When he was three years old twins were born, and died. Other children—Emanuel and Gottfried Bernhard—came in 1714 and 1715. One may assume the uneven cycle of child-birth to have been interrupted by miscarriages. Over and above the memories of more children coming into the restricted quarters in which the Bachs lived in Weimar, and of a mother withdrawn from regular functions of the household from time to time, there was almost certainly at least some vague recollection of his father's discontent with the duke. Particularly would he have come to know of this just prior to the family's remove to Köthen, which took place when Friedemann was seven years old. Three years later his music lessons with his father were immortalized by the *Clavierbüchlein vor Wilhelm Friedemann Bach*,[5] commenced by Sebastian on 22nd January. In this systematic collection of exercises and pieces the care which Sebastian took in inculcating sound habits through his teaching is evident. Apart from the pieces composed by himself (the great majority) there were examples from Johann Christian Richter,[6] Gottfried Heinrich Stoelzel[7] and Telemann. In the summer of that year Friedemann's mother died. He was then ten years old, old enough for this loss indelibly to etch itself on his mind and there to create an emotional turbulence not to be understood by himself nor perhaps anyone else. There followed the need to accept a young stepmother, and to live again with the regular arrival of new half-brothers and sisters. In 1723 the family moved to Leipzig—an exciting occasion for the older children as they went on their way, the family filling two coaches, their household goods four waggons[8]—to a newly renovated house in a great city.

Friedemann, old enough to be companionable, was much in his father's company. 'Well, Friedemann,' Sebastian used to say, 'shall we go over to Dresden to hear the pretty tunes?'[9] This charming glimpse of the father-son relationship is authentic enough; Friedemann himself related it to Forkel in later life. Perhaps the 'pretty tunes' were not quite that to Sebastian himself; but they were much to the taste of Friedemann who, in due course, became a Dresdener by adoption. Sebastian visited Dresden in 1725, and gave an hour-long recital on Gottfried Silbermann's organ in the Sophienkirche.[10] He was there again to give another recital on the same instrument on 14th September 1731—one day after Hasse's *Cleofide* had had its *première*.[11] He also put in an appearance at Court. More than likely Friedemann was with his father on those, as on other unrecorded, occasions.

Meanwhile Friedemann was making his way through the principal educational foundations of Leipzig. Some of his exercises from 1723, 1725 and 1727, in St Thomas's School, remain[12] to show his relative diligence in Latin, Greek and German studies, and a talent for caricature that is demonstrated in sketches done in May 1727. A predilection for the grotesque, as evinced in his drawings, is shown also in his somewhat free translations of Latin maxims into German. For instance, *Sua veritati est acritudo* becomes *Wahrheit reucht in die Nasen wie die Zwiebel, ist unleidlich*.[13] There is a break in Friedemann's exercises during the latter part of 1726 and the first part of 1727, during which period he was lodged with Johann Gottlieb Graun in Merseburg to study the violin. In years to come he remembered Graun's tuition with gratitude, and there is no doubt that the more fluid style of Graun's techniques exerted a strong influence on Friedemann's development as a composer.

Towards the end of his school days, during which he was involved in the multifarious activities of the choir of St Thomas's, Friedemann was often a participant in Collegium Musicum performances, and at less formal musical evenings in his father's house. He played violin, organ and clavier, and—as Emanuel reported in his own autobiography —had the opportunity to meet those musicians of distinction who were his father's colleagues and friends, among whom the Hasses were honoured guests. On 5th March 1729 Friedemann enrolled as a law student in the University of Leipzig. In June, however, he was detached from his studies to undertake a mission for his father who, being sick, was unable to make the journey himself. Friedemann went over to Halle to invite Handel—briefly (and for the last time) visiting his aged mother—to meet the elder Bach in Leipzig. For one reason or another Handel (who by the time Friedemann came was on the point of departure from Halle anyway) had to decline the invitation. No doubt the nineteen-year-old Friedemann had his own satisfaction from meeting the great expatriate.

For the next four years Friedemann attended lectures in the university; he heard Ernesti and Jöcher on philosophy, Rudiger on logic, Kästner on institutional law, Joachim and Stieglitz on other aspects of jurisprudence, and Hausser and Richter on mathematics. He also took over some of his father's teaching commitments, and

Nichelmann, the future colleague of Emanuel, owed some part of his early instruction in keyboard technique to him. Before completing his university studies Friedemann wrote at least one considerable work, a concerto for clavier and strings in A minor (Falck 45), remarkable for its close-knit counterpoint, its brilliant exposition of advanced keyboard techniques and its passionate content. In his last student year Friedemann travelled to Thuringia, to observe his first duties as godfather, to Dorothea Wilhelmine—the younger daughter of Tobias Friedrich Bach (1695–1778)—who was born on 9th December, 1732.

LIFE IN DRESDEN

Owing to the death of Christian Pezold there was a convenient appointment as organist to be filled at the Sophienkirche—the Protestant Court Church—in Dresden, just when Friedemann was on the point of finishing his studies in Leipzig. He duly put in his application, fortified by his father's connection with the church and by Sebastian's assistance in drafting his letter of application (7th June, 1733). It was a time of general change in Dresden, for August 'the Strong' had died in February and August III (otherwise Friedrich August II of Poland) was on the throne. Both Bachs entertained hopes of preferment from the new sovereign, but first of all Friedemann had to be levered into the vacant organ-loft. Although the stipend of the organist was miserably inadequate the post itself was attractive in that, with luck, it could be supplemented by a place at Court such as Pezold had held. There was then keen competition for the succession. After the applicants had been whittled down a short list was drawn up; besides Friedemann Bach there were Christoph Schaffrat (1709–63) and Johann Christian Stoy. At the trial on 22nd June the assessor was Hebenstreit, and he had no doubt that the 'younger Bach' was the best of the three candidates. On the next day Friedemann received his contract, and on 1st August he took possession of his organ. The salary was seventy-four thalers (and a few groschen), with a supplement of three barrels of beer. This latter could be exchanged for five thalers in the unlikely event of the organist having no taste for beer. The duties were confined to playing the organ, the arrangements for the ch al music resting in the hands of the Kantor of the Kreuz Chor, at that time, and until his death, Theodor Christlieb Reinhold (c. 1682–1755).

Although Friedemann was at the bottom end of the salary scale (Hasse was said to be earning six thousand thalers a year) life in Dresden held both attraction and opportunity. The intellectual climate was freer and less earnest than in the Hohenzollern establishment farther north. A warm wind blew from the south and especially through the melodies of Hasse. Reinhold—one of the great Kreuz Chor Kantors—maintained the Italianate tone that was the legacy of his predecessor Grundig, willingly accommodated his choristers to the requirements of the Court Opera, and organized memorable performances within the Church of the Holy Cross[14]. There were, for example, great goings on in Dresden in 1736, in which year the Elector of Saxony finally gained recognition as King of Poland on the return of Friedrich August from Warsaw. The Bolognese composer and chamber organist at Dresden, Giovanni Alberto Ristori (1692–1753), wrote the festal opera *Le Fate*—standing in for Hasse who, at the time, was away in Italy. Reinhold organized 'an excellent vocal and instrumental music for three choirs . . . with a fine echo effect resounding from the top of the cupola',[15] in his church. And during the three days in which the city was specially illuminated he performed his cantata, *Gaude, Dresda*, from the top of the tower, whence the mingled jubilation of voices and trumpets and drums rang across the inner city.

Friedemann Bach settled happily into his duties and began to lay the foundations of his formidable reputation as a virtuoso. Nor did he put aside his inclination to mathematics, finding a congenial tutor in one Waltz—later to be appointed *Hofmathematikus*. Already well acquainted with Hasse, he cultivated the society of the members of the Dresden orchestra, occasionally taking particular friends back to his father's house in Leipzig.[16] He maintained good relationships with Pisendel and Buffardin, the one-time tutor of his uncle Johann Jakob. The Russian ambassador, the insomniac Count Hermann Karl von Keyserlingk, was enthusiastic over Friedemann's musicianship, and helped him by recommending pupils. Of these the most celebrated was Johann Gottlieb Goldberg, whose connection with the Bach family has already been told (page 138). If Sebastian Bach was proud of his eldest son, Friedemann was also delighted to see how well his father was received in Dresden. On at least four occasions Sebastian was able to stay with Friedemann in Dresden. On 1st December 1736 the elder Bach, now composer to the Elector, gave a recital on Silbermann's new organ in the Church of Our Lady, in the presence of von Keyserlingk and other notabilities. He was in Dresden in May 1738, possibly on family business—for this was a period of anxiety concerning Johann Gottfried Bernhard at Sangerhausen. At the end of November 1741 (in which year a bourgeois Collegium Musicum was started) he was in Dresden again, on this occasion accompanied by Johann Elias who recorded his pleasure at the compliments paid to his kinsman. The intimacy between father and son is implied in the number of recorded occasions on which the two met, or travelled together. From this may be deduced a strong temperamental affinity between the two. Friedemann developed his father's 'artistic pride' to a high degree and, also inheriting a disposition to obstinacy, proved to be not always amenable as a subordinate.

In 1737 Marperger, the senior Court chaplain, took up his preaching duties at the Sophienkirche. So far as Friedemann Bach was concerned the zeal of Marperger for the services of the church meant that he had twice as much organ-playing to do as previously, although his stipend remained at its existing level. Even in 1740, when the organ-tuner received an addition to his earnings, those of the organist were kept where they were. Between 1737 and 1760 organ-playing in the church was in any event no pleasure. Since there was a rebuilding scheme in hand the interior of the building was in a chaotic condition, and Friedemann was—not unreasonably—concerned at the deterioration of the organ on account of the accumulating dust, and the impossibility of giving a proper recital.[17] In 1742 Ch. A. Gräbner (one of those who applied for the Sophienkirche post in 1733 and recommended by a testimonial from J. S. Bach!) moved from the Church of Our Lady to the Kreuzkirche, thus leaving vacant an attractive opening for Friedemann, as he thought. He duly applied for the post, but, to his chagrin and disgust, was turned down. Gottfried August Homilius (1714–85), who had been a pupil of Friedemann's father and was later to become Kantor in succession to Reinhold, was preferred. Disappointed in this ambition, Friedemann was also disheartened by the impossibility of obtaining any kind of Court appointment, and by a general reluctance to appreciate his efforts as a composer.

In this respect he was industrious according to the family tradition. His output included pieces for flute (for Buffardin?), miscellaneous keyboard works, concertos and symphonies. Since most of Friedemann's works of this time exist only in copies (some with doubtful ascriptions), and undated, it is difficult precisely to chart his progress as a composer. The clavier concertos in D major (Falck 41) and F major (Falck 44), the sonata for two claviers in F major (Falck 10), later edited by Brahms, and the D major sonata (Falck 3), were certainly composed at Dresden, where the last-named was published in

1745. Dedicated to Georg Ernst Stahl,[18] counsellor at the Court of the King of Prussia, and to be obtained from the composer in Dresden, from his father in Leipzig, or from his brother in Berlin, this work was appraised by Hubert Parry as of great significance.[19]

In looking for the link between the past and the future, between the intensity of the intellectualism of J. S. Bach and that of the expressionism of Beethoven, one finds it in the slow middle movement. The twice interpolated *adagio* of the first movement, paralleled by similar gestures in Emanuel Bach's manner, anticipates, of course, the dramatic Beethoven. It is, however, the middle movement *adagio* that commands attention, by the 'unvocal' character of melodic phrases, by the close-knit part-writing and by the way in which the second section discusses the opening bars in inversion.

MOVE TO HALLE

Friedemann Bach, after thirteen years, felt that he was getting nowhere in Dresden. As the Dedication of that in D major shows he had intended issuing a set of six sonatas, but lack of enthusiasm on the part of subscribers left him without the means of fulfilling his intention. And his prospects in the field of practical music in Dresden were dim. A worldly wise man might also have calculated at the end of 1745 that the prospects of Saxony, following military defeats by Prussia at Hennersdorf (on 24th November) and Kesselsdorf near Dresden, (15th December), were also beginning to look bleak. There was perhaps something to be said in favour of moving to Prussia. Although largely peopled by Saxons, the city of Halle belonged to the state of Prussia. In 1712 Friedemann's father had considered the post of Director of Music in Halle, but in the end allowed it to go to Gottfried Kirchhoff. Kirchhoff (another of the 1685 vintage of German musicians) died at the end of January 1746, leaving open one of the more attractive appointments in eastern Germany. The director of music—who was nominally organist of the Market Church—had the responsibility for superintending the music there and also in the other two great churches of the city—of St Ulrich and of St Moritz. Since there was no independent director of music in the university the organist of the Market Church supervised occasions there, as also for the municipality.

Friedemann Bach applied for the post of organist and *Director Musices*. On 16th April 1746 he received the appointment—the last permanent one of his career. To what extent he was helped by his father is not known, but it is likely that help from this quarter was not inconsiderable. At any rate, after his father's death Friedemann never applied for any job with success.

Then a place of some 14,000 inhabitants, Halle was provincial compared with Dresden or Leipzig. It had long since ceased to be a *Residenzstadt*, and economically it had made slow progress towards the recovery of economic prosperity since the Thirty Years War. But the university, favoured by the king as a nursery for future civil servants, was a powerful influence in the country. The Enlightenment, stemming from Thomasius and Francke, swung on, and when Friedemann Bach arrived in the city the outstanding scholar was Christian Wolff (1679–1754), philosopher, mathematician, interpreter of Leibniz and close friend of Frederic the Great. J. S. Baumgarten, Professor of Theology, was also an important teacher, and the founder of a new school of critical theology. Among his pupils were Samuel Gotthold Lange (1711–81), Jacob Immanuel Pyra (1715–44) and Johann Melchior Goeze (1717–91), who were important figures in the literature of the period.

Friedemann Bach was brought into the inner circle of writers and scholars particularly through his friendship with J. J. Gebauer the publisher, who undertook a complete edition of the works of Luther, and also issued the first three cantos of Klopstock's *Messias* in 1748. A further phase of Enlightenment was represented by the partial emancipation of women in Halle. In 1754 Dorothea Christiane Erxleben was the first of her sex to be admitted to the degree of Doctor of Medicine. Such was the state of Halle when Friedemann Bach came to the city in succession to Kirchhoff.

Kirchhoff, apart from his compositions for organ, was not a noteworthy composer, but he had done a good job in his official post. There were two *Chori symphoniaci*, one from the Grammar School (the so-called *Stadtchor*) and one from the other schools (the *Schulchor*), the first based on the churches of St Ulrich and St Moritz, the second on the Market Church. (Each church had its own Kantor, responsible for some general school-teaching, and answerable to the overall *Director Musices*.)

On special occasions the two choirs combined. The whole situation regarding school and church music looked more promising when the king issued instructions on 12th October 1746 that proper attention should be paid to music lessons. Kirchhoff had also looked after the instruments that belonged to the Market Church.

In those performances for which instrumental music was required[20] the orchestra consisted of four first and two second violins, two violas, one double-bass, two flutes, two trumpets, drums and organ. (In Halle the cembalo was not used for church cantatas, according to Petri.) Four town-musicians were on regular call; for the rest the director relied on members of the Collegium Musicum and free-lance players. It was similar to the set-up in Leipzig.

Friedemann was practical in his demands—more than his father was—and rarely exceeded the statutory limits in respect of instrumental or vocal resources. Occasionally he used horns as well as oboes, as in the Circumcision Cantata, *Der Herr zu deiner Rechten* (Falck 73); and in the Easter Cantata, *Erzittert und fallet* (Falck 83), he introduced a *Flauto d'amour* into the duet 'Komm, meine Hirte, lass Dich küssen'. A full complement of three trumpets is only to be found, however, in *Wer mich liebt*, a cantata for Pentecost.

The repertoire of church music in Halle was made up of works by the more fashionable composers. In 1746 the standard cantatas were by Telemann, J. F. Fasch, Görner, Kauffmann, Stoelzel, Christoph Foerster, Keiser, J. H. Rolle, J. C. Vogler (J. S. Bach's Arnstadt pupil) and Zachau. Works by any of the Bachs were conspicuous by their absence.[21] Friedemann set about repairing this deficiency. At the Whitsun Festival of 1746 he presented his own *Wer mich liebet* (Falck 72), a demonstration to the Hallenser that he had throughly learned the techniques of the Dresden church composers—in particular Hasse and Johann Zelenka (1679–1745). Friedemann's music has the amiable flow of the Saxon-Italian style, the flexibility of melodic outline that belonged to the opera aria, a feeling for the interdependence of vocal and instrumental sonorities linked with instrumental figurations that give clarity and spaciousness to the texture. A fine example of his relaxed yet disciplined style is the cantata *Dies ist der Tag*. In the tenor aria 'Süsser Hauch von Gottes Throne' there is a sense of spiritual elevation that may be felt also to belong to Haydn (see page 193).

The fine, three-movement symphony which introduces this cantata is cited by Leopold Nowak[22] as an example of music in transition from 'spiritual' to 'worldly'. He also quotes this as a fine specimen of

'lively, German baroque'. The difficulty about the first definition is that it presupposes a real distinction between 'spiritual' and 'worldly' which is denied by the music of the last example—which is as spiritual as one wishes to make it. The symphony, from without, is neither German nor baroque, but Italian and early classical. On the other hand the D minor symphony (of 1758?)[23] with its stern fugal writing, would appear both more spiritual and more German—except that in style it is French.

One returns to Friedemann's grasp of counterpoint, for its singularity was that he could shelter artifice from view, with a singular talent for introducing canonic devices that register in sound rather than on paper; but he was able to induce a sense of the mysteries that is expressed in not always obvious harmonies. Friedemann imbibed his father's teaching, and, it would seem, shared his father's enthusiasm for Johann Ludwig Bach, and settled their attitudes within his own independent experiences. Friedemann was extremely active as a composer in Halle, and his church music of that period (such as remains) represents an important department of the German liturgical music tradition. He also performed a filial office by performing works of his father—not always in the form in which they were written, but adapted to the taste of the day.[24]

Until 1750 Friedemann Bach was to some extent sheltered by his father's name, and he was, it would seem, also dependent on his

father's counsel. Such dependence implies a certain emotional inse-
curity, or immaturity, which conditions were impediments to marriage.
The death of Sebastian was a great blow, and it was from that time that
Friedemann's problems and reported eccentricities seem to have
increased. When his father died Friedemann went immediately to
Leipzig. As the eldest son much of the responsibility for controlling
the estate fell on him, and since he was near at hand he acted on behalf
of Emanuel as also of his sister Catharina. (The interests of the mentally retarded Gottfried Heinrich were protected by Gottlob Hesemann, a student of the university.) By agreement with Emanuel—and
presumably the rest of the family—Sebastian's music was withdrawn
from the general body of the estate and divided between the two elder
brothers. In time to come Friedemann, who held a large part of the
manuscripts of the church cantatas on the grounds that they might be
of more use to him at Halle than to Emanuel in Berlin,[25] was obliged
to sell off some of his holding in order to maintain himself. In 1750 the
only one of Johann Sebastian's sons (apart from Gottfried Heinrich)
who was not yet independent was the fifteen-year-old Johann Christian. According to family tradition he was deposited on an elder
brother. Friedemann, as yet unmarried, was in no position to enter-
tain him, whereas Emanuel was. So Friedemann took the boy up to
Berlin. With a scant regard for his Halle obligations, however, he
absented himself from his official duties for five months, and when he
returned at the end of December was not unreasonably welcomed
back with a reprimand.

At this juncture Friedemann decided to marry, and on 25th February 1751 his wedding to Dorothea Elisabeth Georgi, eldest daughter
of a local official, took place in the Market Church. The Bachs moved
into a house, purchased from Georgi, behind the church and overlook-
ing the River Saale. Of the three children born to Dorothea Elisabeth
two sons died in infancy, and only the daughter, Friederica Sophia
(born 7th February 1757), reached maturity.

In 1753, as already related (see page 168), Friedemann applied for
the post of organist at Zittau, but was unsuccessful. During the next
few years the chances of leaving Halle were reduced by the Seven Years
War, during which the city suffered greatly.

Many citizens were reduced to a state of indigence, of which a poign-
ant symbol was a letter from Friedemann Bach, dated 20th October
1761, asking to be excused from the payment of his contribution to the
War Tax. He received, however, an unsympathetic reply from the

church committee responsible for collecting such levies, a negative response to his supplication for an increase in salary, and a sharp reminder that his conduct had not been entirely satisfactory. The memory was still fresh of an occasion in 1760 when Friedemann had loaned one of the church drums to the Collegium Musicum, and— through the zeal or destructive instinct of a student—the skin had been broken. Bach was ordered to pay the cost of repair himself. Once again Friedemann stirred himself to consider moving.

Christoph Graupner—who almost became the Leipzig Kantor far back in 1723—died at Darmstadt in 1760. The Count of Hesse-Darmstadt, Ludwig VIII, was a long time in appointing a replacement. In 1762 an invitation came to Friedemann to succeed Graupner. He received this unexpected invitation with initial enthusiasm, but this enthusiasm waned and, for no very apparent reason, he failed to finalize a contract, although he subsequently was pleased to use the title of Kapellmeister at Darmstadt. During his Halle years Friedemann, whatever his defects, was a zealous teacher, his most conspicuous pupils being Friedrich Wilhelm Rust (1739-96), who spent the years 1758-62 in Halle, and J. S. Petri, who left his own testimony to the excellences of his teacher.

> Bach of Halle [Friedemann], who subsequently went to Braun-schweig and whose friendship and instruction I enjoyed in Halle in 1762-3, is the finest organist I have ever heard. It is only a pity that so few of his most artistic and profound compositions are published.[26]

In another place Petri, lauding the organ as the king of musical instruments, drew particular attention to the organs in the Market Church in Halle and in Görlitz, and to their great organists. Bach and Nikolai, he wrote, were 'two masters whose names deserved to go down to posterity'.[27] Some of the most characteristic of Friedemann's qualities are to be appreciated in his chorale preludes for organ,[28] in which the old style of contrapuntal techniques is refashioned according to the prevailing harmonic principles of his day, but without detriment to the dignities inherent in counterpoint. Friedemann left few organ works by which his bolder qualities may be judged, since these, it seems, were most evident in his extemporization.

In addition to Petri there were others who appreciated Friedemann. For some time, probably since meeting Marpurg and others of the 'scientific' school in Berlin, he had had the intention of publishing a textbook. He got so far as to complete at least a considerable part of the text and announced its title as the *Abhandlung von harmonischen Dreyklang*. Marpurg commented on its imminence in 1754.[29] Friedemann advertised it in the *Leipzig Zeitung* in 1758, and indicated that it would be out in time for the Easter Fair. Since he then solicited for subscribers it is to be presumed that, as in the case of the Dresden sonatas, insufficient were forthcoming. At any rate the work did not appear. On 19th January 1760 Marpurg gave another prod. He also tried to give a helping hand to Friedemann by observing that while the taste of the time was directed towards odes (songs) such as those contained in a collection he was presently reviewing, there was always the chance that taste would change. Then perhaps the contrapuntal excellence of Friedemann Bach, exemplified by his 'Fugue with three subjects', would be understood.[30] The triple fugue, in F major (Falck 36), is a masterly performance, compact yet fluid, an amalgam of the earnest principles of baroque polyphony with the relaxed manner and clarity of exposition of the classical. During his time in Halle Friedemann reflected much on the values of contrapuntal techniques, and it was on his facility for handling these that his reputation (through Marpurg's advocacy and citation) then depended. Of his choral fugues, which have a Handelian quality, one of the finest is the double-fugue in the first movement of the Advent Cantata, *Es ist eine Stimme eines Predigers* (Falck 89).

As the city's chief official musician Friedemann Bach was called on to celebrate auspicious occasions. These related principally to the king and his military progress—thus was the composer drawn into the ambience of developing patriotism whether he wished it or not—and to the university. Of such compositions not all are extant. On 5th November 1757 Frederic the Great, with 22,000 men, defeated a joint French and Imperial army numbering more than 60,000 at Rossbach, just outside Leipzig (thereby becoming a popular hero, and the defender of the Protestant cause, in England). A fortnight later a celebratory cantata composed by Bach was sung in the Market Church. On 8th January the defeat of the Austrians at Breslau was the cause of another cantata, while a fortnight later there was need for special music in honour of the king's birthday. This, the secular cantata *O Himmel, schone* (Falck 90), sponsored by the university, was preceded by ceremonial in the Market Place, for which the city brass players played from one of the towers of the Market Church. The cantata is a superb piece of laudation in D major, athletic in rhythmic structure and alive with optimism in the triadic gestures of the melodic motivs and the spring of the instrumentation. Both of these features belonged to the new world of the symphony rather than to the old world of the cantata.

From 1758 until 1762 there was little reason for exceptional rejoicing, but the brighter atmosphere of 1762 brought Friedemann back into action—in spite of the fact that he and his colleagues had been so hardly hit by the war. He wrote a work (lost) to mark the peace treaty signed between Prussia and Russia on 5th May 1762 and it was performed in June. Almost a year later the end of the war, signified on the one hand by the Peace of Paris and on the other by the treaty agreed between Saxony and Prussia, at Hubertsburg outside Dresden, was marked in Halle by Friedemann Bach's *Auf, Christen, posaunt*, for which he borrowed material from the Birthday Cantata of 1758. Celebrations in 1763 came one after the other, on 18th April, on 27th and 28th May. The last was organized by the Society for Arts and Science and—presumably since he had been much engaged for the previous occasion—Friedemann was not commissioned to compose the works in the performance of which the amateur musicians of the city were much involved.

> After everyone had taken his place Psalm 103 was performed, and afterwards a fine, resonant, performance, including trumpets and drums, was given by the local Collegium Musicum.[31]

Everyone, it seems, was pleased at that time; with the exception of Friedemann Bach. He stuck it out in the Market Church for another year, and then, on 12th May 1764, tendered his resignation. For four years he remained in Halle, befriended by Gebauer, until, on 13th August 1770, the notice of sale by auction of property belonging to his wife (valued at 630 thalers) indicated to the citizens of Halle that Friedemann Bach was about to fold his tents and depart. After presenting Gebauer with a Fantasia in E minor in October, he and his wife and their thirteen-year-old daughter prepared to take their leave, and a few months later moved to Braunschweig.

BRAUNSCHWEIG

In looking for permanent appointment at the age of sixty Friedemann was defying the general rule. But, like his father, he had no doubts concerning his own ability. He was a celebrated performer and he knew that in Braunschweig there were those who appreciated his worth. Among them were two professors of the Carolineum; Friedrich

Wilhelm Zachariä and Johann Joachim Eschenburg. The former—according to Burney a good practical musician—was a disciple of Gottsched, one of Telemann's librettists and a friend of Gellert and Lessing. A conspicuous champion of the cause of 'German song', and loud in his praises of J. S. Bach's chorales, he had applauded the 'melodious' sons of Bach in his *Tageszeiten*. Eschenburg, a friend of Emanuel Bach, translated a number of English treatises on poetry and music into German as well as the works of Shakespeare. Both he and Zachariä were prepared to exert themselves on behalf of Emanuel Bach's gifted, but unfortunate, elder brother.

On the death of J. D. C. Graff, then, influence was brought to bear to promote Friedemann's candidature for the post of organist in the town church in Wolfenbüttel (a few miles away from Braunschweig). But nothing came of this. Nor of his application (underwritten by a personal plea from Friedemann to the Duke of Braunschweig-Lüneburg) for the succession to Beyer, the deceased organist of the St Ägidius and St Catherine churches in Braunschweig. In his report on the competition for the latter appointment Johann Schwanberger (1740–1804), Court music director at Braunschweig, a prominent north German symphonist, and an opera composer of the school of Hasse, drew attention to the fact that Bach's 'reputation and talents were known by all who were knowledgeable in music throughout Germany', and found nothing in his performance that was other than praiseworthy. The committee responsible for the appointment chose Carl Friedrich Wilhelm Lemme—who seemed well qualified by having three members of the ducal family as godparents.

Having arrived in Braunschweig Friedemann determined to stay there—at least for a while. He was befriended by notable persons in the city, including Eschenburg and Georg David Matthieu (1737–78), then Court painter at Mecklenburg-Schwerin—one of the best German portrait painters of the age. Schwanberger—whose father had known Friedemann's father—was friendly; so too were the members of the Court orchestra, and the amateur musicians of the city. A zest for music was due in no small measure to the personal enthusiasm of the duke and duchess. The latter, Charlotte, was a sister of Frederic the Great, a woman of high intelligence and charm, who maintained close contact with her brother.

At this juncture Friedemann made a new acquaintance, and in so doing may be said to have changed the cultural history of Germany, if not of the world. He met Johann Nikolaus Forkel (1749–1818), the first biographer of J. S. Bach and as such the effective influence behind the movement that raised Johann Sebastian Bach to the dignity of a national hero.

JOHANN NIKOLAUS FORKEL AT GÖTTINGEN

Forkel, son of a shoemaker in Meeder in the duchy of Saxe-Coburg and the nephew of Kantor Johann Heinrich Schulthesius, followed an old Thuringian tradition when, in 1766, he was given a place in the Johanneum in Lüneburg and taken into the choir of St Michael's Church. There he was under the direction of Kantor Schumann (1724–77), but after only a year he was made choir prefect in the cathedral in Schwerin. Two years later he was admitted to the University of Göttingen, a special arrangement being made for the remission of his fees on account of his poor circumstances.[32] Later that same year a representative of the Ohrdruf Bachs, Augustinus Tobias Bernhard (1740–89), was admitted as a student—at a somewhat advanced age, and also as a non-fee-payer.[33] The fourth son of Johann Christoph (1702–56), Augustinus Tobias, went into the family business and became a Kantor in Langenburg (where his brother, Johann Georg Friedrich (1736–1818), was a Court official), and sired six children. Of the sons one became a pastor, the other an apothecary. In 1773 another Bach—a remoter connection?—was entered on the matriculation list.[34] The attractions of the University of Göttingen were considerable, for Gessner's spirit had inspired a new conception of the place of the university in society. At Halle the pioneers of the *Aufklärung* had liberated thought from the tenets of theological dogma and laid the foundations of a literature in the German language. Of late, however, Halle had become a rather specialized vocational training school for Prussian civil servants. Gessner's principle was the cultivation of the mind; his philosophy was all-embracing, so that all branches of experience were necessary subjects for study and discussion.

In 1770 Forkel became organist of the university church; two years later he was appointed music instructor; in 1779 he succeeded Kress, a violinist of the Benda school, as director of the university concerts. These had taken place since the foundation of the university.[35] All of this owed very much to Gessner's successor, Christian Gottlob Heyne (at Göttingen 1736–1812), who was not only a philologist of distinction, but the founder of the German school of classical archaeology, and so built up the university library that in the eighteenth century it was regarded as the best in the world. He was also a friend of the Bachs.[36] Forkel was a true son of the Göttingen extension of the *Aufklärung*, and believed in the necessity for a combination of theory and practice. It cannot be said but that some of his successors in the field of musical scholarship would do well to refer back to his precepts in this respect. He was, however, a stubbornly patriotic Thuringian, with an inbuilt conviction that whatever was best came out of Thuringia. As proof of the dogma he evinced the works and the methods of J. S. Bach. He was one of the few who 'preserved the method of clavier playing of Sebastian Bach in all its purity, and came (thereby) to be called a "Bachianer" '.[37] Already in 1771 'he had a rare capacity for playing Bach's fugues, which was all the more remarkable since it was the result of his own industry'.[38] Knowing that a son of J. S. Bach was near by in Braunschweig, and that he was in poor circumstances, Forkel invited him to Göttingen to perform. With great generosity— for he was by no means well off—Forkel gave a small contribution towards Friedemann's living expenses from his own pocket. He described Friedemann's clavier playing as 'elegant, delicate, and pleasant', his organ playing sent a thrill of 'holy' ecstasy through him.[39] But the main purpose of his entertainment of Friedemann was to learn about Sebastian at first hand. Already the intention to be that great man's memorialist had formed in his mind, and he laudably commenced on his project by consulting the facts rather than the legends. In the end of course he created a new legend, but that was not to emulsify until a generation had passed. Forkel ransacked Friedemann's filial recollections, borrowed a year's set of church cantatas from him (he paid Friedemann two louis d'or for the privilege, but Friedemann tried to make the transaction final by offering the set to his host at an all-in price of twenty louis d'or,[40]) and sent him back to Braunschweig.

BACH IN BERLIN

Having returned to Braunschweig Friedemann gave performances in the cathedral and also in Wolfenbüttel in the late summer of 1773. Then (and no specific reason can be adduced) he decided to go to Berlin. He travelled lighter than he had come, leaving behind his precious collection of his father's manuscripts. Eschenburg took charge of them on the understanding that he would arrange for them in due course to be auctioned.

Recitals on the organs of St Mary's Church on 29th April, and of the Garrison Church on 4th May, were advertised.[41] Neither, it seems, took place. The Berlin newspaper *Berlinische Nachrichten* of 17th May, however, gave a glowing account of Friedemann's performances on the previous Sunday—in the morning at St Nicholas's Church and in the afternoon at St Mary's. The report indicates perhaps rather more what the public was looking for than a critical appraisal.

> ... Wilhelm Friedemann Bach, one of the greatest organists in Germany ... was received with extraordinary applause. Everyone was carried away by the feeling [of the music], the novelty of the ideas, the astonishing contrasts, the dissonant sections that finally resolved into a kind of Graun-like harmony— force and delicacy were united by the fingers of this master. Joy and sorrow transported the spirits of the audience—could it have been possible not to have recognized a son of a Sebastian?

Friedemann was well received in Berlin, not only by the public but also by the leading musicians. Thus encouraged he set up house and, again, hoped for the best. Domestically it was a restless existence. In ten years he changed houses five times, living finally in the parish of Luisenstadt. Among his pupils the most noteworthy was Sara Levi (*née* Itzig), an aunt of Felix Mendelssohn. Another of the Mendelssohn connection whose association with Friedemann had fruitful consequences was Carl Friedrich Zelter (1758–1832)—a pupil of Kirnberger and Carl Friedrich Fasch, and Mendelssohn's teacher—who frequently heard Friedemann play, and reported his experiences to Goethe. In the 'scientific', academic, national-conscious, climate of Berlin in the last years of the lives of Frederic the Great and Friedemann Bach (the king outlived the musician by only two years) the ideas from which a new image of J. S. Bach was to be formed were accumulating round the presence of Friedemann. His 'learning' was a great asset, in so far as his reputation was concerned. Among the foreign diplomats in Berlin when Friedemann lived there was Gottfried van Swieten, Austrian Ambassador to the Court of Prussia from 1770–7. A particular admirer of the works of Handel and J. S. Bach he, like Forkel, honoured the sons of the latter because they were their father's sons. From Emanuel he commissioned a set of six symphonies, and he was deeply impressed by Friedemann's musicianship. Like Forkel, he learned what he could from the Bachs and what he learned he used to good effect on his recall to Vienna. Friedemann's talents also guaranteed a welcome at the assemblies of Princess Amalia in the Wilhelmstrasse. Copies of Friedemann's works made by Kirnberger existed in the library of the princess.[42] On 24th February 1778 Friedemann expressed his appreciation to her in the Dedication of a set of eight fugues. These fugues, by their arrangement, propose an unfulfilled intention. They are in C major, C minor, D major, D minor, E flat major, . . . E minor, F minor and B flat major. The two-fold implication is clear. His father's son, Friedemann projected another 'twenty-four', but he lacked resolution. What he did not lack, however, was genius. 'He could have replaced our father,' Emanuel once said sadly. These fugues of 1778 are works of importance; strenuous (with sharp definition in the rhythm of the subjects), unyielding in contrapuntal argument, calculated for the keyboard and therefore instrumental rather than vocal in essence, and wholly expressive. Certainly J. S. Bach lives behind the impulse of the music, but the road to Brahms and to Reger, and beyond, is opened up. As by this searching passage from the chromatic fugue in F minor:

The apostolic succession, thus worthily maintained, was emphasized increasingly throughout the early years of the nineteenth century, and Friedemann Bach duly honoured by posthumous beatification by the Berlin Academy of Arts, in the *Auswahl vorzüglichen Musik-Werke . . . zur Beförderung des höhern Studium der Musik* published in 1835, where his G minor fugue for organ (wrongly noted by Falck as unpublished) appears.[43]

One would like to think that in his last years Friedemann enjoyed to the full the appreciation of his colleagues. Alas! it was not so. Hardly had he taken possession of a silver coffee service (and an even more welcome gift of money) from the princess—her response to his 'Amalia-Fugues'—than he fell into disfavour. 'Mr Bach', wrote Kirnberger to Forkel in 1779, 'has not recognized any good feelings, but has gone to the Princess, calumniated me in the most unfair manner, believing that thereby he would put me out of my place which he would get.' A sad story—the truth of which is not open to reasonable doubt—and one which indicates the strong neurotic strain that was Friedemann's worst enemy. In an age of change there are frequent casualties. Friedemann, subjected to the inner pressures that were his inheritence, was under the strain of living near to the catastrophes that resulted from the internecine wars wished onto the German people by Frederic the Great. The end of the life story of Friedemann Bach was written in the register of the Luisenstadt church in Berlin:

> On July 1, 1784, the Leipzig-born musician Wilhelm Friedemann Bach, 73 years of age, died of a disease of the chest [tuberculosis?], leaving a widow, Dorothea Elisabethe Georgii and a 26-year-old daughter, Friederica Sophia.

A more ample obituary appeared in the newspaper a few days later:

> On the first of this month Mr Wilhelm Friedemann Bach, son of the imperishable Sebastian, died here of a severe 'exhaustion'. Germany has lost in him her first organist, and the musical world in general a man who is irreplaceable. All who honour true harmony and real greatness in music will be deeply affected by his loss.

The saddest footnote on Friedemann Bach is provided by the last news of his daughter, who had (it would seem) sacrificed herself to the care of her parents. In the same year that her father died she married a musketeer, one J. Schmidt. The marriage took place five days after she gave birth to a child,[44] the first of two daughters. Friederica Sophia died in 1801.

Friedemann Bach suffered more than his brothers from the fact of having been the son of his father. In his lifetime because of the very particular understanding that existed between himself and his father; posthumously because he did not live up to the ideal that hagiography invented for the sons of Bach. He was (like his father) an enigma. He may, however, be better understood in the light of twentieth-century psychology than in that of nineteenth-century morality. He disposed of Sebastian's manuscripts carelessly. But—except in the musicological calendar—this was no crime. He put his own name on certain of his father's manuscripts,[45] and his father's on some of his own.[46] Certainly these actions would now be considered reprehensible. But in the eighteenth century? Friedemann was of course just as careless of his own manuscripts as of those of his father. From this he has suffered also.

The fine clavier concerto in F minor, for example, of which the opening motivs follow, was attributed to Emanuel.[47]

This work, fiercely energetic in the melodic and rhythmic patterns of the first movement, is a cry from the heart. It is the voice of one who had known pain, but of one who was compassionate. The accent of the slow movement is that of Sebastian, but the attitude is that of Friedemann.

NOTES TO CHAPTER NINE

1. Gustav Schilling, *Encyclopädie der gesammten musikalischen Wissenschaften oder Universal-Lexicon.* Stuttgart, 1835, p. 379.

2. *A New General Biographical Dictionary*, London, 1857, 12 vols., II, p. 439.

3. 'Bachs Mutter und ihre Sippe', in *BJB*, Jg. 22, 1925.

4. Erwin Barr, Eugen Fischer and Fritz Lenz, *Menschliche Erblehre und Rassenhygiene (Eugenik)*, Munich, 1936, 2 vols., 4th ed., I, ('Die Erblichkeit der geistigen Eigenschaften'), p. 680.

5. The MS. eventually came into the possession of J. C. Bach (the 'Clavierbach') of Halle. *See* p. 123.

6. No. 25, *Allemande* and *Courante*: Johann Christian Richter (1689–1744) was an oboist in Dresden.

7. *See* p. 176.

8. *Relations-Courier*, Hamburg, 29th May 1723.

9. Forkel (*see* Chapter 3, Note 18 above).

10. Silbermann agreed to a contract to replace the much altered organ of 1624 on 10th December 1718, and completed the work in 1721. It was his twelfth instrument, and contained thirty-three registers. *See* Ernst Flade, *Gottfried Silbermann*, Leipzig, 1953, p. 106 f.

11. See *Relations-Courier*, Hamburg, 1st October 1731.

12. In the Bachhaus, Eisenach. *See* illustration between pages 74 and 75.

13. 'Truth reeks in the nostrils like an onion, [and] is intolerable.'

14. Rheinhold also developed a Collegium Musicum among his choristers.

15. *Dresdner Merkwürdigkeiten*, 1736, quoted by Erna Hedwig Hofmann, *The Dresden Kreuz Chor*, Leipzig, 1962, p. 52.

16. Johann Elias Bach reported the visit to Leipzig of Friedemann, and Johann Kropfgans and Weiss, the Dresden lutenists, in 1739, in a letter of 11th August of that year. Kropfgans was employed by Count Heinrich von Brühl.

17. *See* Flade (Note 10 above).

18. The Stahl family lived in Weimar when the Bachs did.

19. *Grove's Dictionary*, 3rd ed. (1928), in 'Sonata', p. 819.

20. At Christmas, Easter and Whitsuntide, performances were spread over three days: on the first day in the Market Church, on the second in St Ulrich's, on the third in St Moritz's. On the three High Feasts the Market Church performances, which took place in the morning, were repeated in the afternoon in the *Schulkirche*, the official church of university and garrison.

21. *Wöchentlicher Hallischer Anzeiger*, 1946, p. 195, quoted by C. Zehla, 'W. Friedemann Bach und seine hallische Wirksamkeit', in *BJB*, Jg. 7, 1910, pp. 103–32.

22. Leopold Nowak, *see* Preface to his edition of *Dies ist der Tag*, Musikwissenschaftlicher Verlag, Leipzig and Vienna, 1937.

23. Copy in B.M. Add. MS. 32,147.

24. Cantatas by J. S. Bach of which the scores have been lost were performed in Halle, while there were adaptations of *Man singet mit Freuden, Es ist das Heil*, and probably other works. *See* Martin Falck, *Wilhelm Friedemann Bach*, Lindau, 1956, pp. 27 and 141.

25. Forkel (*see* Chapter 3, Note 18 above), p. 103.

26. Petri, *Anleitung zur praktischen Musik*, Leipzig, 1782, p. 106.

27. *See* Note 26 above, p. 285.

28. See *Choralvorspiele alter Meister*, ed. K. Straube, Leipzig, Peters, 1907, and *Les Oeuvres pour Orgue (Orgue et Liturgie 37)*, Paris, n.d.

29. *Beiträge* (*see* Chapter 6, Note 13 above), I, p. 430 f.

30. *Kritische Briefe über die Tonkunst, XXXI Brief: an Herrn Wilhelm Friedemann Bach:* 'Jedes Alter hat seine Lust, und jeder Zeitpunkt seinen Geschmack. Wer weiss, ob nicht viele unsrer Odenliebhaber in einigen Jahren ihren Geschmack verändern, und an nichts als an Fugen mit drey Subjecten Belieben tragen werden? Glück zum voraus!'

31. 'Nachdem ein jeder seine Stelle eingenommen hatte, wurde der 103 Psalm gesungen, und hernach eine wohlklingende Musik, unter Trompeten- und Paukenschall von dem hiesigen Collegio Musico aufgeführet'. *Wöchentlicher Hallischer Anzeiger*, 1736, p. 384.

32. *Die Matrikel der Georg-August Universität zu Göttingen*, 1734–1837: '1769, Ap. 17, Joann. Nic. Forckel, Coburgens, jur.; ob paupertat. testim. Dn. Prof. Beckmanni prob. iura fisci illi remissa sunt.'

33. *See* Note 32 above. '1769, Sept. 6; Augustinus Tobias Bernhardus Bach, Ohrdruffio Hohenloensis, jur.; testimonio paupertatis munitis quoad iura fisci gratis.'

34. *See* Note 32 above. 1773, Mai 3; 'Johannes Adolphus Bach, Vicenhusa Hassus, jur.'

35. *See* Kapellmeister Frohwalt Hardege, 'Grosse Musiker in Göttingen', *Göttinger Jahrbuch*, Jg. 2, 1953, p. 90.

36. Heinrich Edelhoff, *Johann Nikolaus Forkel*, Göttingen, 1935, p. 23.

37. Becker's *National-Zeitung der Teutschen*, 3, p. 15.

38. *See* J. W. Hässler, Autobiography in *6 Leichte Sonaten* (Nagel's Musik-Archiv No. 20).

39. Hardege (*see* Note 35 above).

40. Haacke (*see* Chapter 8, Note 9 above), p. 42.

41. The organs in the Garrison and St Mary's churches were both built in the 1720s by Joachim Wagner, a pupil of Schnittger. J. S. Bach had played on the former, and probably on the latter, in 1747. *See* Gustav Leh, *Die St-Marien-Kirche zu Berlin*, Berlin, 1959, pp. 36–42.

42. The catalogue of Princess Amalia's library was prepared in 1800 by Zelter. Subsequently the collection became the property of the Joachimsthale Gymnasium, but was later dispersed. *See* Eva Renate Bleckschmidt, *Die Amalia-Bibliothek: Musikbibliothek der Prinzessin Anna Amalia von Preussen* (1723–87), Berlin, 1965.

43. *Auswahl vorzüglichen Musik-werke . . . zur Beförderung des höhern Studium der Musik*, 1835, p. 19, No. VI.

44. Haacke (*see* Chapter 8, Note 9 above), p. 48.

45. E.g. D minor organ concerto, arr. from Vivaldi.

46. *Kyrie* and clavier concerto in C minor (pub. Schott).

47. Pub. Sikorski, Hamburg, 1959.

10

Emanuel Bach in Hamburg

MUSIC IN A 'DEMOCRATICAL' SOCIETY

In moving to Hamburg from Berlin Emanuel Bach was not only moving from one city to another, but from one state to another. Administered by a Senate—comprising lawyers and merchants elected by the three Colleges of Burghers—the 'form of Government [was] mixed, and [had] something of the *Democratical* and something of the *Aristocratical*'.[1] This definition of the government of the city-state may also be extended to describe the character of the organization of the musical life of the community during the period of Telemann's long office as music director, and indeed to that of the music of Telemann. The task of Bach, when he exchanged Berlin for Hamburg, was to extend further the tendencies of music towards the 'Democratical'. That in fact was what the argument among musicians was really about.

The independence of Hamburg (which had drawn Telemann there in the first place) was one of the important facts of German political life. In 1768 this independence was symbolically recognized by its final release from an ancient Danish connection which had once kept Hamburg within the hereditary territories of the duchy of Holstein. Emanuel Bach had been born and brought up in the confinement of a little *Residenzstadt*. At the age of fifty-three he found himself in a community which was on the edge of the wide world. Hamburg, rather larger than Berlin with a population of 150,000, was an international city; of the 2,000 ships that came in and out of the port each year only 160 were Hamburg-based, the rest being foreign; during Bach's life in Hamburg trade with America developed and so too did sympathy for the newly independent United States of America—a fact obliquely registered in the setting by Emanuel's half-brother, Johann Christoph Friedrich of Bückeburg, of von Gerstenburg's *Die Amerikanerin*. This work was performed in Hamburg by Emanuel in 1787.

Emanuel was ceremonially welcomed into his new dignity by Johann Melchior Goeze, the chief pastor of Hamburg, at St Catharine's

Church on 19th April 1768. Having no disinclination to speech-making on a public occasion Goeze read a paper, *De harmonica coelesti*, suitable to the occasion, and Emanuel responded, also in Latin, with *De nobilissimo artis musicae fine*. In office he promptly disengaged himself from the more onerous duties of his Kantorate and engaged a deputy to teach the three upper classes of the Johanneum. The office of Kantor was not as it had been in Leipzig in his father's day (Telemann had seen to that), and Emanuel Bach was under no illusions as to what was expected of him. He was to be the inspiration of the musical life of the bourgeoisie, and in so far as he was concerned with sacred music, that should be unmistakably liberal in tendency (see p. 211). Church music had been shifted away from dogma, and any large-scale works were to be thought of rather as contributions to public entertainment (on the highest level of 'taste') than as expositions of theological tenets. There is a paradox here to be remarked. The religious music of Haydn and Mozart contemporary with that of Emanuel Bach is super-ficially more worldly than his, but—rooted in liturgical language and the worshipping attitudes of south European Catholicism—it is in fact more positively inspirational in a religious sense. Emanuel Bach, it may be suspected, was towards being a free-thinker. His oratorios therefore begin to belong to the Romantic order. They were often conceived for secular performance and given by the members of a musical society. If they had been left to the church musicians they would have come off rather badly; Burney went with Bach to hear the music at St Catharine's Church, and was unimpressed by the standard of execution.[2]

Whatever the nominal conditions of Emanuel's engagement those citizens of Hamburg interested in such matters looked forward to the stimulation to their recreation (both public and private) that the presence of so famous a man would afford. Emanuel Bach was not only celebrated in Germany, but also abroad (see pages 172–3). When the news of his appointment was known the *Wöchentliche Nachrichten* of Hamburg, for 3rd November 1767, greeted 'this great master of clavier playing' enthusiastically, and it was as clavier player that Bach first appeared at a concert—in the *Drillhaus*, on 28th April 1768, with a programme of piano concertos and songs.[3] After this he began to plan for the subscription concerts for the next season. Of these there were twenty, the first taking place on 31st October. Public subscription concerts, at which Bach played and conducted, continued until 1782, when a wave of flippancy swept the prosperous into balls, masquerades and 'clubs', and diverted interest from the assurances of classical music towards the ephemeral excitement of public lotteries. An index to Bach's own original contributions to the concerts lies in the publication of important works, such as the six clavier concertos of 1772 (dedicated to Duke Peter of Curland, Wtq. 43), the four symphonies of 1780 (dedicated to Prince Friedrich Wilhelm of Prussia) and the oratorios. The four symphonies were first heard in the summer of 1776, and a larger than usual orchestra was required. There being insufficient professional players available—and no ban on playing with amateurs—it was augmented by non-professionals:

> The day before yesterday—August 17—Kapellmeister Bach rehearsed four of his recently completed great symphonies in the Concert Room *auf dem Kamp*.[4] The orchestra was larger, perhaps, than any seen in Hamburg for a long time. It consisted of some 40 people—our Hamburg professionals with a few amateurs— and performed those incomparable and, of their kind, unique symphonies with accuracy and enthusiasm. So much so that Mr Bach made public reference to their skill, and the audience present showed its lively appreciation.[5]

As well as public concerts there were many of a more private nature of which Bach was the centre. Especially important were those given in the *Handelsakademie* (High School for Commerce). The sponsors were two particular friends of Bach, Professors Johann Georg Büsch and Christoph David Ebeling. Büsch, educated in theology at Göttingen, and who had visited England, Holland and Scandinavia, was a mathematician and the founder of the High School for Commerce. Ebeling was a historian, a classical scholar, the official city cartographer and deeply interested in literature. To Ebeling Burney was especially indebted, both for his hospitality in Hamburg and his readiness to establish contacts, and for the fact that he had already made a German translation of the first (Italian) part of Burney's *The Present State of Music*.[6] In addition to Büsch and Ebeling, Johann Christoph Westphal, the principal music dealer in Hamburg, was a staunch supporter of private concerts. Many young musicians were grateful to these citizens for their support; among them Johann Friedrich Reichardt who, in 1774, played the viola in a chamber orchestra assembled at Büsch's house to run through the symphonies that Bach had composed for van Swieten. Burney gives a nice account of an evening arranged by Ebeling in the course of which some parts of Bach's *Passion* were given.[7]

The cultivation of the knowledgeable amateur was not only part of progressive educational philosophy but a sound business undertaking.

The tyro pianist was obliged to Bach for his *Versuch über die wahre Art das Clavier zu spielen*, which was as a bible to the earnest teacher. To none more so than Christian Gottlob Neefe (1748–98), who dedicated a set of twelve sonatas to Emanuel Bach in 1773, but who is better known to posterity on account of his most celebrated pupil—Ludwig van Beethoven. The effect of Bach's instruction thus absorbed and the influence of his works on Beethoven was considerable, as Beethoven himself indicated.[8]

The care which Bach bestowed on his easier pieces in order to make them intelligible is instanced by their advertisements—as in the *Schwerin Anzeiger* of 10th February 1776:

> Kapellmeister C. P. E. Bach's Clavier-Sonatas, which are easy and, according to present-day practice, arranged into parts for violin and violoncello, will be published soon after Easter, 1776; subscription price 1 thaler. Because the piano part will be printed in the soprano as well as the violin [i.e. treble] clef there is a choice for the honourable music-lovers; but they are requested to indicate their choice before 25 February.[9]

Pohl observed that the best of Emanuel Bach appeared in his collections of sonatas for amateurs,[10] and while this is an overstatement in one sense it is not in another. The geniality he dispensed took the edge off the high seriousness of music lessons and was a powerful agent in socializing the practice of music. At the end of the line of clavier works came Bach's more or less frivolous sets of variations, which tended to go round in manuscript copies. Among these were a cantonette with fifteen variations, *Was helfen mir tausend Ducaten*. Written in 1786, this is the prototype of many piano-teaching pieces of the next hundred or more years. But the old man's sometimes Mozartian fancy was charming:

THE ORATORIO CULT

If Emanuel Bach encouraged music lovers in general he was also aware of his responsibility towards his younger, or less well-circumstanced, colleagues. His programmes in Hamburg were catholic in character, not least in respect of what was to become the 'oratorio tradition'—towards which from time to time he got a push from friends from England.

The programmes of the Hamburg subscription concerts combined the sacred and the secular. Thus on 6th March 1769 a *Passion* 'by a famous Master' (Telemann?) was performed, as well as a piano concerto. Just before Christmas of the same year, in addition to 'piano concertos', *Die Hirten bey der Krippe zu Bethlehem* was given. Advertised as a new work, this was probably the setting of a text by Ramler (that became very popular[11]) by Carl August Westenholtz (1738–89), a native of Lüneburg and a pupil of Emanuel, who was Kapellmeister at the Mecklenburg-Schwerin Court at Ludwigslust. The members of this musical establishment had close contact with Hamburg. In 1774 another oratorio on Ramler's text was given under Bach's direction, the music on this occasion being by Johann David Holland (*b.* 1746), Director of Music in St Catharine's Church and therefore one of Bach's subordinates. First performed on 16th November 1774, Holland's work was repeated a month later when Emanuel's setting of Psalm VIII (from the volume of *Cramers Psalmen* published in 1774) and a *Te Deum* by K. H. Graun were also given. A more or less complete record of the choral music performed at concerts of the High School for Commerce is given in a letter of 12th November to Gerstenburg[12] from Matthias Claudius—a poet with a musical ear, who was one of those on whose works the Lied tradition was built. There were operas and oratorios by Hasse, Salieri, Gluck and Jommelli, as well as Handel's *Messiah* and (Dettingen?) *Te Deum*, and Bach's own new oratorio—*Die Israeliten in der Wüste*. In his Preface to this work Bach made it clear that oratorio had no confined significance: '. . . this oratorio is so designed that it is not only suitable for a kind of Festival, but for all times both in and out of church; it is solely to the praise of God and can be performed without offending any Christians'.

Hamburg was the first city in Germany in which Handel's *Messiah* was performed. The first performance took place on 15th April 1772 under the surprising direction of Michael Arne (1740–86), son of the more famous Thomas Augustine Arne. It was three years before

Messiah was performed again in Hamburg, in which time Klopstock, helped by Ebeling, had completed his version of the text. An account of Bach's performance of the same oratorio was given by the poet Johann Heinrich Voss in a letter (5th January 1776) to his fiancée.[13]

ENGLISH INTERESTS

The year in which *Messiah* was first introduced into Germany was particularly important in respect of Anglo–German musical affairs, and Emanuel Bach (his support to Michael Arne's venture being understood from his subsequent action in respect of the work) was a central figure. He was host to Burney, to whom he presented 'three or four curious books and treatises out of his father's collection . . .' and 'promised, at any distant time, to furnish me with others, if I would only acquaint him by letter, with my wants'. To this Burney footnoted a subsequent gift of works of Sebastian and Emanuel Bach.[14] These gifts included Ammerbach's *Orgel Tabulatur* and the 1538 edition of the Moravian Brethren Hymn-book, a MS. copy of the Credo of the *Mass in B Minor*, the *Inventions* and *Six Suites from le Clavecin*[15] and a copy of the '48'. Eleven of the fugues from this collection were also in the possession of Lord Fitzwilliam[16]. Bearing the signature 'R. Fitzwilliam' and the date '1772' this MS. is now in the Fitzwilliam Museum, Cambridge (32. G. 18). John Stafford Smith (1750–1836) also visited Hamburg in this year and called on Emanuel Bach, from whom he returned with a copy of the *Ulm Gesangbuch* of 1538 that had belonged both to Sebastian and Emanuel. Peter Beckford was the owner of the so-called London Autograph of the '48' (B. M., Add. MS. 35021), which Muzio Clementi came across when he was Beckford's protégé in Dorsetshire[17]; while three pieces in the Royal College of Music MS. 814, attributed by Benjamin Cooke to John Robinson, are copies of works by J. S. Bach[18] which had been taken from some migrant original probably acquired in Germany by an English traveller.

An English connection with Emanuel Bach, by implication at least, was more than slender. There is his presumed acquaintance with Burney's English friends resident in Hamburg; John Hanbury, at whose villa 'true English hospitality reigns'; and Emanuel Mathias, Minister Plenipotentiary of the British Government. So far as Burney himself was concerned, Bach went further than Burney's own countrymen were prepared to go by giving a performance of his Doctoral Exercise.[19]

PICTURE COLLECTION

Bach's picture collection, so far as we know its contents from his will, is some index to his general interests as also to his appreciation of the art of painting. He had a portrait of the senior of the Meiningen branch of the family, Johann Ludwig—with whose gifted sons he was well acquainted (see page 236). His friendship with the Hamburg artist Andreas Stöttrup (1754–1812) resulted in a drawing that shows Bach and Stöttrup with Christian Sturm, the preacher, as well as others of Bach himself. As he knew Andreas Ludwig Krüger, the architect and painter of Potsdam and Berlin, it is natural that his second son, Johann Sebastian (1749–78), should commence his studies with that master. And since Johann Sebastian (the younger) went to Leipzig in 1770 to become a pupil of Adam Friedrich Oeser—who was also Goethe's instructor—it is probable that Emanuel was well acquainted with his work too. Certain of Emanuel's portraits related to his enthusiasm for the outward-looking tendencies of German letters and philosophy. There were, for instance, representations of Hölty (after Chodowiecki, also a Berliner), Leibniz, Lessing and Moses Mendelssohn. He possessed a wood-cut of Melanchthon, after Cranach; portraits of Orlando di Lasso, Hammerschmidt, Frescobaldi, Scheidt, Daniel Eberlin, Buffardin and a number of his own ancestors. Of famous Britons he had pictures of King James (I ?), Milton, Thomas Browne—'Dr. Med. in Norwich', and Robert Fludd—a doctor also, but more famous as a Rosicrucian. Of musicians who were English, or lived in England, there were some whose presence in Bach's gallery is understandable. Thomas Simpson, the seventeenth-century violist, for instance, lived for some time in Germany and published works in Hamburg; Pepusch, before emigration, had been a Prussian Court musician; John Frederick Lampe, a Saxon, brother-in-law of Thomas Arne, had once worked in Braunschweig. There was also a portrait of Handel. Other prominent English musicians were in one way or another more or less closely connected with Handel—John Beard, Richard Leveridge and the anglicized Fleming, William Defesch. Karl Friedrich Abel (1723–87) was in a special category. His family, of Köthen, was closely attached to the Bachs. Sebastian was godfather to Karl Friedrich's sister, while it was for their father that he wrote the cello suites. Karl Friedrich Abel left Dresden in 1759 and, having reached the safety of London, remained there. He was a close friend and business partner of Emanuel's youngest half-brother, Johann Christian.

Another picture of some Anglo-German interest in Bach's possession was an engraving—after a portrait by Joshua Reynolds—of a Miss Fordyce, catalogued in Bach's will as a 'Lautenistin', but otherwise described as an opera singer.[20]

A MANY-SIDED MUSICIAN

Emanuel Bach, then, in Germany at least, was a musician of a new order, for finally he was independent of the patronage of Court or Church. In view of his standing in his profession he was also a free agent so far as his Hamburg employment was concerned. From the social point of view he was of unimpeachable middle-class respectability, with broad interests that conformed to the pattern accepted by an enlightened bourgeoisie. He lived comfortably, entertained well and enjoyed life. Highly professional, as in his dealings with publishers and in his capacity for exploiting the market, he was less an eighteenth-century musician than a prototype for the successful composer of the twentieth century. In brief, although a distinguished composer he neither looked nor behaved like one, except when he was playing. The versatility of his talents and the diffusion of his interests maybe lessened the force of his genius. Thus we are brought back to the comparison between him and his elder brother. Wilhelm Friedemann was much more his father's son in the intensity of his expression. Emanuel inherited Sebastian's methodical tendencies. What he set out to do he generally achieved. He also resembled his godfather Telemann in being able to adapt himself to socio-musical requirements. But in so doing he rarely allowed the commonplace to take control. His originality is generally evident—though in different degrees—in whatever he composed. Many Bachs of his period composed works that could have been (and sometimes were formerly thought to have been) by Emanuel. Apart from Wilhelm Friedemann those who most resembled him in style—Johann Ernst and Johann Christoph Friedrich —possessed a comparable efficiency, but lacked the dramatic sense that distinguished his expression. One may, for example, compare the charming Double Concerto for Fortepiano, Viola and Orchestra in E flat by the Bückeburg Bach[21] with Emanuel's Double Concerto for Cembalo, Fortepiano and Orchestra (Wtq. 47) in the same key.[22] The first work is effectively classical in figuration and design, but lacking in variety. It is also longer (it lasts about half an hour) than its ideas can properly support. Emanuel's concerto centres on the behaviour of the fortepiano, which progressively grows in significance throughout the work. Apart from Emanuel's greater flexibility of tonal structure within separate movements he realizes in this work the compelling effect of a complete switch of tonality. The second movement, *Larghetto*, from which the horns are omitted, is an island of C major surrounded by the E flat of the opening *Allegro di molto* and of the concluding *Presto*.

The many-sidedness of Bach is illustrated by the fact that, had he not been accepted as the most important exponent of keyboard music of his time, he would certainly have been regarded as a significant master of vocal forms and techniques. As it is, his virtues as an oratorio composer on the one hand and as a song composer on the other have been largely obscured. It so happens, however, that in his vocal music he was most particularly the representative composer of his time and environment. It is thought that the sons of Sebastian Bach spent most of their lives trying to escape from their patrimony. In so far as they did, they did not really succeed. The tensions of baroque expression, as exposed by Sebastian, left their mark on the work of his sons.

Emanuel—in spite of Burney's strictures on the performances he heard—was a fine composer of church music, but music that fitted the climate of his day.

> The splendid music for Michaelmas, *Holy, Holy, Holy*, by our worthy Kapellmeister Bach, which includes a masterly and elaborate double-chorus of angels and men, was performed several Sundays ago in our principal churches. Tomorrow, Saturday, and on Sunday, this double-chorus will be performed in the great Church of St Michael so that the Chorus of Angels can be placed high up over the body of the church, which is not possible in the other churches on account of the limitations of space.[23]

This piece was much thought of in north Germany, as Kantor Roemhild of Güstrow signified on 28th December 1779:

> In response to the requests of so many music lovers, I have decided to perform the famous *Holy, Holy, Holy*, of Kapellmeister Bach, on the Sunday following the Feast of the Three Kings on 9 January, 1780, in the great room of the Town Hall. I shall also perform *The Death of Abel* [J. H. Rolle, 1771]. Because I am aware that large numbers of admirers of Bach's work, both local and in distant places, have expressed a wish to hear it I did not wish to fail in making public my intention.[24]

In the larger field of oratorio Emanuel Bach commanded much attention, and through his essays in this form he exerted a powerful influence on communal music-making and on musical appreciation in Germany. For his works of this nature came just in time for the large-scale development of choral societies. He was of course faced with situations other than those with which his father had been faced. The hold of doctrine on music had loosened early in Hamburg, which was one reason for the wide disparity between the church cantatas of Telemann and Sebastian Bach. By the time Emanuel came to contemplate oratorio seriously (in 1770 he had composed the first of three Passiontide works) the Handelian influence had begun to take hold. Hamburg oratorio therefore was not designed for the church but the concert room, and the intention of the composer was not to stimulate conventional religious response but to awaken a general sense of wonder. The most celebrated of his oratorios was *Die Israeliten in der Wüste*, published in 1775. Large in dimension, the proportions of this work are different from those of a Handel oratorio in that the medium for expression is the orchestra rather than the chorus. There are in fact only six choruses in the work, of which the first is a splendid two-sectional movement of considerable power, and the penultimate a chorus with appended chorale. The element of colour is an ever important consideration, and throughout the oratorio Bach releases emotional situations and reveals landscapes by means of a variety of instrumentation. The instrumental introduction to the opening chorus is for muted strings, *pianissimo*, with two flutes wandering an octave above the violins. Concerto-wise this ritornello is taken up by the chorus which, however, extends the sense of desolation by a piece of direct realism:

Schering observed that Emanuel Bach remained true to the 'old style of Hamburg and was little influenced by the Italian cantata'.[25] It is of course in his expressionist essays that he recalls the old style, as is shown in the soprano aria—for the first Israelite woman—'Will er, dass sein Volk verderbe?' In a movement that in general terms has a good deal of Italian spirit in it the sudden interpolation of a word rich in significance within the German musical tradition causes a return to the delineatory processes of an earlier generation. The idea of 'suffering' is spelled out by a row of chromatics.

Like Handel in *Israel in Egypt* Bach generalizes, and individual characterization plays only a minor part. But the hero, Moses, is energetically projected in a strenuous aria, 'Gott Israels', at the beginning of Part II.

If Bach in other respects is a transitional composer, so also is he in this sphere, recollecting older practices (notably in the inevitable chorale insertion) and the direct intimations of Handelian method (especially in the *obbligato* bassoon that accompanies Moses' 'Gott sieh dein Volk im Staube liegen'), but also forecasting the pantheistic references of Haydn and Beethoven and the near sentimentality of certain of Mendelssohn's choral movements in *Elijah*. This is shown in the facile effectiveness of the Israelites' chorus, 'Du bist der Ursprung unsrer Noth'.

Bach's oratorios were also welcomed in Vienna, where the new-style oratorio was developing under the influence of van Swieten—to a meeting with whom Bach referred in a letter to Artaria of 14th July 1779.[26] On 7th April 1785, Bach's setting of Klopstock's *Morgengesang am Schöpfungsfeste* (published 1784) was performed during Lent at a concert in the National-Hoftheater in Vienna. This work again illustrates Bach's exposition of the principle that music exists to reflect nature. And it gave him opportunity to start with another effective piece of tone-painting.

Among the other oratorios the late *Auferstehung und Himmelfahrt Jesu*, to words by Carl Wilhelm Ramler, was highly thought of and was described by Schering as the setting of this text that 'put all the rest in the shade'.[27]

Bach's church music, as he himself suggested, was not intended to be cloistered. And because the more liberal theological tendencies of the 1770s and 1780s took the values of religion into the world, so Bach projected his collections of 'spiritual songs', of which the most familiar were those of settings of poems by Gellert (1758, 1764), Christoph Christian Sturm (Pastor of St Peter's, Hamburg) and Johann Andreas Cramer (1723–88). The last, published in 1774, were versions of Psalms, and they were extremely popular. Being so, but also of a serious nature, they helped to bridge the gap between the song of the classical period and the later Lied.

The full title of this collection indicates the new direction which solo song was to take: *Herrn Doctor Cramers übersetzte Psalmen mit Melodien zum Singen bey dem Claviere*. These were not only intended to be accompanied by pianoforte; the instrumental part was an essential part of the scheme, an adjunct to expression. In exploitation of an effective *motiv* Bach, not unmindful of the *ritornello* principle which he dealt with in summary form, hinted at the future function of *Leitmotiv*. Moreover, with the ample support of pianoforte tone he extended the vocal range, again to the general benefit of expressive purpose. Voice and pianoforte will be found to establish a new kind of unity, in that although each is independent both are interdependent. This collection (as others by Bach) is a staging-post on the high road of German Lied.

Some of the Psalms are reflective—*choralmässig, sehr langsam und nachdrücklich*—as, for example, Nos. 6, 25, 42 and 130; some are delicate and tender, particularly No. 23; some are of a refined simplicity, as No. 67 with its sinuously curving melodic line; a number are strong and durable. Of these Nos. 93 and 110 are outstanding; the first on account of its exaltation of mood, the second—but a short step from Beethoven's *Die Ehre Gottes*—because of its strenuous vitality.

In those of his works which employ the voice Bach was both at his most conservative and at his most progressive. Conservative because he stood firm by the precept that German music existed most effectively when attached to the German language, which led him to understand that it was the undertones and not the superficialities of verbal meaning that were significant; progressive because he recognized the inevitability of new techniques and fresh purposes. He infused a new seriousness into domestic song and in so doing prepared the way for the domination of the Lied over the bourgeois appreciation of music in Germany during the nineteenth century. Song, in this case, extended on the one hand to opera, and on the other to symphonic music.

REPUTATION OF EMANUEL BACH

Emanuel Bach was a tolerant man, and helpful to the young or the necessitous in his profession. He was sufficiently successful to have aroused envy; but he did not. His eminence was conceded without reserve. He was passionate by nature, but his passions were controlled. Their outlet was through his playing. Burney recorded his impressions of Emanuel's playing, and so did Carl Ludwig Junker, a Swiss writer, some four years later:

Bach played the pianoforte with sweetness, with precision, and with the utmost fire. So far as expression is concerned he is, perhaps, the best player of the present time. If he has a long note to press out in slow pathetic movements he knows how to produce an affecting mood, of grief and complaining, of which he alone is capable. He often catches fire, and a true enthusiasm, and takes on the appearance of one out of himself with rapture.[28]

A sociable man, Bach was helped towards fame by his willingness to conform to the general pattern. In Hamburg he was highly esteemed because he had become a typical Hamburger.

It was when the name of Sebastian became more widely discussed that that of Emanuel became less familiar. Twenty years or so after his death he had already been relegated to the position of a secondary composer—an interesting transitional figure. That notable Bach-lover, Samuel Wesley, in England, wrote of him in his memoirs as follows:

The Compositions of Emanuel Bach although not generally elaborated to that pitch of sublime excellence which characterises the effusions of his transcendant [sic] Father, Sebastian, are never the less entitled to high consideration and estimation. They consist principally of Music for keyed instruments and are generally remarkable for polished elegance and fluid execution. —The following Anecdote is an instance of the mild and gentle disposition of Sebastian.—The son above mentioned found himself perplexed and embarrassed in a certain modulation and signifying the same to his Father, the latter took the pen from his hand and having set all to rights returning the pen with these words—'My son, suppose, you were to try it this way.'

NOTES TO CHAPTER TEN

1. Thomas Lediard, *The German Spy*, London, 1738, p. 179.
2. Burney (*see* Chapter 8, Note 13 above), II, p. 251.
3. *Neue Zeitung*, No. 61.
4. i.e. Valentinskamp; a new concert room was built in 1761.
5. *Hamburgische Correspondent*, 27th September 1768, No. 155.
6. *Carl Burney's der Musik Doctors Tagebuch einer musikalischen Reise durch Frankreich und Italien* (Hamburg, 1772); the German edition of Burney's second part followed in 1773. Clearly Ebeling had been hard at work.
7. *See* Note 6 above, p. 255.

8. *See* Donald W. MacArdle, 'Beethoven and the Bach Family', in *M. & L.*, 38, No. 4, October 1957, p. 353 f.

9. *Erste Sammlung* of three Sonatas, Leipzig, 1776; a *Zweyte Sammlung* of four Sonatas followed in the next year.

10. Carl Ferdinand Pohl, *Joseph Haydn*, Berlin, 1875–82, 2 vols., I, p. 133.

11. J. C. F. Bach set Ramler's text in 1785, but the score was lost.

12. Quoted in J. Sittard, *Geschichte des Musik- und Concertwesens in Hamburg*, (Hamburg) Altona and Leipzig, 1890, p. 108.

13. *Briefe von Johann Heinrich Voss*, Halberstadt, 1829, vol. I, p. 205 f.

14. *See* Chapter 8, Note 13 above, II, p. 273.

15. The first two items are in the Euing Library, Glasgow University; the last three were listed in the Sale Catalogue (1814) of Burney's Library. *See* Stanley Godman, 'Bach's Copies of Ammerbach's "Orgel oder Instrument Tabulatur"', *M. & L.* 38, No. 1, 1957, p. 21 f.

16. Richard Fitzwilliam (1745–1816).

17. *See* Walter Emery, 'The London Autograph of "The Forty-Eight"', *M. & L.* 34, No. 2, 1953, p. 106 f. Clementi lived at Beckford's house until 1773.

18. *See* Peter F. Williams, 'J. S. Bach and English Organ Music', *M. & L.* 44, No. 2, 1963, p. 140 f.

19. *See* C. F. Pohl, *Haydn in London*, Vienna, p. 326.

20. This engraving is now in the Staatsbibliothek, Berlin, II, 1; 'Fordyce —Sängerin am Theater in London um die Mitte des 18 Jhdts.'

21. Recorded by DGG Archive 3280 (Stereo 73280).

22. Pub. Bärenreiter, 2043.

23. *Hamburgische Correspondent*, 23rd October 1776.

24. *Mecklenburgische Intelligenzblatt*, 1st January 1780. *Heilig, mit zwei Chören und eine Ariette, zur Einleitung von C. P. E. Bach*, was published by Breitkopf, 1779.

25. A. Schering, *Geschichte des Oratoriums*, Leipzig, 1911, p. 343.

26. *See* Chapter 8, Note 8, above, pp. 64–71, where nine of C. P. E. Bach's letters are published.

27. *See* Note 25 above, p. 373.

28. Carl Ludwig Junker, 'E. Bach', in *Zwanzig Componisten: eine Skizze*, Bern, 1776, pp. 7–13.

I I

The Classical Bachs

THE BÜCKEBURG TRADITION

Disputation about terminology is often a sterile operation; none more so than in respect of the word 'classical'. Nevertheless, as has been seen, the Bachs provide a useful index to changes of attitude, not only in regard to music but to artistic and social affairs in general, and in relation to some of them 'classical' has particular significance. On the whole—and this derived from their innate obstinacy which in turn came down from Thuringian antecedents—they were slow to change. Although seen in retrospect as pioneers of a new age Carl Philipp Emanuel and Wilhelm Friedemann carried a good deal of the apparatus of an age that was gone with their equipment; which was precisely the reason why they were in some respects ahead of their more patently modern contemporaries.

Carl Philip Emanuel and Wilhelm Friedemann were of one order, their half-brothers, Johann Christoph Friedrich (1732–95) and Johann Christian (1735–82), were of another. In the case of Christian the one distinguishing feature is made patent by reason of his close connection with Mozart; by Mozart's high regard for him, and by clear analogies in style and expression in their works. Christian was further separated from the family tradition by expatriation and by his ultimate concessions to English values. He was of course relatively famous. Johann Christoph Friedrich, on the other hand, is the forgotten son of Sebastian Bach, of whose works the generally well-informed musician would be hard put to it to mention a single one. Without making extravagant claims it may be observed that Johann Christoph Friedrich —the 'Bückeburg' Bach—deserves better than to be thrust into oblivion, if only because he was a signal exponent of the charm that in the classical era was taken to be one of its predominant qualities.

In itself the classical ethos—the conclusion of processes of refinement within refinement—is particularly aristocratic, as was unequivocally pointed out by Frederic the Great (see page 166). Lessing found a spiritual home at the Court at Wolfenbüttel, Goethe at that of Weimar; Johann Christoph Friedrich Bach lived the whole of his adult life in the little Parnassus that was Bückeburg under the rule of Wilhelm, Count of Schaumburg-Lippe; the Bachs of Meiningen, who were painters, lived under the protection of the Thuringian hills and the benevolent House of Saxe-Meiningen. The anachronism of the smaller German states (as distinct from those controlled by the major ruling Houses) probably justified itself towards its end by a frequent care for values that were, before long, to be obliterated.

Bückeburg, between Hannover and Minden, is one of those little towns, of an infinite charm, in which time stands still. To this day it is half medieval, half baroque, and permeated with a sense of grace in living that is still inherent in the quiet parkland and the restrained rhythms of the buildings and the decorations of the Schloss. The town itself is crowned with the splendour of the Stadtkirche, built by Ernst, Count of Holstein, Schaumburg and Sternberg in the early seventeenth century. Ernst, who altered the Schloss and added its *goldene Saal*, was the inspiration of the musical tradition at Bückeburg. Heinrich Schütz was Kapellmeister to the Count between 1615 and 1617, and among the works he wrote especially for this musical establishment was the *Psalmenbuch* of 1619. Schütz's successor as Kapellmeister was Johann Grabbe (1585–1655), also a student of the school of Venice, a madrigalist and composer of instrumental music. A great-grandson of Grabbe, named Münchhausen, was also a Court and town musician in Bückeburg. His daughter, Lucia Elisabeth, a singer at the same Court, became the wife of Johann Christoph Friedrich Bach.

THE INFLUENCE OF COUNT WILHELM AT BÜCKEBURG

The second great period in the cultural history of Bückeburg was that into which this Bach was introduced. The then reigning count was Wilhelm (1724–77), whose reign lasted from 1748 until his death. Wilhelm set out to make Bückeburg a centre of cultural influence. Having ensured a proper regard for the arts of war by the foundation of a military school he turned to the arts of peace, and in 1765 called Thomas Abbt (1738–66) to Bückeburg to devise a new educational programme.

Abbt, a Halle-trained theologian, sometime Professor of Philosophy at Frankfurt/Oder, was in general sympathy with the aims of Gessner at Göttingen. He was devoted to Frederic the Great (and the cause of Prussia), was a disciple of Lessing and a collaborator with Nikolai and Moses Mendelssohn. In 1763 he visited Voltaire in Switzerland. A new *Schulordnung*, particularly declaring war on all sorts of useless 'mythology', was decreed by the Court on June 29th 1766. Five years later Johann Gottfried Herder (1744–1803) came to Bückeburg as the principal preacher and as a member of the Consistory. Yet another of the brilliant young men then emerging, Herder—'decided, clear, pedagogic, knowing his own aims and fond of communicating his ideas'[1]—came to Bückeburg, with a fine reputation as philosopher and teacher. Not greatly loved, for he could be 'rude, sarcastic and bitter',[2] Herder none the less made friends in Bückeburg, not least with Johann Christoph Friedrich Bach.

COURT MUSIC AT BÜCKEBURG

Count Wilhelm of Schaumburg-Lippe was not only enthusiastic for music in a general way, but, like Frederic the Great, also a practising musician, well able to play the pianoforte efficiently for chamber music performances. It was by this means, and through his attendance at music parties at Potsdam, that he became aware of the younger Bachs. In 1751 Emanuel published two all-purpose trios (with alternative instrumentation) in Nürnberg, and dedicated them to Wilhelm of Schaumburg-Lippe. At this time Johann Christoph Friedrich was nineteen years of age, and had been in the service of the count since the beginning of 1750. His recommendation had come by way of Emanuel, whose recognition of the count's acceptance of the recommendation is implied by the Dedication of his trios. That Friedrich had gained a place at Bückeburg was the last great joy of his aged father's life.

Friedrich was a pupil at the Thomasschule, and for a brief period essayed a course in law at the university. He learned music from his father, and in some respects at least was the most apt of the sons. It was he, according to Forkel (relying on the testimony of Friedemann), who was the ablest keyboard player among them, and the one who was most expert in the presentation and interpretation of their father's works. Friedrich also had lessons from Altnikol, Agricola,

Homilius and Kirnberger. When he left home it must have been a wrench to his parents, who, however, rejoicing in his good fortune, were glad to take Müthel (later Herder's friend) into the household as pupil and assistant.

When Friedrich settled in as Court musician at Bückeburg he found the place dominated by Italian influence, Angelo Colonna being leader of the orchestra and Giovanni Battista Serini being Court composer. Favourite composers at Bückeburg at that time were Tartini, Alessandro Scarlatti, Pergolesi, Porpora, Jommelli and Hasse. In 1752 Lucia Münchhausen was appointed to the staff of musicians as a singer, a circumstance congenial to Bach, who married her in the summer of 1755. His stipend was 200 thalers, hers 100 thalers (according to custom with certain extra emoluments in kind), but their living expenses were considerably reduced by the count's wedding present of a large kitchen garden. Since, however, this was in time of war there were certain complications; not for the newly married Bachs, but for the Italians. In 1756 they packed up and went home, and the times being unpropitious for the appointment of Italian successors their places temporarily were left vacant. It was not until 1759 that the count came to a decision concerning his musical staff. When he did, he did the sensible thing, by naming Friedrich Bach *Konzertmeister*, whose stipend eventually reached 1,000 thalers (Colonna had received 600) a year (with firewood, etc.). In the same year a son, Wilhelm Friedrich Ernst, was born, the first of eight children. There is a rather touching little note from Bach to the count, written on 3rd January 1761, indicating that at this time he was not in good health and that he needed to take particular care for his diet.[3]

In 1765 the count, belatedly, married; his bride being the twenty-one year old Marie Eleonore who developed a warm understanding of, and friendship for, the Bach family. It is notable that both the count—to Herder—and the countess—to Friedrich Bach—dispensed with the usual formalities in their correspondence with those of their staff for whom they had a particular regard; an unusual practice in days when differences of social status were, according to convention, keenly emphasized.

There is extant one particularly charming letter from Countess Marie Eleonore. Couched in the most personal terms—it accompanied a gift—it shows how, in the final issue, distinctions of station become irrelevant.

Bückeburg,
April 25, 1774

Well-born and Worthy Music Director:

If you would be so good as to accept the trifle sent herewith, regard it as a mark of esteem against each piece of music whereby you are able to lift up the heart, and to inspire noble sentiments and actions. In the first place all thanks are due to you yourself. I have done nothing more than to show from a distance that I am, perhaps, a not entirely unworthy listener to your excellent songs; my interest is considerable, and only imperfect in relation to what you have given us. If Nature had endowed me with a better courage and voice then by now I would be singing in your choirs; but since that is not possible here, then I hope in a better world to take part in the great 'Hallelujah', for which you prepare us and give us so much happiness.

In esteem and gratitude I wish that all the blessings of Heaven may be with you and on your dear home.

Marie Eleonore
Countess of Schaumburg-Lippe

FRIEDRICH BACH AND HERDER

By 1774 Bach was in full spate as a composer, his works of this period being stimulated by his close association with Herder. Already in 1768, when M. C. Bock of Hamburg (persuaded by Emanuel Bach?) issued his six quartets for flute, violin, viola and (figured) bass, Friedrich had shown himself to be a composer of distinctive gifts. His handling of the medium, in which he demonstrated a tact similar to that of Haydn in allowing a more than usual independence to the participating instruments, was more expert than his manipulation of thematic and harmonic resource. In the proper spirit of 'house-music' he preferred to remain with a kind of casual, Italianate charm to adventuring in the by-ways of introspection. Part of the business of composition of course was to know what was wanted. This Friedrich Bach did know, and his responses were inerrant. In this he resembled his younger brother, Johann Christian. Coming to Bückeburg under the supervision of Italian colleagues, at first he did his best to furnish music after their manner. The solo cantata, *Cassandra*, is, however, the solitary surviving example of a setting of an Italian text by him.

Karl Geiringer, who notes the originality and felicity of the instrumentation, refers to the 'warm tenderness' of the music while noting at the same time that Bach was some way behind the *Sturm und Drang* of the text.[4] When Herder arrived in Bückeburg in 1771 this was one of the first works of Bach that he heard. Johann Friedrich owed a good deal to Emanuel, who helped to popularize him through frequent inclusion in the issues of the *Musikalisches Vierlerley* (which became an excellent show-case for the works of the Bach family). Here Friedrich demonstrated his submission to the new principles of German Lied (in the establishment of which his contribution was not negligible) by settings of poems by Lessing and C. F. Weisse. These songs were with pianoforte accompaniment, and of more subtlety than superficially they may appear. Bach was a master of the elegant vocal contour; but his inflections, his variation of tessitura, his expansion and contraction of rhythmic figuration display a keen sensitivity to verbal considerations. The dialogue between Age and Youth in the setting of Lessing's *Die Gespenster*[5] falls somewhat short of Schubert's in *Death and the Maiden*, but that was the direction in which Friedrich Bach was moving. Johann Ernst Bach, of Eisenach, was also moving in this direction.

In 1773 Herder married Caroline Flachsland from Alsace, and both he and his wife took part in Bach's musical evenings. In that year the first Herder–Bach work was performed: *Die Kindheit Jesu*. By this time, as has been seen already, the place of oratorio in German musical life had been re-assessed, and some up-grading had taken place. This was due in large measure to developments in Hamburg (see pages 215–218), with which, through his brother, Friedrich Bach was in close contact. In 1769 he had made his own contribution to the Hamburg-type oratorio by emulating Telemann and Graun and setting Ramler's *Der Tod Jesu*, into the introduction of which—*Du, dessen Augen flossen*—a chorale of Sebastian's, from the *St Matthew Passion*, was inset. On 11th February 1773[6] *Die Kindheit Jesu* was performed at Bückeburg and the countess was enchanted by its 'heavenly music'. Well she might be. The opening movement of the oratorio, in which two shepherds, one a bass, the other a tenor, prompted by an angel, hear music—described in the score as 'himmlische Music'—which comes nearer and nearer. Thus the strings, muted, and without cembalo, introduce a motiv which takes on the character almost of a *Leitmotiv*. Repeated twice, each time a fifth higher, it culminates in a chorus of praise:

After this there follows a *da capo* aria of great tenderness from Maria (alto)—'Schlummre sanft in deiner Krippe.' Friedrich worked quickly at this oratorio—it was completed within a month—and throughout endeavoured to realize Herder's concept. Herder opposed realism and dramatics in church music, preferring the persuasive power of lyricism supported by the subliminal influences that he perceived in musical *Tonmalerei*. Once again, however, Friedrich paid his respects to his father by means of a chorale movement.[7]

A month after the performance of this Christmas Oratorio came *Die Auferweckung Lazarus*, which has notably fine opening and closing arias in F minor that contain a characteristic depth of Bachian feeling. The collaboration with Herder led further to cantatas for Whitsuntide (1773), Michaelmas (1775)[8] and Ascensiontide (1776), and in the latter year also a Passiontide work, *Der Fremdling auf Golgotha*. *Die Auferweckung Lazarus* is published in a modern edition,[9] but the music of the Whitsuntide Cantata[10] and *Der Fremdling auf Golgotha* (like much of Friedrich Bach's music) is lost. The Michaelmas Cantata is one that would appear to have been performed in Hamburg, the score in Tübingen[11] bearing the inscription *das Bass accompagnato von C. P. E. Bach*. In 1785 Bach returned to Ramler, and his second Christmas Oratorio, *Die Hirten bey der Krippe Jesu* (no longer in existence), was also well thought of in Bückeburg. It was indeed for his oratorios that he was most remembered in the town.

This period of his life was generally productive. Between 1768 and 1770 nine symphonies and a great deal of chamber music were composed, and in 1773–4 Breitkopf of Leipzig issued a set of fifty-one settings of 'spiritual' poems by Baltasar Münter of Copenhagen. Comparable with the 'spiritual' songs of Emanuel they were praised for their beauty by C. H. Bitter, but, a little unjustly, described as having less 'depth'.[12]

In 1776 Herder accepted Goethe's invitation to become Court Preacher and General Superintendent in Weimar—not to the entire satisfaction of the people of Weimar who had heard stories of how the philosopher-poet was in the habit of ascending the pulpit in hunting attire. The loss to Friedrich Bach was considerable. Not only had Herder stimulated his interest in the sphere of oratorio but also of opera. Unfortunately the scores of *Brutus* and of *Philoktetes*, both of the year 1774, are lost. The so-called solo cantata, *Die Amerikanerin*, also belongs to this period, being printed by J. F. Hartnock of Riga in 1776. It has been surmised that this may have been intended for an opera and to have been sung by Bach's wife. She must have found it pleasant to sing. It is warm (moving always to tonalities on the flat side) and lyrical, with two especially charming arias—'Schön ist mein Mädchen' in A flat and 'Mein Herz' in B flat—which are as *gemütlich* as anything by any of the Bachs. In 1777 Count Wilhelm died, being succeeded by his nephew Philipp Ernst. Wilhelm and his countess had imposed on the Bückeburg Court a pattern of culture that derived both from the *Aufklärung* and also from the climate of *Pietismus*. The spirit of the former was with the count, while that of the latter with the countess. A keen and efficient musician, Wilhelm preferred the rationalism of instrumental forms, Marie Eleonore the mystical attributes of 'sacred music'. Herder complained of Wilhelm's audible conversation during the performance of *Der Tod Jesu*, but observed the rapture shown by Marie Eleonore over *Die Kindheit Jesu*.[13] Under the governance of Philipp Ernst liberal tendencies continued, but the echoes of Pietism became more faint. So far as music was concerned that was handed over to the new countess, Juliane,[14] whose jurisdiction lasted until Bach's death, since on the death of her husband, in 1787, she acted as regent.

A VISIT TO THE 'LONDON' BACH

With the change of regime Friedrich Bach concluded that he was owed a real holiday. Bound, as all the Bachs, by family ties, he sought permission (which was granted on 15th April 1778) to visit his brother Johann Christian in London. There was a particular reason why he wanted to see Johann Christian at that time. His eldest son, Wilhelm Friedrich Ernst, was now nineteen years old, and proposing to follow in his father's footsteps. Conscious of his own conservatism (which most commentators have not been slow to observe) Friedrich realized that in order to succeed some acquaintance with the world beyond Bückeburg was desirable. Together, Friedrich and Wilhelm Friedrich Ernst travelled to London by way of Hamburg, where they spent a little time with Emanuel. In London they had the great pleasure of hearing Christian's 'new serious opera, with Grand Choruses', *La Clemenza di Scipione*, and of appreciating the esteem in which the London Bach was held. The consequences of the expedition were twofold. Wilhelm Friedrich Ernst stayed behind as a pupil of his uncle. As for Friedrich:

> After his journey to London, which made him acquainted with the works of Handel, Haydn and Mozart, he devoted himself increasingly to the composition of instrumental works. Between 1792 and 1794 there were ten symphonies. In respect of its instrumentation and its excellence of technique and musicianship his last work—a symphony in B flat major—can stand beside the symphonies of Haydn.[15]

By the 1780s the two poles of German music (as distinct from German-Austrian music) were represented by Emanuel Bach on the one hand and by Christian Bach on the other. In the first case the revolutionary character of the music—if so it may be described—came from within the composers of the German tradition. In the second, modernity derived from a strong and patent respect for Italian style. Friedrich Bach admired both his talented half-brother—whose encouragement was near at hand to support his self-confidence—and his famous brother in England. He himself, of a complaisant temperament, placed his creativity somewhere between the two. This was congenial to his patrons at Bückeburg, since the reality of a temperate conservatism allowed the suggestion of a purposeful forward-looking outlook. Friedrich Bach may not have been the greatest of the sons of Sebastian (a conclusion reached by every critic, whether aware of his musical output or not), but he was not the least able. More than any of the others he understood exactly where he stood in relation to his environment and the nature of his function.

COMPETENCE OF A KAPELLMEISTER

Like all of his profession Friedrich was a teacher, and his pedagogic interests are shown in the four books of *Musikalische Nebenstunden* (Rinteln, 1787–8). These volumes were well subscribed and there are interesting names among the subscribers, including Forkel at Göttingen, the organist Lemme at Braunschweig, who had taken the place that Friedemann Bach had coveted, a 'Herr Candidat Bach' of Ambleben and a Demoiselle Delius of Bielefeld. The fact of Forkel's name on the list indicates that he was indefatigable in his cultivation of every Bach contact. The name of Delius here appears in music for the first time, to furnish an unexpected and fortuitous link with English music. Ernst Wilhelm Friedrich Delius of Bielefeld—who fought under Blücher in the Napoleonic Wars—was the grandfather of the English composer Frederick Delius. The Demoiselle Delius acquainted with Friedrich Bach was (it would seem) an aunt of Ernst Wilhelm Friedrich. In the first volume of his *Nebenstunden* Friedrich Bach neatly acknowledges the musicality of the English by three pretty dances, Angloises, of which the most charming (see below) matches up with the inventions of, say, James Hook, whose *Guida di Musica* belonged to the same period.

The *Nebenstunden*, preceded by a short guide to the proper practice of ornamentation, also contained songs—settings of words by Klopstock, Ludwig Heinrich Hölty (1748–76), Matthias Claudius (1740–1815) and Friedrich Wilhelm Gotter (1746–97), and of other less familiar or unspecified poets. In these Bach, together with the poets, shows the decline of the bright principles of German classicism into the sub-tropics of nineteenth-century Romanticism: in, for instance, the settings of 'Als Gellert starb', or 'Ich bin ein teutsches Mädchen':

Ich bin ein teu-tsches Mäd-chen,mein Aug ist blaw und sanft mein Blick!

of which the words run on—'Ich hab ein Herz das edel ist und stolz und gut'. In this manner was the cause of nationalism served. Of his other, last period, vocal works interest centres on the extended setting of Ramler's *Ino* (published by Breitkopf in Leipzig in 1786) for the comparison it affords with Telemann's *Ino* of some twenty years earlier. Telemann's work, intense in dramatic conception, requires a virtuoso singer; it also requires fine orchestral playing. This is music that has the promise of *Sturm und Drang*. Friedrich Bach's handling of the theme is more classical in two senses: it has an elegance that is within the concept of classicism held by Lessing, and the stock patterns of the early classical symphonic school. It is, however, interesting in its extensive range of tonalities—from G major to B flat, to B minor (for the aria 'Wo bin ich'), to A major, and finally back to G major. The lyrical element runs into a charming dance interlude—the kind of movement that Wilhelm Friedrich Ernst was also expert at (see page 279)—which is a preface to the song of the tritons and nereids:

Bach was a not inconsiderable symphonist, and his extant works are a useful and attractive index to the provincial progress of symphony between *c.* 1768 and 1794. Of his twenty or so works in this form less than half have survived. Three only are in his own hand—in C major, *c.* 1770 (Staatsbibliothek, Berlin); E flat major, *c.* 1770; and B flat major, 1794 (Marburg-Lahn). The parts of the E flat symphony were recovered from a Dutch antiquarian book dealer and restored to the Bückeburg Archives in 1963.[16] The B flat symphony is the only one existing in score.

Until 1792 Bach composed symphonies in three movements, well formed and in liveliness of manner and deftness of scoring similar to those of Christian Bach. Occasionally, however, Johann Christoph Friedrich wrote more or less expansively, as in the 1770 E flat symphony, of which the contrasted first movement themes are:

The earliest of Bach's symphonies, showing no lack of modesty, are those in D minor and E major (Peter collection Nos. 76 and 80), of which the parts are preserved in the Moravian Music Foundation, Winston-Salem, N. Carolina, and in F (No. 77), B flat (No. 78), A (No. 79) and F (No. 39), in the Moravian Music Library, Bethlehem, Pennsylvania. All these works (together with others by Johann Christian and Johann Ernst of Eisenach) were copied by Johann F. Peter when he was in Europe *c.* 1768, and later used by the Moravian Collegium Musicum at Winston-Salem, which Peter conducted. Showing the same kind of easy manner as his concertos, cantatas and oratorios, all these symphonies reflect the pleasant circumstances of life in Bückeburg.

In his symphonies in F (1792), D, C, G minor, D minor (1793–4) and B flat (dated by a copyist, September, 1794), however, he fulfilled the symphonic design of the later classical period by writing four movements. In the B flat symphony—the only one of this group extant—he followed Haydn in prefacing the first movement with a slow introduction. In the earlier symphonies the scoring was for strings only (D minor, A major, F major—Bethlehem 39), horns and strings (E ma.), or flutes (or oboes), horns and strings. Clarinets are added in the B flat symphony, and with his enlarged woodwind section Bach somewhat broadened the emotional properties of his style. A craftsman after the order of the Bachs of an older tradition, Friedrich was impeccable in the technique of scoring. On the other hand he lacked the talent for compelling thematic (or harmonic) development. His strength lies in lyrical statement rather than in dialectic. The merits and shortcomings of his music are the result of remaining for almost forty-five years in one place. Apart from his application to succeed Telemann in Hamburg he appears never to have tried to move. Perhaps we cannot blame him. Bückeburg was a very charming place, and the conditions of work not far from ideal.

On 1st February 1795 the *Schaumburg-Lippische Landesanzeiger* reported as follows:

> On 26 January Music Director Johann Friedrich Bach died of a chest complaint, in the 63rd year of his life and the 45th year of his service in Bückeburg.
> ... Through his excellent compositions, of which connoisseurs

reckon *Die Hyrten bey der Krippe* and *Die Pilgrime* [sic] *auf Golgotha* as the finest, and also through his devout disposition and upright way of life, he has ensured that he will not be forgotten by the world.

The most equable of the Bachs was buried in the Jetenburgh graveyard in Bückeburg, content that one son—the last composer of the long line—was honourably maintaining the family tradition. He was succeeded at Bückeburg by Franz Christoph Neubauer (1760–95), one of many Bohemian musicians then active in the orchestras of northern Germany. A violinist, who went to Vienna from Prague and who was acquainted with both Haydn and Mozart, Neubauer enjoyed his office at Bückeburg only for a short time. He died of drink.

PAINTERS IN THE FAMILY

One branch of the Bach clan carried German music, across the bridge of the *Aufklärung*, from baroque to classical. During the same period another branch helped to introduce and to fortify classical, and German, principles within the sphere of the visual arts. The two branches were linked during the classical period by Emanuel Bach—as patron and connoisseur—and his younger son, Johann Sebastian. Johann Ludwig of Meiningen was admired by his cousin, the first Johann Sebastian, for his musicianship. Ludwig's second son, Gottlieb Friedrich, however, was praised by Emanuel on account of his skill in portraiture. Emanuel spoke as a satisfied client. Not only had he commissioned a portrait of himself from Gottlieb Friedrich, but he owned a painting of Johann Ludwig (which went to the Royal Library, in Berlin, after Emanuel's death) by Gottlieb Friedrich, and also a pastel of Sebastian.

The case for heredity which is normally adduced to account for the musicality of the Bachs may also be invoked in respect of the artistic talents of the Meiningen branch of the family. Johann Ludwig was an artist as well as a musician, and his wife was the daughter of a distinguished artist. Thus Gottlieb Friedrich (the second of Ludwig's sons) had initial advantages, which were enhanced by his environment. The conditions at Meiningen—in a landscape of melting beauty—were comfortable, and not only was the reigning duke, Karl (1754–82), busily encouraging his artists and craftsmen to add rococo embellishments all over the interior of his Schloss, but the court officials and townspeople, now absorbed in the establishment of middle-class values, were intent on having their portraits painted. Gottlieb Friedrich spent the whole of his life at Meiningen. He married Juliane Friederike Charlotte Anthing—an aunt of a French general of that name. The house in which he lived, in Schlossgasse 4, having escaped the fire that destroyed some buildings in the town in 1874, is still to be seen.

Gottlieb Friedrich was reputed to have painted a portrait of Sebastian Bach—presumably during the time he was in Leipzig. A former attribution of this pastel study to Konrad Geiger, of Erlangen,[17] being impossible in that Geiger was not born until the year of Sebastian's death, the authenticity of Gottlieb Friedrich's claim may be upheld. This portrait remained with Sebastian and after his death became the property of Emanuel who indeed informed Forkel, on 10th April 1774, that he owned such a pastel portrait. Already possessing an oil portrait of his father, Emanuel exchanged the pastel with Johann Philipp, son of Gottlieb Friedrich, for the aforementioned portrait of Johann Ludwig. The picture of Sebastian (which was not signed by the artist) remained in the possession of the Meiningen Bachs, eventually passing to the great-grandson of Johann Philipp, Paul Bach.[18] Gottlieb Friedrich, whose chief claim to fame this portrait is, painted numerous portraits of members of the local and of nearby ducal houses.[19] It is, however, in studies which demanded less formality that Bach showed his interpretative capacity. In, for example, the lively portrait of Johann Wilhelm Treiber (1711–92) of the famous academic family of Arnstadt, where he too was Director of the Grammar School.[20] Or in the delicate handling of subdued lights in the *Porträt einer Dame in grauweissen Seidenkleid mit Rüschen verziet*.[21]

Gottlieb Friedrich had two sons, Johann Philipp (1752–1846) and Samuel Friedrich (1755–1841). The younger became assistant minister at Neuhaus in 1782, and from 1785 until his retirement in 1815 was pastor of the parish. The elder, godson of Emanuel Bach, inherited the posts of organist, cembalist and Court painter at Meiningen. He also inherited the recurring Bach characteristic of indefatigability. Johann Philipp, a robust character, is reported to have painted more than a thousand pastels, and there were few of the bourgeoisie of Meiningen and district who did not possess one or more examples of his work. He was, as it were, the Telemann of German pastel art. Some of his works were official portraiture, but most were done without the compulsion to flatter a fashionable patron. Johann Philipp was, however, not indifferent to the value of his work, and his meticulous book-keeping shows him to have been in economic matters a typical German small-town bourgeois. His energy went not only into his art, but also into his life. The longest lived of all the Bachs (his great-grandson Paul coming next in order of longevity), he would seem to have enjoyed life more than most. His first wife, Amalie Briegleb, was the daughter of the Director of the Grammar School in Coburg. By her he had three children, of whom only one reached maturity.[22] Secondly he married the daughter of a merchant of Schweinfurt, Johanna Rosina Frankenberger, who bore him four children.[23] The extent to which Bach involved himself in the recreational affairs of the community is indicated by his enthusiasm for marksmanship, and the atmosphere of *Der Freischütz* is evoked by Johann Philipp Bach's record as a huntsman in the wooded glens of Thuringia. In 1825 his fellow members of the Meiningen Shooting Club celebrated his jubilee as one of their company. Ten years later the sixtieth anniversary of his membership was marked by an anonymous commemorative poem.[24]

The high tide of absolutism had passed from the little courts when Johann Christoph Friedrich Bach worked in Bückeburg and Johann Philipp Bach in Meiningen. Power rested in Vienna, in Berlin and to a lesser extent in Dresden. The dukes in the satellite states, left with local authority, sometimes followed the tendency inherent in the *Aufklärung* towards a liberal philosophy. But—to do him justice—the influence of Frederic the Great had in some respects also encouraged attitudes of tolerance. The last years of the eighteenth century were congenial to the artist with a Court appointment which permitted as much of freedom as was possible at Bückeburg and Meiningen. Such congeniality is reflected in the music of J. C. F. Bach, and also in the pictures of Johann Philipp. There is a similarity of feeling in the works of these two highly civilized artists. Each, in his own medium, handled form with ease, and colour with imagination. Each was responsive to the prevailing aesthetic considerations of the period, but restrained in their application. Liveliness, charm and sobriety add up to less than genius; but in a disordered world their virtues are not inconsiderable. And their cultivation in small, self-contained communities was of lasting benefit to those communities.

As a young man, Johann Philipp Bach spent some time in Erlangen, where he came to know Konrad Geiger (1751–1808). In the paintings of Bach and Geiger, as well as of Johann Friedrich Schröter (or Schröder) (1757–1812), there was a common preference for clear bright colours, that suggested acquaintance with the works of the English artists Gainsborough and Reynolds. (The former was connected, a little tenuously, to the main Bach tradition through his friendship with Johann Christian Bach and Karl Friedrich Abel.) Schröter, to whom certain pictures by Johann Philipp Bach were attributed,[25] undertook commissions for English patrons, and his portrait of the Duchess of York (daughter-in-law of George III) was engraved by Henry Hudson.

Johann Philipp Bach handled his subjects with sympathy, his capacity for being able to reveal the personality of his sitter being especially shown in his portrait of Major von Uglansky of Meiningen,[26] while his delicacy in the harmonization of discreet colouring—after the manner of his father—is evident in his *Porträt einer Dame mit schleier in rosen Seidenkleid mit weissen Spitzen*,[27] and in his various studies of the Duchess Luise Eleonore. In the exhibition of works in the Meiningen collection of 1904 Bach was represented by 120 examples, ranging from the companionable study of a Meiningen Court musician named Tischer and realistic reflections of Court functionaries (particularly of members of the Bibra family) and the solid Thuringian burghers and their wives, to the classicism of *Pan, einem Ziegenbock auf der Schalmei vorblasend*, which could have been by Oeser or by his pupil, Johann Sebastian Bach the younger.

That Johann Philipp Bach did not receive the credit due to him (because it was doubted that Bachs could be expert otherwise than in music?) was recognized by Lothar Briegel, who regarded him as the outstanding master in pastels of the German tradition.[28] He had more strength and more personality, remarked Briegel, than the more favoured (Johann Heinrich?) Tischbein. Otherwise, by an unnamed critic quoted by Ulrich Nicolai, he was the German La Tour.[29]

JOHANN SEBASTIAN BACH II

Johann Sebastian Bach the younger (1749–78)[30] spent his youth in Potsdam and Berlin. Showing an early talent for painting, he was a pupil of Andreas Ludwig Krüger (1743–1803). At the age of twenty-one he was sent to Leipzig, where Adam Friedrich Oeser (1717–99) had for the last seven years been Director of the Academy of Art. Oeser, who had worked for many years in Dresden (from which he was a refugee at the time of the attack on the city by Frederic the Great), was the most important artist in Germany at that time. A close friend of Winckelmann, praised by Herder, and drawing-master to Goethe, Oeser stimulated a far-reaching enthusiasm for all that was classical and all that was antique, all that was Greek and all that was Roman.

Oeser instructed his pupils in the philosophy of Winckelmann, that truth and beauty lay in the works of antiquity, that beauty was a liberating force, and that it was the duty of patriotic German artists to build a new Athens on their own soil. Oeser, who had a strong affection for Sebastian Bach the younger, gave him much personal attention and directed him to study and to make copies of the Bacchanalian studies of Giulio Carpioni. One such exercise by Sebastian was exhibited in Dresden in 1771. In the following year, on the eve of the opening of the annual Dresden Exhibition, on 27th February, Oeser wrote to Christian Ludwig von Hagedorn in the Saxon capital, complaining of a lack of creative talent in Leipzig, but adding that Bach was excepted from his strictures.[31] In the following two years Bach exhibited a canvas of 'historical impressions', two 'landscapes' and 'a historical drawing and a landscape in moonlight'. The last may well have been that which was engraved by J. F. Bause in Leipzig in 1787 under the title of 'Der Sommerabend, Landschaft mit Mondbeleuchtung'.

In music the passage from the cult of sensitivity towards that of avowed Romanticism is noticed in the progress of the Lied—through Emanuel, Johann Ernst and Johann Friedrich Bach, for example. Johann Sebastian Bach's studies of moonlight are at the beginning of a process that led to D. F. Caspar's more evocative 'Baüme im Mondschein',[32] while his idylls were the prelude to classically posed essays in actuality such as J. A. Hurlein's 'Bauergesellschaft'.[33]

In 1774 Sebastian wrote from Dresden to Oeser's daughter (who was helping him then financially), and the tone of the letter (which shows that he had acquaintance with the music publisher Breitkopf who also dealt in works of art) demonstrates the familiar relationship he enjoyed with the Oeser family.[34]

In February 1776 Oeser wrote once again to Hagedorn, giving a full description of Bach's landscape, 'Monument in Arkadien', which was to be shown in that year's Dresden exhibition. To his description he added these words, which suggest a high degree of independence, to be expected of a Bach, on the part of the young artist:

> So far as I am concerned Bach is altogether a new Phoenix in the world of art. I have placed him in different kinds of art, and after the most stringent tests, decided that I must let him go where he displays the most of his talents. I recommended him to [Francesco] Albani and to the study of Nature. I once said to him that he should look at [Albani's] pictures from life and carefully

consider all that was good in the works of that master. He went into this with the greatest enthusiasm and looked at the best drawings and copper engravings in [Gottfried] Winkler's collection [in Leipzig]. He came back, all cold, and said that he had found first-rate landscapes, but no interesting pictures from life. To this I replied that he must not stop looking; for if he did not find any of the ideas that were in Nature in art then he would not find them in Nature either.

The 'Monument in Arkadien' was Sebastian Bach's last exhibit in Dresden, for in that same year he took the road, taken by many young German painters, that led to Rome. He was supported by a subvention from Hagedorn. Here, according to his friend Karl Wilhelm Dassdorf (1750–1812), the Court Librarian in Dresden, his work was appreciated by all those who could tell a good artist when they saw one. During this time he contributed drawings to C. F. Weisse's three-volume *Komischen Opern* (Leipzig 1777). In the same year he illustrated a scene from Thomson's *Seasons* (*Damon und Musidora*), which was also engraved in Leipzig by Bause. Full of enthusiasm for his art, and full of promise, Johann Sebastian Bach, artist, died in Rome in 1778 at the age of twenty-nine.

Not only was he influenced by Oeser, but also by Solomon Gessner, whose *Idyllen* had appeared in 1756. Gessner's motivation of the 'Zephyrs' was imitated by virtually every classical German artist, Sebastian Bach included, for half a century at least. Bause engraved Bach's 'Les Zephyres, aus den Idyllen von Gessner', while other engravings after Bach by him included 'Die büssende Magdalena Battoni's' and a 'Landschaft mit der Ansicht einer Mühle'.[35]

In 1790 J. F. Goldschmidt of Hamburg issued a catalogue of the works of Bach, detailing 103 pages of drawings (lightly coloured), antique scenes—with trees, temples, nymphs, fauns, shepherds, shepherdesses, representations of ruins and interpretations of mythological subjects.

The *Ideale Landschaft* illustration shows the attitude and style of a minor master who might, had he lived, have become a major figure in the history of German painting. This work, typical of the artist and the period, shows a lake backed by an aqueduct. On the hill to the left a temple ruin looks across at the tree that borders the right-hand side of the scene. Just left of centre a marble goddess appears to listen to the entreaties of a group of women and children. It is a far cry from the world and the thoughts of Johann Sebastian Bach I. But the artist was his grandson, and this picture was painted only a quarter of a century after the great Kantor's death.

In 1782 Dassdorf wrote of his friend:

> He was one of the finest of Oeser's pupils. He loved Oeser very much, and promised great things in the future for him. Already this talented young artist had fulfilled Oeser's high hopes, since under his tutelage he had taken gigantic strides forward in his art, and was very gifted in drawing landscapes full of feeling and spirit.[36]

JOHANN ERNST BACH OF EISENACH

The words 'full of feeling and spirit' have occurred so frequently in one form or another during this survey of the 'classical' Bachs that accepted terminologies appear to have had their accepted significance reversed, or even lost. If so, however inconvenient, it is probably a good thing in that attention is thereby directed to the particular 'thing in itself': to the man, to the man in his environment, to his works, to a specific work. In a network of relationships final consideration is of the individual, of the work of the individual, of the quality of uniqueness inherent in each. Each Bach was himself and no other. At no time was this more markedly the case than in the second part of the eighteenth century. That this was so was of course a consequence of the revaluation of personality that came with and from the *Aufklärung*. Even in the greatest musical dynasty ever known in the Western world music itself was not then so exclusive a calling as it had been. The Meiningen Bachs, and Emanuel's second son in particular, show the devolutionary process by which musical instincts were metamorphosed, at the end of which process were painters where there had been musicians. The process was ineluctable. Also ineluctable was the changing importance of particular centres of musical interest. For the greater part Thuringia had been evacuated of its musical significance. But there still remained in Eisenach one Thuringian Bach of no inconsiderable talent: Johann Ernst, son of Johann Bernhard (see page 71).

A pupil of the Thomasschule in Leipzig and of Sebastian, Johann Ernst lived a quiet life as organist, Court conductor at Weimar and Church Registrar in Eisenach. His one disappointment was that although he was a trained lawyer (and, unlike other Bachs who had been schooled in that faculty, keen to put his knowledge to good use) the

Duke of Weimar, Ernst August Constantin, was sceptical of the competence of a lawyer who was also a musician and unwilling to give him a
legal office. In 1756 he was appointed to take charge of the musical
establishment. His administration of this was marked by a strong
practical sense, for his memoranda on staffing were far more realistic
and economical than those of Georg Benda of Gotha, whose advice
was also sought. The rearrangement of the music at Weimar was
undertaken in honour of the Duchess Anne Amalia (of Braunschweig)
—later the patroness of Goethe—who, however, disbanded the establishment when her husband died some two years later. Ernst Bach did
not suffer. Indeed he gained, in that he was given an allowance and
much free time. After 1758, when he was thirty-six years old, Ernst
enjoyed an enviable leisure backed by his pension from Court funds.
From a distance he watched the development of musical trends to the
north, and in the quietude of Eisenach marked the margins of musical
history with his own annotations on changing conditions.

Already some part of Bach's *Passion Oratorio* has been annotated,
and from the example quoted on page 149 it is clear that he was a
composer of some depth of feeling. He was also a composer whose
assurance in technique encouraged flexibility of expression. On the
one hand he was capable of putting on a show of strength (the training
he received in Leipzig left its mark); on the other he was aware of the
gracious properties within music that were being revealed, particularly
in Italy and Austria. The two poles are to be seen in his setting of the
eighth Psalm.[37] The first of the two following excerpts is after the
accredited examples set before him in youth (and could of course be by
Emanuel Bach), though a lack of discordant argument leads to a kind
of Mendelssohnian conception of contrapuntal purpose. This indeed is
properly to be defined as academic in presentation:

In contrast, however, is this pure piece of Mozart in an aria which
would happily have fitted into a Mass for Salzburg—or into the
Requiem:

The sensibility of the second fragment is here derived from a purely musical origin—from the pattern of four tones followed by three half-tones in the rising melodic formula, with a realization of its harmonic implications. But a similar sensibility also came elsewhere from considerations of poetry. Of Johann Ernst's works the best known in his time were his songs, and of them his *Sammlung auserlesener Fabeln mit darzu verfertigen Melodeyen. 1. Theil* (Im Verlag Joh: Ulrich Haffner's, Lautenisten in Nürnberg: Dresden, 1749). Dedicated (with a fulsome inscription) to the Duke of Saxony, these songs were to varied and charming texts by Johann Josias Sucro (1724–60), Christian Gellert, Johann Adolf Schlegel (1761–93) and other less distinguished poets.[38] Described in Bach's Introduction as 'moral fables' the poems tended to go over the edge from sensitivity into sentimentality. So too, from time to time, did the composer.[39]

But, aware of the implications of the song with keyboard accompaniment, he was alive to the desirability of developing new zones of interest. In the movement of his ideas there are distinct hints of the Schubertian manner.[40]

Ein Häuf - ling, des - sen Ar - tig - keit___ im

Sin - gen___ man - ches___ Ohr er - freut

This sympathy for the role of the accompanist is further extended in the three violin and clavier sonatas, published in Eisenach in 1770 (reprinted 1780),[41] and the further set of three issued in 1772. In these sonatas of course a fresh balance of sonorities is achieved, not by the emancipation of the clavier but of the violin, which hitherto in such works had been generally condemned merely to 'fill in'. Of Johann Ernst's works few remain. Other than those mentioned there are ten or so cantatas, a Lutheran Mass, a charming symphony in B flat (of which the only extant parts are in the Moravian Music collection at Winston Salem, see page 234), organ and clavier works. Of the latter two sonatas were published in the *Oeuvres mêlées* of Ulrich Haffner of Nürnberg in 1760 and other pieces by Emanuel Bach in the *Musicalisches Vielerley*. A *Fantasie*, published in this collection, shows a purposefulness that attracted not only the attention of Emanuel Bach but also of Clementi. Even in Eisenach the dramatic properties of Romanticism were becoming evident.

NOTES TO CHAPTER ELEVEN

1. G. H. Lewes, *The Life and Works of Goethe*, London, 1855, Everyman, p. 82.

2. *See* Note 1 above.

3. *See* Hannsdieter Wohlfahrth, 'Johann Christoph Friedrich Bach', *Schaumburg-Lippische Mitteilungen*, vol. 17, Bückeburg, 1965, p. 58.

4. Karl Geiringer, *Music of the Bach Family, An Anthology*, Cambridge, Massachussetts, 1955, p. 179. Geiringer quotes a recitative and aria from *Cassandra*.

5. *Musikalisches Vielerley*, Hamburg, 1770, Part 6, p. 21.

6. *See* BM. Add. MS. 32039.

7. *Die Kindheit Jesu* was revived at a City of Birmingham (England) Symphony Orchestra concert, on 21st December 1967. An article by N. Fortune in *The Musical Times* (February 1968), did scant justice both to the music at Bückeburg and to J. C. F. Bach.

8. *Michaels Sieg.*

9. Together with *Die Kindheit Jesu* in D.D.T., vol. 56.

10. *See* Herder's *Sämtliche Werke*, ed. Bernhard Suphon, vol. 28, p. 554.

11. MS. St. 266.

12. C. H. Bitter, *C. P. E. Bach und W. F. Bach und deren Brüder*, Berlin, 1868, 2 vols., II, p. 134.

13. M. C. von Herder, *Erinnerungen aus dem Leben Johann Gottfried von Herder*, ed. J. G. Müller, Stuttgart/Tübingen, 1830, 2 vols., I, pp. 185, 186, II, p. 98.

14. *See* the instruction from Philipp Ernst to Court councillor von Landesberg (1782) quoted by Wohlfahrth, *see* Note 3 above, pp. 57–8.

15. Hermann Salzwedel, 'Vom Rezitativ bis zum Arioso', in *Die Esche*, Bückeburg, 1964. This is the house magazine of the firm of Hans Neschen of Bückeburg, which celebrated its jubilee on 20th November 1964 with a performance of Bach's (new-found) Symphony in E flat and *Der Tod Jesu.*

16. See *Drei Sinfonien von Johann Christoph Friedrich Bach zu Bückeburg*, *Schaumburger Faksimiledrucke, nr. 2*, ed. Franz Engel, Bückeburg, 1966, in which the original material of the three symphonies is reproduced together with an annotation by Hannsdieter Wohlfahrth.

17. *See* E. Doebner and W. Simons, *Meininger Pastell-Gemälde (Neue Beiträge zur Geschichte deutschen Altertums Nr. 19)*, Meiningen, 1904, pp. 9–10.

18. *See* Heinrich Besseler, *Fünf echte Bildnisse Johann Sebastian Bachs*, Kassel, 1956, pp. 33–6.

19. Of Emil Leopold August (1772–1822) and Friedrich IV, of Sachsen-Gotha (1774–1825), Christian August of Hohenlohe-Langenburg (1768–96), Karl of Sachsen-Meiningen (1754–82) and Duchess Luise of Sachsen-Weimar, in addition to those in the Meiningen Collection, shown in Appendix 4. *See* H. W. Singer, *Neuer Bildnis-katalog*, Leipzig, 1938.

20. No. 491 in the present collection in the Schloss Elisabethenburg, Meiningen.

21. No. 270.

22. (1) Johanne, died in infancy. (2) Juliane (Julie), who married Karl Schwanitz, Commissioner of Taxes in Eisenach; the son of this marriage, Karl, was a Commissioner of the Peace, who died in 1902. Karl married Laura Fritzsche, daughter of the Pastor in Magdala. Their daughter married a man named Steinmann. (3) Ludwig (1805–7).

23. (1) Eduard, born in 1813 and died in the next year, (2) Friedrich Carl Eduard (1815–1903), Head Forester in Liebenstein and then in Coburg. From his marriage with Alma Wilhelmina Hilfert, daughter of a physician in Wasungen, came Karl Bernhard Paul Bach (1878–1968), a postal official in Coburg, and an artist (*see* Bibliography), (3) Amalie, died in infancy, (4) Rosalie, who married Eduard Lotz (*d.* 1892), merchant of Meiningen. The two sons of this marriage were Rudolf, whose son Hermann inherited some pictures from his grandfather, and Eduard, of Hildburghausen, who also inherited pictures which, like those of his nephew, were exhibited in 1904. A daughter of Rosalie and Eduard Lotz, Sophie, married into the Aschermann family of Erfurt.

24. 'The artist's greatest pleasure is enjoyment of the delight afforded by his image of woman's beauty; you have succeeded well in pressing the soul into this, as a speaking likeness, and have unveiled it as even more beautiful.'

25. Doebner and Simons (*see* Note 17 above), p. 9.

26. Nr. 156, Schloss Elisabethenberg, Meiningen.

27. Nr. 477, Schloss Elisabethenberg, Meiningen.

28. Lothar Briegel's article in the *Leipziger Illustrierte Zeitung*, for 28th May 1929, was quoted by Paul Bach, 'Die Meininger Bache', in *Johann Sebastian Bach in Thüringen*, Weimar, 1950, pp. 217–19.

29. *See* Paul Bach, Note 28 above.

30. There is some doubt as to whether Sebastian was Sebastian or Samuel. Gustav Wustmann opts for Samuel on the grounds that he was named after Johann Ludwig's son, Samuel Anton. In general, however, the majority of authorities prefer Sebastian. *See* G. Wustmann, 'Ein Enkel Johann Sebastian Bachs', in *Wissenschaftliche Beilage der Leipziger Zeitung*, 23rd February 1907, Leipzig, p. 33.

31. *See* Wustmann, Note 30 above.

32. Wallraf-Richartz Museum, Köln.

33. Mainz, Gemäldegalerie und Altertumsmuseum.

34. This letter, dated 11th July 1774, is given in full in Wustmann (*see* Note 30 above), p. 34.

35. *See* Julius Meyer, *Allgemeines Künstler-Lexikon*, Leipzig, 1878.

36. *Beschreibung der vorzüglichsten Merkwürdigkeiten der Churfürstlichen Residenzstadt Dresden*, Dresden, 1782, p. 584.

37. *Hamburg Staats-und-Universitätsbibliothek*, MS. 7706 (copy of *c.* 1810, inscribed 'di J. E. Bach').

38. A second part never appeared.

39. Concluding bars of *An die Geissigen*, from *Musikalisches Vielerley*, V, p. 20.

40. From *Fabeln*, No. 12, *Die Unzufriedenheit* (Carsted).

41. *3 Sonaten für das Klavier und I Violine*, Eisenach, Griesbach's Söhne, 1770.

The London Bach

AN ODE FOR THE QUEEN'S NUPTIALS

For the sake of his reputation within English music, Christian Bach came to London either twenty years too late or twenty years too soon. Missing the first full flush of oratorio enthusiasm, he was at a disadvantage in respect of the large choral works that the English had come to relish because he had to live through the period of consolidation of the Handel cult. On the other hand, the condition of secular instrumental music was not such that it afforded an effective point of departure towards a complete realization of Bach's skills. Overshadowed from the start by the greatness of one German—Handel—he was pushed into respectable oblivion soon after his death by that of another —his father. In the programme of the Concert of Antient Music for 16th March 1796, for example, the aria 'Se possono tanto' from Christian's *Alessandro nell' Indie* was carelessly attributed to S. Bach. This misprision was a sizeable straw in the wind.

Yet Bach was one of the two or three most influential figures in the history of English music. He popularized the pianoforte and (together with Abel) he established the 'symphony concert', by which means he helped to revolutionize British musical habits and attitudes. Before Bach—although its hold was weakening—the aristocracy still had some influence on taste. After Bach the aristocratic influence, for all practical purposes, had ceased to exist.

During the eighteenth century it was assumed in Europe that for the non-British musician London was a gold-mine.

> The greatest part of the foreign musicians who visit London remain there: for as that great city is actually a PERU to them, they do not choose to deprive themselves of the lucrative monopoly which they there enjoy, in regard to their own profession.[1]

This was certainly the case when Bach proposed to visit (if not to settle in) England for the first time in the summer of 1762. In fact his preparations were pretty thorough, and it is clear that his selection as a royal music master had been under discussion for some time.

On 8th September 1761 King George III married Sophia Charlotte, the seventeen-year-old daughter of the Duke of Mecklenburg-Strelitz. At an early age (for in those days girls of intellectual accomplishment were rated high in the marriage market) Charlotte was precipitated into the department of German ducal bluestockings—to whom music was indispensable. After the king had announced his intention of marriage he sent Earl Simon Harcourt to Strelitz to inform Charlotte. From Strelitz, where Friedrich Albert (father of Mrs Papendiek)—who was to be a close friend of Christian Bach in London —was among the Court officials responsible for arranging a fitting reception for the English milords, Harcourt wrote:

> This little Court has exerted its utmost abilities to make a figure suitable to the Occasion, and I can assure you they have acquitted themselves not only with magnificence and splendour, but with a great deal of good taste and propriety.[2]

On the day that this letter was written—two days after the conclusion of the treaty of marriage—Charlotte set out for England accompanied by the Duchesses of Ancaster and Hamilton, Mrs Tracy, General Graeme and Lord Harcourt. Lord Anson, in the flag-ship *Charlotte*, was in command of the naval squadron assigned to the duty of bringing the new Queen to England. After a stormy crossing, in no way made more bearable by the sailors being specially dressed in red uniform, gold-laced hats and light grey stockings, she arrived there on 7th September. The wedding was solemnized in the German Chapel Royal at St James, and the anthem was *The King shall rejoice* by the Chapel Royal composer, William Boyce. Mence, Savage, Cooper, Beard and one of the chapel boys were soloists, and the enlarged orchestra included Vincent the oboist and Karl Friedrich Weideman(n) (*d.* 1782) the flautist.

> After the wedding ceremony and while the august company waited for supper the Queen bride sat down, sang and played, conversed with the King, the Duke of Cumberland and Duke of York in German and in French.[3]

During the evening an Entrada for horns, trumpets and drums, composed by Weideman(n) (who had been in London since 1726) and minuets, by the violinist Salvatore Galeotti and by the Duke of York, were played.[4]

The fact that the queen was musical had been noted previous to this by one John Lockman (1698–1771), Secretary to the British Herring Fishery, who had written the text of an *Ode on the Auspicious Arrival and Nuptials . . . of Queen Charlotte*, which was set to music by J. C. Bach. Not among the more distinguished works of Bach, this ode is nevertheless interesting in the manner in which the composer seemed to have picked up an English accent—that of T. A. Arne—for the occasion.

What is perplexing is how the text came into the hands of Bach who, in 1761, was still organist of the cathedral in Milan. Though—in conformity with a family tradition—for the greater part of 1761–2 he was absent for a long stretch from his official duties. He was in fact supervising the production of his operas, *Catone in Utica* and *Alessandro nell' Indie*, in Naples. Consequent upon his success with these works in Italy overtures were made to him to come to London where the Italian Opera, in its usual parlous condition, was awaiting salvation from abroad. Managed from 1759 until 1764 by the prima donna Colomba Mattei, it was in 1761 under the inconspicuous musical direction of Gioacchino Cocchi of Venice. For the next season, of 1762–3, Mattei engaged 'Mr John Bach, a Saxon Master of Music'. The analogy with Handel is close. Bach made it closer by picking up the royal connection already established by his setting of Lockman's *Ode*. Wrapping up his duties in Italy he travelled to London where he remained until his death.

EARLY YEARS IN PRUSSIA AND ITALY

Of the earliest years of all the sons of Sebastian Bach least is known of those of Christian. Where, in Leipzig, he went to school, and to what extent he benefited from his father's tuition, are not documented. On the death of his father—from whose estate he claimed three claviers with pedals, a number of shirts and a few thalers—he was taken into the care of Emanuel. Moving from Leipzig to the lively atmosphere of Berlin and Potsdam brought a new set of influences to bear. In general the tone was conducive to stimulating the broad interests that in later life distinguished Christian. From the musical point of view the most effective factors were the instruction of Emanuel and the Royal Opera. Under Emanuel he developed into a competent clavier player. That he was in any sense brilliant is not really borne out by the evidence of later years, and when Gerber wrote how his performances of his own music had won applause in Berlin it is to be doubted that this had represented more than encouragement to a young man with a famous name. Christian's first compositions—of which Emanuel preserved a small number—were various, but no more exceptional than might have been expected from a well-trained musical apprentice of that workmanlike age. Among them however, were five clavier concertos—each in the established, post-Vivaldi, three-movement manner regularized by Sebastian Bach—which, in addition to moments of tension reminiscent of the baroque, showed a fluidity of melodic outline that was Italian and operatic. At the Royal Opera the principal works to be heard during Christian's Berlin years were by Graun, Agricola and Hasse. But, since singers were imported from Italy, there was much opportunity to become acquainted with the Italian manner of performance. One notable characteristic of Christian's music was that it was always conceived from the performer's point of view. Both Gerber and Forkel declared that Christian struck up acquaintance with Italian singers in Berlin and became enamoured of the idea of making an expedition to Italy. It was also said, at an inconveniently late point in time to be accepted as historical fact, that he became enamoured of one (or more) of the female singers. In 1754 (according to Emanuel) or 1756 (which Terry prefers) he duly set out for Italy. Either way, in view of the fact that in Berlin he was a Saxon in Prussia, he was well advised to go. By so doing he avoided the hardships that were imposed by Frederic the Great on his, and other, subjects in the Seven Years War.

As Handel had done half a century earlier, Christian Bach proved that a German (provided he was a Saxon) could succeed both socially and professionally in Italy. For five years or so Bach was assisted, both morally and financially, by a Milanese nobleman, Count Agostino Litta. At first Christian lived in Naples, but then moved to Milan, at the same time transferring himself from the Evangelical to the Roman Catholic Faith. To this no especial significance need be attached. Religious passion among the Bachs lay dormant in the second half of the eighteenth century, and Christian—speculating on the best means of promoting his interests as a composer—found that certain opportunities were more likely to come his way if he was a paid-up member of the local church in Italy. Encouraged towards church music by his patrons, and also by the famous Bolognese priest-musician Giovanni Battista Martini (with whom he was on excellent terms and by whom he was instructed), Christian composed a number of works for liturgical use. Living now in Milan, but visiting Martini fairly regularly in Bologna, Bach worked determinedly, producing a number of ecclesiastical works between 1757 and 1760 that both deserved and compelled attention.

As German composers a hundred and fifty years before his time had done, so did Christian Bach learn effectively to marry German and Italian methods. More effectively perhaps than even Handel had done at the same stage of his development. The *Dies Irae* of 1757, the *Magnificat* and the *Te Deum*, both dated 1758, do in fact retain characteristics of tonal dispersal that had long ago passed into the early German motet and remained in the general tradition of Lutheran music. The expressive homophony of Bach, and particularly the refinements of instrumentation surrounding it, are directly comparable with those of Leonardo Leo (1694–1744) and Francesco Durante (1684–1755) (whose music no doubt was heard by Bach in Naples), and with those of Hasse, whose works were familiar throughout Europe. The sum of Bach's early achievements often seems as a deduction from Handel, except in so far as solo melodic lines were inspired by the more recent sophistications of the Italian opera house. This is exemplified by the *vocalises* of the first aria of *Si nocte tenebrosa*.

Also by the suave figuration of 'O Clemens, O Pia', and the emotive details of this passage, in a *Salve Regina*:

In the summer of 1760 Bach, who had also embarked on his career as a composer of chamber music, was appointed organist of the cathedral in Milan. He owed this appointment to the good offices of the solicitous Litta. But by now Bach had set his sights in another direction. The whole object of going to Italy in the first place had been to pursue his interest in opera. In that field lay both fame and fortune.

In the Carnival Season of 1761 Bach's first opera, *Artaserse*, was produced in the Teatro Regio in Turin, with Carlo Nicolini in the title role and Gaetano Guadagni in that of Arbace. These were two of the most celebrated castrati of the century, the one a soprano the other a contralto. International artists, both were known throughout Europe. Guadagni had sung in London, where he had made his reputation under the tutelage of Handel, for whom he sang the oratorio arias composed in the first place for Kitty Clive. Guadagni had many friends and admirers in England, and distinguished himself by his ability to sing convincingly in English.[5] The subject of *Artaserse* was a familiar one, having been treated by Gluck (whose first opera it was) in 1741, Graun (produced in Berlin in 1743), and Hasse (Venice, 1730). Shortly after Christian Bach's Turin production Thomas Augustine Arne's *Artaxerxes* was produced at Covent Garden on 2nd February 1762: a holding operation—to demonstrate to any intending immigrant composer that an Englishman could do the job as well as any foreigner. By this time Bach had produced his second opera—*Catone in Utica*—in San Carlo in Naples. The star of this opera was Anton Raaf, the celebrated German tenor, for whom Bach also composed motets, including *Si nocte tenebrosa* (see page 252). On a rising tide of popularity, he proceeded to his third opera, *Alessandro nell' Indie*, which was also given its *première* in Naples, on 20th January 1762. Raaf was in this cast too, and the manner in which he inspired the composer is shown in the liquidity of the most famous aria in the work, 'Non so d'onde viene'. Although Bach was content to accept the prevailing conventions (and why not?), he learned how to write just enough and not too many notes into a vocal melody.

With three operatic successes in a row, Bach thought he knew where his destiny lay. Oblivious of his duties as a cathedral organist—concerning which Litta wrote to Martini with some anxiety on 7th April 1762[6]—Bach (so it would appear) began seriously to consider the attractions of England. In a few months' time, his permanent ties with Milan severed, he was composer-elect to the Italian Opera in London. He had worked intensively in Italy, polishing his melodic style under the influence of great singers and adjusting his feeling for instrumentation to the requirements of the theatre. In both cases the result was a distinctive limpidity and clarity, a kind of actuality of experience considerably removed from the metaphysical elements of the more solid German style. So far had Christian Bach forgotten his former habits that he had, as he told Burney, given up playing, except to accompany singers.[7] On 13th November 1762 'Mr John Bach, a Saxon Master of Music' appeared in public in London for the first time. He directed the first performance of *Il Tutore e la Pupilla*, or *Il Matrimonio alla moda*, a pastiche, to which he contributed an overture and two airs. This sort of entertainment was a come-down after Italy. But if this was how the English liked it, then Bach would play it their way.

THE OPERATIC SITUATION IN ENGLAND

No one but a born optimist would have invested his future in opera in England during the eighteenth century (or, for that matter, at any other time). The catastrophic record of Italian opera during Handel's lifetime should have been a sufficient warning. But it was not, and Bach proceeded to plough his way through a succession of pasticcios towards the production of his first proper opera in England. This was *Orione, ossia Diana Vendicata*, to a libretto by Giovanni Gualberto Bottarelli, and it was produced for the first time on 19th February 1763. Three days later the Court attended a performance. *Orione* ran, on and off, for three months, and it commanded much attention, the 'favourite songs' being published by Walsh. Bach's melodious style made a favourable impression on those to whom music at its best was represented by the most popular tunes of Handel, Thomas and Michael Arne, and Jonathan Battishill (whose *The Fairy Tale*, of 1763, and *Almena*, of 1764, were the hits at Drury Lane). He was helped by the popularity of his prima donna, Anna Lucia de' Amicis. Those of a more analytical turn of mind admired Bach's orchestration, which appeared the richer through the introduction of the clarinet. This was the first time that this instrument had been used in an English opera house.[8] Emboldened by initial success, Bach forged ahead on a second major work, and on 7th May 1763 *Zanaida*, an ambitious *drama per musica* which required larger ballet, choral and orchestral forces than were usual, was put on. In *Zanaida* Bach showed his real appreciation of the clarinets, with effective embellishment in thirds (taken over from oboe practice) above Guadagni's aria, 'Se spiego le prime velle', and a distinctly romantic inclination in the figuration of de' Amicis' 'Che pieta'. *Zanaida* went a long way beyond expectation (which militated against immediate popularity) by introducing such truly affecting moments as this:

In 1764 there was no opera by Bach. His next work of this kind was *Adriano in Siria*, which was performed on 26th January 1765, with Ferdinando Tenducci in the title role, Giovanni Manzuoli in that of Farnaspe and with Arne's niece, Polly Scott, singing the part of Barsene. This was a fine theme—of Hadrian's Syrian campaign and subjugation of the Jews, and half way towards oratorio. For the first performance the house was packed, but the reception of the work was less than enthusiastic. Quarrels among the cast, feuds between Italians and Germans, as indicated in the following quotation, discomfort caused by the fact that many of the audience were unable to get seats, all contributed to a relative failure. And as always there was the unpredictability of the English in respect of opera. Nevertheless

> Many of the songs . . . were so frequently sung at concerts; (public and private) and with such rapturous applause, as to give birth to the expectation that the German musicians would become almost as obnoxious to the Italians as Englishmen, and be deemed equally worthy of their hostility.[9]

A day of two after the production of *Adriano* Samuel Arnold's ballad opera, *The Maid of the Mill* (a 'musical' based on Samuel Richardson's *Pamela*), was staged at Covent Garden. This was much more to the taste of the public. Not unmindful of Christian Bach's general popularity as a melodist, Arnold included two numbers by him, 'Trust me, trust me, would you taste true pleasure', and 'My life, my joy, my blessing', which varied only from Italian arias by reason of the fact that their texts were English. At the end of that year a second work of this kind, *The Summer's Tale*, contained three songs by Bach that had a much more distinctive English character. Indeed, it would be possible to assign the melodies of 'So profound an impression' and 'Yes, 'tis plain' to Thomas Arne on the one hand, and to Arthur Sullivan on the other. The second of these arias was, in fact, a transcription of the duet for Cleofide and Poro, 'Se mai turbo', in *Alessandro*.

After the production of *Adriano in Siria* Bach made a deliberate concession to native feeling by selecting a British subject for his next opera. Although Caractacus was not among the most successful of heroes, the story of his legendary nobility in defeat (and the fact that he was Welsh) stirred many hearts when it was retold by William Mason in 1759.

At this point it is worth looking back to notice how, from Handelian times, there had been strong forces at work among the English intelligentsia to refashion opera in the direction of dramatic plausibility. Mason (whose musical interests have already been shown) wrote a dramatic work, *Elfrida*, in 1751, and in a sequence of prefatory letters discussed drama and music in general. Observing in Letter V that in Paris performances of Racine's *Athaliah* and *Esther* were done without chorus, he asked:

> To what is this owing? To the refinement most certainly of our modern music. The art is now carried to a pitch of perfection, or, if you will, of corruption, which makes it utterly incapable of

being an adjunct to Poetry. .... Our different cadences, our
divisions, variations, repetitions, without which modern music
cannot subsist, are intirely improper for the expression of poetry,
and were scarce known to the ancients.

Bach was the victim partly of his own fluency, partly of the social
conventions that contained *opera seria*, and he was not really the man
to go all the way with Mason. Nevertheless he went some of the way
by diminishing the *da capo* tradition, by infusing vocal parts with
palpable emotion and by considerably enlarging the function of the
orchestra. Of this there is a fine example in 'Sposa raffreno il pianto',
where, with muted strings, the introduction shows this kind of
spaciousness:

Carattaco was first performed on 14th February 1767 and gained this
measure of approbation:

Methinks the Poet, Author of *Carattaco*, deserves Commendation
for bringing before us a Hero whose Memory does Honour to the
English Name, and also thence most dear to Englishmen. En-
comiums on Mr Bach would be superfluous, as he has already
distinguished himself so much among us by the Invention, the

Spirit, and Dignity of his Composition. . . . His Choruses elevate
the Soul and put us in mind of those of the immortal Handel. . . .[10]

It is thus made clear what a 'serious' composer was really expected
to do in England. To put the clock back; to repeat the familiar formulas
of Handelian oratorio. This being the case, coupled with the generally
invalid condition of the Haymarket Theatre, it is not surprising that
Bach only composed one more opera for the English—*La Clemenza di
Scipione* (4th April 1778), a *succès d'estime*, but of little general significance. In between his third and fourth operas for London, Bach composed *Temistocle* and *Lucio Silla* (1776) for Mannheim, and in the year
following the production of *La Clemenza* he wrote his operatic masterpiece, *Amadis de Gaule*, for Paris.

This was a work of considerable power. In this opera—based on a
libretto prepared by Quinault for Lully, and chosen to avoid involvement in the current Gluck-Piccinni contention—Bach excelled in
expressing mood and atmosphere. He employed a large orchestra
(two fl., two ob., two clar., two fag., two cor., two tr., three tromb.,
timp., str.), and used the chorus more frequently and more effectively
than in his London operas—with an offstage group of singers for the
storm scene. His accompanied recitatives are taut and compelling and
the arias effectively theatrical. The finale—an ariette and chorus—in
A major is an exceptionally fine concluding movement. It was unfortunate for Bach that the curtailment of Quinault's libretto aroused bad
feelings among the more patriotic French critics, and that he was
disadvantageously compared both with Gluck (whose style he ap-
proached quite closely in this work) and Piccinni.

As a composer of opera Christian Bach ranks among those who
failed. A few airs survived as separate concert items, but the operas
themselves almost immediately passed out of hearing. Their influence
was minimal. In so far as he was an English composer, Bach was trying
to exploit his particular skills in this connection at the wrong time and
in the wrong place. Italian opera, long regarded with xenophobic
suspicion by the influential English middle class, was an irrelevance.
As an entertainment, ballad opera was preferred, as being nearer to
reality, while morals and religious sensibility were still mightily
sustained by oratorio. On the whole Bach also came to see opera as
an irrelevance—or at best a luxury to be indulged in but seldom—and,
in spite of his early ambitions, he was prepared from the outset to
come to terms with the general cultural situation in his new environment.

CONCERT PROMOTION

Since 1759 Abel had been a conspicuous figure in the concert world. Friendship with Abel, which led to the two of them living together in Soho, brought Bach into the centre of public music-making, and a profitable business partnership developed which gave a new impetus to concert organization in London. Bach brought into this partnership a number of assets. He was young, his early reputation as an operatic composer was both glossy and enviable, and he stood high in the affections of the royal family. King George III was a keen music-lover, whose conservative tastes (his principal enthusiasm centred on Handel) helped to establish his right to be considered the first truly English of the Hanoverian monarchs. According to German precedent, however, he played the flute. The abilities of his consort have already been noticed.

Concerts were held at St James's Palace on Tuesdays and Thursdays, some two or three hundred guests being invited to music and cards. The private band was in attendance and the other well-known performers were engaged. At various times these included the famous blind organist, John Stanley; Giacomo Cervetto and John Crosdill, the cellists; John Parke, the oboist; and the talented Linley girls. When Bach set up his own establishment in Richmond in 1776 Abel used to come down to visit him each Wednesday to plan the next day's concert.

> On one occasion Bach had totally forgotten that it was his turn [to write a work], so after dinner he sat down and wrote an enchanting first movement of a quintett in three flats. He sent off for two copyists, who wrote down the parts from score over his shoulders, while he wrote the harmony, after having composed the melody.

Mrs Papendiek, one of the Court ladies, who left this in her memoirs, was a little girl at the time—but the picture is both charming and clear enough.[11]

On 17th March 1763 Bach published his first set of six harpsichord concertos (Op. I) and dedicated them to the queen. The last movement of the last of the set consists of variations on the theme of 'God Save the King'. Although hardly epoch-making in one sense, these lucid little essays in rondo-concerto form were in another. They were, *par excellence*, music for 'the dilettantes in whose hands the concerts lay for a decade'.[12] On 1st February 1764 were published six trios (Op. II), also attractive to amateurs, on the title-page of which the composer was described as *Maître de Musique de S. M. La Reine d'Angleterre*. Music of this temperate, orderly nature was acceptable to many, whose point of view was nicely expressed in the *Annual Register* of 1772.

> It is therefore perfectly obvious, that music ought to address itself to the affections and passions; and that it ought never to be degraded to express difficulties. That music has little merit, where we only admire the execution of the performer.[13]

It was later in the month in which Bach's Opus II was published that Bach and Abel gave their first concert—a benefit concert in the 'Great Room' in Spring Gardens, at which an unspecified serenata by Bach and various instrumental works by Abel were performed. Some weeks later, in April, Leopold Mozart arrived in London, with Wolfgang and Nannerl. Pitched into the rigours of the life of a prodigy in a new and vast city—with concerts at Hickford's Room, at Spring Gardens, at Ranelagh and at Court, Wolfgang was appreciative of the great kindness shown to him by Christian Bach. He also appreciated the clarity and melodiousness of Bach's music, to which he was introduced almost immediately on arrival in London. One day in May, according to his father's testimony, he was busy playing through Bach's—presumably newly published—trios. The long-term effects of Mozart's early contact with Bach were considerable. Long years afterwards Mozart recollected his acquaintance, and how he learned a minuet from Bach (letter to Leopold, 5th December 1780). On hearing of Christian's death he exclaimed: 'What a loss to the musical world' (letter to Leopold, 10th April 1782). Immediately, when he was a boy of nine, Bach's music opened his eyes to new possibilities of assimilating significance of idea within significance of form. Bach was no anonymous composer (none of the Bachs were). The felicities of statement that he had acquired through Italian music, and in Italy, were not merely repeated as polite commonplaces. He was, opined Burney, 'the first composer who observed the law of *contrast*, as a *principle*'.[14]

The same point was made by W. T. Parke (1762–1847), an oboist and viola player, with recollections of a particular work.

> He seems to have been the first composer who maintained the law of contrast as a principle. . . . His symphony for a double orchestra in the key of C (composed for his own concerts) is perhaps one of the most original, noble, and effective compositions I have ever heard.[15]

Bach united the elements of song and dance, and his symphonic expression is underwritten by a feeling for immediate statement in orchestral terms. On the one hand he understood that the *buffa* idiom was not necessarily synonymous with flippancy; on the other that gravity was not the same as pretentiousness. The transition from *buffa* towards symphonic melody is shown by this graceful outline in the ritornello of 'Sposa adorata' in *La Clemenza di Scipione*:

whereas the passage from the third Act of *Catone in Utica* preludes the intensity of feeling of a slow movement by Beethoven.

This is a frequent incipit procedure of Bach, both melodically and rhythmically (cf. opening of Sinfonia concertante in A major, Eulenberg No. 765, and of the *Andante* of the E flat Sinfonia concertante, Eulenberg No. 768).

At his best (like most prolific composers Bach was not always at his best) he could stir the emotions as few among his contemporaries. A not unfamiliar, and very characteristic, work composed sometime in his first ten years in London is the symphony in E flat (Op. 9, No. 2). In temperament this fine work is Mozartian. But Mozart learned how to be Mozartian through his study of, and affection for, Bach. He went home from London and set about turning three sonatas from Bach's Opus V (dedicated to the Duke of Mecklenburg) into concertos: *Tre Sonate del Sgr. Giovanni Bach ridotte in Concerti dal Sgr. Amadeo Wolfgango Mozart* (K. 107). (At the same time Mozart applied the same procedure to sonatas by Emanuel Bach and other composers.) He also took Bach's symphonies, especially in regard to their dynamic properties and their tonal contrasts, as his models, as will be understood from hearing the familiar E flat symphony (Op. IX, No. 2) of Bach, with its gay elegance offset by a pensive melancholy in the C minor slow movement.

The character of a composer's work is affected by environment.

In London Bach spent his time in unconscious pursuit of the compromise that is English music. His Italianate facility was moderated by the claims of the market. The opera composer was the composer of the Pleasure Gardens. The appeal to the 'man of taste' was made less clamant by the fact that most Englishmen of that period were inclined to be more proud of their lack rather than their acquisition of taste. Bach was employed by a Court in which the attitudes to matters of culture for the most part were those of the community in general. The centre of English music (apart from the oratorio, and that comes under a separate heading of 'music and morals') was the subscription concert, of which the last important musician-promoter had been Giardini.

At the beginning of 1765 Bach and Abel began a series of six concerts at Carlisle House, an establishment made both notorious and popular by Mrs Teresa Cornelys—a lady of obscure German origins whose name was adapted from her one-time Dutch protector, Cornelis de Vanderboom, and whose lovers had included the great Casanova—who maintained the house as a centre for entertainment. At these concerts Bach's Opus III Symphonies were performed—works which began to operate against the interests of William Boyce, whose more solid style suddenly appeared old-fashioned. The concerts of Bach and Abel—surprisingly perhaps—proved no less popular than Mrs Cornelys's other ventures. In 1768 they were transferred to Almack's Great Room, in St James's. Seven years later Bach and Abel moved their headquarters again—to the new Hanover Square Rooms, which became the principal concert centre in London for a hundred years. Supported by a talented body of free-lance orchestral musicians (including the mainly German *ensemble* belonging to the royal band), and by the peculiarly co-operative professional attitude of these players (united and to some extent protected by the Society of Musicians), Bach and Abel were able to make a great success out of their venture. Not only did they command the attention of the London public, they drew in visitors from the provinces.

Towards the end of his career Bach's concerts—their popularity now on the wane—were subsidized by Lord Abingdon, a peer of revolutionary views, and a composer, who later became a friend of Haydn. Friendship with the Abingdons is commemorated in the dedication of the *Four Sonatas and two Duets for the Piano Forte or Harpsichord*... (Op. XV) to the countess, and the Opus XIX quartets and two trios, posthumously published, to the earl. The importance of

Bach's concerts (apart from affording him ample opportunity to perform his own works) lay in the fact that by introducing a wide range of European symphonic music (much of which was published in London), and by regularizing concert and orchestral conditions, they made London into a European centre. 'The concerts in London', observed J. W. von Archenholtz, 'are allowed to be very grand, and the English in general prefer them to the music of the opera-house.'[16] After Bach's death professional concerts were undertaken by William Cramer, formerly of Mannheim, a member of the royal band, and by Johann Peter Salomon.

The cult of the infant prodigy was an integral part of eighteenth-century concert life. As an impresario Bach was not unaware of the publicity value of exhibiting the talents of gifted children. At the beginning of his London career he helped Mozart. Later on he gave encouragement to certain English children, one of whom was later to help in the discovery of the works of Christian Bach's father. On 20th May 1777 a benefit concert (for a musician named Rauffe) took place in Hickford's Great Room

> Under the direction of Mr Bach. The vocal parts by Signora Balconi, and Signor Savoi. The instrumental by Messrs Cramer, Fischer, Master and Miss Weichsel, with concertos on the violoncello by Messrs. Rauffe.
> End of Act II a young gentleman will perform extempore on the organ.[17]

Charles Weichsell and his sister Elizabeth were the children of a German oboist at the Haymarket. Elizabeth was an especial friend of Bach, and in 1773 she was invited to play a piano concerto at one of his concerts. Later on she became his singing pupil, and ultimately one of the most popular singers in England. The young gentleman who extemporized at the end of Act II was Samuel Wesley, whose regard for Bach was tempered by a critical precocity that in later life was to inhibit his own advancement. Of one of Bach's concerts that he attended as a boy he approved the works and the manner of their performance, but complained of bad programme-building since the four works were all in the same key.[18] Twenty-six years after the death of Christian Bach Samuel Wesley was giving the first public performance in England of music by Sebastian Bach: in the same Hanover Square Rooms that had accommodated Christian's activities.

A WIDE RANGE OF MUSICAL INTERESTS

The stabilization of London concert life—the same was true in Manchester and Leeds, which were prominent centres of symphonic music in the latter part of the eighteenth century—was brought about by an unofficial Anglo-German consortium. (That opera made no progress was partly due to the general tendency—already hinted at—for the English and the Germans to gang up against the Italians, and vice versa.) It was also as a consequence of Anglo–German associations that the pianoforte began to take a prominent place in English musical life. The credit for popularizing the instrument is normally given to Bach; but equal credit must be allowed to Johann Christoph Zumpe—who came to England from Saxony during or immediately after the Seven Years War. He was the leading manufacturer of the pianoforte in England for a time.

On 2nd June 1768 a concert took place in the Thatch'd House, St James's, to introduce to the public Johann Christian Fischer, lately arrived from Germany. As part of this concert there was advertised a 'Solo on the Piano Forte by Mr Bach'. Since Bach made a payment of £50 to Zumpe in June 1768, there is no doubt of the kind of instrument that Bach used.

Although—as Burney observed—Bach's technique was not extraordinary, it is clear that his preference for the pianoforte was entirely due to its capacity to 'discourse very eloquent musick'—as Thomas Gray observed.[19] At this point the deeper instincts of the Bachs may be seen emerging. The Italo-English Bach could not entirely disguise his authenticity within the tradition. And—as in the fine fugue on B A C H[20] —in the last of the Opus V sonatas a passionate nature is revealed in a statement inappropriate to the harpsichord but proper to the pianoforte.

Bach was a very varied composer, who might be considered to have increased a natural tendency towards versatility from the circumstances of his English environment. He may in this context be described as a pragmatist. Of all the more celebrated Bachs he was the one who conformed least to precedent, the one to whom dogmas—whether in religion, politics or art—were unimportant. A man of the world, Bach took things as they came, only careless in respect of his own security. Like a good professional composer of his age he was amenable to local styles. His German musical accent was softened, but it remained. He took to Italian forms of expression as a duck to water. By judicious selection, however, it would be easy to present a number of his works—without advancing the composer's name—as authentically 'English'. Within such a complex of contrariety lies a set of unacknowledged paradoxes. The paradoxes become more potent when Bach's music is seen as a whole. He covered a very wide range: different kinds of church music (though the English liturgy passed him by); operas and ballad operas; serious songs, popular songs; and folk-song arrangements; ceremonial music for court and military occasions; chamber music of many sorts; and (that which remains most secure) symphonic music. Sir John Hawkins, who was often weighed down by rather ponderous prejudices, looked at the music of Bach (and of Abel) somewhat aslant. To do him credit he was displeased at the public indifference to the fine orchestral music of Boyce. Although probably unaware of the views of Frederic the Great in the matter, he echoed them in protesting against what he considered flippancy. He was all for 'Adagio-music', which he feared had been 'exploded' and replaced by 'the noise and rattle of an unisonous *Allegro*', or the 'intoxicating softness of that too oft iterated air, the *Minuet*'.[21] He was all against composers who wrote 'for the gratification of the many'.[22]

But it was precisely because he crossed the strains that Bach became a vital figure in English musical life. If he made the *idea* of serious music popular, he also helped to make popular music serious. That is, if he may be adjudged to some extent guilty of levelling-down, he must also be applauded for levelling-up. At the centre of this was the fulcral power of an acute sensitivity; the quality that communicated itself to the young Mozart. And combined with this was a sense of humour. It was always on the cards that the ebullience of Bach would produce a kind of barn-dance for a courtly entertainment:[23]

The Court of George III was a robust institution and excesses of elegance were not welcomed. That the English Court had always moderated enthusiasm for culture was one of the reasons why English music, at least since the sixteenth century, had been the most bourgeois in character in Europe. Bach of course did his stint at Court, and the results of his teaching may be seen in permanent form in the dances occasionally composed by the Dukes of York and Gloucester.[24] As an official composer Bach was also required to write regimental marches. Of these a number are contained in a collection—which names some forty-seven regiments—to which Abel also contributed,[25] while there were others in the Mecklenburg–Schwerin Library.[26] Military music was of course a familiar adjunct to the eighteenth-century way of life, and added a good deal to the general amenities. Sebastian Bach himself had in 1747 been sufficiently inspired by the Prussians to write a *Marche pour la Première Garde du Roy*, while Emanuel, following the old *Lustige Feldmusik* tradition, composed a set of 'outdoors sonatas' in 1775. At about the same time Christian Bach composed symphonies for wind quintet or sextet—the combination depending not on aesthetic considerations but on what was practicable for cavalry regiments. These works, for two clarinets, two horns and bassoon, are conspicuous less for their virility than their frequent excursions into a beguiling romanticism, and for the felicitousness of the scoring and the exploitation of the clarinet.

Bach's conspicuous talent for revealing new sonorities gives especial interest to his 'songs for the Gardens', so many of them written for his friend Tenducci, or for his pupil Mrs Weichsell. For a nicely orthodox piece of scoring one may look at the arrangement of the Scottish, pentatonic, song (the pentatony provoking some unusual and diatonic discords from Bach which belong to the twentieth rather than the eighteenth century), *The Broom of Cowdenknows*. This piece—sung at the Pantheon and at the Bach–Abel concerts—is neatly instrumentated for flutes, strings and continuo. The popularity of Scottish idiom at that time was considerable and is otherwise attested by Bach in his variations on *The Yellow Hair'd Laddie*, in Op. XIII, No. 4, and his setting of *Lochaber* (1785 ?). There is a charming description, in Henry

Silhouettes of Tobias
Friedrich Bach II (1723–
1805), Kantor in Erfurt,
and his wife Sophia
Christina

J. C. F. Bach, drawing by Friedrich Rehberg

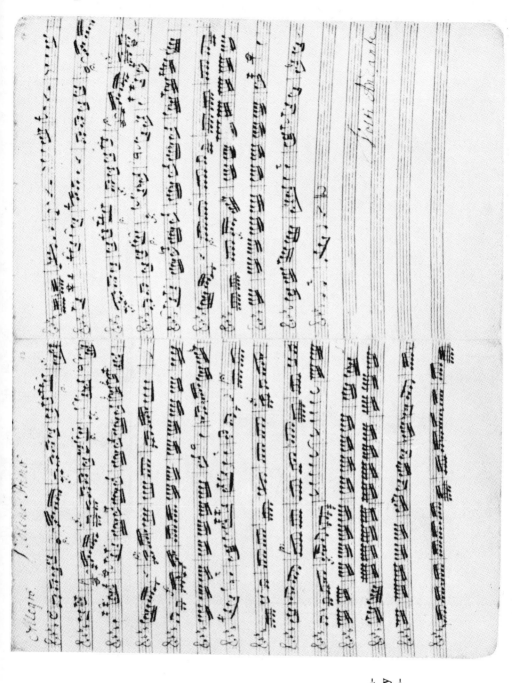

Violin I part from Symphony in E flat by J. C. F. Bach (autograph)

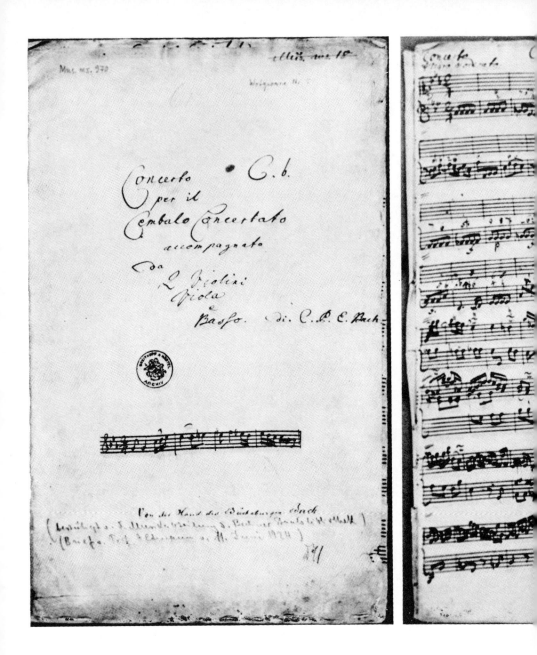

Concerto in C minor by C. P. E. Bach, copied by J. C. F. Bach

J. N. Forkel, anonymous drawing

K. F. Zelter, lithograph by
Count Anton Radziwill

A German copy (late eighteenth century) of an unaccompanied sonata by
J. S. Bach, brought to England

Opposite page: Signs of the English 'Bach Revival', 15th June 1840

MR. CIPRIANI POTTER'S

MORNING CONCERT,

MONDAY, JUNE 15, 1840,

TO COMMENCE AT TWO O'CLOCK, AND TERMINATE AT FIVE.

VOCAL PERFORMERS ENGAGED.

Madame DORUS GRAS,

Miss CLARA NOVELLO,

Signor TAMBURINI.

Mr. POTTER

WILL PERFORM ON THE PIANOFORTE

A CONCERTO BY MOZART

As arranged by J. N. HUMMEL,

(*Never performed in this Country*),

ONE OF S. BACH'S PEDAL FUGUES

With Signor DRAGONETTI,

AND

HIS OWN CONCERTO IN E FLAT.

In the course of the Concert will be performed, complete,

BEETHOVEN'S FAVORITE SYMPHONY IN A,

WITH THE

CELEBRATED ANDANTE;

C. M. von Weber's Overture to Preciosa ;

AND MR. POTTER'S

Overture to Shakespeare's Play, Cymbeline.

THE ORCHESTRA

Will be numerous and complete in every department, selected from the

PHILHARMONIC AND ROYAL ACADEMY OF MUSIC

(*By permission of the Committee*).

Leader, Mr. F. CRAMER.   Conductor, Mr. C. LUCAS.

The Orchestra will consist of the following eminent Performers :

Messrs. DRAGONETTI, LINDLEY, ANFOSSI, WATTS, MORALT, TOLBECQUE, DANDO, WAGSTAFF, A. GRIESBACH, W. THOMAS, WILLY, PHILIPS, HOWELL, HILL, THOMAS, WATKINS, GATTIE, W. CRAMER, HATTON, J. CALKIN, CARD, WILLMAN, PLATT, BAUMANN, HARPER, G. COOKE, KEARNES, GLEDHILL, BANISTER, J. BANISTER, C. SMART, KEATING, NICKS, PATEY, ALSEPT, SMITHIES, SMITHIES, Jun. BOWLEY, RAE, TULLY, CHIPP, F. HILL, ALBRECHT, RICHARDS, H. GOODBAN, T. HARPER, S. SMITH, C. HARPER, HOPGOOD, W. BLAGROVE, DUNSFORD, STEVENSON, J. CALKIN, Jun. NOBLE, DOYLE, BULL, MACCULLOCH, BAKER, MC LEWEE.

Tickets, 10s. 6d. each, to be had of Mr. POTTER, 27, Osnaburg Street, Regent's Park, and at the principal Music Shops.

PRINTED BY J. MALLETT, WARDOUR STREET, SOHO.

*Morning Hymn at
Sebastian Bach's*, by
T. E. Rosenthal,
Berlin

Angelo's *Reminiscences*, of how his mother—at whose house the musicians were frequent guests—used to sing *Patie's Mill*, a Scottish song, to the accompaniment of Bach and Abel. Scottish songs indeed were all the rage in London, and there were many popular anthologies to be had. Nor was Bach allowed to forget the renascence of Welsh musical culture. A contributor to Edward Jones's (1752–1824) *Musical Remains*,[27] he was a colleague of that distinguished harpist and pioneer of folk-song research in the royal household, where Jones was employed in the Office of Robes.

The cultivation of an enthusiasm for landscape was part of the late eighteenth-century way of life and, like his nephew Johann Sebastian the painter, Christian was amenable to suggestions that faithfully to reflect landscape in art was a proper thing to attempt. A good example of his accessibility to the idea is the cantata *Aurora*,[28] also composed for Tenducci. The scoring—by which Bach always announced his intentions—is ample, with flutes, clarinets, bassoons, horns, strings and continuo.

The introductory symphony is a charming pastoral that could have picked up from Handel's landscapes in *Solomon* or, more directly, from Arne's *Morning Cantata*, where a similar, Watteauesque delicacy appears. Bach's *tour de force* in this movement, however, is the Rossini style *crescendo* (taken in the first place by Bach from Mannheim practice) which runs through the symphony and up to the opening recitative. Above this the flutes and clarinets alternate in imitation of bird-song. In *A Collection of Favourite Songs Sung at Vaux Hall* (by Mrs Weichsell, mother of Elizabeth), of about 1756, there is a considerable variety of scoring—with instruments deliberately selected for their evocative quality. So 'By my sighs' is supported by clarinets, horns and bassoon, in addition to strings. In 'Cruel Strephon' the same scoring is used, but the clarinets—as Bach's enthusiasm for this instrument increased so also did his skill in its imaginative handling—are allowed much more scope. In the pretty, pastoral 'Come, Colin, pride of rural swains' *traversi* replace clarinets to lighten the atmosphere. In the last of the set, 'Ah why shou'd love', there are violins with violas (hitherto absent) and bassoons.

In the popular field Bach did not believe in writing down to his audience, and his songs, whether independently conceived or written for ballad operas, are not unimportant aspects of his genius, nor of English eighteenth-century music. He had a genius for composing what was obvious but not commonplace, as in this opening of a song

published in *Clio and Euterpe* (John Welcker, *c.* 1778), a five-volume
anthology of the best songs of the age:

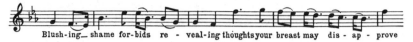

Blush-ing— shame for-bids re - veal-ing thoughts your breast may dis - ap - prove

On the whole it can perhaps be claimed that at that period England
provided the best popular music, whether for one voice, or for groups
of singers, of any country. This was a reflection of a social attitude to
music. The London Bach's contribution to its repertoire was considerable. It is perhaps surprising that it was on only one occasion that
he invaded the territory of English hymnody, which was also a branch
of popular music. His *Let the Solemn organ blow* (composed for the
Magdalene Chapel and published in the *Christian's Magazine* (March
1765, page 140) is a splendidly broad piece after the manner of Croft—
patently Church of England.

The interest of this lies more perhaps in the author of the text than
in the music itself. The words were written by one of the royal chap-
lains, William Dodd, who, having forged a bond for £4,200 in the
name of the Earl of Chesterfield, was executed in 1777.

SOCIAL CONTACTS

This unhappy event stimulated a great deal of agitation, and a petition
for a reprieve was organized by Samuel Johnson. Abel and Bach took
opposite sides on the matter of capital punishment. Abel, in this case,
was against the death penalty. Bach—saying that while he like
Dodd was always in debt, that did not give him warrant to forge
bonds—was in favour. Yet Abel took a day off to witness the execution.
Bach responded to what he considered an unpraiseworthy example of a
double-think by observing:

> I am thankful for not being a sentimentalist. I cannot boast of any
> finer feelings, God help me, but—my dear Mr Abel—excuse me;
> for though you cry to the amount of a pail brim-full of tears, I
> cannot admire the man who shall take a front seat in the Tyburn
> boxes to behold a human being die like a dog in a string.[29]

The age was one of brutality, and this slender evidence of the concern of Bach and Abel for humane issues detaches them from the unconcern with which the many viewed moral and ethical matters. Bach's involvement in social affairs was sometimes involuntary. An intimate friend of the painter Thomas Gainsborough, Bach was returning with him from Bath by coach (Gainsborough's coach, following Bach's) on 7th June 1775 when two highwaymen—Henry McAllister and Archibald Girdwood—set on them, removing from Bach a gold watch valued at £20, a chain valued at £3 and a guinea, and from Gainsborough his watch and two guineas. The criminals were caught, taken before Sir John Fielding and committed for trial to the Old Bailey; Girdwood for robbing Bach, McAllister for robbing Gainsborough. In his evidence before the Recorder Bach stated:

> [Girdwood] cried, 'Stop, your money or your watch!' That waked me, for I was asleep in my carriage. He took my watch and a guinea; the business was very soon over. I should not know the person who robbed me. It was about half past nine or near ten o'clock.[30]

Despite Bach's inability to recognize his assailant, Girdwood, together with his partner, was condemned to death on 17th July.

As a consequence of Bach's friendship with Gainsborough his portrait was painted by that master. They shared many common interests. Bach was a connoisseur of painting, while Gainsborough's keenness for musical performance was so strong that he could hardly be prevailed upon to refrain from demonstrating it, even when his lack of ability gave acute pain to his not always willing audience. Gainsborough's daughter Mary married the oboist Johann Christian Fischer—a frequent performer at the Bach–Abel concerts—in 1780. Bach was friendly also with other artists, including Joshua Reynolds, John Zoffany, the Anglo-American Benjamin West, Giovanni Cipriani and George Stubbs. Gainsborough, West and Cipriani provided murals for Bach's concert-room in 1775.

Soho at that time was an excellent social centre and, living there, Bach had opportunity to get to know a good cross-section of English society. He knew George Colman, dramatist and sometime manager of the Haymarket Theatre, and Colman's friend David Garrick; Richard Brinsley Sheridan, whose elopement with Elisabeth Linley gave him a certain standing in the world of music; John Horne Tooke, whose revolutionary ideals led him to support John Wilkes, who was also of Bach's acquaintance; Sir William Young, Governor of Dominica and a friend of the Papendieks; and the eccentric Lady Glenorchy. To Sir William Young Bach dedicated his *Six Instrumental Quartets*, Op. VIII (later Op. IX), of 1770–5; to Lady Glenorchy a set of six, so-called, *Canzonets*, or duets (Op. IV) in 1765.

COUNTRY EXCURSIONS

England was not only London, and Bach was not unacquainted with the West Country. It was convention that a man of fashion should visit Bath, then the most exciting example of town planning in the country. Bach obeyed this convention; once, as has been seen, with unhappy consequences. But he also knew other parts of the west and south-west—in the cathedral city of Salisbury. The musical life of Salisbury had for long depended on the energy and enthusiasm of James Harris (1709–80), a local worthy who was Secretary to the Queen. Harris instituted a musical festival (with the main intention of promoting the cause of Handel) as far back as 1744. The festival having established itself became a prominent event in the social and musical calendar. The compilation of pasticcios being a normal English practice, it is not surprising to find one such concoction in the Salisbury programme of 1764. This, *Menalcas*, was constructed by Harris, who drew on Bach for five numbers from his operas. In 1770 Bach was invited to contribute a work to the Salisbury Festival, when a 'New Overture' of his was performed. Otherwise:

> Mr [John] Stanley favoured the company with an Organ Concerto ... Mr Malchair, Simpson, Richards and Lates displayed their taste and execution in playing two elegant quartettes—composed by Mr Bach.[31]

Three years later Bach took part in the festival, and 'favoured the company with an elegant performance on the harpsichord'.[32] This was soon after his visit to Germany, when he had produced *Temistocle* in Mannheim at the end of 1772; it is possible that during this German visit Bach met Harris's son, later Lord Malmesbury, who inherited his father's taste for music and who, at this time, was British Ambassador in Berlin. In Mannheim Bach had dallied with the idea of marrying the daughter of Johann Wendling the flautist. But he also had a strong attraction towards Cecilia Grassi, an Italian singer well established in London. Grassi was engaged for the Salisbury Festival of 1773, and on this account Bach, who soon afterwards married her and proceeded to help to dissipate her accumulated savings of £2,000, found it difficult to refuse the invitation, even if he had wished to do so. Previous to appearing at Salisbury Bach, Cecilia Grassi and other musicians from London gave a concert in the Great Assembly Room at Blandford, Dorset, on 14th July. This concert was arranged as a diversion during the annual horse-race meeting, on the second evening of which it took place. On 8th, 9th, 10th September Grassi and others (Bach is not named) moved into Hampshire and performed in Winchester. The Salisbury Musical Festival came at the beginning of October. Among the visiting artists were Stephen and Nancy Storace, later to become intimates of Mozart in Vienna.

In 1781 (in which year the last of the Bach–Abel concerts were given in London) at each of the so-called 'Miscellaneous Concerts' during the Salisbury Festival a serenata by Bach was performed. And a year later—that is, nine months after Bach's death—another 'MS Serenata of Mr Bach' graced the same festival.[33] Thereafter the memory of Bach was kept alive there by his last favourite pupil, Anne Cantelo, who used to sing duets with Cecilia Bach and was a frequent guest with the Bachs on Zoffany's boat on the Thames.

MAN AND MUSICIAN

In the last quarter of the eighteenth century Bach's music was the hinge of London musical experience. It represented the means whereby public taste adapted itself to the challenge of later classical expression. And as in London he altered an ingrained conservatism that had for so long clung to Corelli, Handel, Geminiani, Stanley and to the out-dated *concerto grosso*, so he brought new vistas before the music-loving public of the provinces. Bach's 'overtures' and opera excerpts were the chief contact with the wider world of European music; in Chichester, where the musical society was run by John Marsh[34]; in Leeds, where subscription concerts were promoted by the German-born Herschel; in Manchester, as the city began to build its musical eminence through the Gentlemen's Concerts; at the St Cecilia's Music Hall in Edinburgh; and at Aberdeen, where the players borrowed the music belonging to Sir Archibald Grant of Monymusk.

In Exeter William Jackson was alive to Bach's importance, and was importunate in chasing answers to his letters. A friend of Gainsborough, Jackson used him to prosecute inquiries as to why he had received no answers to his communications. 'I have', Gainsborough wrote to Jackson on 25th January 1777, 'been from time to time after Bach and have never laid eyes on him . . . but surely I shall call on Bach soon to get you an answer to your letter. . . .' This of course fits in with the impression of the careless Bach.

Of Bach's pupils the best known were Mrs and Miss Weichsell for singing, and his Bückeburg nephew and Joseph Mazzinghi (1765–1844) for composition. Mazzinghi, like Samuel Arnold, James Hook, William Shield, Stephen Storace and Thomas Attwood (also a pupil of Mozart) carried on the graceful tradition of J. C. Bach—a tradition of urbanity unusual in British music, especially in the realm of keyboard music where, in England, the classical seed took strongest root. Bach had a considerable European reputation—manuscripts of his works are widespread, from Wolfenbüttel to Novo Mesto, in Slovenia,[35] but his long residence in London tended effectively to cut him off from the main stream. Thus in the end, like Handel, he merits attention as an English composer. Handel created an 'English' form—that of the oratorio—and established such mastery that no one could surpass him in this field. John Christian Bach did not even try, perhaps because he was a Catholic (though this did not deter Arne), more likely because he saw that the market was too well stocked. So far as the English were concerned Bach created symphony and concerto; but a dozen years after his death his slender genius was overwhelmed by the mature works of Josef Haydn.

Christian Bach was a composer of infinite courtesy—in this resembling his Bückeburg brother—but one who rarely expressed deeper thoughts than those covered by the then vogue word *pathos*. He was a man of his own time, beyond the frontiers of which he was not prepared to speculate. This was the reverse of a virtue in his personality. He was ever amiable, and greatly esteemed by his friends. It is significant that his coachman was in his service from the time of his arrival in England until his death. Mrs Papendiek loved him as Mary Delany loved Handel, from childhood, and remembered how when she was a small girl she had the chance to dance in front of the French balletmaster Noverre. 'I made Bach come to see me dance . . . and so delighted was he that it gave me a lift in his affection', she wrote long afterwards.[36] Bach was also a little naïve in his humour. He was quite capable of teasing his friend Fischer unmercifully, and the anecdote told of his embarrassing Fischer prior to his playing the oboe by squeezing a lemon before him passed into the general folklore of orchestral players, to be repeated by Samuel Wesley, but in respect of another oboist and another lemon-squeezer. Bach's capacity for friendship was one foundation of his success in establishing the public concerts that he controlled, as also the semi-private morning concerts that became an unusual feature of social activity, and of his Court duties.

In the end Bach suffered the fate of being taken for granted. But this perhaps was as he wished it. Carl Ludwig Junker proposed to weave jasmine and myrtles into the funeral wreath of Emanuel Bach; for John Christian he thought forget-me-nots, violets and anemones more suitable. The symbolism is apt.

NOTES TO CHAPTER TWELVE

1. J. W. von Archenholtz, *A Picture of England*, Dublin, 1791, p. 235.

2. Simon Harcourt, letter to Andrew Mitchell, diplomat then in Berlin, 17th August 1761. BM. Add. MS. 4857.

3. H. Walpole, *Reminiscences*, III, p. 432.

4. *Entradas and Minuets for the Balls at Court*, 1761–87, 3 vols., British Museum, R.M. 24 i 16. This collection contains various pieces by J. C. Bach composed after his Court appointment had become effective.

5. Burney, *A General History of Music*, IV, pp. 495–7.

6. Terry (*see* Note 21, Chapter 5 above), p. 57.

7. *See* Note 5 above, p. 482.

8. *See* Burney, Note 5, p. 481.

9. T. Busby, *A General History of Music*, London 1819, 2 vols., II, p. 450.

10. 'Harmonicus' in *The Public Advertiser*, 28th February 1767, quoted in Terry (*see* Note 21 in Chapter 5 above), p. 107.

11. *Court and Private Life in the Time of Queen Charlotte, being the journal of Mrs Papendiek*, London, 1887, 2 vols., I, pp. 76–7.

12. *See* Chapter 8, Note 18, p. 6.

13. *Annual Register*, 1772, p. 184.

14. Burney (*see* Note 5 above), IV, p. 483.

15. W. T. Parke, *Musical Memoirs*, 2 vols., London, 1830, I, p. 350.

16. *See* Note 1 above, p. 244.

17. Advertised in *The Public Advertiser*, 20th May 1777.

18. Daines Barrington, *Miscellanies*, London, 1781, p. 303.

19. *Correspondence of Thomas Gray*, ed. P. Toynbee and L. Whibley, 3 vols., London, 1935, III, p. 957.

20. See *Fugen über BACH von J. G. Albrechtsberger, J. C. Bach & G. A. Sorge*, ed. Percy M. Young, Bärenreiter Verlag, 1970.

21. John Hawkins, *An Account of the Institution and Progress of the Academy of Ancient Music*, etc., 1770, p. 20.

22. John Hawkins, Preface to Boyce's *Cathedral Music*.

23. BM., R.M., 24 h 15.

24. *See* BM., R.M., 24 i 16.

25. BM., R.M., 24 k 15.

26. *See* Otto Kade, *Die Musikalien-Sammlung des Mecklenburg-Schweriner Fürstenhauses*, Schwerin, 1893, 2 Vols., I, p. 119.

27. *Musical Remains*, ed. Edward Jones, *see* p. 28, 'Sonata VIth: for the Harp . . . Composed by G. C. Bach on purpose for the Editor to play'. London, 1796.

28. BM., Add. MS. 24310, also quoted in William Shield, *Rudiments of Thorough Bass*, p. 83.

29. *Reminiscences of Henry Angelo, with memoirs of his late father and friends*, 2 vols., London, 1828–30, I, p. 467. Bach's statement is given in Angelo in the kind of pidgin English that Bach, like Handel, was supposed to have spoken.

30. W. T. Whitley, *Thomas Gainsborough*, London, 1915, pp. 117–19.

31. *Salisbury Journal*, 8th October 1770.

32. *See* Note 31 above, 11th October 1773.

33. Regarding Bach's activities in and about Salisbury, *see* Betty Matthews, 'J. C. Bach in the West Country', *Mus. T.* 108, August, 1967, pp. 702 f., and Douglas J. Reid 'Some Festival Programmes of the eighteenth and nineteenth centuries—I Salisbury and Winchester', in *R.M.A. Research Chronicle*, No. 5 (1965), pp. 51 f.

34. *See* Stanley Sadie, 'Concert Life in Eighteenth Century England', in *P.R.M.A.*, vol. 35, London, 1959, p. 25 f.

35. Wolfenbüttel, Herzog August Bibliothek, MSS. 11 and 12, Symphonies in D and E flat; Novo Mesto, Franciscan Monastery, MSS. 295, 299, 301, 302—six concerti, and two sets of six divertimenti ascribed to Johann (Christian?) Bach.

36. *See* Note 11 above, p. 117.

37. *See* Chapter 10, Note 28 above.

13

End of an Old, and Establishment of a New, Tradition

THE PASSING OF THE OLD ORDER

The last of the Bachs—that is, of those who were practising musicians and composers—went out with something nearer a whimper than a bang. Wilhelm Friedrich Ernst Bach (1759–1845) is almost the only one of the whole long line who can, and then by stretching courtesy, be ranked only among the minor composers; those who are but marginal notes on the careers of the great. Nevertheless he was sufficiently active to cover a few pages of the Bach tradition with examples of music one further stage removed from the dominant strains within that tradition. It is just possible to perceive that Wilhelm Friedrich Ernst Bach was the contemporary of Beethoven and Weber, both of whom he outlived, and that he looked round the corner from the style he inherited tentatively to essay some elementary Romantic procedures.

On 23rd April 1843 the monument to Sebastian Bach—designed by Eduard Bendemann 'in old German style' and executed by a local sculptor, Knauer—was unveiled in Leipzig. The initiative had come from Mendelssohn, who made the day more memorable by arranging a morning concert in the Gewandhaus of which the programme consisted entirely of Bach's works—an orchestral suite, a motet, a cantata, the D minor clavier concerto and the Sanctus from the *Mass in B minor*. The dedication of the statue was at noon. There was a speech from a city councillor, two chorales and a motet. The day belonged to Sebastian Bach—'the indispensable Master and the teacher of all musicians', as Hermann Hirschbahn wrote in the *Neue Zeitschrift für Musik*. But after him the honours went to

> his only surviving grandson, an old—but still active—man of 81 with snow white hair and expressive features. He had come to the ceremony with his wife and two daughters from Berlin. No one— not even Mendelssohn himself, who had long lived in Berlin—

knew anything about him . . . even though he had lived in Berlin for 40 years [but there is] honour due to a man of worth who bears such a consecrated name.[1]

Wilhelm Friedrich Ernst Bach was among those who were forgotten before they were ever remembered, a figure of no importance in his own right in the brave new world of Mendelssohn, Schumann, Chopin and Liszt, and ignored even by the J. S. Bach revivalists. In music, as in statesmanship, heredity eventually runs out of ideas. The miracle of the Bachs is that the principle of heredity (if such it may be called) persisted for as long as it did. Wilhelm Friedrich Ernst simply did not have the strength to help maintain it. Nor was he educated to face the rigours of an age of change.

Born at Bückeburg, the godson of the ruling count from whom he derived his first name, Wilhelm Friedrich Ernst was taught music by his father, Johann Christoph Friedrich. At the age of nineteen he was taken by his father first to Hamburg, where he was put through his paces by his uncle Emanuel and given opportunity to perform in public, and then to London. Here he was left with his uncle John Christian, from whom he was expected to acquire the modish early classical techniques that seemed to pay off so well. That he appeared at Bach–Abel concerts is attested by a note on his Grand Sonata in E flat of 1778, saying that it had been 'first performed at Bach's Concert, Hannover Square' (B. M., Add. MS 3204d). Gifted with a singular capacity for proving himself unobtrusive, Wilhelm Friedrich Ernst slid out of London after the death of John Christian, not having found any niche in English professional music that he could fill. In view of the strong disposition of the English at that time to employ foreign, and particularly German, musicians it is a reasonable deduction that John Christian's nephew did not show any signs of outstanding talent. Or it may be that his uncle's successor, Schroeter—according to Mrs Papendiek a 'fascinating, fawning and suave' character—ensured that he should not be impeded in his career by a younger Bach. On leaving London Ernst spent some time in France and Holland and then re-turned to Westphalia, according to the flautist Friedrich Ludwig Dulon becoming music director at Minden, on the Weser, a few miles from Bückeburg. Minden was a small town of some forty thousand inhabitants, but important for its industries, of which the chief were mining and cloth manufacture. There, protected by the respectable influence of his father, Ernst led a quiet life. As a composer (of chamber, symphonic and vocal music) he showed a marked disposition to maintain the courtesies offered by the general style of his father's music. So may be noted the temperate tunefulness of the second of the *Six Sonatas for the Harpsichord or Piano Forte, with an Accompaniment for a Violin and Violoncello*, published by John Preston in London in 1785 (?), and the ingenious figuration of the fifth of the set.

These pieces were dedicated to Miss Dumergue, with whom Ernst had presumably become acquainted at the Angelos.[2] They may of course be paralleled by many similar sets expressly designed for young lady amateurs. A Miss Cornewall, of a Herefordshire family, is known to have possessed music by W. F. E. Bach, according to a MS. catalogue complied in 1796.[3]

In 1787 an aria, 'Seyd gegrüsst', was published in Johann Christoph

Friedrich's *Musikalische Nebenstunden* (see page 231), where the composer's name was printed as William Bach. The fact that a German composer should wish so to see his name anglicized in his own country is so rare as to call for emphasis. In the same year Wilhelm Friedrich Ernst, obeying the voice of patriotic duty, composed a

Trauer-Cantate auf den Tod Sr. Majestät Friedrichs des Grossen von Preussen, aufgeführt am Tage des Leichenbegängnisses in hiesiger Reformierter Kirche. Minden 1787.[4]

The king was dead: long live the king. And shortly after his accession the successor to Frederic the Great, Friedrich Wilhelm II, paid a visit to Minden. In his honour Wilhelm Bach composed a ceremonial work—

Westphalens Freude ihren vielgeliebten
König Friedrich Wilhelm bey sich zu sehen

This dull work, which shows the influence of John Christian in the Italianate flourishes in the melodic line and in the easy flow of, for instance, the rondo-aria 'Tönet sanft', was applauded by the king, and not long afterwards Bach was commanded to fill the place of Kapellmeister to the queen in Berlin.[5] In 1791 the cantata was published, and after the names of members of the Prussian royal house among the subscribers were (among others) those of Pastor Stille and Concertmeister Bach of Bückeburg, a Frau von Frenzel from Erfurt (showing that contact with Thuringia was still not entirely lost) and, representing English interest, the Duke of Manchester—who was at that time in Berlin. In 1788 twelve songs by Wilhelm Bach of some social-historic interest were published in

Freymaurer-Lieder mit ganz neuen Melodien von den Herren Kapellmeistern Bach, [Johann Gottlieb] Naumann & [Johann Abraham Peter] Schulz
and in an

Allgemeines Liederbuch für Freymaurer, both being published in Kopenhagen and Leipzig in 1788. These songs (as in Wotquenne) were previously mistakenly ascribed to Emanuel Bach, by whom, so far as style is concerned, they might very well have been composed.[6]

In 1798 Bach married the eighteen-year-old Charlotte Elerdt, who bore him two daughters and, in 1801, having produced the second, soon afterwards died. Less than a year later Bach remarried, his second wife being Wilhelmine Albrecht, who bore a daughter and a son. The latter died in infancy.

Bach was Kapellmeister to the consorts of both Friedrich Wilhelm II and Friedrich Wilhelm III, although after 1810 he retired from regular participation in the Court musical activities. Among his pupils were the future Friedrich Wilhelm IV, and the Princes Wilhelm and Heinrich of Prussia. He lived in Berlin in Linienstrasse 113, and enjoyed a pension of 300 thalers.

For the most part the compositions of Bach belong to an age that was past almost before he came to maturity. He held on to the conventions with a pious regard for the obligations they implied. His chamber music is considerably less interesting than that of his father and in no way to be compared with that of his uncles, even though a kind of Biedermeier charm hangs around the *Sestetto per Due Corni, Clarinetto, Violino, Viola e Violoncello.*[7] In a *Ballet Pantomime*[8] dated 1798, and composed in Berlin for one of the queen's famous and extravagant masquerades, however, Bach did allow himself to be carried towards a warmer climate. With his overture and forty-three dances Bach, by using a full symphonic orchestra (of that day) with discretion, went into a more emotion-laden atmosphere. *On vient inviter Béatrix et son amant à danser*, reads the direction:

In this charming movement—for strings only—there is at least a suggestion of the children's pieces of Schumann. As *les paysannes expriment leur allegresse* there is a hint of Weber, and even of the Pastoral Symphony.

Obliged to consider what was proper to a French ballet, Bach managed to produce his most 'German' music; but in at least one piece, where

Lorenzo se racommode avec Dovira, he manages a neat piece as of Delibes. But that the French Revolution had taken place, that all Europe was in turmoil, the music of Wilhelm Friedrich Ernst Bach is happily unaware.

As it happens there was one Bach of this period who was aware of and affected by political happenings. On 2nd March 1861 a music-teacher, G. Bach, living at Hofkämperstrasse 326, Elberfeld, wrote to Ferdinand Hiller as follows:

> Hoping that I, the undersigned, am not troubling you, may I make so bold as to acquaint you of a notable discovery. All along the most prominent artists have remarked that there must have been a transitional stage between J. S. Bach and Beethoven.
>
> Note this! Because of a death in my family I have come into possession of great works by Michael Bach. He was born on 9th November 1745 near Schmalkalden [Thuringia] and died in Elberfeld in 1820. Through the French Revolution he was robbed of his great destiny in music and between the years of 179?–1800 (at which time he and two of his sons had to serve the Revolution) many of his earlier works—which had been sent into the world under the name of Sebastian Bach—got lost. Perhaps you, my dear Herr Director, are destined to bring the service to music of the departed spirits into esteem. To this end I would like to lay before you a work so that afterwards you may pronounce judgment over the remaining works. I would, therefore, come to Köln to visit you for this purpose if you would arrange a day and hour.
>
> Hoping that this is not inconvenient to you.
>
> I remain,
>
> Yours
>
> G. Bach[9]

In his diary for 10th March 1861 Hiller made the following note:

> Visit from the old music-teacher Bach from Elberfeld, who brought me a work of his father, Michael Bach, which he thought was a work of genius.[10]

Johann Michael Bach, although not nearly related to J. S. Bach, coming from Schmalkalden (he was born in Struth near by), was certainly of the *clan* of Bach and, musically speaking, was closer to the family tradition than, say, Wilhelm Friedrich Ernst. He held office as Kantor at Tonna early in life, but was soon expelled from it for reasons which are not known. He then travelled extensively in Holland,

England, America and various parts of Germany,[11] after which he enrolled as a student of 'Liberal Arts' at Göttingen, on 29th June 1779.[12] On leaving Göttingen Michael Bach practised law in Güstrow and was later a professor in Elberfeld, where he died. While living in Güstrow he composed a secular cantata, *Heil dir! beglücktes Land*, in honour of the birthday of the Duke of Mecklenburg. For reasons stated by his son, J. M. Bach's compositions were dispersed (and there would seem to have been confusion with the earlier Johann Michael Bach of Gehren), but his theoretical work, the *Anleitung zur General-Bass und der Tonkunst*, remains.[13] This little essay—which quotes from Emanuel Bach's *Art das Clavier zu spielen*—was written at Göttingen, presumably under Forkel's inspiration, in 1780. Not in itself extraordinary it is none the less a link between German and English musicology. For it was among those documents that came into consideration when John Wall Callcott (1766–1821) began to investigate the general Bach field in 1800. His aide in this undertaking was August Friedrich Christoph Kollmann (1756–1849).

PLANTING SEED IN ALIEN SOIL

Kollmann is a most important figure in the Bach revival, but the fact that he emigrated to England militated against recognition of this fact in Germany, while in England the derivative influence of Samuel Wesley has been praised without due respect to his mentor in these matters. Kollmann was a link between the authentic tradition and the Romantic era, and between Germany and England. Born at Engelsbostel, Hannover, he was a pupil of a Thuringian organist, Johann Christian Böttner (1731–1800), who was heir to the true style. In 1781 Kollmann was appointed organist at Kloster Lüne, near Lüneburg. From his later writings it is clear that he was well instructed in the works of J. S. Bach, as also those of Marpurg, Kirnberger and Fasch and other members of the Berlin School. He was familiar also with Hamburg, where his uncle Karl Christoph Hachmeister (*d. c.* 1779) was organist of the Church of the Holy Ghost from 1753, and where his brother, Georg Christoph Kollmann, was organist of St Catherine's Church. Georg Christoph was appointed to this post by Emanuel Bach after satisfying that master with his treatment of this theme.

which I suppose to be by Emanuel Bach, because he laid it before my Brother at Hamburgh to extemporize upon, at a public trial of skill for a place, as is the custom in Germany.[14]

In 1784 August Kollmann migrated to England where he received a modest appointment in the royal household as schoolmaster and chapel-keeper of the German Chapel in St James's Palace. In 1792 George III presented an organ to the chapel and Kollmann became organist. A vigorous campaigner in the cause of popular musical education, he published a number of teaching aids, among which *An Essay on Musical Harmony* (1796), dedicated to Burney, and *An Essay on Practical Musical Composition* (1799) are the most important. The latter was inscribed to the king, and Forkel was among the subscribers.

In the *Essay on Musical Harmony*, Kollmann introduces the English reader not only to the main German masters (among whom J. S. Bach is numbered), but less familiar figures such as Hachmeister, Georg Benda and Forkel—whose variations on *God Save the King* (page 118) are mentioned. Emmanuel Bach is applauded as 'one of the great fancy players and writers' (page 121) in an essay on extemporization. Well aware of the predilections of his English audience, Kollmann wisely reserves the highest praise for Handel. In the *Essay on Practical Musical Composition*, however, the stress is on Sebastian Bach. What Kollmann had to say in respect of Bach must have stimulated many minds. Regarding 'duets for two keyed instruments', he wrote

> But two excellent Fugues of this description are in *Seb. Bach's* Art of the Fugue, which might be played on the two sets of keys of the organ. This great Author has also written concertos for two, three and even four Keyed Instruments. (p. 13.)

A few pages later Kollmann announced his intention (which was not fulfilled) of undertaking publication of certain of Bach's works. In discussing the subject of fugue he differentiated between fugues of an academic nature and those of a more free order:

> Proper Fuges therefore are: those six by *Handel*, published for the Organ by Walsh; also twenty-four Fugues by *Sebastian Bach* [probably Book II of the '48', see below] which I wish to publish analysed if I find sufficient encouragement for it ... *Sebastian Bach* also has written a whole collection of improper Fugues, in four parts, for a Keyed Instrument, entitled: Inventions, which deserve to be known and studied. (p. 27.)

Returning to the *Wohltemperirtes Clavier* Kollmann described it as

> This most ingenious, most learned, and yet practicable work [which] is so highly esteemed by all who can judge of it, that as it is grown scarce, I intend to offer it to the public analysed. (pp. 97–8.)

The first prelude and fugue of Book II he published among the copious music examples at the end of the volume (Plate LII). The *Art of Fugue* is dealt with throughout the book (pages 29, 50, 52, 57), and the subject of Canon throws Kollmann aside to discuss an early English master of that science—Elway Bevin (pages 72–3, and Plates XL and XLI). Kollmann, who gave a full analysis of the *Musikalisches Opfer* (pages 71–2), backed his pedagogic intention with a refreshing enthusiasm. The sixth and seventh sections of the *Art of Fugue* he regarded as the 'most sublime pieces imaginable', while the same adjective was applied to the Chromatic Fantasia (illustrated on Plate XIII). He drew attention to the unaccompanied violin sonatas (pages 104, 105) and to works with 'obligato' pedal part, such works being rare in England.

> An example of [this] sort, or of a piece with a whole *obligato part* for Pedals, see at Plate LVIII, *Trio*, by *Sebastian Bach*. This piece is taken from the said great Author's collection of Organ Trios, and is calculated to be performed by one Person, on two sets of Manuals and the Pedals. . . . (p. 99.)

The importance of Kollmann will become further apparent, but here let it be said that by the time he had published his *magnum opus* the English Bach movement was well under way. Kollmann's two books are notable in that, while they make frequent reference to Handel, John Christian Bach is quite ignored. His half-brother Emanuel on the other hand is respected, not only as the great master of extemporization, but as one of the great exponents of contrapuntal techniques.

FORKEL AND ZELTER

While Kollmann was extolling the virtues of Bach in England, there were those in Germany similarly active. The German Bach 'revival' was in full spate. But, although in due time the German and English movements may have been said to have become one, there were different intentions behind these developments. The Germans re-created Johann

Sebastian Bach as a national hero. Forkel wrote in the preface to his biography, of which the English translation was by Kollmann:

> The works which John Sebastian Bach has left us, are an invaluable national patrimony, with which no nation has any thing to be compared.[15]

And he ended his study as follows:

> And this man, the greatest musical poet, and the greatest musical declaimer, that ever existed, and probably ever will exist, was a GERMAN. Let his country be proud of him; let it be proud, but at the same time, worthy of him.[16]

The English musician William Crotch was no less enthusiastic, but restrained himself to this comment to Samuel Wesley:

> You are perfectly right in considering Sebastian Bach the greatest Musician that ever existed.[17]

The German renascence of interest in Bach stemmed from two sources; the one musical, the other literary, theological and philosophical. Both were subject to an overriding concern for the concept of a particular all-German culture.

In Leipzig occasional performances of Bach's motets, such as Mozart heard in 1789, from time to time served to remind the citizens of their greatest Kantor. Doles, who was Kantor at the time of Mozart's visit, was a pupil of Bach and, having succeeded Harrer in 1755, remained in office until 1789. After Doles came Johann Adam Hiller, who retired in 1804 to be followed by August Eberhard Müller. The son of the university organist in Rinteln (not far from Bückeburg), Müller was a pupil of J. C. F. Bach, and his keen interest in the music of J. S. Bach led him to attempt (but without much success) to reintroduce the church cantatas into the repertoire at Leipzig. Müller was followed by Johann Gottfried Schicht—a pupil of Trier in Zittau—who was Kantor from 1810 until 1823. An important figure in the field of choral music in general, Schicht founded the Leipzig Singakademie in 1810. He was also a keen collector of Bach manuscripts and amassed a considerable collection of the church cantatas.

And after Schicht came Christian Theodor Weinlig, the teacher of both Schumann and Wagner. The Bach tradition that had been maintained to some extent by the succession of Kantors to the Thomaskirche was thus communicated to two composers who were particularly responsible for regarding the methods of Bach as being applicable to the problems of musical expression in the high summer of the Romantic era.

The fact was that the whole matter of Bach's life and works came as a godsend to Romantics. The quest for the romantic Bach (and Handel) began in C. F. Cramer's *Magazin der Musik* in 1783 in this way:

> If Bach had possessed the same idea of truth and the same deep feeling for expression as Handel he would have been much greater than Handel. He is, however, only more learned and industrious. If both these great men had more knowledge of mankind, of speech, and of poetry, and if they had been sufficiently critical to put aside all purposeless mannerisms and mere convenience, they would have been the highest ideals of our art. . . .[18]

By the end of the century, however, matters had been put right on this front. The *Allgemeine Musikalische Zeitung* was ready to put Bach alongside Michelangelo.[19] A year later he was compared with Homer,[20] and in 1806, the impulse towards nationalism having become more intense, to Dürer.[21]

The writer responsible for these analogies (on another occasion he compared Bach with Isaac Newton) was Johann Friedrich Rochlitz (1769–1842), who had studied under Doles at the Thomasschule. E. T. A. Hoffmann, a pupil of Christian Wilhelm Podbielski of Königsberg—with an interest in Bach by way of an ancestor who had been a student in Leipzig—gave Bach the full romantic treatment by portraying Kapellmeister Kreisler as 'washing himself clean in Bach's music'. So far as Hoffmann was concerned music itself was as a religious cult, and the high priest of the cult was Sebastian Bach.

Between the 1783 issue of Cramer's *Magazin* and the publication of Hoffmann's *Lebensansichten des Katers Murr* (1820–22) lay the main work of Forkel's mission.

Forkel was a complex personality (too complex for his wife to understand and so she ran away to seek understanding elsewhere). He was, as students tended to see him, possessed of an encyclopedic mind, industrious, pedantic. He had enemies and they disliked most his self-esteem. He was once described as 'one of the top grade egoists, who only enjoys his own excellence; all else comes in for criticism'.[22] (The same writer, however, acknowledged that he 'played the clavier like a Master'.) He had, however, rebellious impulses—directed against the limitations imposed by the apotheosis of 'reason', and against the formal limitations of 'good taste'. He was all for asking questions, for enlarging frontiers.

As a scholar Forkel's ambitions were too great for his capacities. Even so his contribution to scholarly understanding of music was very considerable. His general argument for the proper realization of music-historical studies in a university was promulgated in his first literary work, *Über die Theorie der Musik*. In 1778 Forkel published a three-volume *Musikalisch-kritische Bibliothek*, followed by various pamphlets, and the *Musikalischer Almanach für Deutschland* (1782–3–4–9). In 1788 and 1801 there appeared an *Allgemeine Geschichte der Musik* in which, as did many other German writers, he relied a great deal on Burney and Hawkins. In 1789 he published a two-volume translation of Esteban Arteaga's *Rivoluzioni del teatro musicale italiano*. Three years later came the *Allegemeine Literatur der Musik*. By this time Forkel's position was firmly established. W. H. Wackenroder wrote to Ludwig Tieck at the beginning of November in that year:

> Let me know if, when you are in Göttingen, you will make the acquaintance of Professor Forkel, who has written a *History of Music*, a *Critical Music-Library*, etc., and is a very good music critic. Write to me if he holds music seminars. I find him an interesting man.[23]

But Tieck, replying on 6th November, merely noted that there was a lot of Dittersdorf played at Forkel's concerts and that he himself was too much tied up with his own researches into art to find time for meeting Forkel.[24]

A musician as well as a writer, Forkel was indefatigable in searching out source material. In 1801 he undertook a grand tour through the libraries, monasteries and schools of middle and southern Germany to find manuscripts, and he reported to Zelter in Berlin what a vast amount of unknown music there was.[25] At that time he was preparing the music examples to accompany his *History of Music*, a project that was intended by Joseph Sonnleithner, the Viennese scholar, to develop into a general history of music through music—under the supervision of an editorial committee of Albrechtsberger, Haydn and Salieri. In 1803 a prospectus concerning the work was issued. Despite the war the engraving of the first volumes—of Netherlands Masses to the time of Isaac—continued. The proofs of the first volume were in Forkel's hands in 1805, but the plates were in Vienna. The French soldiery discovered them, shortly before the battle of Austerlitz, in 1805, and decided that they could serve a better use. So they were converted into bullets. Although this work never saw the light of day it was the basis on which the later *Denkmäler Deutscher Tonkunst* was raised.

Forkel's career so far marks him out as a hero-scholar, familiar in the German tradition. But two other facets of his personality turned him into the particular kind of hero he became to posterity: a sort of gentleman's gentleman, the permanent attendant on the shade of the great Bach. First, he was a Thuringian, and a pupil at Lüneburg, circumstances which ensured that he was among those to whom the name of Sebastian Bach was not unfamiliar. Second, he had an engaging habit of showing generosity to unknown musicians, or those who were out of luck's way. So far as Forkel was concerned, Bach was not (as others had previously opined) the end of a tradition, but the beginning of a new tradition. Immediately Bach was the first great German master from whom all German music derived. This point found instant appeal. But Bach was the master from whom all (then) modern music derived. The exposition of this faith was of course *Über J. S. Bachs Leben, Kunst und Kunstwerke*, which was dedicated to van Swieten, addressed specifically to 'musical patriots' and published in Leipzig in 1802. The English edition appeared some eighteen years later. The London publisher was Thomas Boosey, who had for some time been importing German books and music.

While Forkel was thus preparing the ground for a reassessment of the significance of Bach, Zelter was dedicating his practical gifts to a similar end in Berlin. A pupil of Kirnberger, Zelter was one of the few authentic performers of Bach's keyboard works (which he taught to Mendelssohn, who, as a boy, played them to Goethe) and as the Director of the Berlin Singakademie he was able, in 1829, to give Mendelssohn the opportunity to perform the *St Matthew Passion* on 11th March.

In view of the fact that Mendelssohn interpreted the *St Matthew Passion* in a manner deemed improper by present-day musicological criteria it is perhaps surprising that the work should have made the impression that it did on Karl von Holtei, who wrote with unbounded enthusiasm to Ludwig Tieck on 22nd March 1829[26], and to many others. However, the credit that was formerly given to Mendelssohn for his initiative was not all quite merited. The lion's share should have gone to Zelter; but Mendelssohn was acclaimed as the youthful wonder-worker of his country at that time and it was tactically correct to put him in charge of the Singakademie singers and orchestra for what was hoped would prove an epochal occasion.

Zelter's devotion to Bach had led him to a long sustained effort to bring back into use the choral works—even though he had reservations about the archaic theology contained within many of the texts, especially of the chorales. He was encouraged by the opportunities afforded him by the circumstances of the times. In 1809 he was called upon by the Royal Academy of Arts and Sciences 'to attempt the revival of a taste for church music, which had sunk to a very low ebb'.[27] In the same year, in order further to develop the art of choral music, he formed twenty-four of the best men among his singers into a *Liedertafel*. Following on the militarily satisfactory end of the 'Wars of Liberation' there came the Reformation Festival of 1817 (the stimulus to choral societies in other parts of Germany also), and a strengthened link between Church and State. In 1822 a Royal Institute of Church Music was established under Zelter's direction. Among the leading Berlin church musicians who assisted Zelter was Mendelssohn's organ teacher—August Wilhelm Bach (1796–1869), a Berliner, who succeeded Zelter as Director of the Institute in 1832. Blessed with such a name it was sometimes wrongly assumed that August Bach belonged to the clan proper.[28] In fact he did not.

It is said that Zelter 'knew about 100 of the Cantatas, the two Passions, the *Mass in B minor*, the shorter Masses, the *Magnificat*, and the Motets'.[29] Many of these works he studied with his singers, and although he was doubtful of the public viability of the major works, he rehearsed the *Mass in B minor* in 1811 and 1813, and the *St Matthew Passion* in 1815.

In 1827 Zelter wrote to Goethe, and in memorable language set out the apotheosis of Bach in these terms:

> Everything considered which might be held against him, this Leipzig Cantor is a divine phenomenon, clear, yet inexplicable. I could cry out to him: 'thou gavest me a task to do, and I have brought thee to light again'.[30]

Forkel, Rochlitz and Zelter exerted influence in every field, and the pressures for the recognition of Bach as a native hero grew more intense. C. F. Schubart's naming of Bach as the Orpheus of the German people and the Newton of music (Edward Holmes was another who went in for the Newton analogy) was contained in an essay published in Gentz's *Deutsche Monatschrift* of 1793 (pages 40–1); not only Goethe, but also Schiller and Wilhelm von Humboldt, took up the theme of Bach as a national hero. On 20th April 1821 Carl Maria von Weber contributed an essay on Bach to the Encyclopedia of Ersch and Gruber. Bach he hailed as a 'hero of art', as one whose modernity contrasted with Handel's more conservative manner, and whose individuality was strongly romantic, fundamentally German.[31] G. W. F. Hegel, at the time Professor of Philosophy in the University of Berlin, was also among those present at Mendelssohn's performance of the *St Matthew Passion*, and he too subscribed to the theme of Bach's greatness.[32] By 1835 it was impossible to write an article on Bach in any encyclopedia without paying the kind of homage normally reserved for the saints.[33]

The fact that Bach had been raised up as an object of veneration by writers of strong romantic proclivities helped the growth of a new mystical cult. The rejection of the rationality of the eighteenth century, the onset of nationalism and its intenser cultivation under the impact of the Napoleonic Wars, and a potent influence stemming from religious revivalism, all contributed to the emergence of a legendary Bach—the truly *Protestant* genius of Hegel's evaluation. The recognition of Bach as a pillar of Christianity (Forkel supposed that his fugues were implicit with a religious faith, and many others readily accepted the assumption) was established before the choral works were again in use. The revival of these was fraught with difficulties; partly on account of their inherent difficulty, partly on account of the alien style that led Mendelssohn to cut and edit the *St Matthew Passion* unmercifully. Since, for the most part, German churches lacked the resources for performing Bach's works, their resuscitation depended largely on choral societies. Choral societies depended on the goodwill of their members. Not very many were enthusiastic about the actual rehearsal of Bach's music however much they might be in sympathy with the principles that provoked suggestions that they should be performed.

As has been seen, Zelter laid the foundation of a revival of interest in performing Bach's choral works in Berlin. In Breslau Johann Theodor Mosewius, director of the Singakademie of that city, and Carl von Winterfeld took up the cause with enthusiasm. Mosewius heard the 1829 performance of the *St Matthew Passion* in Berlin, and gave a performance in Breslau a year later. Subsequently he worked through the church cantatas, not only giving regular performances of them but also writing about them. In Frankfurt/Main the interest of J. Nepomuk Schelle in Bach led to his performing the credo from the *Mass in B minor* there in 1828, and also a number of cantatas.

In Kassel the cause of Bach was espoused by Ludwig Spohr (1784–1859), whose early interest had been aroused by Gottlieb Schwenke of Hamburg. The latter possessed manuscripts that he had acquired from Emanuel Bach. Spohr organized the St Cecilia Society in Kassel, and from 1824 choral works by Bach, despite occasional opposition by the duke, were included in the programmes. The versions of these works—edited by Spohr—were less than authentic and aroused the ire of Hauptmann, who was as near a purist as it was possible to be in the mid nineteenth century.[34]

Apart from prejudice, such as that of the Count of Hesse-Darmstadt, the growing popularity of Handel (as well as that of works by composers of more recent date) hindered the progress of Bach. The truth was that in Germany there was not—as there was in England—a firm, popular tradition of choral singing solidly based on the reputation and achievement of a composer who, having become one in his lifetime, had no need of posthumous election to the status of national hero. As it happens, the English were a little presumptuous in treating Handel in this way since, after all, he was a German. But in so doing they also prepared the way for the rehabilitation of Handel's greatest contemporary.

SAMUEL WESLEY AND THE BACH TRADITION

It is said that James Hook (1746–1827) was 'the first who had the courage to play the fugues of Bach in public [thus initiating] the work to be carried on in later years by Samuel Wesley, Battishill and Jacob'.[35] But it was Samuel Wesley (1766–1837), one of the most remarkable among English musicians of that period, who was the key figure in the elevation of Bach to a commanding position in English music. Wesley's achievement was the greater since he held no official appointment which he could use to give backing to his unusual views. All he had was his own genius and integrity of purpose. Wesley tells his own story in respect of his Bach campaign in his somewhat disordered and fragmentary, but invaluable, reminiscences[36]:

> The Compositions of the mighty Sebastian Bach were not known in this Country until within the last 30 Years.[37] He was manifestly the most Scientific and Versatile Master that ever adorned the Musical World: it is but Justice to the English Public to say that the more his Works have been circulated, the greater has been their Estimation. . . .[38]

Thro' the late Frederic George [*sic*] Pinto . . . I first became acquainted with the preludes and fugues of John Sebastian Bach, whose matchless compositions I have had the honour of introducing to the English Public . . . When I practised the organ assiduously these pieces were of the most essential benefit, and I could not consider myself a complete master of the instrument until I was able to play them correctly and with facility—I published an edition of them by subscription, and added an explanatory preface, recommending the best and most effectual method of studying and practising them with advantage.[39]

It was ill naturedly reported that I had extolled these Compositions extravagantly only because I alone could play them, whereas I am perfectly conscious that my earnest wish was for their universal Adoption and Practise [*sic*], as I am sure that my Preface to the work clearly proves.—The event justifies what I say.— Moreover by the Exercise of all these Keys it will be found of what great advantage to the proper use of the Thumb is in the Execution of numberless Passages which without it upon the black Keys, would be impossible . . . No sooner did the superior excellence of these Compositions find their own Level in this Country than the most Characters in the Profession eagerly betook themselves to the study and practise of them.[40]

Wesley goes on to specify Vincent Novello and Benjamin Jacob[41] as conspicuous Bach enthusiasts, and how the latter had adapted some of the '48' for two performers and how Crotch had become a leading champion of the cause of Bach. Since the English held fast to the idea that the organ was the king of instruments, it was generally assumed that all Bach's fugues must have been composed for that instrument. But Wesley had his doubts.

As Bach's Organ Music had always an obligato Pedal Bass part, it may be doubted whether the Preludes and Fugues were originally designed for the Organ, although they have so admirable an effect when well performed upon it, and many tied and holding notes seem to prove that the Organ was the instrument first intended for them.

The late C. F. Horn [1762–1832, a Thuringian immigrant musician] also brought to me in manuscript six Organ trios, the bass part of which was originally intended to be performed on Pedals: I also published an edition of these with a preface[42]: they met with universal approbation, and have been found eminently serviceable to all who aspire to excellence in the true organ style.

There are numerous exercises of this mighty Master for the

Harpsichord, printed in Germany, and in single numbers.—His vocal music is quite as extraordinary as his instrumental.—His motetts for a double choir and variations upon Chorales are instances of his fertile and versatile fancy.

There is a Credo for a full Orchestra of voices and instruments, which is a splendid specimen of the most magnificent invention conducted with most learned and scientific mode imaginable . . .[43]

Novello and Wesley used to play fugues from the '48' at the Portuguese Embassy Chapel in South Street as voluntaries after morning service, while Jacob did the same at the independent Surrey Chapel. Here Wesley and Jacob once organized a Bach–Handel programme for a special occasion, with the consent of the Rev. Rowland Hill. In 1814 Novello and Wesley played the so-called 'St Anne' fugues (from that time among the most highly favoured of Bach's organ works in England) with an introduction (since Bach himself had supplied no prelude) composed by Wesley, at the Foundling Hospital for the benefit of William Russell's widow and children.[44]

Anticipating later practice Wesley told how

A late Pupil of mine, desirous of analysing the structure and ingenious Ramification of the forty eight Fugues, was at the pains to set them out in score, whereby he was enabled to distinctly ascertain and as it were anatomize their wonderful tonal combinations, and he had so thoroughly digested their contents, as to prefer performing them from the score he had made, to reading them from the usual copies condensed in two lines. All the Fugues would produce a noble effect if performed by a band of either stringed or wind instruments.[45]

Wesley was altogether indefatigable in propagating the music of Bach, and in due course his enthusiasm met up with that of Mendelssohn. The latter set the seal on the English Bach movement when in 1837 and 1840 he included organ works of Bach in the programmes of the Birmingham Triennial Festival. To Wesley, however, went the honour of first producing one of the choral works in England. This was on 3rd June 1809, when he organized a performance of *Jesu, meine Freude* at a 'Musical Morning Party' at Hanover Square Rooms.

BROADENING OF INTEREST IN ENGLAND

Inspired by Wesley's dedication, the leading organists of London— Jacob, Battishill (see page 290) and Thomas Adams (1785–1858)—in days when church-going was general, made a large number of people aware of the Bach style. But it was not only organists who were effective in the dissemination of knowledge. In his later days J. P. Salomon performed some of the violin sonatas. George Bridgetower (1779–1860)—who played the 'Kreutzer' sonata for the first time with Beethoven—also included Bach in his repertoire; so that Wesley could write:

> It was a rich Treat for a Lover of the Instrument [violin] to hear him perform the matchless and immortal Solos of Sebastian Bach, all of which he perfectly retained in Memory and executed with the utmost Precision, and without a Single Error.[46]

Wesley used to visit Charles Burney at Chelsea Hospital to discuss Bach. There he made a convert in a surgeon named Graham, a former pupil of Giardini, and among amateurs Graham won much respect as an exponent of Bach.

Wesley, whose son Samuel Sebastian Wesley (1810–76) conveyed his father's intentions to a later generation, summed up his thoughts on Bach as follows:

> He is equally matchless & magnificent in instrumental as in vocal Music. His own chief Instrument was the Organ, upon which he was unrivalled both before and since—his skill of Execution on Pedals was marvellous, & every Portion of his Production is an Evidence of Superiority never attained by any other Musician.
>
> His Knowledge of the Violin was complete [Wesley also played the violin], as his sublime & beautiful Solos demonstrate—It was equal as to the Violoncello, for which Instrument he has constructed [an]other Set, shewing a similar Mastery.
>
> It may be truly said of him, 'Quicquid tetigit, ornavit': he never meddled with any Thing that he did not improve.[47]

The curiosity aroused by Wesley created a thirst for knowledge, and the musical journalists were not slow to take the hint. They were given a convenient point of departure by the gradual appearance of published works. In the June issue of *The Harmonicon* of 1823 (page 75), a 'Memoir of John Sebastian Bach' appeared, while in the September number of *The Musical Library* (No. XVIII) of 1835 (page 98) a more critical notice (quoting from the *Allgemeine musikalische Zeitung* of 1823) was printed:

> Bach's compositions, in almost every class, are numerous; of these scarcely any are known out of Germany, except his

Clavecin bien Temperé, or Preludes and Fugues in all the keys. These were composed as exercises for his sons, and while we admit the deep learning and ingenious contrivance they display, as well as the vast labour they must have cost, we are heretical enough to think that, as regards effect—and what is music without?—they have been overvalued. His vocal works are, in our opinion, much more likely to convey his name to distant ages, than those of the instrumental kind. Among the former are a funeral cantata, a magnificat, a motet, several *chorals*, or psalm-tunes, and, above all, his *Passionsmusik*, which show that he possessed genius as well as science; that he could not only write laborious fugues, but create pleasing melodies, and clothe them in harmonies as ravishing as recondite.

The writer of this piece was probably the editor, William Ayrton, who had certainly come on in his appreciation of Bach since 27th July 1816, when he met Wesley and J. C. Bach's acquaintance, Edward Jones, in Chappell's music shop.[48]

At the time of his death Ayrton had in his possession 'Bach's Mass, for 8 voices, pt. 1. full score, 4 copies'[49] as well as five copies of J. C. Bach's Mass in D (formerly the property of Lord Burghersh) and a manuscript score of the same composer's *Carattaco* which had come from Queen Charlotte's Library. Having started a hare in *The Musical Library* by upgrading Bach's choral works he was, as a popular journalist, not displeased to see one 'G.T.', of Oxford, setting off in pursuit—with a letter, dated 29th October 1835, stoutly defending the principles of fugal composition.

As they became more familar, however, it was the big organ works that made the biggest impression. In *The Musical World I* (18th March–10th June 1836, page 46) there was a revealing notice of:

John Sebastian Bach's Grand Studies for the Organ, consisting of Preludes, Fugues, Toccatas, and Fantasias, never before published in this Country, Book I, Coventry and Hollier: . . . . the Fantasia is most wonderful in construction. It is an absolute anticipation of almost every modern invention in harmony. It is as profound as anything that Beethoven ever wrote. The admirers of that astonishing man [J. S. Bach] will readily believe that we do not over-estimate this composition when we pronounce it to be a stupendous effort of genius. The work contains a separate part for the double-bass or violoncello, arranged from the pedals, by a man as remarkable in his way, as the author himself—the inimitable Dragonetti.

Despite Kollmann's installation of an organ with pedals at St James's Palace, the English were generally slow in adopting the pedal-board until after the municipality of Birmingham had shown the advantages in the new instrument in the town hall. So for many the only way to hear the great organ works was through adaptations for piano and double-bass.

In 1838 the *Wohltemperirtes Clavier*, in Czerny's edition (Leipzig, 1837), was made available in England by Boosey, Cocks, Ewer & Co. About this *The Musical World VIII* (5th January–26th April 1838, p. 39) said:

> In some instances he differs from the mode of performance adopted by [S.] Wesley, and, we think, to a disadvantage. Wesley had no hereditary notions on the subject; probably neither has M. Czerny. However, Wesley possessed a kindred spirit with the German giant; and whether from long habit, associations, or affection, we know not; but Czerny's reading, in these instances, does not meet either with our sympathy or approval. ... We perceive M. Czerny has adopted the text of Mr Wesley, and in some instances also his mistakes.

The extent to which interest in Bach developed as soon as published works became available is indicated by the details of various sale catalogues. By far the most interesting collection of Bachiana was that of Rev. Samuel Picart (1775–1835), a Welshman who graduated at Oxford and became a Prebendary of Hereford Cathedral in 1805, and Rector of Hartlebury in Worcestershire in 1817. The works he had owned were as follows:

item 127 Magnificat—score (Bonn)—Motetten, 2 Books, in 1 vol.
    128 Mass for a double choir, score (Leipzig)—Missa a 4 voci, score (Leipzig)—An Eight-part Motett.
    129 Vierstimmige Choralgesänge, 4 vols. in 1 (Leipzig, 1784).
    130 Credo Symbolum Nicenum, MS score, beautifully written, hf. russia.
    131 Choral-Vorspiele für die Orgel, 4 p s in 1 vol. (Leipzig).
    132 Mass in D, vocal score, edited by Marx (Bonn).
    133 Clavier Sonaten mit obligater Violine (Zürich).
    134 Preludes & Fugues, Wesley & Horn's edition, vols. 1 & 3.
    135 Choral-Vorspiele für die Orgel, parts 1 & 2—Six Pedal Fugues and Preludes.
    136 Bach's 6 Trios for the Organ adapted to the Piano Forte, by Wesley & Horn.

137 Concerto a due Cembali, with accompaniments in score—Grand Pedal Fugue, MSS beautifully written.

138 Sonate a Violino solo, senza Basso, MSS.

139 Organ Toccata, various Nos.

140 'Du Hirte Israel' & 'Litany von M. Luther', vocal score.

141 Six Preludes & Six Fugues—Clavier Sonaten—XV Inventions—Toccata no. 1—Orgel Stücke.

142 Five Violin Duetts—Musikalisches Opfer—3 Sonatas for Violin & Bass—Trio for the P. F.—Chorale, vel Thema recte et simpliciter, MS.

143 Forty-eight Preludes and Fugues to all the Keys, 2 vols, in 1, russia (Zürich).

144 Two Trios for 2 Violins & Bass, in Score, MS. believed to be autograph. The second Trio contains the celebrated Canon Perpetuus. Both are UNPUBLISHED.

Picart also possessed scores of Emanuel Bach's *Die Auferstehung, Heilig*, and *Die Israeliten*.[50]

Other collectors of Bach's works included Dr Timothy Essex, who owned the *Passion* edition of 1831, two volumes of church music, edited by Joseph Marx, and *The Art of Fugue*[51]; H. J. Gauntlett (1865–76)[52]; Charles Hatchett, F.R.S., the chemist[53]; and the Duke of Cambridge, once a student at Göttingen, and in later life Viceroy of Hannover[54]; the Rev. Richard Allott, Precentor of the Cathedral of Armagh, in Ireland, is notable as among the first subscribers to the Bach Gesellschaft.[55]

The impact of the Bach cult on English music was not inconsiderable and, coinciding with a renewal of interest in madrigalian techniques, began to pull it back towards its own traditions. That is, towards a bluntness of expression that had been discouraged under the swell of classical ideas. During the greater part of the nineteenth century the strengthening techniques of contrapuntal exposition were kept in view by a small, but increasingly effective, school of organists who were also composers. Composers of the baroque period in England naturally took Handel as their model for fugal writing (except for Thomas Roseingrave, who was a law unto himself), and Arne, Greene, Boyce and others turned out impeccable examples of smooth-flowing fugue. Some of those who followed, such as Thomas Dupuis (1733–96), William Walond (*fl. c.* 1790), Samuel Long (*fl. c.* 1800), William Russell, John Bennet (1790–1830?), showed a greater interest in the rhythmic structure of subjects, in the individuality of counter-subjects and in the tensions of dissonance. In the case of Russell this was directly inspired by acquaintance with Bach's music, in others by the general character of German music that was being imported into England.

Samuel Wesley composed a *Eulogium de Johanne Sebastian Bach* (*ab Horatio desumptum*) for three voices (A.T.B.).[56] The influence of Bach's motet style is audible in Wesley's finest motets, such as *In Exitu Israel* and *Anima nostra*,[57] while the figuration of the 'Goldberg' Variations (which Wesley used to play to Vincent Novello) clearly affected the character of certain of the Voluntaries.[58] The *Six Fugues* (1811) of John Jeremiah Jones patently borrow patterns from the recently available *Wohltemperirtes Clavier*. Crotch stiffened his counterpoint according to what he learned not only from his consideration of Bach, but also from Marpurg and Kirnberger.[59] As for Thomas Adams—the best extempore player of his time in England—there is a self-explanatory anecdote:

> The first time Wesley was introduced to Adams was at a private party; who upon being requested to perform, played one of his own fugues—the one in F minor, we believe, of six which were afterwards published. When Adams had finished, Wesley went up to him and said: 'I forget which of Bach's fugues that is': and when he found it was Adams's own, he expressed himself highly delighted.[60]

Adams had a nimble mind in respect of fugal construction, and a talent for discussing themes that suggested further discussion. For instance, this subject from a fugue dated 14th February 1810:

From this there emerges episodically:

The comment of T. W. Philipps, who owned the manuscript[61] in 1814, was: 'It is very much in the style of Sebn. Bach'.

The first to emulate Bach in providing studies for the young in diverse keys was J. B. Cramer, in *Twenty Six Preludes or Short Introductions in the Principal Major and Minor Keys to the Pianoforte*, which were published by Chappell in 1825. Five years later a more interesting set of *Studies . . . in all the Major and Minor Keys Composed for the Use of the Royal Academy of Music* (*in London*) was published, also by Chappell. The composer in this case was Cipriani Potter, sometime a pupil of Joseph Woefl and (briefly) Beethoven in Vienna, and of Crotch and Callcott at home. Potter became Principal of the Royal Academy of Music in 1832, and the most promising student of that time was to become the next influential figure in the Bach movement in England. This was William Sterndale Bennett (1816–75) who, on Mendelssohn's advice, left the Royal Academy to study in Leipzig.

INAUGURATION OF BACH SOCIETIES

At this juncture the wheel came full circle. English musicians, long accustomed to believe in the superior virtues of German music, began to go to Germany in large numbers to acquaint themselves with techniques of the Germans at first hand. In the twenty-year period preceding the inauguration of the Bach Societies in England and Germany many English music students were resident in Leipzig. During this same period Bach propaganda increased as performing artists began regularly to include Bach in their repertoires. The first to make impact in England (in Birmingham as well as in London) was, as has been stated, Mendelssohn. But Ferdinand Hiller—whose early love of Bach was inculcated by Jacob Schmitt of Frankfurt—and Ignaz Moscheles (1794–1870)—whose attention had been concentrated on Bach by Dionysius Weber in Prague, and Albrechtsberger in Vienna—were both effective agents in the dissemination of the Bach cult. Hiller was also one of the first to play the keyboard works in France, and, although it did not show him at his best as a composer, among those who pinned their own fugues to the method of Bach.[62] On a celebrated day in 1839 Hiller, Mendelssohn and Liszt played one of Bach's concertos for three harpsichords at a Gewandhaus Concert in Leipzig. Liszt, inspired by the general enthusiasm, leapt onto the band-wagon and issued transcriptions of a number of the organ works.

In addition to a growing interest in including the works of Bach in the general repertoire there was an accompanying conviction that composition after the manner of Bach was at least a salutary exercise. The English composers who belonged to an independent Bach revival (Schumann paid tribute to English zeal in 'furthering the circulation of Bach's works'), and who were early in the field, have been considered. In Vienna the practice had been encouraged by Johann Georg Albrechtsberger (1736–1809), whose own knowledge of the works of both J. S. and C. P. E. Bach came from Robert Kimmerling, a companion in the monastery school at Melk. The fugues of Albrechtsberger were not only designed as prefatory exercises for those who would play the fugues of Bach, but also as examples of the diversity of techniques to be acquired by all students in search of competence. Albrechtsberger is among those who acknowledged their debt to the master by composing a fugue on the B A C H theme, published by the Berlin Academy of Arts in 1835.[63] It was under Albrechtsberger's influence that Johann Nepomuk Hummel (1778–1837) studied the complexities of counterpoint, and two of his works in fugal form—a fugue in E flat and a ricercare in G major[64]—are among the most highly wrought essays of their kind to have been composed during the first flush of the Bach revival.

From 1833 the main push to co-ordinating the hitherto scattered Bach interests came from Mendelssohn and Robert Schumann, the latter mainly promoting the cause through the *Neue Zeitschrift für Musik*. The effect of the exertions of Schumann and Mendelssohn was stronger within than without the musical profession (Schumann observed that when Mendelssohn played the D minor concerto at a Gewandhaus Concert admiration was restricted to 'certain individuals') but the number of influential supporters of the cause of Sebastian Bach grew. Schumann was not slow to point out that the then modern music was so because of its spiritual adherence to Bach principles.

> Mendelssohn, [Sterndale] Bennett, Chopin, Hiller, in fact the whole so-called Romantic School (of course I am speaking of Germans) is far nearer to Bach in its music than Mozart ever was; indeed it has a thorough knowledge of Bach ... to my mind Bach is unapproachable—he is unfathomable.

In this manner Schumann wrote to Gustav Adolf Keferstein at the beginning of 1840. His own personal token of respect to the inspirational quality of Bach appeared in 1845 in the form of *Sechs Fugen über den Namen BACH für Orgel oder Pfte. mit Pedal* (Op. 60): the proof of the *modernity* of the theme was most apparent in the magnificent fourth fugue of the set—with retrogression and augmentation displayed as factors in an emotional situation. This is all Schumann—and, in spirit at least, all Bach. In shaping the theme it may be noted how Schumann, escaping the bondage of conventional contours, looks forward to dodecaphonic motivation.

In the same year of 1845 an English singer, Miss Lincoln, sang in Leipzig. Her brother, Henry Lincoln, was present, than whom there was no greater devotee of Bach. Among those who have been forgotten for their pioneering in this field he deserves high place for the catholicity of his intentions. He saw Bach not only as himself but as one among a great company. Thus Lincoln began a series of popular lectures in October 1843:

> At Mr Lincoln's first lecture on the 26th (the subject of which will be the genius and works of Sebastian Bach), the lecturer purposes introducing some specimens of the greatest of the composers of the period immediately preceding Bach, viz. Pachelbel, Buxtehude, and Brühns,—a motett by Christoph Bach (an uncle of Sebastian), the 'Crucifixus' from the Mass in B minor, two chorales—and part of one of the violin sonatas, by Sebastian Bach.[65]

Also in 1843 a Handel Society, formed with the intention of issuing 'a superior and standard edition' of the works of Handel was established in London. Two years later the publishing house of Coventry and Hollier, 'under the superintendence of Dr Mendelssohn', furthered a collateral interest (Mendelssohn was also one of the editors of the Handel edition) by issuing the chorales from the *Orgelbüchlein* of Bach; their initiative was supported, it was considered, by the gratifying results of market research:

> The chorales have never before been published, and will be doubtless welcomed with avidity by the musical profession, and especially the admirers of the illustrious Bach, who, we are happy to say, both in London and the provinces, are sufficiently numerous.

On 27th October 1849 a meeting convened by Sterndale Bennett, and at which Cipriani Potter, Henry Lincoln and Sir George Smart were present, launched a Bach Society with the twofold aim of collecting together the master's works (whether in manuscript or published), and of furthering 'a general acquaintance with his music by its public performance'. A little earlier that year, on 14th June, the *Neue Zeitschrift für Musik*, referring back to the heroic endeavours of Kantor

Müller in respect of performances of the church cantatas, complained how few of those who should be were acquainted with these works. The time was clearly ripe in Germany for an undertaking after the manner of the London Handel Society and, for that matter, of the London Bach Society. The centenary of the death of Bach was the proper occasion to launch such a society. The aims of the Bach Gesellschaft therefore were finally laid out in a special memorial issue of the *Neue Zeitschrift für Musik* on 26th July. Among those who signed the letter of intent were Hauptmann, Moscheles, Mosewius, Schumann, Spohr and Baron von Bunsen, Prussian Ambassador in London. The signatories as a whole represented every major city in Germany. Thus was shown the fulfilment of half a century of effort on many fronts, not only towards a renascence of Sebastian Bach, but also towards the ideal of national unity. This ideal had first stirred in the days of the earliest Bachs in this record, in the time of the Reformation. In the letter of 26th July 1850 the hope of establishing a monument 'worthy of the man and of the nation' was made explicit. In fact the monument was to prove more important than had been foreseen: worthy of the man, its importance transcended nationality.

By the foundation of the Bach Gesellschaft—some four hundred years after the first signs of distinctive musical talent in the family and five years after the death of the last of its line of creative musicians— the end of a tradition was signified. The old tradition, that is, of small-town musicians, controlled by the interests and prejudices of Church, Court and municipality, passing on their craft from father to son. Throughout Europe there were many families in which the principle operated. But there was only one Bach family: a unique phenomenon in the history of Western culture.

NOTES TO CHAPTER THIRTEEN

1. Hermann Hirschbahn, *Neue Zeitschrift für Musik*, Leipzig, No. 18, Jan.–June 1843, 'Die Einweihungsfeier von Bachs Denkmal zu Leipzig', p. 144; See also *Allgemeine Musikalische Zeitung*, No. 19, 10th May 1843, column 350.

2. Cf. *Angelo's Pic Nic; or, Table Talk . . . written by himself* (H. Angelo), London, 1834, p. 114: '. . . waiting on a lady, who had been governess to the late Mr Dumergue, the dentist, at whose house Miss Charpentier . . . formerly resided'.

3. *See* A. Hyatt King, *Some British Collectors of Music*, Cambridge, 1963, p. 17.

4. There was formerly a score of this work in the Stadtbibliothek, Danzig.

5. *Musik. Corresp.* (Speyer), 1791, p. 223, quoted by C. H. Bitter (*see* Note 12, Chapter 11 above), pp. 139–40.

6. *See* Hannsdieter Wohlfahrth, *W. F. E. Bach—Werkverzeichnis* (Typescript), Bückeburg, 1960.

7. *Allegro non troppo, Thema con [3] variazioni, Rondo*, ed. K. Janetzky, Mitteldeutsche Verlag, Halle (Saale), 1951.

8. BM. Add. MS. 32043.

9. The original German published in *Aus Ferdinand Hillers Briefwechsel (1826–61)*, ed. R. Sietz, Köln, 1958, p. 174.

10. *See* Note 9 above, p. 192.

11. *Die Musikalien-Sammlung des Grossherzoglich Mecklenburg-Schweriner Fürstenhauses*, I, pp. 126–7.

12. *Die Matrikel der Georg-August-Universität zu Göttingen*, 1734–1837.

13. BM. Add. MS., 31996.

14. A. C. F. Kollmann, *An Essay on Practical Musical Composition*, London, 1799, p. 34.

15. *See* Chapter 3, Note 18 above, Preface, p. iv.

16. *See* Chapter 3, Note 18 above, p. 116.

17. BM. Add. MS. 27593, f. 41.

18. *Magazin der Musik*, Hamburg, 1783, p. 257.

19. *A.M.Z.*, 1800, II, p. 642.

20. *See* Note 19 above, 1801, III, p. 260.

21. *See* Note 19 above, 1806, VIII, p. 199.

22. *Musikalischer Almanach auf das Jahr 1782* (a parody of Forkel's work of similar title), Berlin 1781, p. 12.

23. *Briefe an Ludwig Tieck*, ed. K. von Holtei, 4 vols., Breslau, 1864, II, p. 215.

24. L. Tieck, *Dreihundert Briefe aus zwei Jahrhunderten*, ed. K. von Holtei, 4 vols., Hannover, 1872, p. 69.

25. Edelhoff (*See* Chapter 9, Note 36), p. 66.

26. *See* Note 23 above, II, pp. 248–50.

27. 'Memoirs of C. F. Zelter', *The Harmonicon*, London, 1833, pp. 45–6.

28. Thus Edward Holmes, in *A Ramble among the Musicians of Germany*, etc., *By a Musical Professor*, London, 1828, p. 230: 'In the church of St Mary there is as organist a scion of the illustrious stock of Sebastian ... a young man of frank and cordial manners, and a very clever artist, as I had reason to know in an evening's organ playing

which I enjoyed with a party at his church.' Bach was also a composer, his chief works being the oratorio *Bonifacius* (1836) and *Psalm 100* (1840). He compiled a chorale book and a useful tutor for organ students—*Der praktische Organist.*

29. Friedrich Blume, *Two Centuries of Bach*, London, 1950, p. 46.

30. Quoted by Blume, *see* Note 29 above, p. 46.

31. *See* Max Maria von Weber, *Carl Maria von Weber: ein Lebensbild*, 3 vols., Leipzig, 1866, III, pp. 226–30.

32. Blume (*see* Note 29 above), p. 50.

33. *See*, for example, the biographical entries in A. Gathy, *Musikalisches Conversations-Lexicon*, Leipzig, Hamburg, 1835, pp. 28–9, and G. Schilling, *Encyclopädie der gesammten musikalischen Wissenschaften oder Universal-Lexicon*, Stuttgart, 1835, pp. 371–8. By comparing these entries with, say, F. C. G. Hirsching, *Historich-Literarisches Handbuch*, Leipzig, 1794, 17 vols., I, pp. 77–80 (in which the great choral works are barely mentioned), the great change in appreciation of Bach may be noticed.

34. *See* 'Spohr and Bach', Appendix 1, Dorothy Moulton Mayer, *The Forgotten Master (The Life and Times of Louis Spohr)*, London, 1959, p. 193 f.

35. W. A. Barrett, *English Glees and Part-Songs*, London, 1886, p. 301.

36. BM. Add. MS. 27593.

37. Since about 1800 in fact. Wesley was speaking in general terms, excluding those (like Burney) who had private sources.

38. BM. Add. MS. 27593, f. 41.

39. *New and Correct Edition of the Preludes & Fugues of John Sebastian Bach with Introduction*, 1810–13, R. Birchall & Chappell & Co.

40. BM. Add. MS. 27593, f. 42.

41. Benjamin Jacob (1778–1829) was organist of the Surrey Chapel 1794–1824. The Bach performances in which he collaborated with Crotch as also with Wesley began in 1808. See also *Letters of Samuel Wesley to Mr Jacobs . . . Relating to the Introduction into this Country of the Works of J. S. Bach*, ed. Eliza Wesley, 1875–8.

42. *A Trio* [Six trios] *composed originally for the Organ . . . adapted for three Hands upon the Piano Forte*, 1810.

43. BM. Add. MS. 27593, f. 51; Cf. Eg. MS. 2159, f. 70, S. Wesley to W. Shield (from Gower Place, Euston Square, 12th September 1815): . . . Pray have the kindness to say whether I left in your safe keeping the *Credo* of Sebn. Bach, which I remember having *brought* with me to Berner's Street but rather think I did *not* take away when I did the Book of Motetts from which the Movements prepared for the Organ have been selected.

I am meditating a Publication of the former noble Work, if I can only secure *seventy* Subscribers, which I think you will judge to be no very arrogant Expectation—My Design is not that of pecuniary profit: I want merely to clear Expences, & this cannot be done under from £60–£70:—even with the best Economy.

44. In BM. Add. MS. 27593, f. 59 (an interpolated fragment) Wesley returns to the subject of an anthology—'. . . A Selection from the sacred music of Sebastian Bach might easily be made which would be sure to prove universally attractive.'

45. BM. Add. MS. 27593, f. 52.

46. BM. Add. MS. 27593, f. 109.

47. *See* Note 46, f. 73 b.

48. *See* J. T. Lightwood, *Samuel Wesley, Musician*, London, 1937, pp. 179–80.

49. Catalogue of Sale of Ayrton's Library, 23rd, 25th and 26th June 1849.

50. Catalogue of Sale of Picart's Library, Puttick & Simpson, 10th March 1848.

51. Catalogue of Sale 27th January 1848.

52. Catalogue of Sale 17th December 1847.

53. Catalogue of Sale 12th April 1848.

54. Catalogue of Sale 28th November 1850.

55. Catalogue of Sale 31st July–2nd August 1858. To date seven volumes, all of which Allott had acquired, had been issued.

56. BM. Add. MS., 14340, f. 56.

57. BM. Add. MS. 14340.

58. *See* Peter F. Williams, 'J. S. Bach and English Organ Music', *M. & L.*, 44, April 1963, p. 140 f.

59. On 13th January 1800, Callcott wrote to Kollmann concerning an English edition of Graun's *Passion*, adding, 'I wish for information regarding the dispute between SORGE and MARPURG'.

60. *The Musical World*, 20th October 1837, p. 90.

61. BM. Add. MS. 34693.

62. *See* two two-part fugues for pianoforte, in F minor and D major, in BM. Add. MS. 32180.

63. *See also* Chapter 12, Note 20 above.

64. BM. Add. MS. 32236.

65. *The Musical World*, 19th October 1843, p. 353.

66. *See* Note 65, above, 27th February 1845, p. 105.

Appendix 1

Johann Jakob Bach in Stockholm

Source material relating to Johann Jakob Bach (Back) and his life in Sweden is to be found in:

(1) *Stockholms Slottsarkiv* (the Royal Archives).

    (*a*) *Kungl. Maj:ts hovstats huvudbok*, 1713 ff, (one ledger and one volume of cash accounts for each year).

    (*b*) *Kungl. Maj:ts hovstats kassaräkenskaper*, 1713 ff, (receipts, petitions, etc).

(2) *Kammararkivet*, Stockholm (Exchequer Archives), *Likvidationer*, series 19, vol. 1.

(3) *Stockholms stadsarkiv* (Stockholm City Archives).

    (*a*) *Nicolai forsämlings 'Cassa Rächning Pro Ao 1719'* (The accounts of the parish of St Nicholas, Stockholm), p. 187.

    (*b*) *Nedre Borgrättens bouppteckningar*, 1720–29, (Inventory deeds from Nedre Borgrätten), p. 69 ff.

(1) 1712, Bach is not mentioned in (*a*) or (*b*): 1713 (*a*, p. 359), Bach's salary, of *150 daler silvermynt* stated; but, there being no receipt in (*b*), he did not receive it. In 1714 (*a*, p. 357) Bach's salary for 1713–14 was given as *375 daler*; (*b*, p. 248) 'Johan. J. Back engaged in Novemb. 1712— *74.8 daler*'; (*b*, p. 276) receipt signed by the Court musicians, Gottfried Bucholtz being Master of the Music, for *928 daler 4 öre*, being pay for the first quarter of the year after deduction of *Centonalen* (i.e. Income Tax); no further payment this year. The accounts in respect of Bach are complete until the time of his death, and show a considerable irregularity of payment [e.g. 1720 (*a*), 'Johan Jacob Back for 1713, 1714, 1719, 1720—*600 daler*']. The last payment made in respect of the third quarter of 1721 (*17 daler 8 öre*), and the receipt, dated 16th April 1722 (*b*, p. 358) was signed—'After the decease of my lamented husband, the musician, Magdalena Norell'.

(2) A summary of the accounts in the Exchequer Archives shows that at his death Bach was owed by the Crown the sum of *675 daler*. An extract from the Minutes of Nedre Borgrätten (Stockholm, 12th July 1728) relates the disposition of Bach's Estate after the death of his second wife:

Since it has been shown that Mrs Sara Nentzel, wife of *hofmästaren* [court official] Petter Weckholm, is the sole heir of her daughter, Mrs Magdalena Norell, who was married first to Olof Suan and then to the court musician Johann Jacob Bach, both deceased without children; it was decided that Weckholm should be entitled, by means of an *Extractum protocolli*, to receive the pay due to the Court Musician Johan Jacob Bach, whose Estate was vested in his widow, Mrs Norell, in virtue of a duly executed Will, and should now, after her death, be vested in her mother, Mrs Sara Nentzel.

(3) (*a*) Referring to the death of Bach's first wife—26th November 1719, '[the bell] was knelled for the wife of the court musician N. [*sic*] Back'.

(*b*) Inventory deed of the Estate of Susanna Maria Gaaft [?], executed on 26th July 1721, there being twice mentioned a four-year-old daughter Mariana [?], who is presumed to have predeceased her father. Above the seal is this note by Bach:

In addition there might have been something more left in the Estate of my late dear wife, but since in these difficult times little pay has been forthcoming, I have had to use several things out of this for my livelihood and to bring up my child, so that now there is nothing else remaining but what is contained in this specification . . . .

For the above information I am greatly indebted to Mr Anders Lönn, of the Svenskt Musikhistoriskt Arkiv, Stockholm.

Appendix 2

Works based on the theme B A C H

J. S. Bach	*Die Kunst der Fuge* (Contrapunctus XI and XIX)
1685–1750	*Fantasie und Fuge*, formerly attributed to J. S. Bach; see Hermann Keller, *Die Klavierwerke Bachs*, Leipzig, 1950, p. 52
G. A. Sorge	Three Fugues, *see* p. 140
1703–98	
J. L. Krebs	*Fuge über B A C H für Orgel*, Ms. in Westdeutsche
1713–80	Bibliothek, Marburg; ed. Norman Hennefield, pub. Liturgical Press Inc., New York, 1944, *see* p. 140
J. C. Bach	*Fuge für das Pianoforte oder die Orgel komponirt von*
1735–82	*Christian Bach über die Buchstaben seines Namens*, *see* p. 264
J. G. Albrechtsberger	
1736–1809	*Fuge für Orgel*, *see* p. 299
R. Schumann	*Sechs Fugen über den Namen B A C H für Orgel oder Pfte.*
1810–56	*mit Pedal*, Op. 60, 1845, *see* p. 299
F. Liszt	*Phantasie und Fuge über B A C H für Orgel*, 1857
1811–86	
H. Bellermann	*Präludium und Fuge über B A C H für Orgel*, Op. 8
1832–1903	
N. Rimsky-Korsakov	
1844–1908	*6 Fugues*, Op. 17, 1875, No. 6 on the theme B A C H
V. d'Indy	'Beuron', no. 11 in *Tableaux de voyage*, Op. 33, 1892
1851–1931	
O. Barblan	*Chaconne über B A C H*, Op. 10
1860–1943	*Variationen und Tripelfuge über B A C H*
M. Reger	*Phantasie und Fuge für Orgel über B A C H*, Op. 46,
1873–1906	1900, ded. to Josef Rheinberger
S. Karg-Elert	'Basso ostinato' in *Madrigale, 10 schlichte Weisen*, 1906
1877–1933	*Passacaglia und Fuge über B A C H*, Op. 150, *c.* 1925
A. Casella	*Due ricercari sul nome B A C H*, Op. 46, 1900
1883–1947	
E. Wellesz	*Partita in honorem J. S. Bach 1965*
b. 1885	

H. Eisler *Präludium und Fuge über B A C H (Studie über ein*
1898–1962 *Zwölftonreihe), Op. 46, for string trio, 1936*
E. Pepping *Drei Fugen über B A C H für Klavier*
b. 1901
V. Bräutigam *Johann Sebastian Bach* (setting of an Epitaph by J.
b. 1939 Brobowski for S.A.T.B.), 1969
Between 1822 and 1825 Beethoven considered the composition of an
Overture on the B A C H theme. Of these some sketches exist in the
Westdeutsche Bibliothek, Marburg.

Appendix 3

Drama per Musica: Das angenehme Leipzig

Chorus of the Four Seasons

Aria: Thou pleasant Athens on the Pleiss, Paradise of thy Saxony! Thy fame must ever blossom, and, day by day, increase. Care and zeal at all times are concerned to make thy praises more beautiful, more worthy.

Spring

Recit: There is no place that I will prefer to thee, Leipzig. Thou art where the treasury of all that is most dear to me shall most often lie. I will steal bliss and pleasure from other places, that thy environment alone may be beyond compare.

Aria: Thy gardens shall flower; and, as if by magic, draw the eyes of all towards thee. Their blossoms, their shades, so beauteous fair, shall drive away nagging cares (*da capo*).

Recit: And now, who has but a leg, or an eye, flocks out. The *Muhmen-Platz* [literally, 'place of aunts'], vast though it may be, for so many is too confined. The beautiful daughters of this city find a summer-house, where, in cool shelter, one may sport with these loving children. The girls in Leipzig are good for sport, and beautiful. Everyone wants to serve them and to spend all the hours with them. The girls in Leipzig are good for sport, and beautiful. All girls in other cities lack something. But—look at Leipzig: her daughters can be called angels. The girls in Leipzig are good for sport, and beautiful.

Summer

Recit: O Leipzig! Have not I given you the most in the way of decoration? In my season you harvest nought but pleasure. To say here all that I am to you would take too long. Here is a carriage, there a waggon and horses; there goes a man with his girl—to Gohlis, Gautsch, Zobicker, Eutritsch, and Lindenau [suburbs of Leipzig], in every place to sample Merseburg beer and cherry- and apple-cakes. And the time for bird-shoots comes. How much citizens—long trained for the sport—enjoy being in their shooting-pits.

Aria: If time hangs, go to the bird-shoot, where the tents are erected.
Play and win tokens for the girls. Then when the day and the sun grow
faint stay no longer in the meadow (*da capo*).

Autumn

Recit: That I am also inclined to thee, Leipzig, many a year has shown,
when I put my treasures of the trees on the table at midday. Many enjoy
the game of ninepins outside your gates; pleasure supreme overflows.
Love, like my fruits, ripens when I make ready the marriage-bed for
those with hearts afire, that in quiet rest they may sport amid the
feathers of love. And because night soon brings an ending to the day,
the Muses' disciples fill the silent lanes with apt serenades.
Aria: Come now! Let your choirs unite and raise their song for the
heavens to hear. Let sweet lovers be lulled to sleep by pleasant sounds
and fall into joyous dreams (*da capo*).

Winter

Recit: I appear to the whole world a terror indeed. The coloured
fields must cower under snow and frost. But, Leipzig, I can awaken
pleasure enough for thee. The more often come frost and ice, the wiser
it is to sit and study.
Aria: In summer one lives well; in winter one studies: so each
season merits its own honour. Now one takes one's books gladly
in hand, which clever men send into the country (*da capo*).
Recit: But when one has had enough of studying, and no desire to
sit longer, one recovers from one's exertions in good company. From
all else one chooses tobacco—and a game of cards. But be moderate in
everything, and when a deep snow has fallen it is time to borrow
money, to pawn one's valuables, in order to pursue pleasure.
Aria: All you mothers! Send money to your sons—and save at some
other time. When the snow falls from heaven and the bells ring loud,
let your old gold spring out from your coffers (*da capo*).

Spring

So Leipzig at all times remains the Idea of gladness.

Summer

There are no hours in Leipzig without pleasures to be found.

Autumn

When there is no joy elsewhere there is abundance here.

Winter

And winter comes with abundant springs never to be exhausted.
Arioso à 4:   There is no greater fortune than here to live and here to die.

Aria-tutti

Leipzig stays pleasing for ever because it gives pleasure. Although the
sun shines bright it must go down when night overpowers the day.
But, Leipzig, let thy pleasures stay free of change—change that burdens
all the world.

Appendix 4

Portraits by Gottlieb Friedrich Bach (1714–85) and Johann Philipp
Bach (1752–1846) in the Schloss Elisabethenburg (City Museum),
Meiningen.

Gottlieb Friedrich Bach:
Portraits of
Rektor Johann Wilhelm Treiber (see illustration between pages
170 and 171)
A lady in a grey–white silk dress decorated with trimmings
Johann Friedrich Herrmann, of Nürnberg

Johann Philipp Bach:
Portraits of
Duke Georg I, in profile
Luise-Eleonore, Duchess of Sachsen-Meiningen, in bright blue dress
(see illustration between pages 170 and 171)
(three other portraits of this Duchess are also in the collection)
Court Surgeon Treiber
A young lady in red dress, with blue trimmings, and hair-ribbon
A lady with veil, and red silk dress with white lace
Major von Uglansky (see illustration between pages 170 and 171)
Fräulein von Furche
Herr von Ultenhofen
Ludwig von Türke
Honourable Mrs von Stein, née von Trümbach
A Herr von Stein
A lady in a black dress with lace collar, and red wrap
Fanny Romberg
Johann Matthäus Bachstein
Auguste Bechstein, née Karsten (probably of the family later to
become famous through the manufacture of pianos. The founder
of the firm, F. W. C. Bechstein, was born in Thuringia, in Gotha,
in 1826)
Maria Catharina Kiessling
Justus Christian Kiessling

Maria Elisabeth Vierling
General Superintendent Johann Lorenz Vierling
A lady with red wrap, and white lace collar on a black dress
A man in a light blue coat
A lady with red wrap over a white Empire dress

Bibliography

ADLUNG, JACOB: *Anleitung zu der musikalischen Gelahrtheit,* Erfurt, 1758; *Musica mechanica organoedi,* Berlin, 1768.

BACH, C. P. E.: *Versuch über die wahre Art, das Clavier zu spielen,* 2 parts, Berlin, 1753–62; *Essay on the True Art of Playing Keyboard Instruments,* W. J. Mitchell, ed. and trans., London, 1949.

BACH, PAUL: 'Die Meininger Bache' in *Johann Sebastian Bach in Thüringen (Festgabe zum Gedenkjahr 1950),* Weimar, 1950.

BEAUCAIRE, HORRIC DE: *Eléonore Desonier d'Olbreuze, duchesse de Zell,* Paris, 1884 (English trans., *A Mésalliance in the House of Brunswick,* London, 1886).

BECHSTEIN, LUDWIG: *Kunstfleiss und Gewerbefleiss,* Leipzig, 1860.

BECK, A.: *Geschichte des gothaischen Landes,* 3 vols. Gotha, 1868–75.

BEINRATH, F. W.: *Musikgeschichte der Stadt Sondershausen,* Innsbruck, 1943.

BERTRAM, Ph. E.: *Geschichte des Hauses und Fürstenthums Anhalt,* 2 vols., Halle, 1780.

BESSELER, HEINRICH: *Fünf echte Bildnisse Johann Sebastian Bachs,* Kassel/Basel, 1956.

BITTER, C. H.: *Carl Philipp Emanuel und Wilhelm Friedmann Bach und deren Brüder,* 2 vols., Berlin, 1868.

BLANKENBURG, W.: 'Zwölf Jahre Bachforschung,' in *Acta Musicologica* xxxvii, Basel, 1965.

BLECKSCHMIDT, EVA RENATE: *Die Amalien-Bibliothek: Musikbibliothek, der Prinzessin Anna Amalia von Preussen (1723–87),* (*Berliner Studien zur Musikwissenschaft,* Bd. 8) Berlin, 1965.

BLUME, FRIEDRICH: *Johann Sebastian Bach im Wandel der Geschichte,* Kassel, 1947; *Two Centuries of Bach, An Account of Changing Taste,* London, 1950; 'Die Musik des Barock in Deutschland', 'Johann Sebastian Bach', in *Syntagma Musicologicum,* Kassel, 1963.

BOJANOWSKI, PAUL VON: *Das Weimar Johann Sebastian Bachs,* Weimar, 1903.

BOUTARIE, E., AND CAMPARDON, E., ed., *Mémoires de Frédéric II Roi de Prusse,* 2 vols., Paris, 1866.

BRUFORD, W. H.: *Germany in the Eighteenth Century: The Social Background of the Literary Revival,* Cambridge, 1965.

BUCHHOLZ, BERNHARD: *Eisenach: aus der Geschichte unserer Stadt*, Eisenach, 1959.

BULLING, KLAUS: 'Bibliographie zur Fruchtbringenden Gesellschaft', in *Marginalien: Blätter der Pirckheimer Gesellschaft*, xx, Berlin/Weimar, 1965.

BURNEY, CHARLES: *The Present State of Music in Germany, The Netherlands, and United Provinces*, or *The Journal of a Tour* . . . *undertaken to collect Materials for a General History of Music*, 3 vols., 2nd ed., London, 1773.

BUSZIN, WALTER E.: 'Luther on Music', in *Musical Quarterly*, xxxii, 1, Jan. 1946.

CANAVE, P. C. G.: *Re-evaluation of the role played by Carl Philipp Emanuel Bach in the development of the clavier sonata*, Washington, D.C., 1956.

CARRELL, NORMAN: *Bach the Borrower*, London, 1967.

CRAMER, C. F.: *Magazin der Musik*, Hamburg, 1783.

CREIZENACH, WILHELM: *Geschichte des neueren Dramas*, Leipzig, 1903.

CRICKMORE, LEON: 'C. P. E. Bach's Harpsichord Concertos', in *Music and Letters*, xxxix, 3, July 1958.

DAVID, HANS, and MENDEL, ARTHUR: ed., *The Bach Reader*: *A Life of Johann Sebastian Bach in Letters and Documents*, New York/London, 1945–67.

DAY, JAMES: *The Literary Background to Bach's Cantatas*, London, 1961.

DOEBNER, E. AND SIMONS, W.: *Meininger Pastell-Gemälde, Neue Beiträge zur Geschichte deutschen Altertums Nr. 19*, (*Katalog der Meininger Gemälde-Ausstellung 1904*), Meiningen, 1904.

DOEBNER, R.: ed. *Briefe der Köningin Sophia Charlotte von Preussen und der Kurfürstin Sophie von Hannover an hannoversche Diplomaten . . .*, (K. preussische Staatsarchive, Bd. 79), Berlin, 1905.

DOWNES, EDWARD: *The operas of Johann Christian Bach*, Doctoral dissertation, Harvard University, Cambridge, Massachusetts, 1958.

DROYSEN, G.: *Das Zeitalter des Dreisigjährigen Krieges*, 2 vols., Berlin, 1888.

EDELHOFF, HEINRICH: *Johann Nikolaus Forkel*, Göttingen, 1935.

EMERY, WALTER: 'The London Autograph of "The Forty-Eight"', *Music and Letters*, xliv, 2, April 1963.

ENGEL, FRANZ: ed. *Drei Symphonien von Johann Christoph Bach zu Bückeburg*, Schaumburger Faksimiledrücke, Nr.2, Bückeburg, 1966.

ENGEL, HANS: *Die Entwicklung des deutschen Klavierkonzertes von Mozart bis Liszt*, Leipzig, 1927; *Musik in Thüringen*, Köln/Graz, 1966.

ENGELBRECHT, CHR. AND OTHERS: *Theater in Kassel*, Kassel, 1959.

EPSTEIN, P.: 'Ein unbekanntes Passionsoratorium von Chr. Flor (1667)', B.J.B., Berlin, 1930.

FALCK, MARTIN: *Wilhelm Friedemann Bach, Sein Leben und seine Werke*, Leipzig, 1913/Lindau, 1956.

FLADE, ERNST: *Gottfried Silbermann*, Leipzig, 1953.

FOCK, GUSTAV: *Die Wahrheit über Bachs Aufenthalt in Lüneburg*, Hamburg, 1949.

FORKEL, JOHANN NIKOLAUS: *Life of John Sebastian Bach*, London, 1820.

FORTNER, WOLFGANG: 'Bach in unserer Zeit (Vortrag anlässlich des 75 jährigen Bestehens des Heidelberger Bachvereins)', in *Musik und Kirche*, xxx, 5, Kassel, 1960.

FREDERICK II, KING OF PRUSSIA: *Memoirs of the House of Brandenburg, by the Present King of Prussia*, London, 1757.

FREYSE, CONRAD: *Die Ohrdrufer Bache in der Silhouette*, Eisenach/Kassel, 1957; *Fünfzig Jahre Bachhaus*, Eisenach, 1958; 'Johann Christoph Bach', B.J.B., 1956.

FRIEDLAENDER, MAX: *Das dt. Lied im 18.Jh., Quellen u. Studien*, Stuttgart and Berlin, 1902.

GEIRINGER, KARL: *Music of the Bach Family, An Anthology*, Cambridge, Massachusetts, 1955; *The Bach Family, Seven Generations of Creative Genius*, New York, 1954; 'Unbeachtete Kompositionen des Bückeburger Bach', *Festschrift Wilhelm Fischer*, Innsbruck, 1956.

GERHARDT, PAUL: *Geistliche Lieder, Jubelausgabe*, Cottbus, 1876.

GODMAN, STANLEY: 'Bach's Copies of Ammerbach's "Orgel oder Instrument Tabulatur",' *Music and Letters*, xxxviii, 1, January, 1957.

GOETHE, JOHANN WOLFGANG VON: *Dichtung und Wahrheit*, Leipzig, 1958.

GOOCH, G. P.: *Frederick the Great: The Ruler, The Writer, The Man*, Hamden, Connecticut, 1947.

[GOTTSCHED, JOHANN CHRISTOPH]: *Der Biedermann (Eine Auswahl)*, Leipzig, 1966.

GRETSCHEL, K. C. E.: *Kirchliche Zustände Leipzigs vor und während der Reformation im Jahre 1539*, Leipzig, 1839.

GRUNOW, HEINZ: *Bezaubernde Residenz* (Wolfenbüttel), Wolfenbüttel, 1960.

GUERICKE, WALRAD: *Friedemann Bach in Wolfenbüttel und Braunschweig, 1771–4*, Braunschweig, 1929.

HAACKE, WALTER: *Die Söhne Bachs*, Königstein im Taunus, 1962.

HAENDCKE, BERTHOLD: *Deutsche Kultar im Zeitalter des 30jähr. Krieges*, Leipzig, 1906.

HARDEGE, FROHWALT: 'Grosse Musiker in Göttingen', *Göttinger Jahrbuch*, 2. Jrg., Göttingen, 1953.

HAWKINS, SIR JOHN: *General History of the Science and Practice of Music*, 5 vols. London, 1776; with additions, 2 vols. 1853 and 1875.

HELMBOLD, H.: *Geschichte der Stadt Eisenach*, Eisenach, 1936; 'Junge Bachs auf dem Eisenacher Gymnasium', *Das Thüringer Fahnlein*, 4. Jrg., Jena, 1935; 'Die Söhne von Joh. Christoph u. Joh. Ambrosius a.d. Eisenacher Schule', B.J.B., 1930.

HEMPEL, EBERHARD: *Baroque Art and Architecture in Central Europe*, London, 1965.

HERBST, WOLFGANG: 'Der Endzweck: Ein Vergleich zwischen Joh. Seb. Bach und Chr. Mariane v. Ziegler', *Musik und Kirche*, 30.Jrg., v., Kassel/Basel, 1960.

HERMANN, WALTER: 'Geschichte der Schauspielkunst in Freiberg', *Schriften zur Theaterwissenschaft, herausgegeben von der Theaterhochschule Leipzig*, Berlin, 1960.

HEYER, HERMANN: 'Der Musikfilm "Friedemann Bach"', Fest. Erstaufführung im "Capitol" in Leipzig', *Neue Leipz. Tagesztg.* Leipzig 1 August, 1941.

HIENTZSCH, J. G.: *Das musikalische Deutschland des neunzehnten Jahrhunderts*, Berlin, 1856.

HOFMANN, ERNA HEDWIG: *The Dresden Kreuz Chor*, Leipzig, 1962.

[HOLMES, EDWARD]: *A Ramble among the Musicians of Germany, etc., By a Musical Professor*, London, 1828.

HOLZ, GEORG; SARAN, FRANZ; AND BERNOULLI, EDUARD: *Die Jenaer Liederhandschrift*, 2 vols., Leipzig, 1901.

JUNKER, CARL LUDWIG; *Zwanzig Componisten: Eine Skizze*, bey der typographischen Gesellschaft, Bern, 1776.

KADE, OTTO: *Die Musikalien-Sammlung des Grossherzl. Mecklenburg-Schweriner Fürstenhauses aus den letzten zwei Jahrhunderten*, 2 vols., Schwerin, 1893, Reprint 1967; *Die altere Passionskomposition bis zum Jahre 1631*, Gütterslog, 1893.

KELLER, HERMANN: *Die Klavierwerke Bachs*, Leipzig, 1950; *Die Orgelwerke Bachs*, Leipzig, 1948.

KING, A. HYATT: *Some British Collectors of Music*, Cambridge, 1963.

KOCH, HERBERT: 'Johann Nikolaus, der 'Jenaer' Bach', *Die Musikforschung*, 21.Jrg., iii, Kassel, 1968; *Geschichte der Stadt Jena*, Stuttgart, 1966.

KÖHLER, KARL-HEINTZ: 'Ein Musikalienfund in der Universitäts-bibliothek und seine Bedeutung für die musikhistorische Erschlies-sung der Anfänge des Jenaer "Akademischen Konzertes"',

Wissenschaftliche Zeitschrift der Friedrich-Schiller-Universität Jena, 41.Jrg., Jena, 1954–5.

KOLLMAN, AUGUST FRIEDRICH: *An Essay on Musical Harmony*, London, 1796; *An Essay on Practical Musical Composition*, London, 1799.

KRAFT, GÜNTHER: *Entstehung und Ausbreitung des musikalischen Bach-Geschlechtes in Thüringen*, Doctoral dissertation, Martin-Luther University, Halle-Wittenberg, typescript 1964.

KRAFT, GÜNTHER: ed. *Mein Thüringen (Lieder, Gedichte, Prosabeiträge und Bilder)*, Leipzig, 1956.

KRAFT, GÜNTHER, AND BOCK, ERICH: *Bach in Eisenach: auf den Werkstätten des jungen Sebastians*, Jena, [1967].

KRAUSE, EMIL: *Zur Pflege der religiösen Vokalmusik im 19.Jahrhundert bis auf die Gegenwart*, Langesalza, 1912.

KREBS, KURT: *Das Kursächsische Postwesen zum Zeit der Oberpostmeister Johann Jakob Kees I und II*, Leipzig/Berlin, 1914.

KRETZSCHMAR, HERMANN: *Gesammelte Aufsätze über Musik*, Leipzig, 1910.

KROKER, ERNST: *Leipzig (Statten der Kultur, Nr.5)*, Leipzig, [1914].

KRUMMACHER, F.: 'Motetten und Kantaten der Bachzeit in Udestedt/ Thüringen', *Die Musikforschung*, 19.Jrg., 4, 1966.

KÜMMEL, WERNER FRIEDRICH: 'Die Anfänge der Musikgeschichte an den deutschsprachigen Universitäten', *Die Musikforschung*, 20.Jrg., 3, 1967.

[LEDIARD, THOMAS]: *The German Spy: In Familiar letters home . . . Written by a Gentleman on his Travels to his Friend in England . . .*, London, 1738.

LUTHER, MARTIN: *Luthers deutsche Messe 1526*, ed. and annotated by G. and J. Rawerau, Leipzig, 1926; *Martin Luthers Briefe*, 2 vols., ed. by R. Buchwald, Leipzig, 1949.

MACARDLE, D. W.: 'Beethoven and the Bach Family', *Music and Letters*, xxxviii, 4, October, 1957.

MAHLING, FRIEDRICH: *Die deutsche vorklassiche Sinfonie*, Berlin, [1940].

MAHRENHOLZ, CHRISTHARD: *Luther und die Kirchenmusik*, Kassel, 1937.

MARPURG, FRIEDRICH WILHELM: *Historische und Critische Beiträge*, Berlin, 1754.

MATTHEWS, BETTY: 'J. C. Bach in the West Country', *The Musical Times*, 108, August, 1967.

MAYER, DOROTHY MOULTON: *The Forgotten Master, The Life and Times of Louis Spohr*, London, 1959.

MEYER, JULIUS: *Allgemeines Künstler-Lexikon*, Leipzig, 1878.

MIESNER, HEINRICH: *Philipp Emanuel Bach in Hamburg*, Berlin, 1929.

MONRO, ROBERT: *Monro, His Expedition with the worthy Scots Regiment (called Mac-Keyes Regiment) levied in August 1626 . . . Colonel Robert Monro*, London, 1637.

MORRISON, DOUGLAS: *Views of the Ducal Palaces and Hunting Seats of Saxe Coburg and Gotha*, London, 1846.

MÜLLER, ERNST: *Musikgeschichte von Freiberg*, Freiberg, 1939.

MÜLLER-BLATTAU, JOSEPH: *Genealogie der musikalisch-Bachischen Familie*, Kassel, n.d.

MÜNTZER, THOMAS: *Die Fürstenpredigt und andere politische Schriften*, ed. by Dr Siegfried Streller, Leipzig, 1950.

MYLIUS, JOHANN CHRISTOPH: *Das in dem Jahre 1743 blühende Jena*, Jena, 1743.

NEUMEISTER, ERDMANN: *Kirchen-Andachten . . .*, Hamburg, 1726; *Neue Geistliche Gedichte*, Eisenach, 1718.

NIEMÖLLER, K. L.: 'Grundzüge einer Neubewertung der Musik an den Lateinschulen des 16. Jahrhunderts', *Bericht über den . . . Kongress Kassel 1962* (Gesellschaft für Musikforschung), Kassel, 1963.

NOHL, LUDWIG: *Musiker-Briefe, Eine Sammlung Briefe von Gluck, C. P. E. Bach, Haydn, Weber, Mendelssohn*, Leipzig, [1867].

NORLIND, T., AND TROBACK, E.: *Kungl. hovkapellets historia*, Stockholm, 1926.

OLEARIUS, JOH. CHRISTOPH., HALL.SAX.: *Rerum Thuringicarum Syntagma, Allerhand denckwürdige Thuringische Historien und Chronicken*, Erfurt, 1703.

PARRY, C. H. H.: 'The beginning of German Music', *Oxford History of Music*, vol. iii, London, 1902.

PETRI, JOHANN SAMUEL: *Anleitung zur praktischen Musik*, Leipzig, 1782.

PETZOLDT, RICHARD: *Der Leipziger Thomanenchor*, Leipzig, 1962.

PFEFFERKORN, GEORG MICHAEL: *Merkwürdige und Auserlesene Geschichte von der berümten Landgrafschaft Thüringen*, (Erfurt?), 1685.

PIRRO, ANDRÉ: *J. S. Bach*, Paris, 1913, 6th edition, 1924.

PISCHNER, HANS: *Musik und Musikerziehung in der Geschichte Weimars*, Weimar, 1954.

PLAMENAC, DRAGAN: 'New Light on the Last Years of Carl. Phil. Eman. Bach', *Musical Quarterly*, xxxv, October, 1949.

RAUSCH, H. J.: 'Der Stockholmer Bach', *Eisenacher Bachtage*, Programme, 1939.

RAUTENSTRAUCH, DR JOHANNES: *Luther und die Pflege der kirchlichen Musik in Sachsen (14.–19. Jahrhundert)*, Leipzig, 1907.

RICHTER, B.: 'Uber die Motetten Seb. Bachs', *d. Wissenschaftl. Beil. z. d. Leipz. Zeitung*, Nr.38, Leipzig, 1912.

ROLLBERG, F.: 'Johann Christoph Bach', *Zeitschrift für Musikwissenschaft*, xi, 1928–9.

SADIE, STANLEY: 'Concert life in eighteenth-century England', *Proceedings of the Royal Musical Association*, lxxxv, 1959; 'Wind music of John Christian Bach', *Music and Letters*, xxxvii, 11, April 1956.

SCHÄFER, WILHELM: *Johann Sebastian Bach* (lecture given in Bremen in 1935), München, 1935.

SCHERING, ARNOLD: *Geschichte des Oratoriums*, Leipzig, 1911; 'Aus der Selbstbiographie eines deutschen Kantors', *Festschrift: Max Schneider zum 60.Geburtstag*, ed. by Hans Joachim Zingel, Halle, 1935.

SCHLEDER, HERMANN: *Johann Nikolaus Forkel*, translated [very badly] by Professor Reinhold Forkel, Trenton, New Jersey, n.d. (after October 1937).

SCHMEIZEL, MARTIN: *Jenaische Städte- und Universitäts-Chronik*, ed. by E. Devrient, Jena, 1908.

SCHMIDT, EVA: ed. *Die Stadtkirche zu St. Peter und Paul (Herderkirche) zu Weimar*, Weimar, 1953.

SCHNEIDER, MAX: 'Themat. Verz. d. musikal. Werke d. Familie Bach', B.J.B., 1907; *Bach-Urkunden/Ursprung der musikalisch-Bachischen Familie/Nachrichten über Johann Sebastian Bach von Carl Philipp Emanuel Bach* (with two letters from C. P. E. Bach to Forkel, annotated by Zelter), N.B.G., xvii, 3, Leipzig, (1917).

SCHOEKEL, H. P.: *Johann Christian Bach und die Instrumentalmusik seiner Zeit*, Woltenbüttel, 1926.

SCHRADER, DR KARL: 'Die Fürstlich-Sächsische Residentzstadt Eisenach 1672–1741', *Beiträge zur Geschichte Eisenachs*, Nr.29, Eisenach, 1929.

SCHUMACHER, CARL WILHELM: 'Professor am Eisenacher Gymnasio', *Merkwürdigkeiten der Stadt Eisenach und ihres Bezirkes*, Eisenach, 1777.

SCHÜNEMANN, GEORG: *Geschichte der deutschen Schulmusik*, Leipzig, 1928.

SERAUKY, WALTER: *Musikgeschichte der Stadt Halle*, 2 vols., Halle/Berlin, 1935.

SERAUKY, WALTER: SASSE, KONRAD; AND SIEGMUND-SCHULTZE, WALTHER: *Halle als Musikstadt*, Halle, n.d.

SITTARD, JOSEF; *Gesch. des Musik- u. Concertwesens in Hamburg vom 14.Jr. bis auf die Gegenwart*, Altona/Leipzig, 1890.

SMEND, FRIEDRICH: *Joh. Seb. Bach: Kirchen-Kantaten vom 8. Sonntag nach Trinitatis bis zum Michaelis-Fest*, Berlin, 1947.

SOHNGEN, OSKAR: 'Die Lübecker Abendmusik als Kirchenge-schichtliches und theologisches Problem', *Musik und Kirche*, xxvii, 4, 1957.

SPANGENBERG, KARL: *Mundartforschung*, Institut fur Mundartforschung und Thüringisches Flurnamenarchiv, Jena University, Jena, 1967.

SPITTA (J. A.), PHILIPP: *Joh. Seb. Bach*. 2 vols., Leipzig, 1873–80; translated by C. Bell and J. A. Fuller-Maitland, 3 vols., London, 1884–5; reissue in 2 vols., New York, 1951.

STRUNK, OLIVER: *Source Readings in Musical History*, London, 1952.

SZABOLCSI, BENCE: *Baustein zu einer Geschichte der Melodie*, Budapest, 1959.

TECHRITZ, HERMANN: *Sächsische Stadtpfeifer*, Doctoral dissertation, Dresden, 1932.

TENTZELN, WILHELM ERNST: *Fürstlicher Sächsischer Geschichts-Calender . . . der Durchlauchtigsten Fürsten zu Sachsen Ernestinischer Linie . . . 1601–1697*, Leipzig, 1697.

TERRY, CHARLES SANFORD: *Johann Christian Bach*, London, 1929, second ed., 1967; [*J. S.*] *Bach: a Biography*, London, 1928.

THIÉBAULT, DIEUDONNÉ: *Original Anecdotes of Frederic the Second*, 2 vols., London, 1805.

THIEME, U., AND BECKER, F.: *Allgemeines Lexikon der bildenden Künstler*, Leipzig, 1908.

THOMAS, F.: *Einige Ergebnisse über Johann Sebastian Bachs Ohrdrufer Schulzeit*, Ohrdruf, 1900; *Die Stammbaum des Ohrdrufer Zweigs der Familie von Johann Sebastian Bach*, Ohrdruf, 1899 (published after Ohrdruf Summer Festival, 1898, to commemorate J. S. Bach's schooldays in the town).

THULIN, OSKAR: *Bilder der Reformation*, Berlin, 1967.

TOLAND, JOHN: *An account of the Courts of Prussia and Hanover*, third ed., London, 1706.

TUTENBERG, F.: *Die Sinfonik Johann Christian Bachs*, Wolfenbüttel, 1928.

VESPER, REINHOLD: 'Junge Bachs auf dem Eisenacher Gymnasium', *Das Thüringen Fahnlein*, Jrg., 4., Jena, 1935.

VOCKERODT, GOTTFRIED: *Misbrauch der freyen Kunste/insonderheit Der Music . . . was nach D. Luthers und anderen Evangelischen Theologorum und Politicorum Meinung von Opern und Komödien zu halten sey?*, Frankfurt, 1697.

VOIGT, W.: *Händels Samson und Bachs Matthäus-Passion*, Göttingen, 1885.

VRIESLANDER, OTTO: *C. P. E. Bach*; München, 1923.

WALTHER, JOHANN GOTTFRIED: *Musicalisches Lexicon oder musicalische Bibliothek*, Leipzig, 1732.

WARBURTON, ERNEST: 'J. C. Bach's Operas', *Proceedings of the Royal Musical Association*, xcii, 1966.

WEBER, MAX MARIA VON: *Carl Maria von Weber: ein Lebensbild*, 3 vols., Leipzig, 1866.

WEIZIUS, ANTONIUS: *Verbessertes Leipzig*, Leipzig, 1728.

WENNIG, ERICH: *Chronik des musikalischen Lebens der Stadt Jena . . . bis zum Jahre 1750*, Jena [1943].

WERNER, A.: *Städtische und Fürstliche Musikpflege in Zeitz*, Bückeburg, 1922.

WERNER, ARNO: *Freie Musikgemeinschaften alter Zeit im mitteldeutschen Raum*, Wolfenbüttel/Berlin, 1940.

[WESTERICH, ADOLF]: *Gymnasium Bückeburg*, Bückeburg, 1939.

WHITE, JOSEPH A., JR: *The concerted symphonies of John Christian Bach*, Doctoral dissertation, University of Michigan, Ann Arbor, Michigan, 1953.

WILLIAMS, PETER F.: 'J. S. Bach and English Organ Music', *Music and Letters*, xliv, 2, April 1963.

WOHLFARTH, HANNSDIETER: 'J. C. F. Bach. Eine Darstellung seines Lebens', *Schaumburg-Lippische Mitteilungen*, xviii, Bückeburg, 1965; 'J. C. F. Bach (1732–1795). Eine Studie zur Musikersoziologie des 18. Jahrhunderts', *Schaumburg-Lippische Mitteilungen*, xvii, Bückeburg, 1965; *W. F. E. Bach—Werkverzeichnis*, typescript, Bückeburg, 1960.

WOTQUENNE, ALFRED: *Thematisches Verzeichnis der Werke von Carl Philipp Emanuel Bach*, re-issue, Wiesbaden, 1964.

WRAXALL, N. W.: *Memoirs of the Courts of Berlin, Dresden, Warsaw, and Vienna: In the Years 1777, 1778, 1779*, London, 1799.

WUSTMANN, GUSTAV: 'Ein Enkel Johann Sebastian Bachs', *Wissenschaftliche Beilage der Leipziger Zeitung*, Nr.8, 23rd February 1907.

ZEHLA, C.: 'W. Friedemann Bach und seine hallische Wirksamkeit', B.J.B., 1910.

BY VARIOUS AUTHORS

Zur Erinnerungsfeier an Joh. Sebastian Bach's Todestag, Jena, 1850.

Johann Sebastian Bach in Thüringen; Festgabe zum Gedenkjahr 1950, Weimar, 1950.

Bach in Thüringen, Berlin, 1950.

Samuel Scheidt, 24 März 1654–24 März 1954; Eine Gedenkschrift zu seinem 300.Todestag (her. Stadt Halle), Leipzig, 1954.

Samuel Scheidt; Festschrift aus Anlass des 350.Geburtstages 1587–1937 (her. Händelhaus, Halle), Berlin/Wolfenbüttel, 1937.

Arnold Schering zum 60.Geburtstag (Festschrift), Berlin, 1937.

Verzeichniss des musikalischen Nachlasses des verstorbenen Capellmeisters C. P. E. Bach, Hamburg, 1790.

Devisen auf deutsche Gelehrte, Dichter und Künstler, Aus deutschen Dichtern gezogen, (?) *1772.*

Court and private life in the time of Queen Charlotte, being the journal of Mrs Papandiek, 2 vols., London, 1887.

Reminiscences of Henry Angelo, with memoirs of his late father and friends, 2 vols., London, 1828–30.

Evangelisches Kirchen-Gesangbuch (Landeskirche Sachsens), Berlin, 1950.

Engelische Comedien und Tragedien . . ./von den Engelländern in Deutschland an Königlichen/Chur- und Fürstlichen Höfen auch in vornehmen Reichs-See- und -Handel Städten seynd agiret und gehalten worden/und zuvor nie im Druck aussgangen, Hamburg, 1620.

Kritische Briefe über die Tonkunst, mit kleinen Clavierstücken und Singoden, begleitet von einer musikalischen Gesellschaft in Berlin, Berlin, 1759.

Einige zum allgemeinen Nutzen deutlicher gemachte Musicalische Erwegungs- und andere eingerichtete Uibungs-Wahrheiten . . . von einem Freunde dieser Wissenschaft, Leipzig, n.d. [1750?]

Kurtze Beschreibung des Kinder-Jubilaei welches an dem Evangelischen Jubel-Feste von den Schul-Kindern in Alt-Dressden . . ., Dresden, [1718].

A Wonderfull and most Lamentable Declaration of the great hurt done, & mighty losse sustained by Fire that hapned; & mighty stormes of Winde, Thunder, Lightning, Haile & Raine, with Inundations of Water, . . . that fell in the Towne of Erffurd and Weinmar; & in the County of Wurten- burgh . . . as also in many other places of Germany, to the great destruction of thousands of Men, Women, & Children; Houses; Cattles, Corne, Money, Household-stuffe, & many other things: In the Month of May, but much more in the month of June last past, Anno, 1613 . . . Written to move all good Christians to pitty and compassion, & to stirre up their hearts to pray unto God to convert his Ire from us. Printed at Collen in High Dutch, and Translated into English, London, 1613.

Alte Thüringische Chronicke, Frankfurt/Leipzig, 1715.

Beiträge zur Hamburgischen Musikgeschichte, Hamburg, 1956.

Bibliographie zur Geschichte der Stadt Leipzig, Sonderband III, Die Kunst, Weimar, 1964.

Briefe auf einer Reise durch Thüringen und Hessen; Geschrieben von einem wandernden Helvetier im Jahr 1800, Altenburg/Erfurt, 1801.

Bürgerbuch (Ms.) of Eisenach, 1673–1725; in the Eisenach Stadtarchiv.

Das jetzt Lebende und jezt florirende Leipzig . . ., Leipzig, 1725.

Die Burg und die Stadt: Die Wartburg und Eisenach im Spiegel graphischer Darstellungen, Thüringer Museum, Eisenach, 1967.

Die evangelische Stadtkirche zu Darmstadt, Darmstadt, 1966.

Die Fürstenhäuser Sachsen-Altenburg, Altenburg, 1826.

Die Matrikel der Universität Jena: I, Jena, 1944.

Gedenkschrift zur Einweihung der wiederaufgebauten Martinskirche in Kassel, 1 Juni 1958, Kassel, 1958.

Historische und geographische Nachricht von der Haupt-Festung und Residenz-Stadt Dressden', in ganzem Churfüstenthum Sachsen, und derer seit ihren Ursprunge her vorgefallenen Merckwürdigkeiten, Nebst dem Schicksal von Dressden von Anno 1745 bis 1760, Dresden, 1761.

Jena, von Seinem Ursprunge bis zur neuester Zeit, Jena, 1850.

Kurtze Nachricht von der Stadt Leipzig und absonderlich von der Universität, Leipzig, [1709].

Lebendes Leipzig, 1730–34, 1735–39 (Ms.).

Leipzig in Wort und Bild, Leipzig, 1928.

Leipziger Adress-Post-und-Reise-Calender . . ., Leipzig, 1750.

Matrikel der Eisenacher Lateinschule 1690–1707 (Ms.), Stadtarchiv, Eisenach.

Sagen und Klänge aus Thüringen, Rudolstadt, 1857.

Index

Index

PEOPLE

Abbt, Thomas, 224–5
Abel, Karl Friedrich, 213, 238, 248, 259, 260, 262, 265, 266, 267, 268, 269
Abingdon, Lord, 262
Adams, Thomas, 292, 297–8
Adlung, Jakob, 60, 114, 116, 137, 158, 160 n.22
Agricola, Johann Friedrich, 114, 138, 141, 170, 172, 173, 225, 251
Ahle family, 10
Ahle, Johann Georg, 45, 79
Ahle, Johann Rudolf, 43–5, 51
Albani, Francesco, 239
Albert, Friedrich, 249
Alberti (Kapellmeister of Merseburg), 102
Albinoni, Tommaso, 104, 107
Albrecht, Wilhelmina (m. W. F. E. Bach), 278
Albrechtsberger, Johann Georg, 286, 298, 299, 307
Algarotti, Count Francesco, 165
Allott, Richard, 296
Alt, Philip Samuel, 114
Altenburg family, 10
Altenburg, Michael, 34, 43
Altnikol, Elisabetha Juliane Friederica (d. of J. S. Bach), 136
Altnikol, Johann Christoph, 136, 138, 141, 156, 168, 225
Amicis, Anna Lucia de', 255
Ancaster, Duchess of, 249
Angelo family, 277
Angelo, Henry, 267
Anhalt-Bernburg, Friederica Henriette, Duchess of, 99
Anhalt-Köthen, Agnes Gisella, Duchess of, 97, 98
Anhalt-Köthen, Leopold, Duke of, 93, 97, 98, 99, 146
Anhalt-Köthen, Ludwig, Duke of, 24–5
Anhalt-Zerbst, Johann August, Duke of, 98
Anna Amalia, Princess of Prussia, 139, 171, 179, 202
Anne, Queen of England, 83
Anson, Lord, 249
Anthing (m. G. F. Bach), Juliane Friederike Charlotte, 236

Apel, Christian Siegmund, 113
Archenholtz, J. W. von, 263
Arighini, Giuseppe, 76
Arne, Michael, 211, 212, 254
Arne, Thomas Augustine, 211, 213, 250, 253, 254, 256, 267, 272, 296
Arnold, Johann Heinrich, 72–3
Arnold, Samuel, 256, 272
Artaria (publisher in Vienna), 218
Arteaga, Esteban, 286
Attwood, Thomas, 272
Austria, Maria Theresa, Empress of, 164
Ayrton, William, 294

Bach, various bearers of the name in Bohemia, 6; at Göttingen University, 199; at Jena University, 128 n.1; in Thuringia at an early date, 6, 7, 18 n.10 and 16; ramifications of the Ohrdruf branch, 161 n.4
(1) Bach, Anna Magdalena (2nd wife of 54), 99, 135–6, 159 n.9, 184;
(2) Bach, August Wilhelm, 288;
(3) Bach, Carl Philipp Emanuel (s. of 54), 1, 17 n.1, 36, 38 n.18, 49, 51, 57, 92, 122, 125, 136, 139, 147, 155, 156, 157, 162, 167–81, 184, 185, 186, 194, 198, 201, 202, 207–21, 223, 225, 227, 228, 229, 231, 235, 236, 239, 242, 244, 251, 261, 266, 273, 276, 278, 281, 282, 283, 290, 296, 299; (4) Bach, Caspar (s. of 13?), 8, 33, 35; (5) Bach, Catharina Dorothea (d. of 54), 92, 99, 185, 194; (6) Bach, Christoph (s. of 59), 8, 33, 35, 45, 47; (7) Bach, Dorothea Maria (d. of 6), 35; (8) Bach, Friederica Sophia (d. of 75), 194, 203; (9) Bach, G., 280; (10) Bach, Georg Christoph (s. of 6), 36, 38 n.18, 47, 57–8, 66, 108 n.18; (11) Bach, Georg Michael (s. of 16), 123; (12) Bach, Gottlieb Friedrich (s. of 47), 125, 235, 236, 312–13; (13) Bach, Hans I, 8; (14) Bach, Hedwig Martha, 62 n.19; (15) Bach, Heinrich (s. of 59), 8, 33, 35–6, 45, 48, 49, 65, 69, 75; (16) Bach, Jakob (s. of 74), 23, 45, 91, 123; (17) Bach,

Johann, 81; (18) Bach, Johann, (s. of 59), 8, 32–6, 45; (19) Bach, Johann Ambrosius (s. of 6), 36, 38 n.20, 49, 60, 64, 65–9; (20) Bach, Johann Andreas (s. of 32), 108 n.20, 161 n.41; (21) Bach, Johann Balthasar (s. of 19), 66, 67; (22) Bach, Johann Bernhard (s. of 35), 46, 50, 70–1, 92, 112, 127, 241; (23) Bach, Johann Bernhard (s. of 33), 95–6, 161 n.41; (24) Bach, Johann Christian (s. of 54), 17 n.1, 136, 181, 194, 213, 223, 227, 230, 231, 248–73, 278, 283, 294, 307; (25) Bach, Johann Christian I (s. of 18), 36, 46, 65; (26) Bach, Johann Christian (s. of 11), 123, 204 n.5; (27) Bach, Johann Christoph (s. of 33), 161 n.41; (28) Bach, Johann Christoph I (s. of 15), 36, 49–56, 57, 60, 63, 64, 68, 70, 75, 80, 300; (29) Bach, Johann Christoph II (s. of 6), 36, 47–9; (30) Bach, Johann Christoph III (s. of 35), 46; (31) Bach, Johann Christoph IV (s. of 25), 60, 67; (32) Bach, Johann Christoph V (s. of 28), 67, 83; (33) Bach, Johann Christoph, of Ohrdruf (s. of 19), 65, 69, 73, 74, 99, 108 n.20, 136, 137, 161 n.41, 181; (34) Bach, Johann Christoph Friedrich (s. of 54), 122, 136, 162, 169, 170, 181, 207, 214, 222 n.11, 223–35, 237, 239, 276, 278, 284; (35) Bach, Johann Egidius (s. of 18), 36, 70; (36) Bach, Johann Elias (s. of 56), 137–8, 189, 205 n.16; (37) Bach, Johann Ernst (s. of 29), 73, 78, 79; (38) Bach, Johann Ernst (s. of 23), 71, 114, 122, 149, 155, 181, 214, 228, 239, 241–4: sons of, 71; (39) Bach, Johann Friedrich (s. of 38), 80; (40) Bach, Johann Gottfried Bernhard (s. of 54), 56, 92, 99, 115–116, 137, 184, 185; (41) Bach, Johann Günther (s. of 15), 36, 49, 60; (42) Bach, Johann Heinrich (s. of 32), 136–7, 161 n.41; (43) Bach, Johann Jakob (s. of 19), 66, 67, 68, 69, 73, 81–2, 188, 305–6; (44) Bach, Johann Jakob (s. of 25), 67; (45) Bach, Johann Jonas (s. of 19), 66, 67; (46) Bach, Johann Lorenz (s. of 56), 95; (47) Bach, Johann Ludwig (s. of 16), 97, 106, 123–8, 154, 181, 193, 213, 235; (48) Bach, Johann Michael (s. of 15), 36, 49, 50, 51, 56–60, 73, 79, 114, 144, 281; (49) Bach, Johann Michael (s. of 28), 82–3; (50) Bach, Johann Michael, of Schmalkalden,

280–1; (51) Bach, Johann Nikolaus I (s. of 18), 46; (52) Bach, Johann Nikolaus II (s. of 28), 50, 67, 70, 78, 110–23, 126, 127, 151, 155; (53) Bach, Johann Philipp (s. of 12), 236–8, 312–13: children of, 246 n.22 and 23; (54) Bach, Johann Sebastian I (s. of 19), 1, 3, 12, 14, 15, 16, 17 n.1, 25, 37 n.12, 38 n.18 and 20, 40, 45, 49, 52, 53, 56, 58, 60, 66, 67–83 pass., 88, 89, 90, 92–107, 111, 114, 117, 119, 122, 123–4, 125, 126, 130–58 pass., 162, 167, 168, 174, 175, 183, 184, 185, 186, 188, 189, 190, 192, 193, 194, 198, 199, 200, 201, 202, 203, 212, 213, 214, 216, 221, 228, 235, 236, 240, 241, 248, 251, 263, 266, 275, 276, 280, 282, 283–301 pass., 307; (55) Bach, Johann Sebastian II (s. of 3), 167–8, 213, 235, 238–241, 267; (56) Bach, Johann Valentin (s. of 10), 95, 137; (57) Bach, Johanna Juditha (d. of 19), 66, 67; (58) Bach, Johanne Carolina (d. of 54), 136; (59) Bach, Johannes (Hans II, s. of 72), 8, 33; (60) Bach, Karl Bernhard Paul (great-grandson of 53), 236, 237; (61) Bach, Lips I (s. of 72), 8, 123; (62) Bach, Lips II (s. of 61?), 9, 23; (63) Bach, Maria Barbara (1st wife of 54), 56, 79, 92, 99, 185; (64) Bach, Melchior (s. of 4), 8, 33; (65) Bach, Nikol (a soldier), 51; (66) Bach, Nikol (s. of 4), 8, 33; (67) Bach, Nikolaus Ephraim (s. of 16), 91, 123, 124; (68) Bach, Regine Susanna (d. of 54), 136, 141; (69) Bach, Samuel Anton (s. of 47), 125; (70) Bach, Samuel Friedrich (s. of 12), 236; (71) Bach, Tobias Friedrich (s. of 32), 137, 159 n.9, 161 n.41, 187; (72) Bach, Veit I, 1, 6–8; (73) Bach, Veit II, 8; (74) Bach, Wendel, 123; (75) Bach, Wilhelm Friedemann (s. of 54), 92, 99, 107, 135, 137, 138, 143, 151, 155, 156, 162, 167, 168, 169, 181, 183–204, 214, 223; (76) Bach, Wilhelm Friedrich Ernst (s. of 34), 226, 230, 231, 233, 275–80

Banér, General, 31
Barblan, O., 307
Baron, Ernst Gottlieb, 115
Bartolomäus, Jakob, 60
Battishill, Jonathan, 255, 290, 292
Baumgarten, J. S., 191
Baurath, Anna Amalia (m. J. N. Bach), 111
Bause, J. F., 239, 240

Beard, John, 213, 249
Beckford, Peter, 212
Beer, Johann, 275, 279, 280, 293, 294, 298
Beethoven, Ludwig van, 172, 174, 176, 190, 210, 217, 219, 261, 308
Bellerman, H., 307
Benda, Franz, 164, 173, 199
Benda, Georg, 173, 242, 282
Bendemann, Eduard, 275
Bennet, John, 296
Bennett, William Sterndale, 298, 299, 300
Berlepsch, Hartmann von, 44
Bernhard, Johann Adam, 114
Bertuch, Georg, 110
Besozzi (oboist of Dresden), 165
Bevin, Elway, 283
Birnbaum, Johann Abraham, 157
Birnstiel, Friedrich, 172, 175
Blume, Friedrich, 101
Bock, M. C., 227
Bodt, Jean de, 88
Boeldicke, Joachim, 131
Böhm, Georg, 74, 102, 104
Bokemeyer, Heinrich, 110
Bonalino, Giovanni, 24
Bononcini, Giovanni, 88
Boosey, Thomas, 287
Bornemann, Heinrich, 75
Borstelmann, Rektor, 68
Bottarelli, Giovanni Gualberto, 254
Böttner, Johann Christian, 281
Boumann, Johann, 166
Boyce, William, 249, 262, 265, 296
Brahms, Johann, 22, 189, 202
Brandenburg, Christian Ludwig, Count of, 98
Brandenburg, Friedrich Wilhelm, Elector of, 78, 87
Brandenburg-Ansbach, Count of, 15
Braunschweig-Lüneburg, Charlotte, Duchess of, 198
Braunschweig-Wolfenbüttel, Anton Ulrich, Duke of, 48, 77, 124
Breitkopf, Johann Gottlieb Immanuel, 229
Bridgetower, George, 293
Briegel, Lothar, 238
Briegleb, Amalie (m. J. P. Bach), 237
Brockes, Barthold Heinrich, 146, 148
Browne, Thomas, 213
Brühl, Count Heinrich von, 158, 165, 168, 205 n.16
Brühl, Count Johann Moritz von, 140
Bruhns, Nikolaus, 74, 300
Buffardin, Pierre, 82, 165, 188, 213
Burghersh, Lord, 294

Burgk, Joachim à, 15–16, 43
Burney, Charles, 173, 176, 178, 198, 208, 209, 212, 215, 220, 254, 260, 282, 286, 293
Büsch, Johann Georg, 209
Buttstett, Johann Heinrich, 38 n.20, 47, 92, 95, 102, 114, 132
Buxtehude, Dietrich, 56, 74, 78–9, 104, 300

Callcott, John Wall, 281, 298
Calvisius, Seth, 134
Cambridge, Duke of, 296
Cantelo, Anne, 271
Carpioni, Giulio, 239
Casanova, Giacomo, 262
Cäsar, Philippine Elisabeth, 124
Casella, Alfredo, 307
Caspar, David Friedrich, 239
Cavalli, Pietro Francesco, 53
Cervetto, Giacomo, 259
Chandos, Duke of, 83
Chappuzeau, Samuel, 42–3
Charles V, Emperor, 24
Charles X, XI, kings of Sweden, 81
Charles XII, King of Sweden, 81, 82
Chodowiecki, Daniel Nikolaus, 213
Chopin, Frédéric, 276, 299
Christian IV, King of Denmark, 30
Christina, Queen of Sweden, 81
Cipriani, Giovanni, 269
Claudius, Matthias, 211, 232
Clementi, Muzio, 174, 212, 244
Clive, Catherine, 253
Cocchi, Gioacchino, 250
Colman, George, 269
Colonna, Angelo, 226
Comenius (Bohemian educationist), 39
Compenius (organ-builder), 94
Corelli, Arcangelo, 89, 104, 156, 271
Cornelys, Teresa, 262
Cramer (of Gotha), 176
Cramer, Carl Friedrich, 285
Cramer, Johann Andreas, 218
Cramer, Johann Baptist, 298
Cramer, William, 263
Cranach, Lucas, 17, 90, 213
Creizenach, Wilhelm, 17
Crodel, Markus, 11–12
Crosdill, John, 259
Crotch, William, 284, 291, 297, 298
Cunzius, Christoph, 94
Curland, Peter, Duke of, 209
Czerny, Karl, 295

Dannemann, Johanna Maria (m. C. P. E. Bach), 167
Dassdorf, Karl Wilhelm, 240, 241

Dedekind, Andreas Christian, 41, 68, 123
Defesch, William, 213
Delany, Mary, 272
Delibes, Léo, 280
Delius, Demoiselle, Ernst Wilhelm Friedrich, and Frederick, 232
Demantius, Christoph, 16
Dieskau, Carl Heinrich von, 151
Dietze, Marcus, 42
Dittersdorf, Karl Ditters von, 286
Dodd, Rev. William, 268
Doles, Johann Friedrich, 150, 154, 284, 285
Drese, Adam, 41
Drese, Johann Samuel, 77, 93, 94, 114
Drese, Johann Wilhelm, 93, 94, 115
Dressler, Gallus, 14
Dulon, Friedrich, 276
Dumergue, Miss, 277
Dupuis, Thomas, 296
Durante, Francesco, 252
Dürer, Albrecht, 285

Ebeling, Christoph David, 209, 212
Eberlin, Daniel, 56, 65, 213
Eccard, Johannes, 15
Edenberger, Lucas, 10, 11
Effler, Johann, 56, 77, 80
Eisentraut, Elisabeth (m. J. Christoph Bach II), 47
Eisler, Hanns, 308
Elerdt, Charlotte (m. W. F. E. Bach), 278
Emmerling, Sophie Dorothea, 56
Erasmus, Desiderius, 4
Erdmann, Georg, 73, 109 n.24
Ernesti, Johann, 40
Ernesti, Johann August, 142–3, 186
Ernesti, Johann Heinrich, 131, 141, 144
Erselius, Johann Christoph, 141
Erxleben, Dorothea Christiane, 191
Eschenburg, Johann Joachim, 198, 200
Essex, Timothy, 296
Esterházy, Prince Nicholas, 165

Faber, Johann, 27
Fasch, Carl Friedrich, 169
Fasch, Johann Friedrich, 132, 169, 192, 281
Ferdinand II, Emperor, 29
Fielding, Sir John, 269
Fischer, Johann Caspar, 74, 107
Fischer, Johann Christian, 263, 269, 272
Fitzwilliam, Lord Richard, 212
Fleming, Paul, 106
Flemming, Count Joachim Friedrich von, 95

Fletin, Jonas de, 56
Flor, Christian, 75
Fludd, Robert, 213
Foerster, Christoph, 192
Fordyce, Miss, 214
Forkel, Johann Nikolaus, 74, 110, 185, 198–200, 201, 202, 225, 231, 232, 236, 251, 281, 282, 283–9
Franck, Melchior, 26–8, 128
Franck, Salomo, 91, 106, 148
Francke, August Hermann, 80, 191
Frankenberger, Johanna Rosina (m. J. P. Bach), 237
Frenzel, Frau von, 278
Frescobaldi, Girolamo, 61 n.13, 213
Friedrich I, King of Sweden, 82
Friedrich I, King of Prussia, 87
Friedrich II (Frederic the Great), King of Prussia, 87, 139, 155, 162–81 pass., 191, 196, 201, 202, 224, 225, 237, 238, 251, 265, 278
Friedrich Wilhelm, Prince of Prussia, 209, 278
Friedrich Wilhelm I, King of Prussia, 163
Friedrich Wilhelm II, King of Prussia, 278
Friedrich Wilhelm III, King of Prussia, 278
Friedrich Wilhelm IV, King of Prussia, 279
Friese, Heinrich, 98
Froberger, Johann Jacob, 56, 61 n.13, 74, 82
Frohne, Johann Adolf, 45, 80
Fugger family, 26
Fürstenau, Philipp Zesen von, 44

Gabrieli, Andrea, 26
Gabrieli, Giovanni, 28, 52
Gainsborough, Mary, 269
Gainsborough, Thomas, 237, 269, 271
Galeotti, Salvatore, 249
Gandersheim, Elisabeth Ernestine Antonia, Abbess of, 91
Garrick, David, 269
Gauntlett, Henry John, 296
Gebauer, J. J., 191, 197
Geiger, Konrad, 236, 237
Gellert, Christian Fürchtegott, 154, 198, 218, 243
Geminiani, Francesco, 271
George I, King of England, 76, 163
George III, King of England, 238, 249, 259, 266, 282
George, Prince of Denmark, 83
Georgi, Dorothea Elisabeth (m. W. F. Bach), 194, 203

Gerber, Ernst Ludwig, 139, 251
Gerber, Heinrich Nikolaus, 80, 138, 139
Gerhardt, Paul, 136
Gerlach, Carl Gotthelf, 141, 150
Gerlach, Theodor, 141
Gerstenburg, Heinrich Wilhelm von, 207, 211
Gessner, Johann Matthias, 91, 141–2, 151, 199, 225
Gessner, Salomon, 240
Geyersbach (student at Arnstadt), 78, 81
Giardini, Felice de', 262, 293
Gleim, Johann Wilhelm Ludwig, 170, 171, 173, 175
Glenorchy, Lady, 270
Gloucester, Duke of, 266
Gluck, Christoph Willibald, 211, 253, 258
Goethe, Johann Wolfgang von, 89, 142, 154, 171, 173, 201, 230, 238, 242, 287, 288
Goeze, Johann Melchior, 191, 207–8
Goldberg, Johann Gottlieb, 138, 188
Goldschmidt, J. F., 240
Görner, Johann Gottlieb, 139, 144, 145, 150, 158, 192
Gotter, Friedrich Wilhelm, 232
Gotthilf, Friedrich, 91
Gottsched, Johann Christoph, 131, 146, 150, 153, 154, 155, 157, 172, 198
Grabbe, Johann, 224
Gräbner, C. A., 189
Gräbner, Christian, 139
Graeme, General, 249
Graff, J. D. C., 198
Grant, Sir Archibald, 271
Gräser, Heinrich, 48, 63
Grassi, Cecilia (m. John Christian Bach), 270, 271
Graun, August Friedrich, 158, 168
Graun, Johann Gottlieb, 163, 167, 168, 170, 186
Graun, Karl Heinrich, 139, 163, 167, 168, 170. 172, 211, 228, 251, 253, 304 n.59
Graupner, Christoph, 106, 107, 132, 195
Gray, Thomas, 172
Greene, Maurice, 296
Greff, Joachim, 17
Guadagni, Gaetano, 253, 255
Gustavus Adolphus, King of Sweden, 29–30, 31, 34, 81, 90

Hachmeister, Karl Christoph, 281, 282
Haffner, Ulrich, 243, 244
Hagedorn, Anna Dorothea, 92

Hagedorn, Christian Ludwig von, 239, 240
Hamilton, Duchess of, 249
Hammerschmidt, Andreas, 51, 213
Hanbury, John, 212
Handel, George Frideric, 52, 57, 83, 94, 128, 133, 147, 151, 157, 160 n.31, 163, 164, 175, 186, 211, 216, 217, 231, 248, 251, 252, 253, 254, 258, 267, 270, 271, 272, 282, 283, 285, 289, 290, 292, 296, 300
Harcourt, Earl Simon, 249
Harrer, Johann Gottlieb, 150, 158, 168, 284
Harris, James, 270
Harsdörffer, Philipp, 44
Hartnock, J. P., 230
Hase, Wolfgang, 39
Hasse, Faustina, 165
Hasse, Johann Adolph, 139, 165, 186, 187, 188, 192, 198, 211, 226, 251, 252, 253
Hassler, Hans Leo, 26
Hatchett, Charles, 296
Hauptmann, Moritz, 301
Hausmann, Nikolaus, 11
Haussmann, Elias, Gottlieb, 94, 158
Hawkins, Sir John, 265, 286
Haydn, Josef, 165, 172, 176, 192, 208, 217, 227, 231, 234, 235, 262, 272, 286
Haydn, Michael, 126
Hayne, Gottlieb, 163
Hebenstreit, Pantaleon, 65, 70, 115, 187
Hegel, Georg Wilhelm Friedrich, 289
Heindorff, Kantor, 49, 56
Heinichen, Johann David, 97, 132
Heinrich, Prince of Prussia (nephew of Friedrich II), 180
Heinrich, Prince of Prussia (son of Friedrich Wilhelm III), 279
Heintz, Wolff, 10
Heintze, Samuel, 114
Hempel, Fräulein, 152
Henneberg, Count of, 3, 124
Hennicke, Johann Christian von, 152
Henrici, Christian Friedrich ('Picander'), 144, 146, 148, 150, 152, 153, 159 n.4
Herda, Elias, 73, 160 n.41
Herder, Johann Gottlieb, 225, 226, 227–230, 238
Herschel, William, 271
Herthum, Christoph, 35, 49, 65
Herthum, Maria Katherina (née Bach), 35, 65
Hesemann, Gottlob, 194
Hesse, Eobanus, 10

Hesse-Darmstadt, Ludwig VIII, Count of, 195
Hesse-Darmstadt, Moritz, Count of, 25, 26, 28, 108 n.14
Heyden, Sebald, 16
Heyne, Christian Gottlob, 199
Hildebrand, Zacharias, 114
Hill, Rev. Rowland, 292
Hiller, Ferdinand, 280, 298, 299
Hiller, Johann Adam, 150, 284
Hirschbahn, Hermann, 275
Hoffmann, Bernard, 115
Hoffmann, Ernst Theodor Amadeus, 285
Hoffmann, Johann Christoph, 33
Hoffmann, Niclas, 7
Hoffmannswaldau, Hoffmann von, 106
Hohenlohe-Langenberg, Christian August, Prince of, 246 n.19
Holland, Johann David, 211
Holmes, Edward, 71, 100, 288, 302 n.28
Holstein, Schaumburg, and Sternberg, Ernst, Count of, 224
Holtei, Karl von, 287
Hölty, Ludwig Heinrich, 213, 232
Homer, 285
Homilius, Gottfried August, 138, 139–140, 189, 226
Hook, James, 232, 272, 290
Horn, Karl Friedrich, 291
Hudson, Henry, 238
Humboldt, Wilhelm von, 288
Hummel, Johann Nepomuk, 299
Hunold, Christian Friedrich, 97, 148
Hurlein, Johann Andreas, 239

Indy, Vincent d', 307
Isaac, Heinrich, 10, 68, 286

Jackson, William, 271
Jacob, Benjamin, 290, 291
Jacobi, Christian Gotthilf, 115
James I, King of England, 213
Janitsch, Johann Gottlieb, 170
Joachim (Professor at Leipzig), 186
Jöcher (Professor at Leipzig), 186
Johnson, Samuel, 268
Jommelli, Niccolo, 211, 226
Jones, Edward, 267, 294
Jones, John Jeremiah, 297

Karg-Elert, Sigfrid, 307
Kästner (Professor at Leipzig), 186
Kauffmann, Georg Friedrich, 102, 109 n.27, 132, 192
Kauffman, Johann Andreas, 92
Kees, Johann Jakob, and Johanna Maria, 144

Keiser, Reinhard, 132, 172, 192
Kellner, Johann Peter, 139, 140
Kerll, Johann Kaspar, 74
Kessler, Georg, 91
Keul, Anna Margarethe (m. J. G. Bach), 60
Keyserlingk, Count Hermann Karl von, 188
Kiesewetter, Johann Georg, 91
Kimmerling, Robert, 299
Kirchhoff, Gottfried, 94, 95, 190, 191, 192
Kirnberger, Johann Philipp, 138, 139, 159 n.16, 171, 201, 202, 226, 281, 287, 297
Kittel, Johann Christian, 138, 139
Klopstock, Friedrich, 191, 212, 218
Knobelsdorff, Georg Wenzeslaus von, 166
Knüpfer, Johann Magnus, 111
Knüpfer, Sebastian, 133
Kobelius, Johann Augustin, 77
Koch, Johann Sebastian, 98, 114, 137
Kochen, Johann Georg, 66
Kollmann, August Friedrich Christoph, 281–4, 295
Kollmann, Georg Christoph, 281
Kortthe, Gottlieb, 151
Krause, Christian Gottfried, 170, 177
Krause, G. (of Zittau), 168
Krebs, Johann Ludwig, 95, 138, 139–140, 158, 159 n.16, 168, 307
Krebs, Johann Tobias, 138, 139–40
Kress (violinist of Göttingen), 199
Krieger, Johann Philipp, 94, 98, 106
Kromayer, Johann Abraham, and Melchior, 72
Kropfgans, Johann, 205 n.16
Krüger, Andreas Ludwig, 213, 238
Kuhnau, Johann, 81–2, 94, 95, 98, 99, 107, 131, 132, 134–5, 145, 160 n.42
Kühnhausen, Johann Georg, 75
Künel, Salomon, 14
Kuntzen, Johann Paul, 174

La Tour, Georges de, 238
Lämmerhirt family, 38 n.20, 92, 184; Caspar, 66; Elisabeth (m. J. A. Bach), 65 ff.; Eva Barbara, 67; Hedwig, 34; Maria, 66; Martha Catharina, 92, 99
Lampe, John Frederick, 213
Lange, Anna Sibilla (m. J. N. Bach), 111
Lange, Samuel Gotthold, 191
Lange (organist of Wittenberg), 41
Lassus, Orlandus, 44, 51, 213
Leddiard, Thomas I, 144–5
Leddiard, Thomas II, 160 n.27
Legrenzi, Giovanni, 104

Leibniz, Gottfried Wilhelm, 88, 191, 213
Lembke, Georg, 132
Lemme, Carl Friedrich, 198, 232
Leo, Leonardo, 252
Leonhardt, Hans, 52
Leopold I, Emperor, 45, 79
Lessing, Gotthold Ephraim, 142, 170, 171, 198, 213, 224, 225, 228, 233
Leveridge, Richard, 213
Levi, Sara (née Itzig), 201
Lilienheim, Moritz Gerhard von, 91
Lincoln, Henry, 300
Lindemann, Cyrianus, and Johannes, 15
Linley, Elizabeth, 259, 269
Lisiewsky, Ch. F. R. von, 139
Liszt, Franz, 140, 276, 298, 307
Litta, Count Agostino, 251, 253, 254
Locke, Matthew, 53
Lockman, John, 250
Logan, Friedrich von, 32
Long, Samuel, 296
Lortzing, Albert, 120
Lotti, Antonio, 89, 114
Louis XIV, King of France, 70
Löwe, Johann Jakob, 77
Lully, Jean Baptiste, 258
Lüneburg-Celle, Christian Ludwig, Duke of, 75–6
Lüneburg-Celle, Eléonore Desonier, Duchess of, 75, 76
Lüneburg-Celle, Georg, Duke of, 75
Lüneburg-Celle, Georg Wilhelm, Duke of, 76
Luther, Martin, 4–5, 7, 9, 10–17 pass., 143, 191
Lyncker, Wilhelm Ferdinand, Baron von, 91, 92

Malmesbury, Lord, 270
Manchester, Duke of, 278
Manzuoli, Giovanni, 255
Marchand, Louis, 95
Marperger (minister in Dresden), 189
Marpurg, Friedrich Wilhelm, 140, 155, 172, 173, 174, 195, 196, 281, 297, 304 n.59
Marschalck, Nikolaus, 10
Marschall, Friedrich Gottlob, 91
Marsh, John, 271
Martini, Giovanni Battista, 252, 254
Marx, Joseph, 296
Mason, William, 256, 257
Mathias, Emanuel, 212
Mattei, Colomba, 250
Mattheson, Johann, 61 n.13, 102, 107, 157, 172, 173
Matthieu, Georg David, 198
Mazzinghi, Joseph, 272

Mecklenburg-Schwerin, Duchess of, 266
Mecklenburg-Schwerin, Duke of, 261, 281
Meder, Johann Valentin, 65
Melanchthon, Philipp, 5, 12, 213
Mencke, Johann Burckhardt, and Otto, 131
Mendelssohn, Felix, 105, 201, 242, 275, 287–9 pass., 292, 298, 299, 300
Mendelssohn, Moses, 171, 213, 225
Menzig (Kantor in Wittenberg), 41
Meyfart, Johann, 27
Michael, Tobias, 133
Michelangelo, 285
Milton, John, 213
Mizler, Lorenz Christoph, 115, 138, 140, 157
Möller, Carl, 93
Möller, Johann Heinrich, 111, 116
Monte, Philippe de, 51
Monteverdi, Claudio, 53
Moscheles, Ignaz, 298, 301
Mosewius, Johann Theodor, 289, 301
Mozart, Leopold, 160 n.45, 260
Mozart, Wolfgang Amadeus, 119, 172, 176, 208, 210, 223, 231, 235, 242, 260, 261, 265, 271, 272, 284, 299
Muffat, Georg, 107
Müller (of Dessau), 176
Müller, August Eberhard, 284, 301
Müller, August Friedrich, 151
Münchhausen, Lucia Elisabeth (m. J. C. F. Bach), 224, 226
Münter, Baltasar, 229
Müntzer, Thomas, 4–5, 7
Muth, Conradus (Mutianus Rufus), 10
Müthel, Johann Gottfried, 138, 139, 226
Mylius, Johann Christoph, 112

Nagel, Sebastian, 66
Nahl, Johann August, 66
Naumann, Johann Gottlieb, 278
Neefe, Christian Gottlob, 210
Neidhart, Johann Georg, 113
Neruda, Johann, 165
Neubauer, Franz Christoph, 235
Neuhass, Johannes, 14
Neumark, Georg, 24–5, 45
Neumeister, Erdmann, 106, 148
Newton, Isaac, 285, 288
Nichelmann, Christoph, 138, 139, 170, 172, 187
Nicolai, Friedrich, 120, 171
Nicolai, Ulrich, 238
Nicolini, Carlo, 253
Nikolai, Friedrich, 195, 225
Nosseni, Giovanni Maria, 24

Novello, Vincent, 291, 292, 297
Nowak, Leopold, 192

Obrecht, Jacob, 10, 16, 68
Oeser, Adam Friedrich, 213, 238, 239, 240, 241
Olearius, Johann Christoph, 35
Opitz, Martin, 29, 44
Osswald, Andreas, 50
Otto, Georg, 28

Pachelbel, Johann, 46–7, 55, 60, 65, 66, 69, 74, 102, 104, 300
Papendiek, Mrs, 249, 259, 270, 272, 276
Parke, John, 259
Parke, William Thomas, 260
Parry, Charles Hubert Hastings, 190
Pepping, Ernst, 308
Pepusch, John Christopher, 83, 312
Pergolesi, Giovanni Battista, 226
Permoser, Balthasar, 42, 89
Peter (Petri), Anna Dorothea (m. J. Christian Bach I), 46
Peter, Johann Friedrich, 234
Petri, Johann Samuel, 143, 192, 195
Pezold, Christian, 187
Pfefferkorn, Georg Michael, 15
Pfeiffer, Heinrich, 5
Pflugg, Georg Dietrich von, 43
Pfuhl, Abraham, 113
'Picander', see Henrici
Picart, Samuel, 295–6
Piccinni, Nicola, 258
Pinto, George Frederic, 291
Pisendel, Georg, 89, 163, 165, 188
Planck, Görg, 10
Podbielski, Christian Wilhelm, 285
Poglietti, Alessandro, 82
Pöppelmann, Mathaes, 42, 89
Porpora, Niccola, 226
Potter, Cipriani, 298, 300
Praetorius, Friedrich Emanuel, 75
Prés, Josquin des, 10, 68
Prussia, see individual monarchs
Purcell, Henry, 53
Pyra, Jacob Immanuel, 191

Quantz, Johann Joachim, 140, 165, 166, 167, 169, 170, 174
Quinault, Jean Baptiste, 258

Raaf, Anton, 253
Raison, André, 104
Rameau, Jean Philippe, 175
Ramler, Carl Wilhelm, 170, 171, 211, 218, 228, 229, 232
Rappold, Gottfried Christian, 91

Ratke, Wolfgang (Rattichius), 39
Raupach, Hermann, 169, 170
Reger, Max, 202
Reichardt, Johann Friedrich, 183, 209
Reifenstein, Johann Friedrich, 173
Reineccius, Theodor, 91–2
Reinhold, Theodor Christlieb, 187, 188, 189
Reinken, Johann Adam, 77, 98, 104
Renerus, 68
Rentsch (painter in Weimar), 90
Reuss-Schleiz, Heinrich XI, Count of, 98
Reutz, Caspar, 114
Reutz, Friedrich, 114
Reynolds, Joshua, 214, 237, 269
Richardson, Samuel, 256
Richter, Johann, 42
Richter, Johann Christian, 185, 204 n.6
Rimsky-Korsakov, Nikolai, 307
Rinckart, Martin, 40
Rist, Johann, 106
Ristori, Giovanni Alberto, 188
Rivinus, Augustus, 151
Rochlitz, Johann Friedrich, 285, 288
Roemhild, Kantor, 215
Rolle, Christian Friedrich, 95, 132, 169, 170, 176
Rolle, Johann Heinrich, 192, 215
Roman, Johann Heinrich, 82
Römhild, Johann Theodor, 129 n.17
Roseingrave, Thomas, 296
Rosenmüller, Johann, 41
Rothenburg, General von, 170
Rousseau, Jean Jacques, 178
Rudolf I, Emperor, 26
Rudolf II, Emperor, 29
Rudolf, Andreas, 42
Rühling, Hans, 14, 37 n.14
Rühling, Samuel, 28
Russell, William, 292, 296, 297
Rust, Friedrich Wilhelm, 195
Rust, Marie Johanne (m. J. L. Bach), 125
Rust, Samuel, 125

Sachsen, see Saxony
Sachsen-Coburg, Casimir, Duke of, 26
Sachsen-Eisenach, Johann Ernst, Duke of, 84
Sachsen-Eisenach, Johann Georg I, Duke of, 63
Sachsen-Eisenach, Johann Georg III, Duke of, 84
Sachsen-Eisenach, Johann Wilhelm, Duke of, 64, 70
Sachsen-Gotha, Emil August, Duke of, 246 n.19

Sachsen-Gotha, Ernst, Duke of, 19 n.20, 71
Sachsen-Gotha, Friedrich I, Duke of, 82
Sachsen-Gotha, Friedrich II, Duke of, 82
Sachsen-Gotha, Friedrich IV, Duke of, 246 n.19
Sachsen-Gotha, Johann Friedrich II, Duke of, 8
Sachsen-Meiningen, Bernhard I, Duke of, 124
Sachsen-Meiningen, Ernst Ludwig, Duke of, 125, 128
Sachsen-Meiningen, Karl, Duke of, 235, 246
Sachsen-Meiningen, Luise-Eleonore, Duchess of, 312
Sachsen-Meiningen, Sophie Charlotte, Duchess of, 124
Sachsen-Weimar, Anne Amalia, Duchess of, 242
Sachsen-Weimar, Ernst August, Duke of, 90, 93
Sachsen-Weimar, Ernst August Constantin, Duke of, 242
Sachsen-Weimar, Johann III, Duke of, 103
Sachsen-Weimar, Johann Ernst, Duke of, 77, 90, 91, 93, 104
Sachsen-Weimar, Luise, Duchess of, 246 n.19
Sachsen-Weimar, Wilhelm Ernst, Duke of, 89, 90, 93
Sachsen-Weissenfels, Christian, Duke of, 93
Salieri, Antonio, 211, 286
Salomon, Johann Peter, 263, 293
Saxony (Sachsen), Christiane Eberhardine, Electress of, 146
Saxony, Ernst, Duke of, 105
Saxony, Friedrich, 'the Wise', Elector of, 5, 11
Saxony, Friedrich August II, 'the Strong', Elector of, 1, 42, 87, 89, 145, 146, 187
Saxony, Friedrich August III, Elector of, 147, 151, 152, 164–5, 187, 188
Saxony, Johann Georg, Duke of, 28
Saxony, Johann Georg II, Duke of, 42
Saxony, Johann Georg III, Elector of, 82, 90
Saxony, Marie Josepha, Electress of, 165
Scandello, Antonio, 16
Scarlatti, Alessandro, 226
Schaffrat, Christoph, 187
Schaumburg-Lippe, Juliane, Countess of, 230

Schaumburg-Lippe, Maria Eleonore, Countess of, 226, 228, 230
Schaumburg-Lippe, Philipp Ernst, Count of, 230
Schaumburg-Lippe, Wilhelm, Count of, 224, 225, 226, 230
Scheibe, Johann Adolph, 109n. 22, 141, 150, 154, 157
Scheidt, Samuel, 29, 31, 47, 112, 213
Schein, Johann Hermann, 41, 134
Schelble, Johann Nepomuk, 289
Schelle, Johann, 132, 133–4
Schemelli, Christian Friedrich, 138
Schemelli, Georg Christoph, 154
Scherer, Hans, 94, 108 n.14
Scheuerstuhl, Michael, 174, 175
Schicht, Johann Gottfried, 284
Schiemert, Peter, 138
Schlegel, Johann Adolph, 243
Schlegel, Joseph, 14, 16
Schlüter, Andreas, 88
Schmid, Peter, 72
Schmidt, Anna Margretha (m. J. Christian Bach I), 46
Schmidt, Andreas, 68
Schmidt, Musketeer J., 203
Schmidt, Johann Jakob, 138, 139
Schmied, Anna Margarethe (m. J. Jakob Bach), 123
Schmiedt, Anna (m. Hans Bach II), 8
Schmitt, Jacob, 298
Schneider, Balthasar, 66
Schneider, Hans Gregor, 56
Schneider, Johann, 138, 139
Schnitger, Arp, 98, 206 n.41
Schön, Johann Jacob, 66
Schöne, W., 130
Schott, Georg Balthasar, 132, 141, 150
Schrittger (organ-builder), 94
Schroeter, Johann Samuel, 276
Schröne, Valentin, 67
Schröter, Christoph Gottlieb, 114–15
Schröter, Johann Friedrich, 237, 238
Schröter (organ-builder), 94, 95
Schubart, Christian Friedrich, 288
Schubart, Eva Christina, 165
Schubart, Johann Martin, 79, 95
Schubert, Franz, 228, 244
Schübler, Johann Georg, and Johann Heinrich, 139
Schulthesius, Johann Heinrich, 199
Schulz, Johann Abraham Peter, 278
Schulze, Johann Sigmund ('Sperontes'), 154, 174
Schumann (of Lüneburg), 199
Schumann, Robert, 178, 276, 279, 284, 299, 300, 301, 307
Schürmann, Georg Caspar, 214

Schütz, Heinrich, 16, 22, 28–9, 44, 51, 52, 133, 134, 149, 224
Schwanberger, Johann, 198
Schwarzburg-Blankenburg, Günther, Count of, 6
Schwarzburg-Blankenburg, House of, 3
Schwarzburg-Sondershausen, Anton Günther, Count of, 41, 48, 77
Schwarzburg-Sondershausen, Günther, Count of, 48
Schwenke, David, and Michael, 24
Schwenke, Gottlieb, 290
Scott, Polly, 255
Sebastiani, Johann, 16
Selle, Thomas, 75
Senesino, 89
Senfl, Ludwig, 10, 51, 68
Serini, Giovanni Battista, 226
Shakespeare, William, 198
Sheridan, Richard Brinsley, 269
Shield, William, 272, 303 n.43
Silbermann, Gottfried, 94, 115, 141, 168, 185, 188
Simpson, Thomas, 213
Slevogt (Professor in Jena), 112
Smart, Sir George, 300
Smith, John Stafford, 212
Sonnleithner, Joseph, 286
Sophia Charlotte, Queen of England, 249, 294
Sophia Dorothea, Queen of Prussia, 103, 166
Sophie Charlotte, Queen of Prussia, 88
Sophie, Electress of Prussia, 42
Sorge, Georg Andreas, 140, 172, 304 n.59
Spalatin, Georg, 11
Spangenberg, Johann, 10
'Sperontes', see Schulze, J. S.
Spitta, Philipp, 52, 126, 147–8, 151
Spohr, Ludwig, 290, 301
Stahl, Georg Ernst, 190
Stanley, John, 259, 270, 271
Starck, Ludwig, 44
Steinbach, Georg Adam, 79
Steindorff, Johann Martin, 132
Stengel, Johann, 113
Sterzing, Georg Christoph, 50, 111
Steuerlein, Johann, 16, 124
Stieglitz (Mayor of Leipzig), 158
Stille (Pastor in Bückeburg), 278
Stock, Friedemann Wilhelm, 111
Stoeltzel, Gottfried Heinrich, 113, 176, 185, 192
Storace, Nancy, and Stephen, 271, 272
Stöttrup, Andreas, 213
Stoy, Johann Christian, 187
Strattner, Georg Christoph, 114

Stricker, Augustinus Reinhard, 97
Strecher, Adolf, 79
Stubbs, George, 269
Sturm, Christoph Christian, 213, 218
Sucro, Johann Josias, 243
Sullivan, Arthur, 256
Sulzer, Johann Georg, 170, 171
Sweelinck, Jan Pieterszoon, 29
Swieten, Baron Gottfried von, 201, 209, 217–18, 287
Syring, Judithe Katharina (m. J. Egidius Bach), 46
Szabolcsi, Bence, 177

Tartini, Giuseppe, 226
Taylor, John, 158
Telemann, Georg Philipp, 27, 57, 65, 70, 92, 93, 106, 107, 108 n.7, 109 n.32, 117, 132, 135, 145, 148, 150, 192, 198, 207, 208, 211, 214, 216, 228, 233, 234, 236
Tenducci, Ferdinando, 255, 266, 267
Thayssner, Zacharias, 111
Theile, Johann, 16, 159 n.4
Thieme, Johann Gottfried, 111
Thomasius, Christian, 88, 131
Tieck, Ludwig, 286, 287
Tilly, General, 30
Tischbein, Johann Heinrich, 238
Tischer, Johann Nikolaus, 174
Toland, John, 88
Tooke, John Horne, 269
Tosi, Giuseppe Felice, 177
Tracey, Mrs, 249
Transchel, Christoph, 138
Treiber, Johann Friedrich, 77–8
Treiber, Johann Philipp, 78, 113
Treiber, Johann Wilhelm, 236, 312
Trier, Johann, 158, 168–9, 284
Tscherning, Andreas, 44
Tufen, Andreas Christoph, 132

Vater, Johann Michael, 120
Vivaldi, Antonio, 89, 104, 107
Vockerodt, Gottfried, 80
Vogler, Johann Caspar, 95, 192
Vogeler, Christiane Regina (m. Jakob Bach), and Michael, 123
Voltaire, François, 163, 225
Volumier, Jean Baptiste, 89, 95
Vopelius, Gottfried, 16, 134
Voss, Johann Heinrich, 212
Vulpius, Melchior, 14, 37 n.3, 68

Wallenstein, Albert von, 30, 31
Walond, William, 296
Walsh, John, 173, 254, 282

Walther, Johann, 10, 11–12, 13, 16, 21–22, 28, 68
Walther, Johann Gottfried, 38 n.20, 61 n.13, 92, 93, 102, 114
Walther, Sebastian, 24
Waltz (mathematician in Dresden), 188
Weber, Carl Maria von, 275, 279, 288–9
Weckbach, Friedemann, 92
Wecker, Christoph Gottlob, 141
Wedemann, Katharina (m. J. Michael Bach), and Maria Elisabeth (m. J. Christoph Bach I), 50
Weichsell, Mrs Carl, 266, 267, 272
Weichsell, Charles, 263
Weichsell, Elizabeth, 263, 272
Weideman(n), Karl Friedrich, 249
Weigel, Erhard, 112, 115
Weinlig, Christian Theodor, 284
Weishaupt, Conrad, 83
Weiss, Sylvius Leopold, 165, 167, 205 n.16
Weisse, Christian Felix, 228, 240
Wellesz, Egon, 307
Weltzig, Adam Emanuel, 92
Wender, Johann Friedrich, 77, 80
Wendling, Johann Baptist, 270
Wentzel, Johann Georg, 110–11
Wesley, Samuel, 221, 263, 272, 284, 290–297 pass.
Wesley, Samuel Sebastian, 293
West, Benjamin, 269
Westenholtz, Carl August, 211
Westhof, Johann Paul von, 90

Westphal, Johann Christoph, 209
Wiener, Anna Cunigunda, 147
Wilhelm, Prince of Prussia, 279
Wilkes, John, 269
Winckelmann, Johann Joachim, 142, 173, 238, 239
Winkler, Gottfried, 240
Winterfeld, Carl von, 289
Wittichius, Jeremias, 2, 19 n.24, 21
Wolff, Christian, 191
Wolff, Johann Heinrich, 152
Wrangel, General Karl Gustaf, 81
Wülcken, Anna Magdalena (see Bach), and Johann Caspar, 99
Württemberg, Karl Eugen, Duke of, 179

York, Duchess of, 238
York, Duke of, 249, 266
Young, Sir William, 269, 270

Zachariä, Friedrich Wilhelm, 198
Zachau, Friedrich Wilhelm, 94, 192
Zang, Johann Georg, 139
Zeidler, Rektor, 68
Zelenka, Johann, 192
Zelter, Carl Friedrich, 201, 206 n.42, 283–9
Zeuner, Wolfgang, 68
Ziegler, Christiana Mariane von, 144, 148, 177
Ziegler, Johann Gottfried, 95
Zoffany, John, 271

PLACES

Aberdeen, 271
Aix-la-Chapelle, Treaty of, 164
Altenburg, 113
Ambleben, 232
Amsterdam, 29
Ansbach, 141
Arnstadt, 6, 8, 23, 31, 34, 35, 41, 47, 48–9, 50, 51, 56, 57, 60, 63, 65, 69, 77–8, 81, 91, 95, 103, 113, 236
Augsburg, 15, 26, 114; Peace of, 5
Austerlitz, battle of, 286

Bad Salzungen, 125
Bath, 269, 270
Berlin, 7, 15, 87–9, 96, 97, 114, 115, 139, 162–81 pass., 183, 194, 195, 201–4, 207, 213, 237, 238, 251, 253, 278, 279, 286, 287–9 pass.

Bethlehem (Penn.), 234
Bielefeld, 232
Bindersleben, 114
Birmingham, 245 n.7, 292, 295, 298
Blandford, 271
Bologna, 252
Bratislava (Pressburg), 6
Braunschweig, 124, 132, 195, 197, 200
Breitenbach, 48, 72
Breitenfeld, 30
Breslau, 289
Bucharest, 138
Bückeburg, 162, 169, 181, 207, 223–35, 237, 276
Budapest, 2, 161 n.41

Carlsbad, 98, 99
Celle, 75–6, 77, 163

Chemnitz, 141
Chichester, 271
Coburg, 26, 139, 237
Constantinople, 82
Corvey, 7

Danzig, 302 n.4
Darmstadt, 132, 195
Dederau, 14
Dessau, 176
Dresden, 2, 7, 12, 16, 25, 26, 28, 36, 40,
    42, 51, 52, 70, 87, 88, 89, 90, 91, 95,
    97, 114, 115, 131, 132, 138, 140, 141,
    151, 162, 163, 164, 165, 167, 183, 185,
    187–90, 191, 213, 237, 238, 239

Edinburgh, 271
Eilenburg, 40
Eisenach, 1, 2, 3, 4, 8, 10, 18 n.5, 23, 24,
    30, 48, 49–56, 60, 63–71, 80, 81, 92,
    111, 112, 114, 115, 123, 149, 241, 244
Eisenberg, 113
Eisleben, 61 n.15, 70, 92
Elberfeld, 280, 281
Engelsbostel, 281
Erfurt, 2, 3, 5, 6, 8, 10, 31, 34, 35, 40,
    43, 45, 46, 47, 56, 60, 62 n.19, 65, 66,
    67, 69, 70, 83, 92, 95, 114, 139, 160
    n.22
Erlangen, 236, 237
Exeter, 271

Frankfurt/Main, 2, 25, 31, 289, 298
Frankfurt/Oder, 7, 167, 170, 179
Freiberg (Saxony), 4, 12, 14, 16, 17, 19
    n.26, 24, 25, 51, 141
Friedrichroda, 2
Fürth, 113

Gandersheim, 91, 161 n.41
Gehren, 2, 48, 56, 58, 60
Georgenthal, 6
Gera, 26, 137
Geraburg, 85 n.26
Görlitz, 26, 195
Gotha, 2, 7, 8–9, 15, 18 n.5, 19 n.22, 42,
    61 n.1, 65, 66, 72, 74, 81, 113, 115,
    123, 176
Göttingen, 43, 110, 142, 199–200, 231,
    281, 286
Grabsleben, 9
Gräfenroda, 3, 6, 140
Grossen-Behringen, 38 n.20
Grossen-Sömmerda, 34
Güstrow, 215, 281

Halberstadt, 94, 171, 173
Halle/Saale, 4, 10, 12, 29, 30–1, 61 n.15,
    80, 88, 94–5, 96, 112, 123, 131, 143,
    168, 169, 171, 181, 183, 186, 190–7,
    199
Hamburg, 50, 74, 75, 76, 83, 98, 102,
    105, 124, 132, 144, 145, 162, 168, 172,
    173, 179, 180, 181, 207–21 pass., 231,
    234, 276, 281–2, 290
Hanover, 76, 77, 224
Helmstedt, 115, 123
Hennersdorf, 191
Hirschfeld, 123
Hof, 30, 69
Hohenlohe, 246 n.19
Hubertsburg, 197
Hustomice pod Brdy, 6

Ilmenau, 2, 56

Jena, 2, 5, 14, 19 n.26, 41, 67, 74, 78, 80,
    91, 94, 110–23 pass., 141, 151, 160
    n.41

Kahla, 10
Kassel, 2, 25, 28, 93, 173, 290
Kesselsdorf, 164, 191
Klosterlüne, 281
Köln, 3, 25
Königsberg, 113, 285
Köstritz, 26
Köthen, 93, 95, 96–107 pass., 110, 146,
    185
Kunersdorf, 169

Lahm, 95
Langenburg, 199
Langewiesen, 2
Leeds, 271
Leipzig, 2, 11, 12, 14, 16, 25, 26, 28, 30,
    31, 40, 48, 70, 80, 94, 98, 99, 101, 102,
    103, 105, 111, 115, 125, 130–58 pass.,
    162, 167, 168, 172, 179, 185, 186, 188,
    190, 191, 192, 194, 195, 196, 236, 238,
    239, 250, 275, 284, 285, 287, 298–301
Ljubljana, 16
Lobenstein, 140
London, 83, 181, 212, 213, 230–1, 248,
    250, 253, 254–73 pass., 276, 282, 290–
    298 pass.
Lübeck, 78–9
Ludwigslust, 211
Lüneburg, 73–6, 160 n.41, 199, 281, 287
Lützen, 31

Magdeburg, 14, 15, 30, 70, 169
Mainz, 3, 31
Manchester, 271

Mannheim, 258, 270
Mansfeld, 94
Marburg, 28
Marksuhl, 63
Mechterstädt, 6
Meeder, 199
Meiningen, 16, 97, 106, 123–8, 213, 224, 235–8, 312–13
Meissen, 25
Mellrichstadt, 7
Merseburg, 31, 102, 132, 158, 167, 168, 186
Milan, 250, 251, 252, 253, 254
Minden, 115, 224, 276, 278
Molsdorf, 81
Mühlhausen, 2, 3, 4, 5, 12, 15, 22, 30, 31, 43–5, 77, 79–80, 83, 92, 103, 114, 116, 123, 137, 156
München, 2, 10

Nantes, Edict of, 131
Naples, 250, 251, 253
Naumburg, 22, 31, 35, 48, 136, 138, 141, 168
Niederzimmern, 60
Nienburg, 93
Nordhausen, 3, 61 n.1, 115
Nürnberg, 2, 10, 13, 16, 25, 26, 31, 32, 113, 225, 244

Oehringen, 137, 161 n.41
Ohrdruf, 2, 6, 7, 47, 69, 72–3, 91, 92, 95, 96, 99, 136, 155, 161 n.41, 181, 199

Paris, 70, 169, 257, 258
Plauen, 141
Poltava, battle of, 82
Potsdam, 155, 166, 168, 178, 213, 225, 238, 251
Prague, 2, 235, 298; Peace of, 31
Presswitz, 7
Prettin, 35
Priessnitz, 18 n.17

Quedlinburg, 94, 95, 132, 180

Regenstauffen, 18 n.10
Reisenstein, 5
Rheinsberg, 163, 164, 167
Riga, 139, 230
Rinteln, 231, 284

Saalfeld, 2
Salisbury, 270
Sangerhausen, 77, 116, 188
Schlafstädt, 94

Schleiz, 98, 99
Schmalkalden, 2, 6, 8, 175, 280
Schweinfurt, 31, 34, 47, 57, 95, 237
Schwerin, 199
Siebenburgen, 138
Sollstedt, 36 n.1
Solz, 22, 36 n.1
Sondershausen, 2, 80, 139
Sonneberg, 2
Steinbach, 123
Stockholm, 81, 82
Strelitz, 249
Struth, 280
Suhl, 2, 8, 33, 34, 47, 57

Taucha, 132
Thal, 123
Themar, 47, 57, 66
Tonna, 280
Torgau, 11–12, 13, 28, 29
Trier, 3
Tübingen, 229
Turin, 253

Udestedt, 60, 137, 159 n.9, 161 n.41

Venice, 28, 250, 253
Vienna, 10, 81, 201, 217–18, 235, 237, 271, 286, 298

Warsaw, 2, 188
Wasungen, 123
Wechmar, 6, 7, 8, 23, 34
Weimar, 2, 14, 24, 31, 35, 40, 41, 47, 62 n.19, 71, 77, 80, 83, 89–96, 101, 102, 103, 104, 105, 106, 107, 114, 140, 181, 185, 224, 241, 242
Weissenfels, 31, 42, 92, 94, 98, 99, 106, 151
Wilhelmsdorf, 175
Winchester, 271
Wittenberg, 4, 11, 18 n.6, 18 n.9, 41, 90, 168
Wolfenbüttel, 125, 198, 200, 224
Wölfis, 18 n.10
Wolfsbehringen, 123
Worms, Diet of, 4
Würzburg, 31

Zeitz, 10, 42, 61 n.15, 99, 158
Zella-Mehlis, 2, 139
Zerbst, 98, 99, 132, 169
Zittau, 9, 25, 26, 51, 168, 194, 284
Zorndorf, 169
Zöschau, 137
Zwickau, 4, 11, 17, 132